The Enigma of Gogol

CAMBRIDGE STUDIES IN RUSSIAN LITERATURE

General editor HENRY GIFFORD

In the same series

Three Russian writers and the irrational: Zamyatin, Pil'nyak, and Bulgakov
T. R. N. EDWARDS

Novy Mir: a case study in the politics of Russian literature 1952–1958
EDITH ROGOVIN FRANKEL

Word and music in Andrey Bely's novels
ADA STEINBERG

Nikolay Vasilyevich Gogol-Yanovsky, 1841

The Enigma of Gogol

AN EXAMINATION OF
THE WRITINGS OF N. V. GOGOL
AND THEIR PLACE IN THE
RUSSIAN LITERARY TRADITION

RICHARD PEACE

CAMBRIDGE UNIVERSITY PRESS
CAMBRIDGE
LONDON NEW YORK NEW ROCHELLE
MELBOURNE SYDNEY

Published by the Press Syndicate of the University of Cambridge
The Pitt Building, Trumpington Street, Cambridge CB2 1RP
32 East 57th Street, New York, NY 10022, USA
296 Beaconsfield Parade, Middle Park, Melbourne 3206, Australia

First published 1981

Printed in Great Britain at the University Press, Cambridge

Library of Congress catalogue card number: 81-3867

British Library Cataloguing in Publication Data

Peace, Richard
The enigma of Gogol. – (Cambridge studies in Russian literature)
1. Gogol, Nikolaĭ Vasilévich – criticism and interpretation
I. Title
891.7′8′309 PG3335.Z8

ISBN 0 521 23824 2

To the memory of Henry Peace

Contents

Preface

In Moscow there are two statues of Gogol a very short distance apart. One is an upright figure smiling confidently on the world: the 'Happy Gogol' (*Gogol′ veselyy*). The other depicts the writer seated, surrounded by characters from his works – it is the 'Sad Gogol' (*Gogol′ grustnyy*), and yet, looked at from certain angles, it is also a 'sly Gogol'. The 'Happy Gogol' stands at the head of the boulevard which bears the writer's name, and was erected at the centenary of his death to replace the 'Sad Gogol', which was relegated to a quiet square on the other side of what is now the Kalininsky Prospekt.

That there should be two Gogols (even three – or more) will come as no surprise to those who know his works. Thus three recent studies have examined his writing from distinct points of view. Simon Karlinsky (*The sexual labyrinth of Nikolai Gogol*) has seen homosexuality as the great key. Donald Fanger (*The creation of Nikolai Gogol*) concentrates more on stylistic considerations, and sees the 'medium' itself as the 'message', whereas James Woodward (*Gogol's Dead Souls*) interprets the writer's major work as a system of arcane symbols.

I would argue that the neurotic preoccupations of Gogol's artistic personality are not exclusively homosexual, nor even exclusively sexual. On the other hand, self-sufficiency of style is a doubtful concept – above all for a writer so far removed from the canons of polished elegance. Although symbolism plays an important role in Gogol's writing, he is not the builder of an intricately coherent symbolic universe. Gogol's artistic concerns are rather with disparity and incongruity. In the present study I have attempted to avoid critical monotheism, but inevitably certain concepts will recur. As well as analysing the texts themselves I have sought to relate them to the tradition of Russian literature which Gogol inherited, and also to point to the rich legacy they represent for those who came after.

I wish to express my gratitude to the editorial board of the *Slavonic and East European Review* for allowing me to reprint an edited and slightly rewritten version of my article on 'The Old World Landowners' which first appeared there. Other articles have appeared in *Russian and Slavic Literature* (Slavica), *Filološki Pregled* (Belgrade), the *Oxford Slavonic Papers* and as contributions to *Exeter Tapes*, but although, inevitably, there are similarities of approach and argument these articles are distinct from the corresponding sections of the present study and have been fully acknowledged in the notes. I am particularly grateful to Henry Gifford for his keen critical eye and for his many helpful suggestions. I also wish to thank John Bernasconi for advice on artistic matters, and members of the Department of Russian Studies at Hull University, in particular Dr Elizabeth Warner for allowing me to quote from her study on the Russian Folk Theatre and for her advice on Russian folklore in general, also Dr Edmund Little, who has his own scholarly interest in Gogol. I owe a special debt of gratitude to the Departmental secretaries, Sheena and Tanya, for their unstinting work in typing the manuscript, and I also wish to acknowledge the help given by the editorial staff of Cambridge University Press.

Hull RICHARD PEACE
June 1981

A note on transliteration

For the convenience of non-specialist readers, proper names in the main text are rendered in the simplified form of the 'British' system, familiar to readers of Russian literature in translation. However the demands of phonetic exactitude necessitate the use of the orthodox British system in quoted matter.

Introduction

Gogol and Russian humanism

Gogol's contemporaries and later biographers largely agree on one fact: the enigma of his personality. Enigma, too, inheres in his writing, so that both his life and works have given rise to many misunderstandings and been the subject of widely divergent interpretations. Gogol himself frequently complained of being misunderstood, but, by and large, his attempts at elucidation have merely deepened the mystery.

To many modern Western critics his immense reputation throughout the nineteenth century as a realist writer seems in itself to be based on a misconception.[1] Nevertheless one fact is undeniable: Gogol exerted an immense influence on the whole course of Russian literature and continues to do so to the present day. There is scarcely a later Russian writer who did not succumb in some measure to his magic, and in many cases (Dostoevsky, Chekhov, Ilf and Petrov) his influence was crucial. In this sense alone, to call Gogol the 'father of Russian prose fiction' is eminently justifiable.

Yet at once we come up against the Gogolian enigma. The Russian prose tradition is outstanding in its psychological analysis and insight: Gogol apparently shuns any inner exploration of his characters. The Russian tradition is realism: Gogol's world is permeated by the grotesque. The Russian tradition is largely built on powerful yet simple prose (Turgenev, Tolstoy, Chekhov): Gogol's style is rhetorical, syntactically involved, and full of words which are not standard literary Russian. How is it that this idiosyncratic and apparently eccentric writer could have wielded such enormous literary influence?

Gogol's apparent lack of interest in psychological analysis raises a more fundamental problem. Russian literature of the nineteenth century is remarkable for its depth of human understanding and compassion, yet it is precisely this which appears to be lacking in the works of Gogol. His characters seem for the most part subhuman;

it is not often that the author arouses sympathy for them in his reader.

Until the nineteenth century there was no humanist tradition in Russian literature (although there are strong glimmerings at the end of the eighteenth century). Russia had not experienced the Renaissance. There had been no Russian Shakespeare or Montaigne to proclaim the richness and complexity of the human personality and its superiority to the rigid abstractions of medieval dogma. In Russia the spirit of medieval Christendom reigned a long time. Literature was principally concerned to record events and miracles (in the Chronicles or the Lives of the Saints). Its protagonists were not ordinary human beings, but exemplars of a caste: princes, heroes, saints; and the same is true of the oral tradition: the heroes of the *byliny* spring from a mould much larger than the mere human.

Behind such literature the dominant assumptions are that established authority is unimpeachable and the individual must submit to it; that society at large is right and there is no room for the dissenter. It is, indeed, significant that Avvakum, the dissident voice of the seventeenth century, embodies these values more clearly than his antagonists. He is the arch-conservative, defending long-established church ritual and traditional dogma against the reformers. The life of Avvakum, with its fanatical drive towards martyrdom, shows only too well how the medieval religious temperament was prepared to sacrifice ordinary human considerations to the 'higher' values of authority and ritual. Yet even in the nineteenth century similar imputations may be sensed in the works of Nikolai Leskov – a writer who was far from hostile to religion, yet in his stories, *The Enchanted Wanderer* and *The Man on Sentry-go* the values of the official representatives of the Orthodox church are seen to be essentially non-humanistic.

This non-compassionate Christianity, which punishes those who break ritualistic codes, be they religious or social, is clearly in evidence in Gogol's precursor and fellow Ukrainian, V. T. Narezhny, and it is worthy of note that such of Gogol's characters who show religious leanings (and they are not many) are imbued with the ritualistic, non-humanist Christianity of the Russian middle ages. This is true of the unspiritual theology students in 'Viy'; it is true of the protagonists of 'The tale of how Ivan Ivanovich quarrelled with Ivan Nikiforovich'; it is above all true of the militant Orthodoxy of Taras Bulba. For the characters of Gogol's early stories religion is principally a matter of ritual. It is often reduced to little more than incantations to ward off the devil and the forces of evil (*Evenings in a village near Dikanka* and 'Viy'); and it is significant that when religious formulae are invoked for fellow human beings the curse predominates rather than the blessing (for instance Pulkheriya Ivanovna in 'The Old World Landowners', the NCO's wife in *The Government Inspector* and the whole basis of the plot of 'A Terrible Vengeance'). For the vast majority of Gogol's characters religion is mere form shorn of human content.[2]

In its narrowest sense humanism represents a tendency contrary to the theism at religion's very core, but in its historical sense it sprang from the Renaissance discovery of the classical world with its concept of man as the measure of all things. Russia's brief period of classicism in the eighteenth century brought with it no such revelations; it was in fact a neo-classicism imported from Western Europe, and its roots were shallow. Rather than humanist values it tended to reinforce the dominance of abstract eternal concepts: glory, patriotism, honour. It was to higher ideals, such as these, that the individual must still be sacrificed.[3]

This is not to say that before the rise of nineteenth-century humanism, compassion and ordinary human fellow feeling did not exist among the simple people, or in the church itself. Nevertheless the dominant ethic promulgated by literature was not the sanctity of the human individual, but the inviolability of higher, more eternal laws. Literature reflected the values of the literate, which meant, in effect, the landowning classes, who, through economic necessity, were debarred from regarding the vast majority of their fellow countrymen as full human beings: their wealth was calculated in terms of the number of peasants they owned. The institution of serfdom, which permitted the buying, selling and owning of human beings as if they were just another form of livestock, increasingly came to be seen as the overriding moral problem. A society based on such an institution could not have a humanist outlook in any meaningful sense.[4] Yet the tide of history had actually been flowing in a contrary direction; for from the early middle ages serfdom was gradually being extended and its conditions made stricter.

Gogol himself came from minor Ukrainian gentry stock. His family owned serfs. He himself, like most men of his class and times, never questioned the institution, even though serfdom in the Ukraine was a fairly recent introduction (1763–83) which seemed at odds with the national ideal of the freedom-loving Cossack (depicted so forcefully in 'Taras Bulba'). Gogol's chief concern in respect of the peasants was that their labour should be exploited efficiently, and that they should not be allowed to cheat their masters. He was interested in their moral welfare, but opposed to their acquiring literacy or any form of education. He was, in other words, a landowner of the old school,[5] and the portraits of peasants that occur in his works (e.g. in *Dead Souls*) are far from flattering.

Throughout the eighteenth century change was in the air. It had begun with Peter I attempting to drag Russia out of her middle ages, to take up a new role as a modern European power; it had continued with the foreign empress Catherine II trying to sow the ideas of the French Enlightenment on Russian soil, much as she had forcibly introduced the potato. Yet radical as these changes were they were still carried out within an ethical framework, in which all authority came from above and the interests of the state and society were paramount. But in the last quarter of the century, just as the ideas of the Enlightenment in Europe led to the French Revolution and the collapse of the *ancien régime*, so too in Russia a revolution of a different order was in preparation: Russia's long-belated Renaissance. A whole shift of consciousness came about under the impact of a literary fashion imported from the West – Sentimentalism.

In England the term Sentimentalism is mostly used in a pejorative sense (even though from its literary roots there sprang a Dickens) but in Russia its impact was momentous, and no figure played a larger part in Russian Sentimentalism than the English writer Laurence Sterne. One of the early champions of Sterne in Russia, M. N. Muravyev, pointed to the central issue, when in an essay in the paper *Morning Light* (*Utrenniy svet*) he praised Sterne for his interest, not in the impersonal life of society, but in the personal life of the individual.[6] The West could easily shrug off Sentimentalism; for, since the Renaissance the emphasis placed on the individual was nothing new. The real impact made on the West was Romanticism which deepened and strengthened the cult of the individual as never before, but its harbinger, Sentimentalism, was for the Russians a new cultural and psychological experience – it unleashed those energies which in Europe had been released long before by the discovery of the classical world.

Sentimentalism in Russia had a political coloration. The first Russian radical A. N. Radishchev was 'remarkable, not for the originality of his thought, but for the originality of his feeling'.[7] He read Sterne's *A Sentimental Journey* in a German translation and largely under its influence wrote his own 'unsentimental' journey: *The Journey from St Petersburg to Moscow*. This is a key work in the fight for the new humanism; in its implied attack upon serfdom it strikes at the very heart of the medieval non-humanist consciousness. Radishchev's *Journey* is in effect a social document showing the terrible material conditions and moral state of the peasantry and lower classes. An interest in such social questions had been fostered by Catherine herself, but she had already been terribly frightened by the peasant uprising led by Pugachev (1773–5), and the events of the French Revolution of 1789 put her liberal ideas to the extreme test, so that in 1790 Radishchev could find nobody prepared to publish his *Journey*. He printed it privately but its appearance was a year too late; he was arrested and exiled to Siberia. In his defence he maintained that he had merely been trying to imitate Sterne's *A Sentimental Journey*, and indeed letters show that he had Sterne in mind when writing his *Journey*. Nevertheless, on the face of it, there is very little the two works have in common apart from the fact that they are both travel notes. Radishchev's *Journey* is grim and serious, written with obvious political intention, whereas Sterne's *A Sentimental Journey* is often considered frivolous.[8]

Radishchev's contemporary, N. M. Karamzin, also wrote travel reflections under the influence of Sterne: *The Letters of a Russian Traveller*, which started to come out in 1791–2 (the first full edition was not published until 1801). At one point Karamzin, in Calais, hunts out the room where Sterne's Yorick stayed, and in an entry, supposed to have been inspired by news of the fall of the Bastille, he quotes (in English) the words of Corporal Trim: 'Nothing can be as sweet as liberty.'[9] Thus not only *A Sentimental Journey* but also *Tristram Shandy* established a libertarian reputation for Sterne, and with these credentials the charges of triviality and frivolity, levelled at him in his own country, could not damage his Russian reputation.

For a literature fettered by censorship, the style of Sterne had even more attraction. It showed the Russians how to exploit ambiguity and paradox, how to make points without seeming to do so, it taught that the reader, too, had his own creative role to play in a work of literature.[10] Elements of Sterne's literary manner became the common places of the minor writers of Gogol's time and they have left deep impressions on the works of both Pushkin and Gogol.

Yet without doubt the most important aspect of Russian Sentimentalism was the cult of sentiment itself, and in this Karamzin's short novel *Poor Liza* played a decisive role. Karamzin not only helped to mould the new Russian language, in *Poor Liza* he also laid the foundations of the modern Russian sensibility.[11] In language, as in literature, Karamzin was a pilot craft, who showed the way to larger vessels of deeper draught. His own apparent shallowness was his strength: he loaded a light fashionable form with just sufficient revolutionary ballast to take him through the shoals and reefs of public opinion and mark out a channel to the deeper waters ahead.

Poor Liza is about a peasant girl deceived in love by an aristocrat, who in her despair drowns herself. The story had an immense impact on Karamzin's contemporaries; it was read through floods of tears and the lake where Poor Liza was supposed to have drowned became an object of pilgrimage. The modern reader is struck by the artificiality of the story: Liza, a peasant girl, speaks in the polished phrases, and with the refined sensitivity, of a French aristocrat, but this artificiality is its very salt; in terms of expression and sentiment a peasant is presented as the equal of an aristocrat; a peasant is, therefore, also a human being: 'For even peasant women know how to love!' In a society where the cultured upper classes derived their wealth and status from the dehumanisation of the common people such an idea was revolutionary. Yet the very artificiality, which made Liza the superficial equal of an aristocrat, was precisely what made the idea palatable: it was, after all, false – only a literary mode. Nevertheless beneath the soft sentimental skin could still be sensed a hard realistic core: the fate of Liza at the hands of Erast revealed the true nature of their social relationship. Liza was not after all a human equal, but a human object to be exploited.[12]

Karamzin had launched a new theme, which was to have a great future. The superficial tears of Sentimentalism for those who are 'insulted and injured' would yield to a deeper, genuine compassion. The new attitude to the peasant would develop to such an extent that ultimately (in the writings of Tolstoy) the peasant would no longer evoke mere compassion, but become a figure to be emulated. This is the Romantic Humanism of a nineteenth-century Renaissance, but its origins lie in Sentimentalism.

In Gogol's predecessor Narezhny the humanely civilising role of Sentimentalism is clearly seen in such tales as *Aristion: or Re-education*[13] and above all in the figure of Prostakov in his picaresque novel *The Russian Gil Blas* (1814). Thus Prostakov insists on taking into his house an unknown man in rags and tatters who is covered in dust and blood. When his wife accuses him of acting without thinking, he retorts that he wants to do everything through feeling, and makes a spirited defence of Sentimentalism:

Sentimentalism is man's true nobility. It places him on a higher rung of creation. A wolf and a bear have enough intelligence to distinguish a tiger from a timid sheep, and fleeing the one chase the other. A man of feeling, if not today then tomorrow or some day, will find hearts which will understand him, will come close to him, and he will be happy even in rags. But as to a hard-hearted man – he is eternally unhappy among riches, fame and greatness, or in a crown and a purple cloak.[14]

Given these views, Prostakov is disconcerted when the ragged stranger claims to be a prince: 'You surely don't think that an unfortunate must indeed be a prince in order to arouse sympathy.'

Here is the direct legacy of the new social attitudes swept in by *Poor Liza*, but Narezhny goes further: even the Jew Yanka is the 'sentimental' equal of the Russian Christian. Thus he protests to the village elder: 'If it's a matter of being a human being then I too can judge. I too have a heart.' But the village elder replies: 'You are a Yid, and therefore you have a Yid's heart.' The hero Chistyakov rushes to the Jew's defence: 'There is more love in his heart for his neighbour, Elder, than you have for bribes.'[15] The precept: 'love thy neighbour', may be Christian, but Christians have no absolute monopoly. Narezhny's attitude to Jews contrasts strongly with the way they are treated by Gogol (e.g. Yankel in 'Taras Bulba' and references in the tale of the two Ivans).

There is in fact a strong anti-clerical, even anti-Christian, strain in *The Russian Gil Blas*. It is as though Sentimentalism is the new morality which has come to replace the old. The village elder is the representative of the old morality. When Chistyakov offends against established custom, by not naming his son after his own father, the village elder quotes scripture against him and considers preventing fellow villagers from visiting his house, 'and thereby irritate the long-suffering patience of God'.[16]

Compassion is the mark of the new morality, whereas intolerance is the mark of the old. For the new, the individual is sacrosanct, whatever his social origins; for the old – it is society itself which must be safeguarded and individuals who do not conform to its rigid conventions will be punished or put to shame.[17] The values of

Chistyakov's fellow villagers are those of the sixteenth-century handbook of manners, *Domostroy* (a work which may be regarded as the Old Testament of medieval morality, just as *Poor Liza* is the New Testament for the modern mind).[18] In *Domostroy* ridicule (*posmekh* = laughter) is a potent social force for conformity, and in Narezhny's novel, *The Russian Gil Blas*, Chistyakov is subjected to pitiless laughter by his fellow villagers, whenever he steps out of line. In this novel there are, therefore, two contrasting expressions of emotion, which equally take on attributes of a social force for the individual: the *laughter* of the old order, and the *tears* of the new.

The shift in social attitude which took place in the early nineteenth century may best be illustrated by an incident in a tale of one of Gogol's contemporaries: *Traveller's Impressions and among Other Things a Pot of Geraniums* by A. Veltman. The hero of this story notices a young country girl in Moscow who is continually crossing herself because she has seen so many fine buildings for the first time and does not know which are the churches (it is Orthodox observance to cross oneself when passing a church): 'Aleksandr Fedorovich wanted to laugh at this rustic simple-mindedness, but he remembered that the age commanded one to laugh at nothing, but have pity on everything.'[19]

The best known cliché ever applied to Gogol's art is 'laughter through tears'. Although it is not usual for it to be interpreted in this light, it is nevertheless obvious that in his writings the old 'laughter' and the new 'compassion' are in precarious balance.[20]

Gogol's father had fallen under the influence of Sentimentalism, yet he was also a writer of slapstick Ukrainian comedies, which were sometimes performed at the home of his influential but distant relative, D. P. Troshchinsky. The Troshchinsky household was almost like a medieval court and at its entertainments laughter reigned with all its pitiless primitive force.[21] It is true that by the time Gogol was writing Sentimentalism had done its work and had been superseded (indeed Vissarion Belinsky said that people already laughed at Poor Liza).[22] Nevertheless Gogol attempted to begin his literary career with a sentimental poem: *Gants Kyukhelgarten*. His debt to Karamzin can be seen in 'The Old World Landowners',[23] and it was the presence of a sentimental passage in the most famous of all his short stories 'The Overcoat' which led to its acclaim as a work with a humanist message.

Sentimentalism had already fused with German Romanticism, the sensitive soul formed by Sentimentalism was now searching for high ideals in life and in art, and was actually shocked by those of his fellow creatures who did not show such refinement of spirit – the Philistines. In essence this is the theme of Gogol's story 'The Nevsky Prospekt' in which strains of Schiller and Hoffmann can be detected. The antinomy of unfeeling 'medieval' laughter and compassionate tears of Sentimentalism should not be seen in too starkly a schematic way. Sterne himself was pre-eminently a humourist, and as F. D. Reeve has pointed out: 'Pushkin and Gogol picked up that half of Sterne Karamzin had left out: the humour, the common sense, the literary gamesmanship itself.'[24]

Moreover in the nineteenth century the middle ages were part of a fashionable romantic cult, which often idealised them as embodying spiritual values lost during the Age of Reason. This is certainly true of the Slavophiles' interpretation of Pre-Petrine Russia, and Gogol was influenced by their thought. A more dispassionate view is provided by D. S. Likhachev: 'The artificial acceleration of cultural development in the reign of Peter I allowed many characteristic traits of ancient Russia to preserve their significance for the eighteenth and nineteenth centuries. This included the type of humour.'[25] Indeed Likhachev's study: *The World of Laughter of Ancient Russia* reveals many facets of medieval Russian humour which are recognisable as those of Gogol himself.[26]

In *Dead Souls* Gogol mocked the 'pure' sentimentalist in the portrait of Manilov as well as the 'Karamzinian' language of the two ladies of the town of N in chapter 9. Yet it is in this work that he talks of the laughter which the world sees and the tears which it does not see. The formula 'laughter *through* tears' is more apt than might at first appear; it suggests that the laughter is basic and that it penetrates the tears. Gogol's outlook is more 'medieval' than modern. His laughter is not conciliatory, it is nearer to the socially punitive laughter of *Domostroy*: 'Laughter is a great thing. It takes away neither life nor property, but the guilty man is like a trussed up hare before it' (*St Petersburg Notes 1836*, VIII, 186). That is why he could claim laughter as the real hero of his comedy *The Government Inspector*.

Laughter for Gogol was a moral force; it preserved the values of society at the expense of the individual. Tears, the moral force for the individual, were enjoined on him by the new attitude of society itself, but he scarcely understood them (except, perhaps, in relation to himself). That is why there is very little genuine compassion in Gogol's works and why, when he put forward his positive ideas in *Selected Passages from Correspondence with Friends*, he produced a work which was entirely out of keeping with the sensibilities of the age; for as Belinsky angrily asserted Gogol had understood neither the spirit nor the form of modern Christianity. In this work he seemed concerned to strengthen and preserve Russian society as it was, and to do so at the expense of the individual, certainly at the expense of the Russian peasant. He was not only out of step with his times, but was lagging behind those of his contemporaries who thought of him as setting the pace. This, in part, helps to explain the 'enigma'. Yet in his art it is the tension between the new and the old which produces richness and ambivalence; the dispassionate eye of the medieval chronicler combines with the emotional, sensitive nature of 'modern' man.

In his writing, and more obviously in his abortive career as a teacher, Gogol felt the attraction of history, in particular the history of the middle ages. Such an interest may, of course, be partly ascribed to the influence of Romanticism (Walter Scott, Schiller, etc.), but Gogol's affinity with the middle ages is deeper than this: there are certain features of his writing which are typical of an earlier Russian literary tradition.

'Medieval' is a term which can be used loosely; often its connotation is merely pejorative. Gogol himself defined it as a period of ten centuries which ended in the fifteenth century.[27] In Russia, however, the medieval spirit can be seen as extending to the seventeenth century, and even two centuries later the values of provincial society were virtually those of *Domostroy*. (Thus the tragedy of Aleksandr Ostrovsky's play *The Thunderstorm* (1860) derives from the clash between the morality of the old order and that of the new with its Romantic emphasis on the individual.) The Russian medieval literary tradition shows both development and diversity, yet a constant feature is the way in which human psychology is presented. Writing of the eleventh to thirteenth centuries Likhachev comments: 'In the chronicles acts and behaviour are described, but not the psychological causes which are responsible for them.'[28] For as he points out 'the inner life of a prince is subordinated to his external depiction'. He makes much the same point for the literature at the end of the seventeenth century (the so-called baroque style): 'The inner life of man interested the writer only in its outward manifestations.'[29]

These observations could be made with equal force about Gogol's writings; he, too, shows concern for external features but very little interest in the inner life of most of his characters. It would, however, be completely erroneous to think that Gogol shuns all psychology, and the same is true of the medieval writer. His method is, as Likhachev puts it: 'psychology without psychology' (*psikhologiya bez psikhologii*).[30] In subsequent chapters we shall see how true this formula is for Gogol's own methods of psychological presentation.

There are other points of similarity. The literature of the middle ages often attributes human motives to a supernatural source ('personality was usually a vehicle of divine will or a vessel of the devil').[31] Thus the seventeenth-century schismatic, Avvakum, constantly attributes the actions of his enemies to the machinations of the devil. Diabolic interference is not only made explicit in many of Gogol's stories (*Evenings in a village near Dikanka*, 'The Portrait', 'Nevsky Prospekt'), but it seems to have been a force in his own life. Thus it was to the devil that he ascribed the burning of the second part of *Dead Souls*.

Likhachev also points out that in the lives of the saints of the fourteenth and fifteenth centuries, emotion was often expressed through rhetoric and a more rhythmical style of prose.[32] Here are devices which the reader will recognise as typical of Gogol's own 'emotional' style: the 'purple passages' scattered throughout most of his writings.

In depicting human characteristics, Gogol frequently makes use of analogies from the animal kingdom. The chronicles, too, often explained human actions in terms of animals. Human beings thinly disguised as animals could be the protagonists of seventeenth-century tales.[33]

Throughout medieval literature there is a strong homiletic element: 'To one degree or another from the eleventh to the sixteenth century an author was always a preacher, and in this respect the sermon was the leading genre throughout the course of several centuries.'[34] Although the tendency to sermonise is absent from Gogol's early writing, it grows from 1841 on. Its presence can be detected in the revised version of 'The Portrait', and behind his ultimate intentions for *Dead Souls*. It is significant that his last finished work *Selected Passages from Correspondence with Friends* is unashamedly homiletic.

The spirit of the middle ages seems to have engulfed Gogol

completely towards the end of his life. It is a bizarre and cruel irony that his death was surrounded by the barbarous rituals of medieval medical practice, which could have formed a fitting subject for Brueghel.

Evenings in a village near Dikanka

The medieval strain in Gogol's writing is clearly apparent in his first collection of stories *Evenings in a village near Dikanka*. It is true that they were written in response to the then current romantic vogue for exotic regionalism, and Gothic horror (and the influence of such writers as Hoffmann and Tieck is clearly in evidence),[35] nevertheless the stories themselves breathe the atmosphere of medieval Russia with its great fairs, its simple ritualised faith and its superstition. It is a world in which the supernatural entirely permeates the grey fabric of ordinary existence; where the devil can appear in many guises, but can be warded off by incantations and by making the sign of the cross.

The protagonists are presented simply, often starkly, and without authorial sympathy. At times the characterisation is pure grotesque and recalls the world of Breughel or even the art of the gargoyle. Thus at the height of the wedding feast at the climax of the first story ('The Fair at Sorochintsy') Gogol chooses to introduce a bizarre *memento mori*:

> All was in motion, all was dancing. But an even stranger, more enigmatic feeling would have stirred in the depths of the heart at the sight of old women whose time-worn faces breathed the indifference of the grave, there, in the throng side by side with new, laughing, living human beings. Unconcerned!, deprived even of childish delight, without a spark of sympathetic feeling, forced by mere intoxication to do something approaching human activity, as is a lifeless automaton by its mechanic, they quietly shake their heads, imitating the steps of the revelling crowd; not even turning their eyes towards the young bridal pair. (I, 135–6)

Immediately after this, the sounds of the feast itself begin to die away, and the medieval tableau yields place to 'tears' designed to appeal to a more modern sensibility:

> Is it not in this way that joy, that beautiful but impermanent guest, flies away from us, and in vain does a lone sound attempt to express gaiety? It can already hear sadness in its own echo, and it listens to it strangely and desolately. Is it not like this that the lively friends of free and stormy youth are lost all over the world, one at a time, one after the other, finally leaving

behind one ancient brother? He who is left behind is sad. The heart becomes heavy and full of grief, but there is nought that can help him. (I, 136)

On the whole such a personal and sentimental note is rare in these stories; more typical is the presentation of grief in a detached or formal way, which at its extreme is the traditional ritualised lament of Katerina for her dead husband in section IX of 'A Terrible Vengeance'.

Laughter, too, permeates these stories. It is the naive, unsophisticated humour of simple people, the crude, rumbustious, slapstick laughter of the medieval fair. But laughter as 'ridicule', laughter as a weapon against the transgressors of accepted bounds, is also present. Again, it is in 'A Terrible Vengeance' that it finds its most striking expression. Thus in section II Katerina relates how the evil wizard feels that everyone is laughing at him. At the end of the story, on the very eve of the terrible punishment which is to be meted out to the wizard, his horse turns round and laughs at him (section XIV) and the monk with whom he seeks refuge also appears to laugh in the same way. Yet most frightening of all is the laughter he hears when retribution itself strikes:

Like thunder the wild laughter rolled across the mountains, and rang out in the soul of the wizard, shaking everything inside him. It seemed to him as though some strong man had got inside him and was walking about there, and striking his heart and his sinews with hammers... so terrifying did this laughter resound within him. (I, 278)

'A Terrible Vengeance' is perhaps the most 'medieval' of all the stories, and it seems significant that this last section is ostensibly told by a blind bard.[36]

The multiplicity of narrators is one of the striking features of *Evenings in a village near Dikanka*. First of all there is the figure whose name appears in the subtitle of the work: 'Stories published by the bee-keeper Rudy Panko'. Gogol is obviously hiding his own authorial personality behind this figure, much as Pushkin hides behind Belkin. But in the choice of name it is possible to see a hint of Gogol himself. In form, the name Panko (*Pan'ko*) is a type of patronymic found in the Ukraine; it is taken not from the father but from the grandfather. Gogol's grandfather was called Panas (which in Russian would be Afanasiy), the name that could be given to his grandson would be Panasenko – shortened to Panko, and therefore Gogol himself could lay claim to the name Panko.[37] The choice of name is in itself indicative: for, as we shall see, Gogol's interest in the Ukraine is in more senses than one 'ancestral'. Rudy (*rudyy*) means red or ruddy haired. The bee-keeper is naive and inept in literary matters, and the presentation of his personality forms a noticeable feature of the stories. The Ukrainians had a reputation for disingenuous naivety, and it is obvious that behind the simpleton, Rudy Panko, lurks the all-knowing Gogol, who is quite happy to hide behind the idiot's mask; such a 'Ukrainian' characteristic was second nature to him.[38]

Panko does not tell any of his own stories, he is the retailer of the stories of others, and editor. Thus 'St John's Eve' has the subtitle 'a real happening related by the sexton of *** church'. This fantastic story could hardly be a 'real happening' (*byl'*) but the device of narrators is of crucial importance in its presentation. Panko is reporting the story of a narrator, Foma Grigorevich, who according to Panko's own introductory words, never tells a story in the same way twice; moreover, it is not really his tale, but one originally told by his grandfather. The effect of a narrator figure reproducing the way a second narrator tells the story of yet a third narrator is of course comic, but there is more implied than this: it is a reflection of how folk-tales become created – a literary reworking of the process at work in the oral tradition, which can transform a 'real happening' into a completely improbable and fantastic story.

Throughout *Evenings in a village near Dikanka* Gogol shows great interest in the comic possibilities of the device of 'narrators'. His use of an uneducated, or at best semi-literate narrator allows him to place emphasis on the way the story is told, with distortions, and lapses both of understanding and taste, as though they arose naturally from the personality and idiosyncrasies of the narrator himself. In his later writing the tone of 'the uneducated narrator' is often present (for example 'The Nose' and 'The Overcoat') even when there is no specific indication of a narrator to be distinguished from Gogol himself.

Historically, the narrator in literature is not so much a 'device' as a natural phenomenon: the inevitable link between the spoken word of the ancient, oral tradition and the written word of the literary forms which replaced it. The West has had its Boccaccios and its Chaucers and, as we have already seen, the sense of a 'Renaissance' in contact with the middle ages was in some degree a concept still relevant for Russia, even at the beginning of the nineteenth century.

The figure of a narrator relating folk-tales was, in this sense, a natural one, but its appeal was reinforced by the prevailing literary vogue for folklore. It must be conceded that the role of the narrator in Gogol owes more to literature than to genuine oral tradition.

In Chaucer's *Canterbury Tales* narrators are of great thematic importance. They constitute a sophisticated literary device, in as much as the story each narrator tells sheds light on his own character and his relations with narrators from other walks of life represented on the pilgrimage. By contrast, in *Evenings in a village near Dikanka* Gogol uses the idiosyncrasies of his narrators more for comic effect. His emphasis is on the story itself rather than on the tale as a means of exploring the character and attitudes of a given narrator. Indeed it is difficult to know precisely who the actual narrator of each story is (though critics have attempted to identify them).[39] In a later work, however, Gogol will exploit the device of the nature of the story told as a means of revealing the character of the narrator and the society in which he moves (i.e. the 'Tale of Captain Kopeykin', told by the postmaster in *Dead Souls*).

F. C. Driessen makes a valid point when he says that the source for 'Ivan Fedorovich Shponka and his Aunty' is not given as verbal narration, but as a story that was actually written down: a piece of literature, and that this also reflects a shift to an entirely different style of tale.[40] Nevertheless this new departure is inevitably surrounded by comic elements which seek to reduce this 'literary' form to the sort of vagaries that condition the oral tradition itself. Thus the story's incompleteness is explained by Rudy Panko as the fault of his 'old woman' who used its final sheets to bake pies. Yet, he says, if the reader wants to hear the rest, he has only to call on Stepan Ivanovich Kurochka in the town of Gadyach, who will gladly relate it to him. In this way, once again, the reader is referred back to the oral tradition. Nevertheless, the point remains that the story of Ivan Shponka is in every sense different from the other tales in the collection: it has no supernatural element, no hyperbolic poetry. Instead it mines a rich new vein of comedy from the drab reality of everyday provincial life. It belongs quite clearly to written literature, and not to the oral tradition.

The story is a work worthy of the mature Gogol. Its central figure is a type, whom, in many guises, we shall meet again in the later writing: a complete nonentity, whose very mediocrity is described in positive terms. Thus the eleven years it took Shponka to rise from the rank of cadet to that of second lieutenant is presented to the reader as a rapid promotion merited by his talents.

This young man of nearly forty leaves the army, and retires to his estate managed by his aunt, a formidable figure in whom 'nature appeared to have made an unforgivable mistake', endowing her with skirts instead of military moustaches and jack books. She dominates his life, and when she suggests that he should get married, he has a nightmare full of symbols equated with wives, such as to gladden the heart of any critic with a Freudian bent.

Evenings in a village near Dikanka is remarkable in Gogol's *oeuvre* for the degree to which sexual themes are openly presented. Unusually, for Gogol, the relationship between the sexes inspires a great deal of good-natured fun, as well as a certain poetry. This is particularly true of 'A May Night or the Drowned Maiden' which in atmosphere and plot at times approaches Shakespeare's *A Midsummer-Night's Dream*. Love has its dark side, too: in 'St John's Eve', in order to appease demonic forces, Petro kills the innocent young brother of his future bride. Here the sexual rivalry between generations which as a theme with many variations characterises all these stories, seems to take on a dark allegorical significance: in order for young love to be consummated (Petro and Pidorka) an old woman must drink the blood of innocent childhood (Ivas).

Even more remarkable is the demonic treatment of love and the generations in 'A Terrible Vengeance'. Because of a curse placed upon another Petro, each successive descendant of his line is to become more vicious than his predecessor – until the ultimate in evil is reached. By its very nature, such a curse of degeneration suggests itself as an allegory of incest, and the ultimate in evil turns out to be precisely this: it is the crime of a wizard (alone of all the characters he has no name) who seeks to marry his own daughter. Yet the allegory is inverted; the progressive degeneration of the line does not begin with incest – it ends with it, as the most terrible of crimes. This is mirrored in a corresponding inversion of the plot, which reasserts the logic of the allegory by placing the story of Katerina and her father before its historical antecedent – the short explanatory tale of Petro and Ivan.

It is significant that the wizard makes his first appearance in the story at a wedding. The raising of holy icons turns him from his disguise as an unknown Cossack into a green-eyed monster with fangs; the first to be frightened by this are children. Katerina's father has a double existence: in the waking domestic world he is a cantankerous father, strict in his view of his daughter's duty; in the world of dream and magic he desires her as a bride. To the outside gaze his crime is public – he is a traitor to the Cossack cause; but as a wizard the evil is private – his crimes are directed against kith and kin.

As with Shponka the sexual implications of the story are conveyed through dream. When Katerina recounts her first dream of her father's incestuous suggestion, her husband, Danilo, comments: 'Yes, dreams tell a lot of truth' (I, 253). Later he himself witnesses her father conjuring the soul out of Katerina's sleeping body to commune with it, and he hears the soul say: 'Poor Katerina! There is much that her soul knows, which she does not know' (I, 259). Danilo returns to his sleeping wife, wakes her, and recounts what he has seen and heard. She recognises much of it as her dream, but not all; she does not remember knowing that her father had killed her mother. At this Danilo repeats the idea of the soul itself: 'You do not know a tenth of what the soul knows.' The section ends with Katerina's ambiguous assertion to her husband: 'You for me are my father' (I, 260).

Earlier Katerina had been the cause of a duel between husband and father, but when Danilo had been about to reach for a pistol with which he never missed, Katerina intervened and dissuaded him from the act. She thus appears to be saving her father, although her ostensible motive is the protection of her husband. Her plea is based on an emotional appeal to Danilo to consider his son.

The wizard, as a traitor to the Cossack cause (it is stressed for this crime and for no other) is locked up in his son-in-law's dungeon, awaiting death. In the name of her dead mother, he begs that Katerina should listen to him, promising to save his soul in a monastery, if she will only set him free. Reluctantly she agrees, and thinks of her act as 'pleasing to God'; that she 'has saved a soul'. Thus on a second and more important occasion, Katerina saves her father from her husband, and the decisive argument is once more the appeal to a filial bond, though it is not now that between father and son, but that between mother and daughter.

Nevertheless, for the first time she has 'deceived' her husband. In her fear she thinks she hears his approach, and falls down in a faint on the spot. The words which rouse her, however, are not those of her husband, they appear to be the comforting words of a mother:

'It is I, my very own daughter! It is I, my dear little heart!' (I, 263). They are spoken, however, by an old serving woman who has carried her out of the dungeon and thus saved her from her husband's wrath.

After his escape, the wizard openly joins the forces of the enemy. Danilo is troubled by a presentiment of his own death, but Katerina cannot bring herself to console him: 'It was bitter for her guilty head to accept a husband's affection' (I, 265). The wizard kills Danilo in battle, and later Katerina confesses that she has brought about her own destruction by freeing her father.

After her husband's death Katerina again dreams of her father: he threatens to kill her baby son if she refuses to marry him. Alarmed, she reassures herself that the baby is alive and well, and goes back to sleep, only to wake up in terror with the words: 'He is killed; he is butchered.' Her child now lies dead in its cot. Katerina goes mad.

A Cossack calling himself Kopryan, and an old friend of her husband, visits her, but when he suggests marriage, she immediately recognises him as her father. She rushes to kill him with a knife, but it is she who is killed instead.

Although the mechanics of the plot allocate the 'ultimate wickedness' to the sorcerer alone, and Danilo grudgingly admits to Katerina: 'all the sins lie on your father', nevertheless, as the last adult of Petro's line, is Katerina totally exempt from the terms of the curse? The wizard's most explicit crimes are political defection and the killing of Danilo. He makes no direct statement that he wishes to marry his daughter;[41] the suggestion is presented through the soul, the dreams, the madness of Katerina herself. It is not clear who kills her child, and the murder of her mother, an act symbolic in the incestuous desires of a daughter,[42] is a fact known to her soul but not to her (in 'St John's Eve' Petro has a complete blockage of memory about the murder of Iva). The twice repeated statement, that her soul knows more than Katerina herself, is striking in its context, and there is more than a suggestion that, subconsciously at least, Katerina bears the guilt of the 'ultimate wickedness'.

If this interpretation is correct, then the daughter's desire for her father is mirrored back in the story as his desire for her, much as the natural world itself is inverted in the magic waters of the Dnepr.

> It is lovely[43] to look from the middle of the Dnepr at the high mountains, at the broad meadows, at the green forests! Those mountains are not mountains: they have no base; beneath them, as above them is a sharp summit; and below them and above them is the high heaven. Those forests

that stand on the hills are not forests: it is hair growing on the shaggy head of a forest grandad. Beneath the head a beard is washed in the water; and below the beard and above the hair is the high heaven. The meadows are not meadows: it is a green belt girdling in its middle a round heaven, both in the upper half, and in the lower half, a moon is riding. (I, 246)

The description is obviously far from realistic. Although nature is observed by moonlight, it still retains its colour – green (the colour of the wizard's eyes) and the light is strong enough to reflect the forests clearly in the water as the image of a wood spirit – *lesnoy ded*: a 'forest grandad'.[44] It is a description built on the concepts of 'above' and 'below'. It is constructed round negatives which deny the true identity of the natural world and assert in its place two strange symbols: one aged, male, ancestral – the 'forest grandad', the other constrained, distorted but suggestively female – a round, girdled heaven with two moons.

The negative constructions are continued in the description of the people in the boat: Danilo does not look to either side, he looks at his young wife; he thinks she is sad, but she is *not* sad, she is thinking of the wizard. She talks of the fear inspired in her by the stories about him, then wipes the face of her sleeping child with a kerchief embroidered in red with emblems of the natural world, leaves and berries.

When Katerina demurs at her husband's desire to rob the wizard of his gold, he becomes inexplicably angry and rudely rebukes her with words of rejection. She falls silent, looks into the 'dreamy' water, and the wind ruffling it makes it appear silvery: 'like a wolf's coat in the middle of the night'.[45] This new image for the river is the prelude to their passing the wizard's hideout and the burial ground of his ancestors, where nothing green will grow. As they row past, corpses rise from their graves. They are all bones and claws, and each is more frightening than the last. Their behaviour seems like a premonition of the terrible vengeance itself, and, indeed, the curse had ordained that ancestors would rise from their graves, after each crime committed by the last in their line – a fact known to the soul of Katerina itself. Moreover, these macabre figures carry on the symbolism of the bearded forest grandfather which is reflected in the river along with the moon. They, too, are 'grandfathers' ('his diabolical[46] grandfathers rot there' says Danilo in describing the wizard's cemetery) and for skeletons they are strangely hirsute: the length of their beards measures the fear they inspire. The appearance of each one is marked by the shattering of a cross, and the last, whose beard stretches to his very heels, holds his hands aloft 'as though he wanted to reach the moon'. At the same time he utters a fearful cry which awakes the child in terror and terrifies Katerina. Yet these 'grandfathers' are also those of Katerina herself, and the nocturnal journey she undertakes with her family down the magic river seems symbolic: it is from marriage to death – from a wedding feast to an ancestral graveyard, and finally to her husband's home where the sorcerer awaits her in the form of a father.

The Dnepr runs as a bright thread throughout the story. Like the wizard it has a double existence: it is the highway of the Cossack warriors, but it is also a 'mirror road', a crystal revealing dark secrets. The wizard is partially reflected in this element, but it is above all for his daughter that the Dnepr presents its mysterious, poetic face. The opening of section IV clearly equates her mood with that of the river itself, and when her husband plans to visit the wizard's castle, the Dnepr is likened to a grumbling old man who finds fault with everything (the mood of Katerina's father after their return from the wedding). At the burning of the wizard's castle the Dnepr runs crimson as with blood, and in section VI when he is locked up in Danilo's dungeon the 'indifference' of the river to his fate expresses the apparent unconcern of his daughter.

Section X describes the Dnepr in three distinct moods. The first is in obvious contrast to the description in section II. There the viewpoint was from the middle of the river, where the moonlight reflected nature in the river as a 'forest grandad'. Now, in bright sunlight, the view is from the banks where the 'greeny-lock' forests admire their image in the water, but 'dare not look into the middle of the Dnepr' (rare is the bird that would fly as far as the middle of the Dnepr).

The second mood is a summer night, but again it contrasts with the summer night of section II. Gone is the moon; it has been replaced by the stars, which have come direct from God, who has shaken them from His holy garment so that not one is lost – they are all reflected in the river. Nature, on the other hand, seems dark and threatening: 'The black forest, dotted with sleeping crows, and the ancient broken mountains, hanging down, attempt to cover it, if possible, with their long shade. But in vain!' (I, 269).

The reader might be tempted to accept such imagery as hyperbole used to convey the great width of the Dnepr. Yet the trees and flowers which 'do not dare to look into the middle', and the forests and mountains attempting to cover it with their shade, are images which in their different ways create the reverse effect. They make a mighty river seem narrow: its centre is too conscious of the pretensions of its banks.

The moon presents nature in strange symbolic forms to Katerina and her family at the river's centre. The waking world with its clarity of vision (the sun) allows nature to admire her own image at the margin, though now she herself fears to look into the depths. When the river reflects the lights of God (the stars) a dark and ominous nature (scattered with crows like the river itself with stars) strives to blot out the divine lights of guidance with its shade. Later, in an almost erotic moment, when the cold of night forces the river to snuggle closer to these banks, the stream it thus imposes on itself is death – the silver strip of a Cossack sabre.[47]

Nature in these scenes is not what it seems ('Those mountains... are not mountains... Those forests... are not forests... Those meadows are not meadows' etc.). Nature is not only personified, it is presented as 'human' in another sense, and the river that reflects it, is like the soul of Katerina which knows more than she does herself; for whether it be dark or light the river's very breadth inhibits full vision: 'In the middle of the night, or in the middle of the day one can see as far into it as the human eye can see' (I, 269).

Section X depicts the Dnepr in yet another mood – a river in turmoil, and a nature torn and shattered by storm. Its illumination is no longer, moon, sun or stars, but lightning which 'in a moment lights up the whole world'. It is then that the Dnepr is terrifying. Yet in this mood of angry revelation the river exhibits two contradictory impulses: the watery hills thunder against the mountains, only to run back crying. The ambivalence is personified in a mother in tears who is following a martial son leaving for the army.

Another figure lurks behind this image of grief. The preceding chapter had ended with Katerina's lament for her husband killed in battle; he, too, like this son, rode a 'black steed', and like this mother, Katerina weeps 'scalding tears'. Katerina 'cries and wastes away from grief' (*plachet i ubivayetsya Katerina*), but now it is the Dnepr which 'cries' and the Cossack mother who 'wastes away from grief' (*tak ubivayetsya staraya mat' kozaka*). The turbulent river refracts Katerina's grief for a husband as a mother's grief for a son, yet it is a father that it actually bears on its warring waves. The wizard is in a boat in the middle of the storm and he is annoyed at the 'funeral feast' prepared at his son-in-law's death – the military losses which the Cossacks have inflicted on the Poles. He attempts once more to summon up the soul of his daughter, but calls forth instead the spectre of retribution.

The image of the grieving mother recurs after the second death: the murder of Katerina's own child. In her madness Katerina sings a garbled song in which death is equated with marriage for the Cossack warrior, as the mother mourns her dead son, but the song has an unexpected ending:

> And who will not love me
> May his mother be struck by fever! (I, 274)

Katerina, in her madness, wanders the banks of the Dnepr at dusk, when there are neither stars nor moon. The dark forest is a terrifying place. Unbaptised children are in the trees and the river is full of maidens who have 'ruined their souls'. Their images fuse into one – a green-haired figure, for whom the water is a transparent shirt. Here is an obvious parallel with the 'forest grandad', but the movement of reflection is from the river to its banks: 'Her hair flows from her green head to her shoulders. The water noisily murmuring runs from her long hair to the land' (I, 274). Her eyes try to entice the soul, she appears about to kiss, and to be burning with love, but the baptised are warned to flee; for her lips are ice and her bed is the cold water.

The water nymph (*rusalka*)[48] is a poetic evocation of suicide. The two occasions on which Katerina had saved her father from her husband had been accompanied by threats of her drowning in the Dnepr. The *rusalka* is an image in the water of Katerina herself: a maiden who 'has ruined her soul', and whose cold love could entice the soul of another to fill the forest with unchristened children. Yet madness preserves Katerina. She is looking for her father, but now it is with a knife.

It is not her fate to kill him. A terrible vengeance is being prepared for the wizard beyond the confines of the Slavonic world. The face of the giant horseman first appears to him after the death of Danilo, but after the murder of Katerina's child the horseman himself (Ivan[49] in the original story) rides out of Hungary to the highest point in the Carpathians. He is a figure of nightmare; once the sun rises, he cannot be seen, though he casts a shadow. He is only visible by night, and, 'whether the stars shine or not', he rides along asleep with an infant page at his back. Like the 'forest grandad' and the *rusalka* darkness does not dim his image in water; for at night he is reflected in the great lakes of Hungary.

The poetic role of the Dnepr ceases with the death of Katerina. In its place are the forbidding heights of the Carpathian Mountains, but there is a link with the Dnepr in the violent mood of section X; for these mountains are compared to lofty petrified waves from a storm-tossed sea. Vision, which the Dnepr seemed to limit, suddenly becomes boundless, and it is possible to see to the ends of the earth. The Black Sea, the Crimea and the Sivash are clearly visible from Kiev, in what appears to be a reflected image (in this perspective Galicia is 'on the left').

The wizard sees the terrible horseman on the mountain top, but he cannot escape. His horse refuses to jump a river, and laughs at him. Nature threatens him in its symbolic forms of bearded forest and righteous stars: 'The trees, surrounding him in a dark forest and as though alive, wagging their black beards and stretching out long branches attempted to throttle him.[50] The stars appeared to run ahead in front of him, pointing out the sinner to everyone' (I, 276). Not only is there a hint here of the 'forest grandad', but after the murder of the ancient holy man, the forests themselves seem to take on the attributes of his own dead grandfathers: 'Something emitted an unbearable moan, and the moan rolled across forest and field. Thin dried-up arms with long claws rose from behind the forest, shook and disappeared' (I, 277).

The Carpathian Mountains, the 'horseshoe' separating Hungarians from Slavs is a fitting place for the giant horseman to stand and exact vengeance on a horseman who cannot escape, but the symbol is not without significance for Katerina herself; for throughout the story she walks on 'silver horseshoes'.[51] The wizard's horse carries him relentlessly towards the rider on the mountain, who, in spite of the increased vision of all around, remains with eyes firmly closed: once they are opened retribution begins.

The figure of the horseman, the strange clarity of vision, and the phrase 'hour of judgement' (*chas mery*)[52] all give the terrible vengeance a sense of apocalypse. The nature of this vengeance, however, is like a paradigm of incest itself: it is a visitation of the sins of the fathers upon the children. The last in the line, and those who have gone before him, are made to pay for the crime of Petro, and the crime itself mirrors its punishment, in as much as Ivan accuses Petro of depriving him of 'honourable breed and issue on earth'.[53] Petro's deed against 'honourable' descendants finds retribution in the crime of incest, punished in a macabre climax of ancestral cannibalism. Forebears, who resemble the wizard 'like two drops of water' gnaw at his bones, while the original malefactor, Petro, in frustration, gnaws at himself: the sin that consumes a line is also self-consuming.[54]

Although incest is not an explicit theme elsewhere in *Evenings in a village near Dikanka*, it is nevertheless true that many of the stories are concerned with 'inbred' relationships, and some seem to hint at more than they express.

In 'A May Night or the Drowned Maiden' the water nymph (*rusalka*) is a young girl who has killed herself because she has been rejected by her father. He is a widower, and when he tells his daughter that he intends to marry again she asks: 'Will you caress me as in the old days, father, when you take another wife?' He replies: 'I shall, my daughter, I will press you even more firmly to my heart' (I, 157). Her stepmother, however, proves to be a witch, who turns herself into a cat in order to visit the daughter in her bedroom at night. When the girl cuts off one of its paws with her father's sabre, the witch does not emerge from her room for three days, and then her hand is seen to be bandaged. After this the father's treatment of the girl becomes progressively worse until, finally rejected, she drowns herself and becomes a *rusalka*. In the same story the village headman is living with a lady loosely described as a 'kinswoman', but this does not prevent him from pressing his attentions on the sweetheart of his own son.

In 'Christmas Eve', the blacksmith Vakula has no father, nevertheless his mother appears to be the 'friend' of most of the town's men (indeed of the devil as well, since she is a witch). One of her lovers, Chub, is the father of Oksana, the girl her son wishes to marry. When Oksana reminds Vakula that his mother is a witch, he makes a statement, quite close to that of Katerina in 'A Terrible Vengeance': 'What is my mother to me? You for me are mother, father and everything that is dear in the world' (I, 414). But Oksana points out complications: *her* father could marry *his* mother.

Ivan Shponka is faced with a similar uncertainty surrounding his parentage. His aunt suggests, very clearly, that his real father was a neighbour Stepan Kuzmich, who has left him some land in his will. Yet to get this land he must marry the sister of his 'father's' heir.

The unifying theme of these stories is the Ukraine, its superstitions, its terrifying legends, its people and its carefree way of life. Most of the tales are set in some legendary past, when the Ukraine was free and independent, the home of doughty Cossack warriors. This sense of a glorious past is evident in 'A Terrible Vengeance', when Danilo remembers the good old times of the hetman Konashevich (Petr Sagaydachnyy who died in 1622) and compares it with the present. The present, however, in Gogol's time had even less to offer Ukrainian national pride: the Ukraine had been reduced to 'Little Russia',[55] a mere province of Great Russia itself.

The degeneration of Cossack descendants in 'A Terrible Vengeance' can be seen as a national as well as a personal punishment. Thus Petro's crime is also interpreted as breaking the bond of comradeship with a Cossack warrior brother, and for this his heirs are doomed to fall further and further away from the Cossack ideal, until we have the wizard who fights with the Poles against his own son-in-law. To this extent 'A Terrible Vengeance' is also a parable which points a moral for the decline of a nation. The Dnepr itself, which, as we have seen, has great symbolic significance for the story, is at the same time the Cossack highway. It is compared to a sabre of Damascus steel.

In 'Christmas Eve' Gogol comes dangerously near to making a political point. Vakula joins a party of Zaporogian Cossacks, who have come to see the empress. They complain about their treatment at her hands: fortresses are being built against them, and there are rumours that the Cossack headquarters (the *Sech'*) will be broken up. (Their fears were justified, Catherine II did destroy the *Sech'* in 1775.)

When the empress asks them what they expect of her, Vakula blurts out that he wants a pair of her shoes. The situation is comic; it is also emblematic. Vakula is carrying out the commission of his sweetheart, Oksana, but at this decisive moment the request for a trivial, female thing (and at the behest of a woman), ironically highlights the Cossacks' plight. Mistrust of women permeates all Gogol's depiction of Cossack life. 'Whoever gets mixed up with you, will himself become a woman', says Danilo to his wife, and adds with sarcasm: 'There would be a great deal to be gained, indeed, if we started to obey wives.' Ironically such fears about women proved to be well-founded: it was at the hands of Catherine II that the Cossacks suffered most. The empress, however, avoids the question of her treatment of them; she asks instead about *their* treatment of women: 'I have heard that in your Sech′, you never marry', and she regards the request for her shoes as an incident worthy of the comic pen of Fonvizin. His reply, that really it is a La Fontaine who is required, suggests that the episode may be taken as a fable: the empress's shoes trampling down the military traditions of the Cossacks.

Evenings in a village near Dikanka, in spite of the overall impression of immaturity which it conveys, contains two significant and remarkable stories. 'A Terrible Vengeance' reveals the roots of Gogol's art rising from oral and medieval literature. This is not only a fairy-tale world, but a world of sympathetic magic where symbol has the force of reality. In contrast to the fictional methods of the nineteenth century, characterisation seems emblematic and thin. The author self-avowedly dare not enter the terrors of the human soul: 'Not a single man on earth could relate what was happening in the wizard's soul, and if he were to peep in and see what was taking place then he would not sleep at nights and would not laugh again' (I, 277). Nevertheless through the methods of an earlier art Gogol is strangely able to give an account of such psychological mysteries.

Katerina is undoubtedly the most convincing female portrait in Gogol's work, yet there is very little physical description of her and even less overt portrayal of her psychology. Her image is poetically evoked through symbol: the moods of the river Dnepr and the nature on its banks. Such oblique presentation of character will become the Gogolian method (in another guise it may be seen in 'Shponka'). The story is also notable for its many dislocations, its mirror inversions, its negative constructions, its hyperbole – all these are the hallmark of Gogol's mature style.

'The Terrible Vengeance' influenced Dostoevsky in his early story *The Landlady*, and the poetic evocation of a river and a tormented heroine could well have served Ostrovsky in his depiction of another Katerina in the play *The Thunderstorm*.

By contrast 'Ivan Fedorovich Shponka and his Aunty' looks forward to Gogol's writing in his so called 'realistic' vein. Not only is the story a comic gem in its own right, but it is the precursor of that whole comic manner identified as 'Gogolian'. *Evenings in a village near Dikanka* contains much in embryo which will be developed later. The theme of the Ukraine will be presented with more subtlety and skill in *Mirgorod*, and the third story in that collection will mark the full fruition of the fairy story as a vehicle for psychological exploration. The short interlude of Vakula's visit to St Petersburg in 'Christmas Eve' looks even further ahead: it gives a foretaste of the view of St Petersburg as a 'fantastic' city which Gogol was to develop in his later tales.

1
Mirgorod

Origins and aims

Gogol wrote the stories, which constitute the collection he called *Mirgorod*, between 1832 and 1834. It was published at the beginning of 1835, yet one of the stories had actually appeared before as a contribution to the Almanac *Housewarming* (*Novoselye*) which the publisher Smirdin brought out to celebrate moving into new premises. This story, 'The tale of how Ivan Ivanovich quarrelled with Ivan Nikiforovich', is the only one actually to be set in Mirgorod, and in the original version in *Housewarming* it was linked quite specifically to the earlier stories of *Evenings in a village near Dikanka*, both by its attribution to Rudy Panko and by the spurious date of 1831.[1] The tale is backward looking in yet another respect: its title and certain elements of plot have a clear relationship to *The Two Ivans or the Passion for Litigation* of Gogol's compatriot V. T. Narezhny (first published 1825 by the same publisher, A. Smirdin). For all the earlier chronology which these facts imply, Gogol chose to place the story last in his collection; there are sound artistic reasons for this, which will be examined later. Critics have long pointed to Narezhny's tale *The Two Ivans or the Passion for Litigation* as the predecessor of the last of the Mirgorod stories. The common factors are striking: the town of Mirgorod; the friendship of two noblemen both called Ivan; a bitter and senseless feud involving interminable litigation. Yet these similarities are entirely superficial. Gogol's story is not only essentially different, it is incomparably better. Nevertheless the presence of Narezhny's rambling and improbable novel can be felt in some measure behind all the stories of *Mirgorod*. Thus, like Gogol in 'The Old World Landowners', Narezhny depicts an aging childless couple, Kirik and Ulita, whom he also ironically calls Philemon and Baucis. The opening of 'Taras Bulba' with the return of Cossack sons from the theological seminary and their immersion into events of great violence is not unlike the opening and subsequent course of Narezhny's novel; there is, too, a similar theme of young love bridging ancient enmities. Moreover a central motif in 'Viy', the reading of scripture over a body, which suddenly rises from its coffin, seems to reflect an incident in *The Two Ivans*, though here it has a comic treatment. It is as though Narezhny's work was a great rough quarry from which Gogol would carve his much finer pieces.[2]

In the original version of 'The Tale of how Ivan Ivanovich quarrelled with Ivan Nikiforovich' cuts were imposed by the censor before it could be printed in *Housewarming*. As the manuscript has not survived it is impossible to say what they were. Nevertheless Gogol was annoyed, and when it was to be published in *Mirgorod*, he wrote a special preface for it, which could be interpreted as irony at the expense of the censors. This preface was removed at the very last moment, indeed the type had already been set up, and Gogol was faced with the problem of how to fill up the unwelcome gap. He solved the problem by adding two extra pages to the preceding story, 'Viy' with the result that 'Viy' now does not end at what appears to be its natural climax, the frozen horror in the church, but goes on to relate what happened to the hero's comrades. That these changes were effected at the very last moment can be seen from the fact that a copy of *Mirgorod* has been discovered already printed with the original preface to the tale of the two Ivans and without the later ending of 'Viy'.

The version of *Mirgorod* which we read today is not, however, that of 1835. Gogol substantially revised the collection for the second edition of his works which came out in 1842. It was the second story, 'Taras Bulba' which underwent most change. New passages and fresh episodes were included, so that the revised version is nearly twice as long as the original, having twelve chapters instead of nine. Significantly, too, the nationalistic sentiments of the first version were reworked into a chauvinism which was Great Russian rather than more specifically Ukrainian. 'Viy' too underwent minor alterations. Belinsky had criticised the detailed descriptions of the monsters surrounding Khoma Brut on the second and final nights of his ordeal,[3] Gogol took note of this, made their depiction simpler, and reduced their number.

Mirgorod invites comparison with the earlier collection of Ukrainian stories *Evenings in a village near Dikanka*. The tale of the two Ivans first appeared, as we have seen, under the signature of Rudy Panko. The name of this inept 'editor' has been banished from

Mirgorod itself, but nevertheless it carries the subtitle 'Tales serving as a continuation of *Evenings in a village near Dikanka*'. Thematically both collections of stories have much in common. There is the same mixture of elements: the supernatural existing side by side with the trivial ordinariness of everyday existence; the comic theme of middle-age amours; the tragic and horrific theme of unnatural sexuality; there is both pastoral idyll and gothic horror, and a similar loose chronology which embraces remote history, legend and the near present. Comparable too is the range of 'modes': the lyrical, the rhetorical, the grotesque, the banal. Despite all these similarities there is one important quality which marks *Mirgorod* off from its predecessor – artistic maturity: what is merely glimpsed in the *Evenings* has come to full fruition in the later collection. *Mirgorod* is a work of real genius.

Both collections designate a geographical location in their titles as a means of unifying what are, on the face of it, quite disparate stories, yet neither the village near Dikanka nor Mirgorod figure as prominently in the stories themselves as the titles would lead one to expect. Their role is, rather, symbolic and emblematic; each stands as a sort of fictional microcosm of the Ukraine itself.

Mirgorod is a real town, but its name is evocative, it is 'Peace-town' (*mir* = peace; *gorod* = town) it is consonant with the somnolent atmosphere of the Ukraine as a province of the Russian empire, but it is in stark contrast to its warlike and violent past as depicted in 'Taras Bulba'. (Ironically, the real Mirgorod was a garrison town.) The title is apt in yet a further sense; for *mir* can also mean 'world',[4] and as 'Worldtown', it hints at that very concept of microcosm, which the four stories, taken together, ultimately suggest.

Each story refracts the theme of the Ukraine through a different prism: 'The Old World Landowners' as idyll; 'Taras Bulba' as epic; 'Viy' as folklore; 'The tale of how Ivan Ivanovich quarrelled with Ivan Nikiforovich' as comedy. The approach is not unlike the many-faceted presentation of a central subject, which Mikhail Lermontov was later to exploit with such success in *Hero of Our Time* (the history of publication, with isolated stories preceding the unified collection is not dissimilar). Yet, if this analogy holds, the great difference, and one which is so typical for Gogol, is that the central theme of Mirgorod is non-human. His first epigraph, commenting on his title, makes this plain:

Mirgorod is an extremely small town near the Khorol river. It has one rope factory, one brick works, four water mills and forty five windmills.

From Zyablovsky's Geography

Here is a town, not of inhabitants, but of a precise number of objects, and as all of these are useful, busy and productive, the list reads like an ironic comment on the actual people who inhabit Gogol's Mirgorod.

In justifying *Hero of Our Time* Lermontov said in the preface to Pechorin's diary: 'The history of a human soul, even though it be the shallowest of souls, is scarcely less interesting and useful than the history of a whole nation.'[5] Gogol in *Mirgorod* is attempting to give us, if not a history, then something of the anatomy of a nation, yet, in so doing, he is in constant danger of turning the human souls he depicts into creatures resembling automata.

'*The Old World Landowners*'

'The Old World Landowners' appears to be a story in the 'sentimental' mode:[6] a nostalgic evocation of the relationship and way of life of an endearing old Ukrainian couple. Yet if the perspective is sentimental, the subject matter itself is nearer to the world of the middle ages, with its enormous meals, its unquestioning self-sufficiency and a religious temperament which finds its chief expression in superstition and a predilection for the terrible curse (compare Pulkheriya Ivanovna's threat to her housekeeper).

The narrator of this story, with his constant note of nostalgia, is far different from those ingenuous narrators of *Evenings in a village near Dikanka*, he is a modern man, a person of some sophistication, seeking to contrast the virtues of this rural life with what he knows of the capital cities. Yet this evocation of Ukrainian life is, in essence, atavistic. The Tovstogubs are apparently based on Gogol's grandparents Afanasiy Demyanovich and his wife, whose maiden name had been Lizogub.[7] Gogol has given his grandfather's Christian name, Afanasiy, to his 'old world landowner', and as we have already seen this is a name, and a relationship, which links the author with his narrator Rudy Panko. Moreover the same inbred nature of relationships which could be observed in *Evenings in a village near Dikanka* seems to be indicated in this tiny, enclosed world by the odd coincidence that the couple share the same patronymic (Ivanovich/Ivanovna).

On the face of it, the story is an idyll; it certainly conforms to Gogol's own definition of the genre:

Although people link the idea of the idyll with the idea of pastoral and rural life, its bounds are wider and can embrace the way of life of many people, given only that simplicity and a modest lot are an integral part of such a way of life. [The idyll] portrays this way of life down to its smallest details, and however shallow its scope may seem, containing neither exalted lyrical mood, nor dramatic interest, nor momentous event, and even though it appears as no more than all that, which first confronts the eyes in ordinary life, nevertheless he who takes it in this sense alone, will be mistaken. For almost always it is directed by some inner idea, which is far too close to the poet's soul, and he has used the way of life and the idyll itself merely as the most convenient forms. The best idylls had some historical significance and were written for some occasion...

An idyll is not a fairy story (*skazka*) and not a tale (*povest'*), although it contains within it something akin to an event, but it is a vivid representation of a quiet, peaceful way of life, a scene having no dramatic movement. It can be called a picture, in the true sense, and, by virtue of the objects it chooses, which are always simple ones, a picture of the Flemish School. (VIII, 480–1)

Pushkin immediately recognised Gogol's story for what it was, when he spoke of 'that comic touching idyll, which forces us to laugh through tears of sadness and tenderness'[8] – a phrase which at the same time forcibly reminds us of the mixed nature of Gogol's art and of the formula: 'laughter through tears'. Belinsky, too, called the story: 'a tearful comedy in the full sense of the word', but the critic feigned anger at being made to weep at the lives of such automata.[9] Indeed, the story always seems to have left its readers slightly perplexed, and it is as well to bear in mind Gogol's own words on the idyll as a genre, which has more in it than first meets the eye.

As we have seen, Gogol thinks of the idyll in pictorial terms, and in 'The Old World Landowners' the narrator says: 'If I were an artist and wished to depict Philemon and Baucis on my canvas, I would never have chosen any other original but them'[10] (II, 15). Philemon and Baucis are the aged childless couple of Ovid's *Metamorphoses*,[11] and it may seem strange that, if Gogol were really depicting his own grandparents, he should have chosen to make them childless (a sort of genealogical death wish akin to the 'terrible vengeance' of *Evenings in a village near Dikanka*). Yet Narezhny before him had depicted an ageing childless couple in his *Two Ivans* whom he too had ironically called Philemon and Baucis, but whereas the sterile relationship of Afanasiy and Pulkheriya is depicted by Gogol as a peaceful idyll, the childlessness of Kirik and Ulita is presented by Narezhny with the violent overtones and starkness which are typical of his novel: Kirik, a tavern keeper, has reached a pitch of violent despair which can only be alleviated by drink:

> Whenever a pregnant woman passed by the windows of his house, he would rush out headlong into the yard; his wife, knowing what this meant, would rush to the bar-counter, and as soon as her husband appeared with a log in his hands, she went to meet him with the most enormous bottle she could find. Kirik would stop, would smile, throw his weapon on the floor, and with parental tenderness would take the bottle out of his wife's hands and into his own embrace, he would kiss her and weep with emotion.[12]

This may seem a far cry from 'The Old World Landowners', and yet there are elements of a latent hostility which Afanasiy Ivanovich constantly expresses towards his wife, and she for her part is always plying him with oral solace in the form of food and drink.

It is indeed food, and hospitality in general which Gogol seeks to present as the chief virtue of these old people, and this is the virtue of the mythical figures Philemon and Baucis themselves who were rewarded by Jove for their hospitality by being allowed to die together and in death become two trees whose top branches were intertwined. Yet in Gogol's story more than five years separate the death of Pulkheriya Ivanovna from that of Afanasiy Ivanovich, moreover in life they already seem more like representatives of the vegetable kingdom than human beings. They are certainly rooted to the spot and surrounded by trees. As the narrator says in his general introductory remarks about such a life: 'Not a single desire flies beyond the paling surrounding the little courtyard, or beyond the wattle fence of the garden full of apple and plum trees, or beyond the villagers' huts which surround it, and which are lop-sided and shaded by willow, elder and pear trees' (II, 13). Critics often link 'The Old World Landowners' to Gogol's first visit home to the Ukraine from St Petersburg (1832), and in particular to a letter he wrote to I. I. Dmitriyev in which he contrasts the fertility of the Ukraine and its luxuriant wealth of nature with the poverty of its inhabitants. 'The lack of communication is to blame for all this. It has made the inhabitants sleepy and lazy.'[13] Lack of communication (certainly the quality of it) is evident in the story. The hatred of mobility is emphasised by the strange *droshky* which is called into motion on only one occasion (so that Pulkheriya Ivanovna can go, not to see her neighbours, but her trees). Presumably because of lack of oil and attention in general this *droshky* produces most of the sounds of an orchestra and can be heard two versts away.

A similar musical effect is produced by all the doors in their house (symbol of communication in another sense) but these have voices and sing:

The door leading into the bedroom sang in the thinnest of descants, the door leading into the dining room wheezed in a bass voice, but the one which was in the hallway let out a strange jingling sound which at the same time seemed to groan, so that if you listened hard you could finally hear very clearly: 'fathers, I am freezing'. (II, 17–18)

The voices of the house tell us all. They sing out the strident immaturity of the values of the bedroom in contrast to the ageing but deep experience of the dining-room.[14] Yet, the third of these voices, that of the hallway, is perhaps the most curious. It appears to refer back to the centre of heat for the whole house. The narrator had told us that it was in the hallway that the stoves were recharged with straw, the fuel which was typical for the Ukraine: 'The crackle of this burning straw and the light it gives, make the hall extremely pleasant on a winter evening, when you are absolutely frozen from chasing after some brunette or other, and run in banging your hands together' (II, 17). Who is the implied 'you'[15] of this little digression? Is Gogol here ascribing to his reader a lust which he denies the central characters of his story? Moreover the 'you' who comes in freezing cold (*prozyabnuvshi*) after his amorous exploits is apparently echoed and parodied about a page later by the door which leads to this centre of heat for the whole house ('*batyushki ya zyabnu*').

The warmth of the hall and the solace of the dining-room all meet in the bedroom:

The room in which Afanasiy Ivanovich and Pulkheriya Ivanovnȧ slept, was so hot, that few would be capable of remaining a few hours in it. But Afanasiy Ivanovich, to add to matters, slept on a stove bench, in order to be warmer, although the powerful heat would often force him to get up a few times during the night and walk about the room. Sometimes Afanasiy Ivanovich would groan as he went about the room. Then Pulkheriya Ivanovna would ask:

'What are you groaning about, Afanasiy Ivanovich?'

'God knows, Pulkheriya Ivanovna, it's as though my stomach is aching a bit,' Afanasiy Ivanovich would say.

'Perhaps you should eat something or other, Afanasiy Ivanovich'.

'I don't know whether it would be a good thing, Pulkheriya Ivanovna, but what could I eat?'

'Some sour milk, or some weak compote with dried pears.'

'Well, perhaps I might just try some', Afanasiy Ivanovich would say.

A sleepy maid would go off and rummage in the cupboards, and Afanasiy Ivanovich would eat a small plateful, after which he usually said: 'It seems to have got a bit easier now'. (II, 23–4)

The passage seems to exhibit a conflict of view about the cause of Afanasiy Ivanovich's insomnia. The narrator clearly tells us it is powerful heat: *sil'nyy zhar* (*zhar* might even be taken in a metaphorical sense of 'passion') which made Afanasiy Ivanovich get up. *Zhar*, it is also suggested, is the cause of his groans. He himself says the groans (and we may remember that the door into the hallway had this same groaning note in its voice) are caused by an ache in the stomach. Nevertheless his wife thinks (apparently with justification) that the whole thing can be cured with the eternal solace of food.

The sleepy maid who has been woken up to cater for Afanasiy Ivanovich's needs, could well be one of those who found that food worked with quite the reverse effect when they went off into a larder and: 'gorged themselves so terribly that they groaned for a whole day, and complained about their stomachs' (II, 19–20). However, the stomachs of Pulkheriya Ivanovna's maids often swell from another and far more mysterious reason:

Pulkheriya Ivanovna considered it necessary to keep them in the house and paid strict attention to their morals. But to her extreme surprise, every few months, one or other of her maids would develop a figure which was much fuller than was usual. This seemed all the more surprising, because there were scarcely any bachelors in the house, with the exception of the young servant boy who went about in a grey tailcoat and bare feet, and who when he was not eating was absolutely sure to be sleeping. Pulkheriya Ivanovna usually scolded the guilty girl and punished her severely in order that it should not happen again. (II, 18–19)

This passage is followed immediately, without any break, by a comic description of the swarms of flies in the house (the bass of the bumble-bee and the high-pitched whine of the wasps seem to be carrying on the musical characteristics of the doors). But in a house which is dominated by food, flies are an obvious symbol of corruption, and it is significant that the description of the flies follows on naturally from Pulkheriya Ivanovna's perplexity at her pregnant maids.

It is noticeable that objects in the house which might be connected with female beauty (a mirror and a portrait) are soiled by flies: 'Two portraits were large, painted in oils. One depicted some bishop or archbishop or other, the other was of Peter III. From a narrow frame peeped the countess de La Vallière, soiled by flies' (II, 17). These two representatives of celibacy and matrimonial incompetence[16] seem odd companions for the mistress of Louis XIV, but then the countess de La Vallière is soiled by flies. Significantly the other pictures in the house are small, and the inmates have grown so accustomed to them that they regard them as nothing more than patches on the walls.

The chairs have the dignified austerity of those in which archbishops sit, and there is a mirror 'in a fine gold frame, with carved leaves, which the flies have speckled with black dots'.

In such surroundings it seems ironical that the mistress of the house should be called Pulkheriya (i.e. 'beautiful woman'). The patronymic she shares with her husband suggests, according to McLean, a relationship nearer to brother and sister,[17] and in this context of general sterility, it seems doubly ironical that Pulkheriya Ivanovna's own room should be so cluttered with what may be taken as symbols of female fertility: boxes and seeds.

After the description of Pulkheriya Ivanovna's pregnant maids, we read that the only burden[18] which she herself bears is to look after the estate. Nevertheless, in this all important area, her incompetence is obvious: the old couple are daily being robbed and deceived; but even large-scale depredation is adequately compensated by the abundant fertility of nature itself – a fertility which seems to mock her own infertility.

Of course, in one sense, she has a child; the childishness of Afanasiy Ivanovich is stressed from the beginning. Moreover when Pulkheriya Ivanovna knows that she is about to die and is concerned about his future, she tells him: 'You are like a child.' Her words to the housekeeper charged with the duty of caring for him are even clearer:

When I die make sure you look after the master, protect him as you would your own eye, like your very own child. Make sure that in the kitchen they cook him what he likes. Make sure that you always give him clean underwear and clothes, that when guests come you dress him up properly for the occasion, otherwise he might come in his old dressing gown, because even now he frequently forgets what are weekdays and what are holidays. (II, 33)

If the housekeeper fails in this duty then dire consequences are promised:

I myself will beg God not to give you a good death, and you yourself will be unfortunate, and your children will be unhappy and none of your descendants will have God's blessing in anything. (II, 31–2)

The barren Pulkheriya Ivanovna seeks to protect her only 'child' by invoking a curse on the generations of those who are fertile.

To the modern sensibility this terrible curse, so reminiscent of 'A Terrible Vengeance', might appear to undermine the goodness which Gogol is keen to ascribe to his heroine, but the narrator steps in immediately to divert our suspicions:

Poor old lady, at a time like that she was not thinking either about the great moment which was awaiting her nor about her own soul, nor about her own future life; she thought only about her poor companion, with whom she had spent her life, and whom she was leaving orphaned and unsheltered. (II, 32)

There is, however, a hint of something a little severe about the 'goodness' of Pulkheriya Ivanovna, as she is first presented to us:

Pulkheriya Ivanovna was a little serious, she almost never smiled; but in her face and her eyes was painted so much kindness, such a readiness to provide you with hospitality from the best of all they had, that you would undoubtedly have found a smile to be far too cloying for her kind face. (II, 15)

This lack of cloying sentimentality in the depiction of the old couple, particularly in their relationship with one another, seems nicely judged by Gogol, and yet it is indicative of far more.

The absence of a smile is a disturbing feature in Gogol's exemplar of kindness and hospitality. The relationship between this Philemon and Baucis is certainly not cloying. Indeed, when one looks closer, their verbal exchanges are full of submerged hostility:

They never said *thou* (*ty*) to one another but always *you* (*vy*).

'Is it you who have broken the chair, Afanasiy Ivanovich?'

'Never mind. Don't get angry, Pulkheriya Ivanovna, it is I'.

They had never had any children and therefore all their devotion was concentrated on themselves. (II, 15)

The polite '*vy*' form in which they always address one another, as McLean suggests, reveals distance rather than intimacy[19] and the curious example chosen to illustrate this form of address, with its very strong elements of a family row, merely serves to reinforce this. Moreover the narrator says thay concentrated their affection 'on themselves' (*v nikh samikh*) not 'on one another' – a phrase which serves to reinforce the ambiguity of the whole relationship; and the cause for this affection (which appears to be not quite what it seems) is given as their lack of children. This short passage tells us far more about the true relationship of the old couple than it appears to do on the surface.

Of course much of the conversation between Afanasiy Ivanovich and Pulkheriya Ivanovna is about food; the bond between them is expressed by the offering and the accepting of food. But even here a note of criticism can be detected, as when Afanasiy suggests that his *kasha* might be burned, or tells Pulkheriya that, just because the water melon she is offering him is red in the middle, it does not necessarily mean that it is good to eat.[20]

Perhaps something of this latent hostility towards his wife comes out more clearly in Afanasiy's jokes, in which he tries to frighten her by suggesting that she could lose the things she holds most dear; first of all the little world in which they live (in a fire) then he himself (in war).

Sometimes if it was fine weather and rather warm indoors, Afanasiy Ivanovich, being in good spirits, liked to make fun of Pulkheriya Ivanovna and talk of something by the way.

'Pulkheriya Ivanovna', he would say, 'what if our house were suddenly to catch fire, where should we go?'

'Heaven forbid', Pulkheriya Ivanovna would say crossing herself.

'But let us suppose that our house were burned down, where would we move to then?'

'God knows what you are saying, Afanasiy Ivanovich! How could our house be burned down? God would not permit it.'

'Yes, but if it were burned down?'

'Well then we would move into the kitchen. You would have, for the time being, the little room that the housekeeper has.'

'But what if the kitchen burned down?'

'May God preserve us from such a calamity as having the house and the kitchen both burned down at once! Well then we would move into the larder while a new house was being built.'

'And if the larder were burned down too?'

'God knows what you are saying! I just do not want to listen to you! It's a sin to say such things. God punishes people for talking like that.'

But Afanasiy Ivanovich, pleased at having made fun of Pulkheriya Ivanovna, smiled as he sat in his chair. (II, 24)

This passage follows on immediately from the description of Afanasiy Ivanovich's troubles in the overheated bedroom, and it is hard to escape the conclusion that the fire, of which he talks, is not merely hypothetical, but also metaphorical.[21] It seems significant, too, that such a fire would drive them from the fortress of the house into the inner stronghold of the kitchen and finally into the innermost citadel of all: the larder.

Whenever the subject of war comes up, Afanasiy Ivanovich has another opportunity to tease his wife:

Then Afanasiy Ivanovich, pretending not to look at Pulkheriya Ivanovna, would often say:

'I myself am thinking of going to war. Why indeed shouldn't I go to the war?'

'There he goes again,'[22] Pulkheriya Ivanovna interrupted.

'Don't you believe him', she said, turning to the guest. 'How could an old man like him go to war? The first soldier would shoot him. I swear he would shoot him. He would just take aim and shoot him.'

'What do you mean', Afanasiy Ivanovich would say, 'I would shoot him too.'

'Just listen to him, what is he saying?', Pulkheriya Ivanovna would take him up. 'How could he go to war? His pistols have been rusty for years and have been lying in the cupboard. If only you could see them. They're in a condition to blow up with the gunpowder, before they would fire a shot. He would blow off his hands and disfigure his face, and be in a bad way for the rest of his days.'

'Well,' Afanasiy Ivanovich would say, 'I will buy myself new weapons. I will take my sabre or a Cossack lance.'

'He's thought it all up. As soon as an idea comes into his head, he must begin to talk about it.' Pulkheriya Ivanovna would interrupt with irritation. 'I know very well that he is joking. But all the same it's not at all pleasant to listen to it. He always talks like this. Sometimes you can listen and listen until you get frightened.'

But Afanasiy Ivanovich, pleased that he had managed to scare Pulkheriya Ivanovna a bit, laughed as he sat bending over in his chair. (II, 25–6)

In this exchange, this 'going to war', Pulkheriya Ivanovna seems to give as good as she gets. She dwells on the fact that Afanasiy Ivanovich will be shot or that he will be maimed and disfigured by his own guns.

When his joke turns sour, and it is not Pulkheriya Ivanovna who is left alone, but Afanasiy Ivanovich himself, he is a broken man, affected by a deep grief even five years after his wife's death. Nevertheless, the narrator leaves us in no doubt about its cause:

Good Lord! I thought, looking at him, five years of all-consuming time. An old man who no longer has any feelings, an old man whose life appears never to have been troubled even once by any strong emotion, whose whole life appears to have consisted merely in sitting on a high chair, and in eating dried fish and pears, in good natured anecdotes – and such long, such sustained grief. What has more power over us passion or habit? Are all our strong emotions the whirlwind of our desires and boiling passions only the result of our bright youth, and, only by virtue of this seem deep and destructive? Be that as it may, it seemed to me then that all our passions are childish, when set beside this long, slow, almost unfeeling habit. (II, 36)

It is habit then, not emotion, which reigns supreme in the world of the old couple; the same habit which causes the smaller pictures on the walls to cease being noticed as anything else but patches. The same habit which governs Pulkheriya Ivanovna's attitude to her pet cat: 'One could not say that Pulkheriya Ivanovna was all that fond of her, she had simply got attached to her, having got used to always seeing her about' (II, 28). Needless to say this relationship between mistress and cat based on habit (which is not unlike that of Afanasiy Ivanovich and Pulkheriya Ivanovna themselves) provokes Afanasiy Ivanovich into more teasing of his wife.

'I don't know, Pulkheriya Ivanovna, what you find in a cat. What use is she? Now if you had a dog that would be another matter. You can take a dog hunting, but what use is a cat?'

'Oh, shut up, Afanasiy Ivanovich', Pulkheriya Ivanovna would say. 'You just love talking and nothing else. A dog is not a clean animal, a dog would make a mess, a dog would break everything, but a cat is a quiet creature. She would do nobody any harm.'

It made no difference, in fact, to Afanasiy Ivanovich, whether it were a cat or a dog. He only spoke like this to make fun of Pulkheriya Ivanovna a little. (II, 28)

The cat becomes involved in a minor incident which, nevertheless, takes on ominous significance for Pulkheriya Ivanovna herself.

Beyond the confines of the garden lies a dark overgrown wood, it is the home of wild, lawless tom-cats: 'These tom-cats and Pulkheriya Ivanovna's gentle pussy had for a long time been sniffing at one another through a hole beneath the barn, and finally they enticed her like a detachment of soldiers entices a silly peasant girl' (II, 29). The cat disappears. After three days Pulkheriya Ivanovna has already forgotten about her. Then one day, as she is about her eternal task of providing Afanasiy Ivanovich with food, she hears a pathetic mewing: 'As though by instinct she called 'kitty kitty' and suddenly out of the undergrowth came her grey cat, thin and emaciated; it was obvious that it had not taken any food for several days' (II, 29). The cat in breaking out from this enclosed world, where food is the surrogate of passion, seems to be implying more: food is the very antithesis of passion. Nevertheless Pulkheriya Ivanovna gives it food and watches it 'almost swell out before her very eyes'. But after her experiences in the wild wood the cat can no longer regard the traditional offering and acceptance of food as a basis for an affectionate relationship. After feeding it Pulkheriya Ivanovna tries to pet it.

She stretched out her hand to stroke her, but the ungrateful creature, it seemed, had already grown too used to the predatory tom-cats, or had got her head stuffed full of the romantic canons that poverty in love is better than palaces, and the tom-cats were as poor as hawks. Whatever the reason, she jumped out of the window and none of the servants could catch her. The old woman became lost in thought: 'it was my death that came for me' she said to herself, and nothing could distract her from this thought. (II, 30)

Thus the cat which escapes from the cossetted, passionless comfort of Pulkheriya Ivanovna's restricted little world, for the wild sexual abandon of life with the forest tom-cats, is interpreted by Pulkheriya Ivanovna herself as a symbol of her own death.[23] It may be that the cat, who has been enticed by the tom-cats 'like a detachment of soldiers entices a silly peasant girl', evokes the memory of a former passion within Pulkheriya Ivanovna herself; for her husband had been a military man and: 'He got married at thirty, when he was a fine young fellow and wore an embroidered waistcoat, he even carried Pulkheriya Ivanovna off rather skilfully, because her relatives did not wish her to marry him. But he scarcely remembered this now. At least he never spoke about it' (II, 16). As if to stress some sort of identification between the passion of the cat and her own death, she insists on being buried in her grey dress (the colour of the cat);[24] but in death, as in life Pulkheriya Ivanovna needs the protection of a barrier: she requests to be buried near the church fence. Yet her dying, which comes as she predicts, is the very negation of the values of her whole life:

After a few days she took to her bed, and was no longer able to take any food. Afanasiy Ivanovich was the embodiment of attentiveness and did not leave her bedside. 'Perhaps you would like to eat something, Pulkheriya Ivanovna?' he would say, anxiously looking into her eyes. But Pulkheriya Ivanovna said nothing. Finally after a long silence it was as though she wanted to say something, she moved her lips – her breath flew away. (II, 32)

The food, which was so absent from her sick-bed, is very much in evidence at the funeral itself: 'the long tables were ranged round the courtyard, heaped up with rice and currants, fruit liqueurs, pies' (II, 32). But there is a new element at the funeral; for the first time in this story we encounter children: 'The sun shone, babies cried in their mothers' arms, the larks sang, children in shirts ran in gleeful play along the roads' (II, 33). Nature in many forms seems to be mocking this sad occasion.

After the death of Pulkheriya Ivanovna, Afanasiy Ivanovich is left a broken old man, and the estate falls into a dilapidation which matches his own. When the narrator goes to see him five years later the house seems to be twice as old as it was before: 'The paling and the wattle fence in the courtyard were entirely destroyed, and I myself saw the cook pulling sticks out of it to light the stove, when she only need have taken a couple more paces to fetch the brushwood that was piled up' (II, 34). Thus those two symbolic bounds of the little world which we encountered at the beginning of the story, the paling and the wattle fence, are completely breached now, and nothing appears to have done more to destroy them than the new values of the kitchen.

The death of Afanasiy Ivanovich has a strange similarity to the death of Pulkheriya Ivanovna, as the narrator himself points out. Walking one day in the garden, he hears a voice call out his name, and knows that it is Pulkheriya Ivanovna who has called him. He accedes to this summons with 'the will of an obedient child', and the death of this lover of great heat is compared with that of his wife – for both it is the burning out of a candle: 'He dried up, coughed, melted like a candle, and finally went out, just as she had done when nothing else had remained which could support her weak flame' (II, 37).

The idyll of love à la Philemon and Baucis is shattered by the existence of another sort of love, which Pulkheriya Ivanovna does her best to suppress within her own household, but in vain. Pulkheriya Ivanovna is at a loss to believe that the mysterious source contaminating her maids lies within the house. Here is a world, in which, as we are told, 'not a single desire flies beyond the paling surrounding the little courtyard', and the life of such people: 'is so quiet, so quiet that for a moment one could lose oneself and think passions, desires and the disquieting things engendered by the spirit of evil which disturb the world, do not exist at all, and that you have merely seen them in a bright glittering dream' (II, 13). Nevertheless there is something animal and wild which lurks in the dark wood on the edge of this still centre. It is this force which symbolically breaks into the household and reveals the idyll in all its insubstantiality. Death leaves this passionless couple without any true heirs. The distant relative who inherits their pastoral paradise soon lets everything go to rack and ruin. The quietness of this bucolic idyll is no proof against the terror which can suddenly enter it with little warning. At the sudden mysterious summons of Afanasiy Ivanovich, the narrator strikes a personal note which seems to lie at the heart of the whole story and here one is reminded of Gogol's own caveat, that the idyll as a genre contains an 'inner idea, which is far too close to the poet's soul'. The narrator recounts how, as a child, he would often hear such a voice calling him, and it would strike fear into his heart, a terror which was greater than anything which could have affected him on the wildest and darkest of nights, yet this was always a clear, bright day when everything was absolutely still, and he was in a garden.

Of course we must not automatically assume that the narrator is Gogol himself, but he certainly is not Rudy Panko. He is a man of two worlds: the rural Ukraine, which he visits from time to time, and the world of the capital cities of Great Russia. When he claims that the air of the Ukraine must have some special quality which enables people to eat such large meals without harm, meals which if eaten 'here' would undoubtedly lead to death, we can see that he is writing in Russia and for a Russian audience. It is this effect of the narrator looking back on the rural Ukraine from a distance of both space and time which creates the all-pervading note of nostalgia.

Yet, for all the apparent distance between him and the old world landowners, their values are really his. His opening words proclaim his great love for the sort of life they lead; he is a frequent guest, who enjoys their great meals. Indeed the obsession with food which so dominates them is characteristic of the narrator too. He finds his heroine 'most interesting of all' when she is offering the blandishments of food to her guests. Even when he digresses on small causes giving birth to great events, his illustrations (the entire forces of a state battling for a scrap of ground not large enough to plant *potatoes*; contrasted with a quarrel between *sausage* makers, which ends up involving the whole state) are both examples in which food plays a qualifying role.

A revealing passage occurs immediately after his description of the voice which can be heard in the creaking door. We have already seen the connection between this 'voice' and the amorous exploits ascribed to the reader, now the narrator goes on to reveal his own attitude:

I know that many people do not like this sound, but I love it very much, and if here I happen sometimes to hear the creak of a door, then I feel a sudden breath of the country: a little low-ceilinged room lit by a candle in an old fashioned candlestick, supper already standing on the table, a dark May night looking in from the garden, through the open window, on to the table laid with places, a nightingale flooding the garden, the house and the distant river with its trills, the terror and the rustling of branches... and Lord what a whole long string of memories comes to me then. (II, 18)

The picture evoked by the creaking door is undoubtedly romantic, but romantic too in an amorous sense: the May night, with its nightingale and its distant river; the setting could be for one of the love exploits of *The Evenings in a village near Dikanka*. Yet the centre of the stage is not occupied by human beings, but by a table laid for supper with food already on it. It is at this that the May night is 'looking in' through the open window. Thus the groaning protest of the door links by a series of associations (some explicit, some implicit) a putatively amorous reader with a narrator who can only conceive of the romantic in terms of food; the emotional world of the narrator is perhaps not so far removed from that of the old world landowners after all. The narrator hears a voice in the door (later he will confess to having heard another and more terrifying voice in the stillness of the garden). The door appears to utter a strange plea for atavistic compassion: 'Fathers, I am freezing!' and the reader is entitled to ask why it should be precisely these words which can be distinguished; for one of the symptoms of the strange illness, which afflicted Gogol himself, was an unaccountable feeling of coldness (*zyabkost'*).[25] Moreover the death of Pulkheriya Ivanovna which comes about through the refusing of food, oddly parallels Gogol's own death.

The picture which the sound of the door conjures up for the narrator seems marred by the curious phrase: 'the terror and rustling of branches' (*strakhom*[26] *i shorokhom vetvey*); for terror lurks in this idyllic setting, just as it lurks in the larger idyll of the story itself, and significantly it is connected in both cases with trees – the concept of the 'wild wood', which seems to play a comparable role here to that of the forest motif in 'A Terrible Vengeance'. The terror which creeps almost unobtrusively into this peaceful scene seems a clear anticipation of the terror which the narrator will describe so vividly, when he recalls the other 'garden scene' from his childhood.

In formal terms the story is constructed round a series of parallels and echoes. The 'singing' doors are echoed in the 'choir' of flies and taken up further in the 'orchestral' sounds of the *droshky*. The death of Afanasiy Ivanovich parallels that of his wife and the idyll of their life is given, in microcosm, in the narrator's evocation of the May night. But terror lurks behind the still centre of the plot as it does in the idyllic May night and in the tranquil gardens of the narrator's childhood. Sexuality is foreign to this world: it is attributed to a 'you' who comes in freezing from outside; to some agent not detectable within the confines of the household which constantly impregnates Pulkheriya Ivanovna's maids; and finally to tom-cats who live in the wild wood and entice her tame pussycat.

In this story nothing is quite what it seems, and this is above all true of the narrator's own interpolations. His anecdote about the young man who lost his true love, is put forward as an illustration of time eventually curing the wounds of passion, but what it shows more convincingly is how a passionate nature can so easily be driven by an irresistible death wish. Once more, as with Pulkheriya Ivanovna and her cat, passion is linked to death.[27]

The narrator's suggestion that habit might be stronger than passion not only throws light on the old world landowners, it also reveals something about himself. He even admits 'habit' as a possibility for the cat's dalliance in the wild wood: 'but the ungrateful creature, it seemed, had already grown too used to the predatory tom-cats or had got her head stuffed full of the romantic canons' (II. 30). Such explanations, apparently put forward by the narrator, seem more like those of Pulkheriya Ivanovna herself.

The narrator also provides a social commentary of his own, which for the most part is designed to set off the old-fashioned worth of his aged couple against the false values of modern life. A note of social criticism is also present in the concluding paragraph of the story, depicting the ultimate destruction of the estate. This comes about through the efforts of the 'terrible reformer', the distant relative who inherits everything, and tries to improve the farming by modern (i.e. Western) practices. Although he is presented by the narrator as the villain of the piece, it is obvious that the estate has been running down for years under the management of the old world landowners themselves. The depredations increase after the death of

Pulkheriya Ivanovna and are even more pronounced after the death of Afanasiy Ivanovich, so that to present the 'heir' as the chief culprit may be emotionally satisfying for the narrator, but it is hardly borne out by the events of the story itself.

The terror, that could suddenly beset a child alone in nature, was well known to Dostoevsky. His short story 'The Peasant Marey', is autobiographical, but it bears a striking resemblance to the incidents related by the narrator in 'The Old World Landowners' from his own childhood. The young Dostoevsky, alone in a thicket on a clear August day, suddenly hears a voice (not calling him) as in Gogol, but calling out: 'A wolf is coming.' He is seized with panic and does not stop running until he comes up to his father's peasant ploughing a field, who comforts him, and dissipates his fears about the wolf.[28] In 'The Old World Landowners' the narrator is also thus reassured by the first person to whom he runs (the incident occurs more than once).

The world of the 'Old World Landowners' is the sort of existence depicted earlier by Pushkin in the life of Eugene Onegin's uncle, though he of course is a bachelor (chapter 2, v. 3). A much fuller development of this sort of life is to be seen in 'Oblomov's Dream', the section of the novel *Oblomov* dealing with the hero's childhood. There is the same nostalgic view of this life seen from a distance and in retrospect, but the device of a dream is used to enter this world rather than the reminiscences of a narrator. Yet the quality of a dream is almost present in Gogol's story: 'Their faces appear to me even now on occasions amidst the noise and the crowd and among fashionable frock-coats, and then suddenly a half-dreamy state comes on me and the past appears to me' (II, 14). Both works describe a similar little world isolated in the depths of the country. The same values of eating and sleeping predominate. Afanasiy Ivanovich is just as inept at running his estate as is Oblomov's father. He too knows very little about what happens to his crops, and superstition reigns supreme. Both works hover between idealisation of this life and implied criticism of it. Yet in Goncharov's story there is one essential difference: this world is seen through the eyes of a child; everything which happens within this charmed, still circle is observed by the young Oblomov, is absorbed by him and this conditions him for the rest of his life. Children are noticeably absent from Gogol's story: there are no direct heirs. 'The Old World Landowners' may well have conditioned Turgenev's portrayal of Bazarov's parents in *Fathers and*

Children, but even closer is the world of Fomushka and Fimushka in *Virgin Soil*.

The story, like so many of Gogol's works, had a fascination for writers who were to follow.[29] It is an evocative picture of an old-fashioned way of life, and yet it is far more than this. It is a story rich in ambiguities suggesting that the fertility of nature may mock the sterility of human life; that generosity and affection may really be narrowness and habit; that the confines of a still world innocent of passion are not proof against the primitive forces without; that in the brightest and calmest of days can lurk a sudden inexplicable terror. Yet most intriguing of all: Gogol in describing what could well be the life of his own ancestors seeks to depict heat, food and habit as the surrogates of passion, and when passion as such is recognised it is identified immediately as death.

'*Taras Bulba*'

The second story of *Mirgorod* depicts a medieval world of barbarous cruelty and crusading idealism, whose values are quite foreign to the modern consciousness. Although it cannot be said that there is any hint of sentimentalism in the portrayal of the Cossack warriors, there is nevertheless a debt to romanticism: to the sort of fictionalised history made popular by Sir Walter Scott. Events of the fifteenth, sixteenth and seventeenth centuries are all fused into the life and exploits of one man.[30] He is not an historical figure, but a hero on an epic scale, who commands a grudging respect rather than our sympathy. If the reader is amazed that such a broad and generous body can house such a narrow and rigid spirit, he has only to acquaint himself with Ukrainian history to see that Taras, as a composite portrait, has a certain poetic justness. Indeed, it is poetic truth, rather than historical fact, which Gogol is after, and as such the work largely conforms to his own definition of the epic: 'The whole world, for a great distance, is illuminated around the hero himself and not individual figures alone, but the whole people' (VIII, 478).

This is the national dimension of 'Taras Bulba', but there is also a personal one, which reflects Gogol's interest in his supposed noble and heroic ancestry. Leon Stilman links 'The Old World Landowners' to the 'Yanovsky' part of the hyphenated surname, Yanovsky-Gogol and 'Taras Bulba' to its last component: the author's claim to be descended from Yan (more properly Ostap) Gogol: 'Taras Bulba...may be regarded as an "anti-Ostap Gogol", as a hero offered in expiatory sacrifice for the deeds of the author's pseudo-ancestor.'[31] This may well be true, but the genealogical sacrifice which is most striking is one nearer to the values of 'A Terrible Vengeance': the killing by Taras of his own son in cold blood.

The influence of Narezhny may be detected behind Gogol's story, but whereas the 'warfare' of his two Ivans is petty and parochial, the violence of Gogol's Cossacks is on an epic scale. Narezhny's heroes are only 'knights' (*bogatyri*) in the mock heroic sense, but Taras Bulba has a serious claim to the title *bogatyr'*. Narezhny gives a more heroic account of the Cossacks in his novel *Church School Boy* (*Bursak*) published in 1824, and this work, too, has influenced 'Taras Bulba'. Nevertheless, V. F. Pereverzev has pointed out that the traditions of the Zaporogian Cossacks were still alive for the generation of Narezhny (1780–1825), but for Gogol they were only history.[32] Narezhny for instance was educated, as a nobleman, at a *bursa* school (like the sons of Taras) whereas Gogol could only write about such *bursaki* at second hand.

In *The Two Ivans or The Passion for Litigation* the 'love' of the younger generation runs counter to the 'enmity' of their parents (the two sons marry the two daughters of Pan Khariton) but in 'Taras Bulba' this clash between love and hostility takes on a deeply tragic sense.

Gogol's treatment of love in relationship to war is extremely enlightening. In 'The Old World Landowners' food had been a surrogate for sexual love, but in 'Taras Bulba' it has been ousted by something far more inimical, the military ethic itself.

The first victim is Bulba's own wife:

Only one brief moment did she experience love, only in the first fever of passion, in the first fever of youth, and her rough seducer soon left her for the sword, for his comrades and for carousing. She would see her husband two or three days a year, and then for several years nothing would be heard from him at all. And when she did see him, when they did live together, what sort of a life was it for her? She suffered insults, even beatings. Affection was shown to her only out of charity. She was a strange, foreign creature in this collection of knights without women, on whom the wild, loose-living *Zaporozhe* cast its own rough hue. (II, 49–50)

The only 'bride' which Taras can respect is a symbolic one, to be wooed by acts of true manliness: 'And you lads! – he said turning to his own men – Which one of you wants to die his own true death? Not behind stoves, or those womanish stove benches, not drunk under the fence of some inn, like any carrion, but an honourable Cossack death, all in the same bed like a bridegroom with his bride' (II, 168). The equation of a Cossack's death with marriage has been seen before in 'A Terrible Vengeance'; it appears to come from the Ukrainian song tradition.[33] Nevertheless Gogol's use of the motif in this particular way seems oddly suggestive: why should a bed full of male comrades be linked to sexual consummation, which is in fact death? The peculiar nature of this image may be further gauged, when it is realised that the simile has replaced (and inverted) the original jibe of Taras, in the 1835 version, that those who returned home would be the sort to be beaten every day by their wives (II, 351).[34]

The *Sech'*, the headquarters of the Zaporogian Cossacks, is an impregnable citadel of masculinity, even as regards the range of diversions it provides for its inhabitants: 'It was only those who were devoted to women who could find nothing here; because no woman dare show herself even in the area near the *Sech'*' (II, 66).[35] The only love between man and woman which appears to be tolerated by this warriors' code (and then grudgingly) is the respectful affection which should exist between mother and son. Even Taras himself is not unmoved by the emotional leave-taking of the mother and their two sons. But the real bond of affection which these men feel is for their own comrades as Taras makes clear: 'There is no bond more holy than that of our comradeship! The father loves his child, the mother loves her child, the child loves its father and mother. But this is not the same, brothers; even an animal loves its child, but only a man can form close ties that are not of the blood but of the soul' (II, 133). It is striking that Taras draws all his comparisons from paternal, maternal and filial love: conjugal love does not appear to be admitted as a possible contender for a close tie which is 'not of the blood but of the soul'.

The love of which Taras speaks is so powerful that even he seems affected by emotion at the mere thought of it. It also has a strong element of chauvinism within it:

'No, brothers, to love as the Russian soul loves is not to love with the mind or anything else, but with everything which God has given you, all that is within you, but...' said Taras and he gave a wave of his arm, shook his grey head, and twitched his moustache, and said, 'No, no one else can love like that.' (II, 133)

It is not merely that the comradeship of the Cossacks and military valour have replaced normal sexual relations in this society, women are actually viewed as a force which is antagonistic to Cossack values. In times of need the Cossack captains swell the ranks of the zaporogian forces by taunting the stay-at-homes with crawling to their wives and ruining the strength of their knighthood (*podbirat'sya k zhinkam i gubit' silu rytsarskuyu*) (II, 47).

The inimical force represented by women is most clearly illustrated by the fate of Taras's second son Andriy. The difference between the elder son Ostap and Andriy is apparent from the opening of the story. The two boys arrive home from the *bursa* after a long absence, and Ostap wins his father's approval by immediately engaging him in fisticuffs, whereas Andriy is rebuked for not offering to fight.

At the *bursa* Andriy had already shown his susceptibility to women; he had been prey to erotic daydreaming, but even worse: he had fallen in love from afar with a young Polish beauty in the town. He contrives to gain access to the house in which she lives, and confronts her in her own room. The daring and ingenuity with which this exploit is carried off is worthy of any Cossack, but his reward at the hands of his lady reads like a symbolic expression of what any Cossack might expect from contact with a woman: ludicrous effeminacy – the Polish girl dresses Andriy up as a woman and laughs at him.

All this is very ominous for the future career of Andriy, and indeed he falls a second time, and now irrevocably, into the clutches of this Polish beauty. The Cossacks are besieging a Polish town, reducing its inhabitants to the last stages of starvation, but the enchantress is in the town and notices Andriy in the ranks of the enemy. She sends out her Tartar maid at night to bring her admirer to her by a secret underground passage, bearing sacks of food to save her from starvation. On their way to the secret tunnel Andriy and the Tartar maid pass Taras who is sleeping restlessly. In a waking moment between deep sleep he appears to notice them and utters the prophetic remark, that women will bring Andriy to no good (in the later version Gogol suppresses authorial speculations which seem to suggest that Taras may be conniving at his son's relationship with a woman).[36]

Once inside the city, Andriy falls utterly under the spell of the Polish enchantress; he undergoes a complete reversal of values. He changes sides and fights for his former enemies against his own father, brother and fellow Cossacks. In a significant declaration to the Polish girl he claims that he now has no fatherland other than her (*otchizna moya ty*) (II, 106).

The defection of his son from the brotherhood of the Cossacks is a great blow to Taras. He vows vengeance on the Polish enchantress in terms strongly suggesting sexual sadism:

> He would not have looked at her beauty, he would have dragged her out by the dense luxurious plait of her hair, he would have dragged her behind him over all the field between all the cossacks. Bloody and covered in dust, her wonderful breasts and shoulders, whose dazzle was equal to the unmelting snows which cover the mountain tops, would be beaten and bruised against the ground. He would sunder in pieces her sumptuous beautiful body. (II, 122)

Taras is not able to act out this fantasy in real life; the Polish beauty does not fall into his hands, but his son does. Taras shoots Andriy in cold blood, saying: 'I gave you birth and I will kill you.' Once more, as in 'A Terrible Vengeance', the power of the fathers to destroy their issue is made evident. That there is something almost ritualistic in this shooting may be deduced from the fact that in the unfinished novel, *The Hetman*, Gogol describes a Cossack religious painting showing Abraham pointing a pistol at Isaac (III, 294).

In contrast to the many heroes on the Cossack side who die with heroic speeches on their lips, Andriy dies in silence, but before the shot he had pronounced one name: 'It was not the name of his fatherland, nor of his mother, nor of his brothers, it was the name of the beautiful Polish girl' (II, 144).

The death of the other son Ostap, when it comes later in the story, serves as a stark contrast to the treachery of Andriy who dies with the name of a woman on his lips. The end of Ostap is an excruciating public execution at the hands of his enemies, which he bears bravely, and we are specifically told that he had no desire that there should be any woman present at his death – he only wanted to see a firm and resolute man who would console him at the end with a wise word.

Taras's own death is noble and heroic and his dying words guide his fellow Cossacks out of danger; to the bitter end he is true to the bond of male comradeship. Indeed, in the first version, the self-sacrifice of Taras was underlined to the point where it assumed the virtual significance of a crucifixion. This unlikely Christ-figure is betrayed, not by a member of his own band, but by a wayward female object. He drops his Cossack pipe (*lyul'ka*) and it is concern not to lose 'his inseparable female companion' (*neotluchnaya soputnitsa*) (II, 170), which brings about his capture and death. In 'A Terrible Vengeance' Danilo had identified his Cossack pipe as a wife, but *lyul' ka* has further significance: it also means a child's cradle. Taras is betrayed by an object, which, while symbolising his Cossack masculinity also has overtones of 'wife and family':[37] it is indeed through women and a descendant that he does feel himself to have been betrayed.

Female beauty is not only something which defeats Taras as a Cossack, it also appears to defeat Gogol as a narrator: 'But let somebody else's words express... but neither the sculptor's chisel nor the artist's brush, nor yet the lofty and mighty word have power to express, what is sometimes seen in a maiden's glances, or yet the tender feeling which envelops him who looks into a maiden's eyes' (II, 103). The mock humility with which he disclaims any ability to describe female beauty is constantly found in Gogol. This passage, in the revised version of 'Taras Bulba', has been substituted for an attempt in the 1835 original, to describe what is now regarded as the ineffable; but the beauty of the Polish girl had been depicted in language so hyperbolic and so stilted as to justify this later contention that the 'lofty and mighty' is powerless to do full justice to such descriptions.

But if the 'lofty and mighty word' cannot cope adequately with feminine beauty, there is another beauty, the beauty of nature, with which it deals superbly. Gogol's description of the steppe by day, in the evening and at night, his description of the river Dnepr, and the July night in the Cossack camp are all passages which are justly famous and have been influential in the description of natural beauty by later Russian writers. Turgenev's lyrical descriptions of nature, though perhaps not as rhetorical, have an obvious predecessor in these passages from Taras Bulba. ('I fill my lungs with country air and I read Gogol' wrote Turgenev to the Aksakovs from Spasskoye where he had been exiled in 1852 for his obituary article on Gogol.)[38] Natural descriptions in Chekhov also owe much to Gogol, especially the early story *Steppe*, in which Gogolian influences are marked, and not merely confined to description.

Gogol's depiction of the Jewish quarters in Warsaw is description in yet another vein: the comic 'naturalistic' method with its concentration on bizarre detail is close to Gogol's treatment of St Petersburg. The description of Andriy's journey through the underground tunnel to enter the starving Polish city, makes use of bizarre detail in a way which is far from comic. It was added to the 1842 edition and, as A. De Jonge points out, its impact is on a symbolic level.[39]

As a work influential in the tradition of the Russian historical novel, 'Taras Bulba', must obviously be placed beside Pushkin's *The Captain's Daughter* and the novels of Aleksandr Bestuzhev-Marlinsky and Mikhail Zagoskin. Its real successors seem not to be Tolstoy (neither Lev, nor Aleksey) but Soviet works such as Aleksandr Serafimovich's *The Iron Flood*, where the poster-like heroism of a central figure is set against the mystique of the group and the flat one-dimensional psychology of the characters goes hand in hand with stirring rhetoric, spurring on collective endeavour. Horror is presented in the same matter of fact way in *The Iron Flood* as in 'Taras Bulba', and Serafimovich even employs the typical Gogolian device of synecdoche in presenting character (although it must be allowed that Gogol himself does not use this fully in 'Taras Bulba'.) Babel's representation of the Cossacks in *Konarmiya*, though quite different in other respects, has something of 'Taras Bulba's violence and poetry combined with an unemotional presentation of brutal and horrific incidents.

'*Viy*'

'Viy' opens with the ringing of a monastery bell summoning the seminary pupils to their studies in the capital city of Kiev: a scene full of bustle and activity. The story ends (or at least did so in Gogol's original conception) with a remote rural church full of monsters struggling to escape, yet frozen in one moment for all eternity by the summons of a cock. The contrast could hardly be more complete: an opening which promises the bustling activity of religious enlightenment, brought into being by the holy sound of a bell; and an ending of dark satanic horror frozen into perpetuity by the summons of a pagan clarion. There is here a reversal of values which is fundamental for the work as a whole; for here everyday reality easily passes into the supernatural; the hero ridden by a witch rides her in his turn, and she, a hideous old woman, becomes a beautiful young girl; her body, three days dead, can come to life for three nights, and the values of the night mock the values of the day. Moreover the story itself falls naturally into two parts, of which the second is the unmaking of the first.

The opening is in a would-be sociological manner. Gogol paints a general picture of life in the Kiev *bursa* in terms of groups rather than individuals, yet the narrative proper is concerned with the fate of an individual out of the context of the *bursa* itself. This shift of focus is more dramatic than the corresponding transition from the general to the particular at the beginning of 'The Old World Landowners', and if in that story a way of life is not what it seems, in 'Viy', the Kiev *bursa* is even more striking in its 'reversal of values'; for the mores of those who are to be educated for the church are profoundly irreligious: stealing, drinking, lechery and physical violence are their chief pursuits, and there is no greater pagan than the hero Khoma Brut (the surname itself is suggestive), nor any greater philistine than this 'philosopher'.[40]

In this depiction of *bursa* life Gogol obviously owes a debt to Narezhny, in particular to his novel, *Bursak*,[41] yet the method he adopts, the differentiation of the various classes of the *bursa*, characterised by the attributes they share in common, and above all by the objects in their possession, is a technique which will come into greater prominence in Gogol's later works, in particular 'Nevsky Prospekt' and *Dead Souls*.

The element of *bytopisaniye* (the description of a way of life) is a feature of 'Viy', it is also present in the description of the Cossack village, though here there are grotesque and comic overtones reminiscent of the depiction of village life in *Evenings in a village near Dikanka*. Indeed of all the stories in *Mirgorod*, 'Viy' is the nearest in mood to the earlier collection, nevertheless, using much the same material, Gogol has somehow managed to transcend many of the limitations and crudities of his earlier romantic style, and has here produced a work of true genius. The juxtaposition of everyday life and the supernatural was never fully convincing in *Evenings in a village near Dikanka*, but in 'Viy' these two apparently disparate elements are linked in a way which is both logically and artistically coherent. This mixture of the naturalistic and the supernatural is the hallmark of the romantic literature of the period, we find it in Anton Pogorelsky, in Veltman, in Vladimir Odoevsky and even in Pushkin; it stems, of course, from the German tradition (Tieck and Hoffmann).

Hoffmann, in particular his story *The Golden Pot*, is an undoubted influence behind 'Viy'. This can be seen not merely in the basic thematic confrontation of reality and unreality, but the German writer has also conditioned the way in which Gogol presents the supernatural. (I.e. flowers which ring like bells, the suggestion that all the market women are witches,[42] and even the incursion of the Germanic 'gnome' into what is ostensibly Ukrainian folklore.)

Yet although this German literary tradition is a conditioning factor, the main influence is Russo-Ukrainian. We have already seen that Gogol's opening description of the Kiev seminary owes much to Narezhny's *Bursak*, and the opening of the narrative proper seems to echo the beginning of *The Two Ivans or The Passion for Litigation*, with its theme of wandering seminarists looking for shelter. 'Viy' reaches its climax in the sequence depicting Khoma reading scripture over a coffin containing a body which 'rises from the dead', and in Narezhny's work, Foma (a deacon with a not unsimilar name) reads psalms over the apparently dead Khariton, but on pronouncing the words: 'Eternal rest to the soul of Khariton', the 'body' replies, 'thank you friend': Khariton is not dead, he has only been sleeping. When he has got over the initial shock, the deacon joins the 'corpse' in drinking and singing psalms, and the noise they make is such that Khariton's wife and daughter think that the deacon is being strangled by the corpse.[43] In Narezhny this bizarre incident is comic, but Gogol divorces the situation from the comic overtones which abound elsewhere in the *bytopisaniye* section of his story and treats it as serious horror. In this he is quite close to yet another possible source for his tale, Robert Southey's ballad 'The Old Woman of Berkeley', translated into Russian by Gogol's friend and protector, Zhukovsky.[44]

Gogol wrote a footnote to the story, in which he claims: 'the whole of this story is a folk tradition, I have not wished to change it in any way, and I tell it in the same simple way in which I heard it'. With this in mind certain critics have tried to relate 'Viy' to the genre of the fairy-tale, with little success.[45] The story is obviously a work of Gogol's imagination, in which, it is true, certain borrowings may have been made from folk tradition, but as we have already seen German and English romanticism have also left their traces. Indeed in defining the literary genre of the fairy-tale (*skazka*) Gogol himself puts least value of all on the mere retelling of a tale, but thinks it a 'lofty creation': 'When it serves in allegorical clothing, decking out an elevated spiritual truth, when, even for the common man, it palpably and visibly uncovers a matter accessible only to a wise man' (VIII, 483).

To the Western reader the fairy-tale element which may seem most familiar is the ending: the magic moment which freezes figures in various poses, whilst the enchanted spot becomes so overgrown with thorns and bushes that all access to it is lost; this is reminiscent of *Sleeping Beauty*. Yet, significantly, this is the dénouement of Gogol's story; for 'Viy' is the very inversion of the sleeping-beauty tale. Here it is not Prince Charming who awakens the sleeping princess with his tenderness, but rather the 'sleeping beauty' who petrifies 'Philosopher Brute' with her horrors.

The tale of *Sleeping Beauty* may be interpreted as an allegorical expression of the awakening of sleeping virginity. If there is a corresponding allegorical significance in 'Viy', then its inversion is suggestive not of sexual awakening but of sexual death.

Sexuality is, in fact, quite explicit in Gogol's story. Thus when the witch first comes to Khoma Brut at night, he has little doubt about her intentions:

> 'Well, Granny, what do you want?' the philosopher asked. But the old woman came right up to him with her arms wide open.
>
> 'So that's it', thought the philosopher, 'but no, my dear, you're too old.' He moved away a little further, but the old woman made no bones about it and came up to him again.
>
> 'Listen, Granny!' said the philosopher, 'it is now Lent, and I am not the sort of chap to break the prohibitions of Lent, not for a thousand in gold.' (II, 185)

Introduced by such a key-signature, the section which follows can only be interpreted in one way. The 'philosopher' loses power over his body, all he can feel is his heart beating; the witch jumps on his back and proceeds to ride him. The marvellously poetic and eerie passage which follows describes their ride through a dream-like landscape, in which the hint of sensuality is ever present.

They appear to be flying over some sort of sea, and looking down Khoma sees himself reflected in the water with the witch on his back. But there is also another female figure in the water, one quite different from the witch, it is the sensuously twisting body of a water nymph (*rusalka*):

> He saw a water nymph swim from behind a sedge. He glimpsed a back and a leg rounded and resilient, all bright and quivering. She turned towards him

and now her face, with its bright eyes shining, piercing, and her singing, all of which penetrated his soul, was already drawing close to him, was already almost on the surface – then quivering with radiant laughter receded, and now she threw herself over on her back, and her cloudy breasts, opaque like porcelain, not covered by a glaze, seemed transparent in the sun all along the edges of their white elastically soft contours. Water, in the form of small bubbles, was scattered all over them like pearls. She was all quivering and laughing in the water. (II, 186)

Yet at the end of their ride, the witch herself turns into a beautiful young girl with long eyelashes and bare white arms.

The ride itself evokes in Khoma the most mixed of feelings:

He felt, welling up to his heart, a sensation which was oppressive and unpleasant, yet at the same time sweet...He felt a diabolically sweet sensation. He experienced a pleasure which was somehow penetrating and terrifying in some exhausting way. He kept thinking that he no longer had a heart, and in fear he would clutch at it with his hand. (II, 187)

The witch's habit of riding young men is later recalled by the Cossacks in the village. Spirid tells the story of the kennel master Mikita, and his account is prefaced by a remark which shows the connection between 'love' and witchcraft: 'Whether he had really fallen in love with her, or whether she had simply cast a spell on him, I don't know, but he was a lost man, he was quite womanized [*obabilsya sovsem*], he became devil knows what. Uh! It's indecent to say' (II, 203). The sensuous element is again emphasised in Mikita's ride: 'The mistress lifted her leg, and as soon as he saw her bare, shapely, white leg, then he said, its charm[46] overwhelmed him. He, the fool, bent his back, and seizing her bare legs in both his hands, he galloped, like a horse, over all the countryside' (II, 203). Thus it is clear that in this story witchcraft is identified with sexuality, and the enchanted ride is the expression of a sexual act. (The link between witches and sexuality has been encountered earlier in Gogol's writing; thus Solokha in 'Christmas Eve' entertains a succession of lovers, and the wizard in 'A Terrible Vengeance' has incestuous designs on his daughter.)

There are, of course, other manifestations of the supernatural in 'Viy': the monsters in the church and the Viy himself. There is no hint of sensuality in their portrayal; all unambiguously inspire fear and horror. Nevertheless the witch is their instigator and it is not difficult to conclude that they, too, are ultimately linked with sexuality.

Narezhny's novel about the two Ivans may again provide a clue. The two wandering philosophers who open his novel at a later stage seduce the two daughters of Khariton. The act takes place in a melon garden, and is described euphemistically in terms of an actual physical fall. On their return home one of the daughters attempts to allay her mother's fears by attributing their delay to their having been frightened by monsters. They had seen a witch, a werewolf and a vampire. The mother accepts this explanation, but when the pregnancies of her daughters are later revealed she says:

Oh how stupid I am. Why did I not guess what really happened on that fateful night, when you my eldest daughter, told me about a witch, a vampire and a werewolf, should I not have drawn the conclusion that it was monsters of quite a different sort which have now turned you yourselves into such changelings [*oborotni*] that all the wizards of the Ukraine cannot undo the spell.[47]

The monsters of Ukrainian folklore are here equated with sexual guilt, and it is this hint which Gogol appears to be developing in 'Viy'.

Gogol's narrative falls naturally into two parts. The first is centred on the 'act' (the enchanted ride); the second on the 'retribution' (the horrors in the church). Unlike Narezhny, however, Gogol's monsters are not noticeably those of Ukrainian folklore. Indeed in the final version of the story their depiction is left purposely vague (with the exception of two monsters on the third night and the Viy itself).

The 1835 version had detailed descriptions of the monsters, which, acting on the criticism of Belinsky, Gogol later removed. Artistically he was probably right to increase the effect of horror by suggestion rather than detail. Yet these monsters of the first version are vividly described and have a surrealistic intensity. Unlike the purely animal monsters of Narezhny and of Ukrainian folklore, they are, for the most part, organs of the human body which have taken on a bizarre life of their own: a pyramid with legs and feet formed from the two halves of a jawbone with a tongue wagging from its summit; a black thing with a multiplicity of thin arms folded on its chest and a dark blue human hand instead of a head; another black monster consisting only of legs; yet another formed entirely of a head (II, 574–5).

The predominance of various human organs in the guise of monsters suggests that the human body itself is the substance of terror. There is moreover an interesting relationship between all these independently living mouths, arms, legs, heads and the device of synecdoche so central to Gogol's art. Thus later in his writing the psychological problems of Kovalev in 'The Nose' will find expression in the loss of that organ and the independent life it leads as a human being.

With the exception of the giant cockroach, the remaining horrors of the second night of the 1835 version are monsters of the body in a negative sense. It is stressed that they lack certain organs for which they have substituted something else: thus there is a white creature with bags instead of legs, arms, ears and eyes and a reddish blue monster which has neither arms nor legs, but has two trunks that seem to be searching for someone.

In the first version Gogol added new monsters for the third night. Most interesting is the 'inverted body', a skeleton with its flesh inside the framework of bones. Two other creatures are monsters of eyes: one is long and thin like a stick and consists entirely of eyes and eyelashes; the other takes up the whole of a wall and stands in its own matted hair as though in a forest: 'through the web of this hair looked two terrible eyes'. The last of these monsters hangs above Khoma Brut like an enormous bladder (*puzyr'*) it has a thousand scorpion-like claws and stings which are covered in earth (II, 583).

These last two bizarre creatures are the only ones to be included in the final version, and their retention in preparation for the introduction of the ultimate monster, the Viy, is artistically sound: each of these creatures prefigures an essential characteristic of the Viy himself – seeing, but only with difficulty, and being covered with earth.

The fact that it is finally an internal human organ which is suspended above the philosopher is perhaps not without significance. The word, *puzyr'* can have more meaning than one; Constance Garnett translates it as 'bubble',[48] yet, given the corporal nature of the monsters in the first version, 'bladder' would seem more likely. Be that as it may, the word in Russian is virtually synonymous with emptiness, and as such is almost the symbol of the typical Gogolian hero (e.g. Chichikov, Khlestakov, Pirogov). Khoma Brut himself is just such a *puzyr'*, a man without any apparent inner content, a man without psychology: 'The philosopher Khoma Brut was a man of jolly disposition. He liked to lie about and smoke his pipe, and if he drank, he would always hire musicians and would dance a trepak. He frequently tasted the hot pease pudding,[49] but he did so with complete philosophical indifference, saying that what had to be, had to be' (II,

181). Here, Gogol is punning on the words 'philosopher' and 'philosophical' ('philosopher' as a grade in the seminary, and 'philosophical' as the equivalent of stoic), the appellation 'philosopher' throws into ironic relief the almost complete lack of thought processes in the hero's psychology. The enormous bladder/bubble suspended over Khoma on the night of retribution is symbolic of his own internal emptiness. Yet, from its very middle stretch a thousand claws and scorpion-like stings, and the fact that these are covered with earth suggests that the real threat is from something buried.

The traumatic events Khoma undergoes in the story appear to have no effect on him; he is introduced as a man 'of jolly disposition' and this is what, in spite of everything, he will always be.

After the eerie night ride with the witch, whom he eventually leaves dying, he very soon finds consolation and financial support from a widow in the market, and that very same evening he can be seen in a tavern lying on a bench smoking, with a mug in front of him: 'He looked at those who came and went with eyes that were stoically indifferent and contented, and gave no thought at all to his unusual adventure' (II, 188). Again after the horror of the first night spent with the corpse, his recovery is almost immediately complete. Food and drink restore him to his normal state of mind: 'The philosopher was one of that number of people, who if they are well fed, will show unusual philanthropy. He lay with his pipe between his teeth, looked at every one with unusually benevolent eyes, and kept continually spitting to one side' (II, 209). The horror of the second night is more intense. It leaves its marks physically on Khoma. His hair turns grey, yet psychologically he appears to be able to make a complete recovery without much difficulty. He drinks heartily with the Cossack Dorosh and then, as is his wont, calls for musicians, but without waiting for them he plunges into a dance, which goes on so long that the servants eventually stop watching him in disgust. It seems that the psychological resilience of Khoma Brut may be attributed to that supremacy of habit over passion which we encountered earlier in 'The Old World Landowners'. Belinsky saw in this behaviour stoic qualities worthy of admiration:

Oh, unforgettable Dominus Khoma! How great you are in your stoic indifference towards all that is earthly, apart from brandy! You have endured terrible grief and anxieties, you have almost fallen into the devil's clutches, but you forget everything when you have a deep wide mug, on the bottom of which your wisdom and philosophy are lying hidden. When they ask you about the horrors you have seen, you make a gesture with your hand and say: 'You come into contact with all sorts of rubbish in the world': one half of your hair has turned grey in one night, but you dance a trepak such that people who look at you spit on the ground and exclaim: 'How terribly long that fellow dances.'[50]

This judgement can only strike a modern reader as naive. The stoicism of Khoma Brut is 'unreal'; there is about it a strange quality of dissociation which is typical not only of many of Gogol's characters, but is also a fundamental element of his style: his sentences often progress by dissociative, rather than consecutive, logic. Lieutenant Pirogov, in 'Nevsky Prospekt', is subjected to the great indignity of a beating at the hands of German tradesmen. He is highly incensed, yet strangely enough, the insult seems less after eating puff pastries and reading the *Northern Bee*. It is entirely forgotten when, like Khoma, he distracts himself in the excitement of a dance. Pirogov's ability to forget is essentially the same as Khoma's 'stoicism', yet of Pirogov, Belinsky comments that he is: 'contented and happy even after unsuccessful philandering and a terrible beating. Yes, Gentlemen the world is boring.'[51]

Khoma Brut easily forgets. He is a man not haunted by memories, but yet the striking thing is that he is haunted in the literal sense. An inner spiritual world which appears to be completely lacking has instead been transformed into an outer world of spirits. Gogol depicts the psychology of Khoma Brut, not by getting inside him, but by portraying a fantastic external reality which is metaphorically the reflection of an inner psychological world.

There is the sense of a suppressed knowledge behind the adventures of Khoma Brut. Thus after his nocturnal ride, when the witch lies dying, he experiences normal human emotions, but yet we are told there is some strange element in them of which he is not fully aware: 'Khoma began to quiver like the leaf of a tree. Pity and a sort of strange agitation which he could not himself explain[52] seized hold of him. He set off running as fast as he could' (II, 188).

When the rector of the seminary summons him to see him and tells him he must go to read prayers over the body of a young girl, Khoma is again prey to feelings which he cannot explain: 'The philosopher shuddered because of an unaccountable feeling, which he could not explain to himself. A dark presentiment told him that something unpleasant awaited him. And, not knowing why himself, he announced point blank that he would not go' (II, 189). The witch's dying words, as they are reported by her father, break off at a very significant point – the point of Khoma's 'knowing':

'If you had lived only a moment longer', said the sotnik in grief, 'then undoubtedly, I would have known everything –
"Do not let anyone read prayers over me, but send immediately, daddy, to the Kiev seminary and bring back Khoma Brut. Let him pray for three nights over my sinful soul. He knows..." But what he knew I did not manage to hear.'[53] (II, 197)

Even more strange is the fact that Khoma cannot bring himself to tell anyone about his experiences in the church, even though the witch's exploits have been discussed before quite openly by her father's Cossacks: 'However, he could not bring himself to speak about what had happened to him in the church – from a feeling of which he himself could give no account, and to the questions of the curious he replied: "Yes, there were all sorts of wonders"' (II, 209). The terror to which Khoma is subjected during his nightly vigils is, it would seem, a purely private affair which he can discuss with no one. The lack of a wise counsellor worries critics who try to fit 'Viy' into the various categories of the fairy story.[54] Yet this omission which seems to cast doubt on one level of authenticity merely reinforces the view that the 'fairy-tale' plot is, in fact, a vehicle for the hero's psychology. Khoma, without any doubt, is the chief protagonist of the tale, yet quite unlike the other stories in *Mirgorod*, there is no mention of this central figure in the title: his place has been usurped by the main representative of the supernatural world, the Viy.

The bizarre events of the story are not forced on Khoma in a purely gratuitous way by the forces of evil; there are hints that he himself must bear some responsibility for his fate.

When the seminarists are lost at the beginning of the story, the witch is extremely loth to take them in and give them shelter, until she hears these words: 'Take pity, granny! Is it possible that Christian souls should perish for absolutely no reason at all. Put us up wherever you want and if we should somehow do something that is not right, or anything else, then may our arms wither on us and may something, God knows what, happen to us. There now!' (II, 184). The seminarists appear to have bound themselves to good behaviour by some vague but terrible oath. The witch consents to take them in but refuses Khoma's request for food, even though he makes another promise: 'And in return for all this, the philosopher continued, we would settle up tomorrow properly in cash. Yes! He added quietly, Devil take it, you'll get something' (II, 184). The seminarists are, of course, destitute and Khoma's ironical comment to himself acknowledges that she will not get a penny, yet it also suggests another vague and unspecified form of payment.

The old woman refuses to give him anything to eat. But the seminarists have already broken their oath for good behaviour by stealing food. Khalyava has taken a carp from one of the wagons in the yard. Khoma puts his hand into his friend's pocket 'as though into his own' and appropriates the stolen fish. Alone in the sheep pen assigned to him by the witch, Khoma devours the carp, and almost immediately the witch appears to him as though for payment (Driessen has pointed to the ambiguity of Khoma's turning over in order to sleep the sleep of the dead, and the suggestion that the witch's demands could be taken as a dream).[55] Khoma rejects her advances, but then it is as though the earlier oath comes into effect. First the withering of the arms: 'The philosopher wanted to push her away with his arms, but to his amazement he noticed that his arms could not raise themselves' (II, 185). The numbness, however, extends to all parts of his body and finally something, 'God knows what', happens to him: the witch proceeds to ride him.

In the second part of the story there is a similar hint that the horrors Khoma experiences in the church may also be self-induced. Before he undertakes his vigil on the first night, his imagination is already overwrought by the Cossacks' stories of the witch's powers, and when the body finally rises from the coffin, it seems almost the result of auto-suggestion:

> 'What is there to be afraid of?', he thought to himself in the meanwhile, 'she won't rise out of her coffin because she will be afraid of the word of God. Let her lie there. What sort of a Cossack would I be if I got scared? It's just that I have drunk too much. Let's have a pinch of snuff, marvellous snuff, fine snuff.' However as he turned over each page, he would look out of the corner of his eye at the coffin, and a feeling, over which he had no control, seemed to whisper to him: 'Any moment now she will rise up, any moment she's about to get up, any moment she will peer out of her coffin!'
>
> But there was a deathly hush. The coffin stood motionless. The candles shed a whole flood of light. A church lit at night, with a dead body in it and not a soul about is terrifying.
>
> Raising his voice he began to sing in various keys wishing to quell the remnants of fear. But every other minute he would turn his eyes towards

the coffin, as though asking a question he could not help asking: 'What if she should rise, if she should get up?'

But the coffin did not stir. If only there were a sound, a live creature, even a cricket chirping in a corner. There could only just about be heard the slight crackling of a candle far away, or the faint, gently plopping sound of a drop of wax falling on the floor. 'But if she should get up?'

She raised her head... (II, 207)

Khoma seems uniquely prepared for such an occurrence; he reads the prayers and imprecations taught to him by a monk 'who had seen witches and evil spirits all his life'. Once he has had a good sleep, the events of the preceding night seem like a dream. During the second vigil the rising of the witch again seems linked with his taking snuff (on the first night he had expressed regret that he could not smoke his pipe in church). The events of the second night are even more traumatic than the first, and yet in the daylight world he can still dismiss them as rubbish: 'There is a great deal of rubbish of all sorts about in the world, and terrifying things do happen. So?' The advent of the Viy on the third night, however, proves too much for him: the horrors of that satanic vigil are frozen in perpetuity.

A similar frozen tableau occurs at the end of *The Government Inspector* where it marks out the hour of retribution. Gogol later interpreted the arrival of the real Government Inspector, and the ensuing dumb show, as the advent of conscience, and it is not hard to see that the Viy has an analogous role in the story which bears his name: he arrives and with him comes a judgement lasting for all eternity. He appears to have the same eschatological significance as the giant at the end of 'A Terrible Vengeance'. Yet the Viy himself does not deliver a judgement: his only function is to see, and it is this moment of recognition which is perpetuated in all its pristine starkness as a potent metaphor for the retribution of an awakened conscience.

'Raise my eyelids for me, I cannot see!', said the Viy in a subterranean voice, and the whole troup of monsters rushed to raise his eyelids. 'Do not look!' whispered some inner voice to the philosopher. He could not restrain himself and he looked.

'There he is' cried out the Viy and pointed to him with an iron finger, and they all, every one of them, threw themselves at the philosopher. Lifeless he crashed onto the floor, and from fear gave up his spirit on the spot. (II, 217)

It is fear, then, at the moment of recognition which kills the philosopher, a point which is emphasised again in the final section by his friend Tiberiy Gorobets: 'But I know why he perished; it was because he became afraid. If he hadn't been afraid then the witch would not have been able to do anything to him' (II, 218). Had Khoma himself not looked, he would not have seen, and have been seen. The Viy is the most terrible of all the monsters because he represents a quality of blindness which can ultimately reveal the most penetrating power of sight. His name may be related to the Ukrainian word for eyelash – *viya*, and eyelids are his most prominent feature; they reach to the very ground, and have to be lifted up for him by all the other monsters in order that he may see. His voice is described as subterranean, but the whole of his being seems connected with an underground existence: 'He was all covered in black earth, his arms and legs, spattered with earth, protruded like strong fibrous roots' (II, 217).

The Viy is led to his confrontation with Khoma in much the same way as Khoma himself has to be led to his final confrontation with the witch, and if the corpse represents a guilty secret, Khoma is engaged in ritualised preparation for its burial. By contrast the Viy is a monster which appears to have been long buried. It seems the very epitome of blindness, with its incredibly long eyelids and its subterranean existence. Yet once it can be summoned forth from the earth and its eyelids lifted, its powers of vision are penetrating. The Viy is not 'the colossal creation of the imagination of the common folk', it is the fantastic embodiment of Khoma Brut's own conscience. The paradox of 'seeing and not seeing' is linked to Khoma's encounters with the witch. Thus the dream-like features, paralleled in the division of night and day,[56] of their nocturnal ride seem to be reflected in nature: 'The forests, the meadows, the sky, the valleys, everything seemed as though it were sleeping with open eyes' (II, 186).

In the 1835 edition Khoma did not look at the witch whom he had left dying in the fields, but in the final version he notices that she has turned into a beautiful young girl with eyelashes as long as arrows. When he sees her on the first night of his ordeal, lying dead in her coffin, his first reaction is to shut his eyes with a shudder, and he feels that she too is looking at him through closed eyes. Later when she rises from her coffin her eyes are still shut, but she cannot see him, not even when she opens her 'dead eyes'; for Khoma has drawn a magic circle around himself. The other monsters, too, are at a loss to see him. It is only the Viy who can force Khoma 'to look' and thereby to be 'seen'.

Outside the charmed circle which protects him, there is another circle which hems him in: the bounds of the sotnik's village, with its incredibly steep hill and impenetrable wilderness of a garden. The enclosed atmosphere of the second part of the story is in contrast to the dominant theme of 'wandering' in the first part. Khoma Brut is forced into this enclosed world in spite of himself. Authority insists that he fulfil his obligations or else face harsh punishment. this is made clear to him by the rector of the seminary and later by the sotnik.[57] It seems as though the hero is in a situation where he has only two choices: to accept a harsh physical punishment or to undergo something analogous in psychological terms.

The third possibility – escape – never appears a reality. He thinks of flight immediately after his interview with the rector, but he is overtaken by events. The Cossacks are already waiting for him. Moreover he seems overwhelmed by a sense of fate: 'What is there to be done? What has to be cannot be avoided.' On the journey out to the village he begs the Cossacks to let him go. All, apart from Dorosh, are prepared to do so. However, the inability to escape turns out to lie within himself – he is too drunk: 'But this escape could scarcely have come about, because when the philosopher took it into his head to get up from the table, his legs had become as though made of wood, and so many doors began to appear in the room, that he would scarcely have found which was the real one' (II, 193).

The following day, having arrived in the village, he again thinks of flight. Beyond the wattle fence he sees a little path all overgrown with weeds. He is about to set foot on it 'mechanically' when he is stopped by Yavtukh who suddenly appears behind him: 'Don't think of running off from the village Mr Philosopher', he said, 'it isn't the sort of establishment that one can run away from. Even the roads are bad for walking' (II, 196). After his second interview with the sotnik, Khoma again thinks of escape. But once more there is some power which appears to be holding him back; a force which, it is strongly suggested, comes from within:

> When the philosopher wished to step over the wattle fence, his teeth began to chatter and his heart beat so strongly, that he himself grew afraid. It seemed as though the hem of his long cloak kept sticking to the ground, as if someone had fixed him down with a nail. As he was stepping over the wattle fence a voice appeared to crack in his ears with a deafening whistle: 'Where are you going? Where are you going?' The philosopher ducked into the

undergrowth and broke into a run constantly stumbling over old roots and crushing moles beneath his feet. (II, 214)

This bizarre detail of the crushing underfoot of moles is realistically improbable, but it has symbolic validity. The inner power which seems to inhibit Khoma's escape and the voice in his ear challenging his flight, are both expressions of his own conscience, whose supernatural manifestation is ultimately the Viy itself. The Viy is represented as having legs like roots, is a 'blind' underground creature who is constantly stumbling. In his flight Khoma constantly stumbles against roots and crushes moles, because his attempt to escape is an act against his own conscience.[58] This strange overgrown garden proves to be just as effective a barrier to escape and contact with the outside world as that incredibly steep hill by which he first entered the village. A thorn thicket takes a heavy toll of his clothing, but he finds a clearing in which there is a pure silver spring. He is just recovering, drinking from the spring, when he is surprised, once again, by Yavtukh, who tells him that he has gone a long way round, whereas he, Yavtukh, has taken a direct route and caught up with him.

There is no escape for Khoma from this village. Indeed Yavtukh seems to be some kind of guardian watching over him.[59] He it is who takes him to the church in the evening and relieves him in the morning. He is like a second self. When we first meet Yavtukh he is crying, in spite of his grey hair, over the fact that like Khoma Brut himself he has neither father nor mother. After the ordeal of the second night Khoma's hair has turned grey, and Spirid draws a comparison: 'You have indeed gone grey, like our old Yavtukh.' It is Yavtukh who on two occasions prevents his flight through the overgrown garden, and Khoma's reaction to being thus thwarted seems to evoke the violence which characterised his first encounter with the wtich: '"The Devil's own Yavtukh!" the philosopher thought to himself in anger. "I would like to take you by the legs and beat that vile mug of yours and all the rest of you with an oak beam"' (II, 214).

The claustrophobic world of guilt, in which Khoma finds himself in the second part of the story, is associated not only with the dead body, but also quite explicitly with the earlier nocturnal ride. A reference to 'riding' precedes nearly every confrontation with the corpse.

When Khoma is first brought before the sotnik he is asked why it should be he alone whom the daughter had requested for the three-night vigil. Khoma is at a loss to know himself and can only explain it as a whim typical of the 'masters', but the folk-saying he quotes to back this argument hints at the theme of 'riding': 'Gallop, enemy, as the master commands!' (*skachi*, *vrazhe*, *yak pan kazhe*!).[60] Khoma is regaled with stories about the daughter's deeds in which 'riding' figures prominently. Dorosh claims that the mistress has ridden him and Spirid tells the tale of Mikita ridden by the mistress until all that was left of him was a pile of ash on the stable floor. After these stories Khoma undergoes the first of his nightly ordeals alone.

Before the second night, he is again diverted by the simple entertainments of the Cossacks and once more the theme of riding looms large. They are playing a primitive form of skittles in which the winner has the right to ride around on another's back. The description of these antics is in a comic vein, but Khoma himself cannot share in the hilarity: 'Khoma in vain tried to get involved in this game. Some dark thought was sticking in his head like a nail' (II, 209).[61] No overt allusion to the 'ride' occurs before the third and final night. Instead, after his futile attempt to escape, Khoma seems to be trying to assert his freedom of movement and independence in the long solo trepak[62] he dances to the disgust of the watching Cossacks.

The strange nocturnal ride which ends in the death of the witch is the key to the haunting of Khoma in the second part of the story, and it is obvious both from the way it is introduced and from its further development that the motif is unmistakably sexual. Yet is it an expression of that dark power of women so inimical to Cossack manhood which we find in 'Taras Bulba'? There is perhaps something here which is even more abnormal: the advances of an old woman result in her riding Khoma; he then rides her; finally he kills her and she changes into a beautiful young girl. But there is another female figure present in Khoma's nocturnal ride – the water nymph. The description of her beauty is unusually sensuous for Gogol. It may be contrasted with the description of the outstanding beauty of the dead witch (it is not merely that she is lifeless, Gogol's description is lifeless, with its comparisons to snow, to silver, to arrows and to rubies).

The sensuous body of the water nymph openly mocks the reflected figure of Khoma with the witch on his back; she seems to be rising towards him, but then sinks back into the water in laughter. Sensuality mockingly rejects the strange image inverted in her element. Significantly each of Khoma's subsequent encounters with the witch is accompanied by a countervailing motif, illustrating normal sexual appetites.

Thus after the ride Khoma returns to Kiev, but finds nothing at all to eat in his lodgings. He soon redeems the matter by strolling through the market and winking at a young widow who takes him into her house and feeds him royally, even providing him with money for the tavern in the evening. This female figure is in direct contrast to the old woman who had refused to give him anything to eat and had grudgingly provided him with the worst of accommodation, a sheep pen occupied by a pig.

When later he is brought before the witch's father, Khoma rejects the sotnik's assumption that he has been summoned because of his saintly life: 'Good gracious, Sir, what are you saying? It is not decent even to mention it, but I visited the baker's woman on the eve of Maundy Thursday itself' (II, 197). Words which seem to take up those he had used to repel the old woman in the first place: 'It is now Lent and I am not the sort of chap to break the prohibitions of Lent, not for a thousand in gold' (II, 185). Such religious scruples were not to keep him from the arms of the market-place widow.

After the first night of ordeal it does not take Khoma long to recover. He has a good drink of vodka, something to eat and once more he becomes the questing male, but he has less success in the village than he had earlier in the market:

> After the meal the philosopher was in completely good spirits. He managed to go round all the village, and get to know almost everybody. They even chased him out of a couple of huts. One good-looking young woman fetched him a heavy blow on the back with a shovel, when he took it into his head to show curiosity and feel what sort of material her blouse and skirt were made of. (II, 209)

Again after the second night, the counterpoint hint of normal sexuality is once more present. One of the people who meets Khoma as he comes out of the church is a woman, 'not quite past middle age', but 'a terrible coquette'. She greets Khoma as someone she knows, and then points out what no one else has noticed: his hair has turned grey. Khoma goes rushing off to look at himself in the scrap of mirror which she keeps hanging in the kitchen, adorned with various flowers and 'even a wreath of marigolds showing that it was assigned for the toilet of a showy coquette'.

Just as the witch's power over Khoma rises in crescendo with each successive stage of their encounter, there is a parallel diminuendo in Khoma's 'normal ' relations with women. It begins with the high point of his liaison with the widow (immediately after the apparent defeat of the witch); then follows the unsubstantiated avowal of an amorous escapade (on arriving at the sotnik's house); then his rejection by the village women (after the first night of ordeal) and finally there is the 'terrible coquette' who does not flirt with him but lets him see his own half-grey image in the glass she uses to preen herself: a reminder of that hideous conjunction of age and youth reflected in the mirror-like element of the seductively mocking water sprite. Yet the motif of 'the marigolds' (*nagidka*) suggests a further link; for the sotnik had called his daughter 'little marigold' (*nagidochka*), and the 'terrible coquette' of ambiguous age and uncertain beauty seems to embody an erotic ambivalence reminiscent of the witch herself.

It is clear then, from this descending counterpoint of natural sexuality that the witch and her nocturnal ride must represent some form of unnatural sexuality. At this point speculation becomes fraught with pitfalls. The literary critic is in danger of deserting the authority of the text for the theories of Freud or Jung, but nevertheless the interpretation as it has so far advanced seems to point in that direction. The critical problem is not unlike that encountered in Dostoevsky's *Crime and Punishment*. Why does Raskolnikov commit his crime? The explanations which he himself advances are, each in its own way, valid up to a certain point, but ultimately the reader feels there is something deeper and more mysterious which lies behind the hero's motives and his assertion, when pressed: 'I killed for myself.'[63]

The analogy with *Crime and Punishment* is more apt than may at first appear. The similarities are formal, superficial perhaps, but none the less striking. In both works an impoverished student who is also a 'philosopher' beats to death an old woman who exploits him. But this act in both cases turns out to be a double murder. In killing the morally repulsive Alyona, Raskolnikov also has to kill her younger half-sister Lizaveta, who is good and kind. Khoma in killing the ugly old witch, at the same time kills the beautiful young daughter of the sotnik.[64] But the hero is not allowed to forget his crime; he is hemmed in more and more in a claustrophobic world of spiritual torment. Admittedly Dostoevsky offers Raskolnikov resurrection, whereas Gogol condemns his hero to an eternity of limbo. Both works fall naturally into two parts: the *act*, full of symbolic overtones; and *retribution* in terms of spiritual anguish. Why there should be this formal similarity is perhaps not hard to see; the real substance of each is the psychological exploration of a tormented central character, and for this purpose Gogol has made use of the Gothic fairy-tale, much as later Dostoevsky was to press into service the more expansive vehicle of the mystery novel. 'Viy' is Gogol's *Crime and Punishment*.

Representatives of various psychological schools concur in seeing Raskolnikov's murder as the killing of a mother-figure; some go as far as to suggest the motive of incest.[65] Gogol in adapting the Gothic tale, had an even more explicit vehicle; for as H. M. Nebel has pointed out, a frequent element found in the genre is illegitimate love, and he suggests Karamzin's *The Island of Bornholm* as the first Russian Gothic tale.[66] It is significant that in *The Government Inspector* Gogol has Khlestakov quote from this tale the words: 'The laws condemn', when he is making amorous advances to a mother-figure who is already married.

An undoubted influence on 'Viy' is Zhukovsky's translation of Southey's ballad, *The Old Woman of Berkeley*. Karlinsky in pointing to this debt nevertheless persists in seeing the theme of 'Viy' as homosexuality,[67] even though, if the parallel with Southey is pursued, incest would seem the more probable. The monk in the ballad (Khoma Brut, it may be remembered, is a seminary student) reads prayers over the body of a witch for three nights, but the witch is his own mother.

Gogol had already dealt openly with the theme of incest in his earlier 'gothic fairy-tale', 'The Terrible Vengeance'. There are many similarities between this tale and 'Viy'. Thus in both, the surrealistic portrayal of nature plays a symbolic role. The night journey down the Dnepr and Khoma's nocturnal ride invite comparison, with their moons, which are not moons and their strange reflections and inversions. In both works forbidden desires are associated with magic: with a wizard in 'The Terrible Vengeance' and a witch in 'Viy'. When the wizard claims he will force his daughter to love him, her soul protests 'Oh, you are a monster and not my father', and it is obvious that in both works the 'unnatural' is being projected as the 'supernatural'.

In 'Viy' the curse on the generations is only adumbrated in the sotnik's oath to God, that he, who had as much as insulted his daughter, should not see his own children, and although the working out of retribution is entirely different, and even involves dissimilar figures, nevertheless the wizard, like Khoma Brut, appears to be the prisoner of a charmed circle. He is physically unable to escape his ordeal, however hard he might try. The motif of 'earth' of 'buried underground',[68] is also common to both stories, and like the Viy, the giant horseman also opens his eyes at the moment of judgement. Indeed the whole sequence of retribution is accompanied by an unusual and far-reaching clarity of vision, which, while it takes on a dimension far greater than that of Viy, nevertheless has the same metaphorical quality. Moreover the wizard, like the witch, 'sees' with dead eyes.[69]

When the witch first makes advances to Khoma he sees her as a grotesque matriarch, a 'granny' (*babusya*) who wishes to embrace him. She rides him and he is aware of a strange sweet sensation, he then rides her and finally he kills her. As she dies he becomes aware of her as a beautiful young girl, and it is this beautiful maiden who later becomes the focal point of his torment, and whose presence alone with him at night profanes a church. The witch is at the same time both ugly and repulsive; young and desirable.

Although it is claimed that both Dorosh and Mikita have been ridden by her, it is perhaps significant that it is only Khoma who has been ridden in her guise of an old woman.[70] The other criminal act ascribed to her by the villagers is the murder of a baby and the savaging of its mother, both acts against the concept of motherhood and reminiscent of crimes committed by the wizard of 'The Terrible Vengeance'.[71] Strangely, too, Khoma is a young man who can give no real account of his parents:

'Who are you, where are you from and what is your station, my good man?' said the sotnik in a manner neither friendly nor stern.

'I am a seminarist, the philosopher Khoma Brut.'

'And who was your father?'

'I do not know, noble sir.'

'And your mother?'

'I don't know who my mother was either. Of course common sense would say I had a mother. But who she was and where she came from, and when she lived, God is my witness, sir, I do not know.'

The sotnik was silent a while, and appeared plunged in thought.

'How did you get to know my daughter?' (II, 196)

Yavtukh, the guardian figure, also echoes him in this. In spite of his grey hairs Yavtukh wept when he was in his cups because he had no father and mother.

The story is permeated by an atmosphere of demonism. The devil is constantly on the lips of Khoma Brut and the mood is sustained by ominous auditory effects, such as those on the third night when Khoma is being taken to the church for the last time:

> The night was hellish. Wolves were howling in the distance, a whole pack of them. Even the very barking of the dogs was somehow terrifying. 'It seems as though something else is howling. it's not a wolf', said Dorosh. Yavtukh kept silent. The philosopher could find nothing to say. (II, 215–16)

The howling of wolves is straight out of gothic fiction, but yet the howling of dogs is also presented as terrifying, and in this story they are representatives of forces inimical to the hero. Thus the witch herself turns herself into a dog to attack human beings, and the young man she rides to his death is Mikita – the kennel master who 'knew each dog like his very own father'. The village itself is full of dogs, when the Cossacks lead Khoma to the church at night they have to fight them off with whips, and Khoma, contemplating flight from the sotnik, boasts: 'I will get such a move on, that you and your dogs will not keep pace with me.'

At the beginning of the story the three seminarists have lost their way in a night black as pitch:

> The philosopher, searching with his feet in all directions, said at last, abruptly: 'Where on earth is the road?' The theologian was silent for a while, and then after much thought he said: 'Yes, the night is dark.' The rhetorician moved away to one side and tried on all fours to feel for the way, but his hands only kept dropping into foxes' holes. (II, 182)

When the philosopher attempts to shout his voice seems to be muffled on all sides, all he hears in reply is a faint moaning like the howl of a wolf. It is finally the barking of dogs which brings them to the witch's house. Thus the eerie atmosphere of the night is reinforced by hints of foxes, wolves and dogs, but the improbable detail of finding only foxes' holes instead of a path seems almost as bizarre as Khoma crushing moles under his feet when, later in the story, he is trying to find a way out of the sotnik's garden. Both these details are symbolic rather than realistic: they hint at an underground way and its denizens. The true path of the story, as we have seen, does lead underground below the surface horror of the gothic tale to the psychological underground of the earth-covered Viy.

'The tale of how Ivan Ivanovich quarrelled with Ivan Nikiforovich'

'A wonderful *bekesha* has Ivan Ivanovich.' With these words Gogol's narrator opens his tale of the two Ivans. The word order is not fortuitous, it warns the reader of his entry into a world where possessions have a strange ascendancy over their owners. The whole opening is a eulogy of this *bekesha* (a type of winter coat): its virtues seem to have supplanted any qualities Ivan Ivanovich might have as a person. It is only much later in this passage that the narrator turns his attention to the man himself, and even here admiration seems to be founded on possessions: 'A fine man is Ivan Ivanovich! And what a house he has in Mirgorod.'

Much the same is true of Ivan Nikiforovich, who in spite of an almost permanent physical estrangement from his clothing, psychologically at least seems to be identified with his wide Cossack breeches (*sharovary*). This is how the narrator contrasts the characters of the two 'friends': 'Ivan Ivanovich was of a somewhat timid nature. But Ivan Nikiforovich, quite the contrary, had breeches with such wide pleats that, if they were blown up, the whole of his courtyard with its barns and buildings could have been housed there' (II, 227). This identification is further developed when Ivan Ivanovich watches the possessions of his friend being hung out to air by his servant: '"The stupid woman", thought Ivan Ivanovich, "she'll bring out Ivan Nikiforovich himself next to give him an airing." And in truth Ivan Ivanovich was not entirely wrong in his surmise. Some five minutes later the nankeen breeches of Ivan Nikiforovich were hoisted aloft and took up almost half the courtyard' (II, 229–30).

The narrator's exaggerated admiration of the sterling qualities of the two 'friends' is contradicted by the facts as he presents them. This discrepancy is exploited for comic effect, yet at the same time it leaves open the possibility of an almost tragic interpretation of their relationship, reflected in the note of gloom on which the story ends.

The physical descriptions of the two protagonists are comic and yet they are also suggestive of some essential reality of personality which is far from funny. Gogol draws his imagery from the vegetable kingdom: Ivan Nikiforovich has a nose like a ripe plum, and: 'The head of Ivan Ivanovich was like a radish tail down; the head of Ivan Nikiforovich like a radish tail up' (II, 226). Such resemblances may be physical but they hint at an inner reality: these two men, who lie about all day, lead a vegetable existence. The narrator calls Ivan Ivanovich a 'fine man' because of his house, and the same admiration is called forth by his passion for melons: 'A fine man is Ivan Ivanovich. He loves melons very much.' Animals, too, play a part in their characterisation. The thin, pompously strutting Ivan Ivanovich is called a 'gander' by his corpulent friend, and he in turn, for some reason, feels insulted at the offer of a pig.

The presentation of character by vegetable and animal analogies looks forward to the depiction of provincial life in *The Carriage* and in *Dead Souls*. This latter work also sheds light back on the tale of the two Ivans; for there Gogol divides the guests at the Governor's reception into fat men and thin men, each group occupying different ends of the room as there are no common interests between them. A physical antinomy thus expresses a psychological gulf which is equally as unbridgeable, and although Ivan Ivanovich and Ivan Nikiforovich are of the same basic vegetable matter, they are nevertheless of contrasting shapes: they are radishes 'tail up and tail down'. The friendship between them, of which the narrator speaks so warmly, seems at best a very fragile affair. Even before the quarrel has begun the 'broad' expressions of Ivan Nikiforovich seem to offer constant offence to the narrow-mindedness of Ivan Ivanovich.

The quarrel begins when the acquisitive instincts of Ivan Ivanovich are aroused by a clothesline of Ivan Nikiforovich's effects airing in the sun. The sight of a gun, brought out to air among these objects, prompts him to abandon the rest he is taking under the awning outside his house and confront Ivan Nikiforovich inside his darkened room, where he is also resting. But the objects are also visible to Ivan Nikiforovich, for a chink of light coming into the room creates a *camera obscura* effect, which presents his possessions in an inverted image. There are thus two views of the objects: one 'tail up', the other 'tail down': one from under the sunlit awning of Ivan Ivanovich, the other from the darkened room of Ivan Nikiforovich. It is not surprising that in the conversation which follows neither can appreciate the position of the other. In Narezhny's story of the two Ivans a gun had also been instrumental in starting the feud, but significantly it is the active use of a gun. The whole train of violent acts stems from the original fact that Khariton Zanoza had shot the rabbits which belonged to the son of Ivan the younger.

In Gogol's story, however, possessions define human beings, and it is significant that it is over the *possession* of a gun that Gogol's two Ivans quarrel. Ivan Ivanovich says he wants it for sport (he talks of quail, but his real sporting trophies seem to be melons; for he saves the seeds of each one, noting the date and circumstances of its dispatch). Ivan Nikiforovich claims he needs to retain it to shoot burglars (but in chapter 4 the narrator tells us that neither theft nor swindling is known in Mirgorod). The practical value of the gun is, in any case, dubious since it is broken. Its significance is more symbolic. It is a mark of their Cossack past, an emblem of their very nobility, and, in casting round for reasons why he cannot give it up, Ivan Nikiforovich almost says as much: 'But allow me Ivan Ivanovich, a gun is a noble object' (i.e. *veshch' blagorodnaya*) (II, 236).

Thus the argument which begins over a gun is really about social status, noble origins and ultimately the claim to be a true Cossack. This argument is presented by Gogol in comic terms and with much irony, yet its serious implications are never far from the surface. It is ironical, for instance, that it should be Ivan Ivanovich who needs the gun, for he is the more 'refined' of the friends, and yet it is his claim to nobility which is called in question, whereas the coarse Ivan Nikiforovich for all his roughness of speech and manners seems less vulnerable socially. Even before the matter of the gun is raised an argument nearly develops over Ivan Nikiforovich's expletives when discussing the innocuous topic of the weather. Ivan Nikiforovich cannot understand the violent reaction of his friend: 'In what way have I insulted you, Ivan Ivanovich? I have not touched either your father or your mother. I don't know how I have offended you' (II, 232). Thus in his reference to a possible affront through parentage, the ticklish question of Ivan Ivanovich's social origins is adumbrated (significantly the title of Gogol's tale, unlike that of Narezhny, includes the patronymics of the two protagonists).

When the argument develops over the gun, it is another unguarded word from Ivan Nikiforovich which generates the real heat: he calls Ivan Ivanovich a 'gander'. His 'friend's' reaction to the insult is unexpected – he takes it, not as a gibe at his stupidity, but as an attack on his social status: 'How dare you, sir, forgetting all decency and respect to a man's surname, name and his rank, dishonour him with such a defamatory name?' (II, 237). Ultimately Ivan Nikiforovich seeks to terminate this argument by having Ivan Ivanovich thrown out of his house by the servants. A threat which is yet a further affront to social position: '"What! To a nobleman?" Ivan Ivanovich shouted with a sense of dignity and indignation' (II, 237). In the complaint which Ivan Ivanovich files against Ivan Nikiforovich, his constant theme is the insult to his rank, name and surname (*chin*, *imya*, *familiya*). He claims that he has never been 'named' a gander before and does not intend to be so 'named' in future. After this statement he feels called upon for some reason to produce evidence of his noble birth: 'As proof of my noble origin there is the fact that in the parish register, to be found in the church of the Three Prelates there is recorded both the day of my birth, and equally too the baptism which I received' (II, 249). Unfortunately, however, in the second point of his complaint where Ivan Ivanovich deals with the all important matter of 'possessions' the real facts of his social origins slip out inadvertently: 'This very same obscene and indecent nobleman has moreover made an attempt on my ancestral property, which I received from my father, of blessed memory, a man of clerical calling, Ivan, son of Onisiy, Pererepenko' (II, 249). Ivan Ivanovich's difficulties with 'official style' (the contorted nature of these sentences defies adequate translation into English) and the passions roused over property seem to have left Ivan Ivanovich unguarded where it matters; for if his father was, as he himself says, 'of clerical calling', then his own claim to nobility is, to say the least, tenuous.

In his own counterclaims Ivan Nikiforovich brings up the question of the dubious social origins of his 'friend', but his logic is equally as absurd:

> Moreover the frequently cited frenzied nobleman and cut-throat Ivan, son of Ivan, Pererepenko is of very shameful origins. His sister was known to the whole world as a trollop, and she went off after the company of chasseurs which was billeted in Mirgorod five years ago; and had her husband ascribed to the peasant class. His father and mother were also extremely lawless people and both were unimaginable drunkards. The aforementioned nobleman and cut-throat, Pererepenko, through his animal-like and reprehensible acts has surpassed all his relations and under the guise of piety commits the most corrupting acts. (II, 253–4)

The style of Ivan Nikiforovich's official complaint is remarkable not merely for its absurd logic, but also for its suggestive use of 'elevated' words.[72]

For his part Ivan Ivanovich permits himself no such innuendoes about the social status of Ivan Nikiforovich in his official complaint. The nearest he comes to this is to say 'whose name and surname inspire all sorts of loathing'. But the social theme is dominant in Ivan Nikiforovich's charges. He accuses Ivan Ivanovich of cursing him like a peasant (a surprising statement in view of his own language) and one of the punishments he wishes to see inflicted on his enemy is that he be deprived of the status of nobleman.

When the inhabitants of Mirgorod make their final attempt to reconcile the two erstwhile friends, the social insecurity of Ivan Ivanovich seems to be symbolically suggested by the presence of a comic double in the role of a one-eyed peacemaker.[73] It is this Ivan Ivanovich who seems to take precedence in the narrator's social roll-call of honour:

What a ball was given by the Governor! Allow me to recite all who were there: Taras Tarasovich, Yevpl Akinovich, Yevtikhiy Yevtikhiyevich, Ivan Ivanovich, not that Ivan Ivanovich but another, Savva Gavrilovich, our Ivan Ivanovich, Yelevferey Yelevferiyevich, Makar Nazaryevich, Foma Grigoryevich. I can go no further. I have not the strength. My hand is tired of writing. (II, 264)

Nevertheless this does not deter the narrator from expatiating further on the full glories of this social occasion. There is, however, one figure of local society who is missing:

Finally Ivan Ivanovich, not that Ivan Ivanovich but the other, the one who had one eye, said:

'It seems strange to me that my right eye' (the one-eyed Ivan Ivanovich always spoke ironically about himself) 'cannot see Ivan Nikiforovich Dovgochun Esq.' (II, 265)

It does not augur well that the initiative for reconciliation with Ivan Nikiforovich comes not from 'that Ivan Ivanovich but the other, the one who only had one eye', and sure enough, when the confrontation takes place, the real Ivan Ivanovich is still harping on the fact that his rank and calling, his rank and surname have been harmed by Ivan Nikiforovich's insulting word. Unfortunately Ivan Nikiforovich in his protestations to the contrary actually pronounces the word 'gander' again, and in front of all the representatives of local society. All is lost.

Why should Ivan Ivanovich react so violently to the word 'gander'? In his official complaint he even regards it as having been attached to his real surname by Ivan Nikiforovich (i.e. '*prisovokupleniye k familii moyey nazvaniya Gusaka*'). It seems significant that Ivan Ivanovich spells this 'Gander' (*Gusak*) 'attached to his name' with a capital letter and Leon Stilman has pointed to Gogol's own mystifications over his noble ancestry. Like Ivan Ivanovich, Gogol's real antecedents were clerical, and a similar 'bird' a *gogol′* (a golden eye duck) had been added to the family name of Yanovsky in order to claim noble descent. Could it be that in the reaction of Ivan Ivanovich to the identification with a gander, we have a comic reflection of the author's own anxiety about social status?[74]

It is not merely the chief protagonists who are reduced to the status of livestock or articles of clothing, these two elements figure prominently in Gogol's methods of social criticism in a wider context. Thus the fact that the court takes bribes is given concrete expression in the number of hens on the porch (those who come to petition bring 'gifts' of grain and the inevitable loss of small quantities from the sacks attracts the hens). Moreover thrushes and methods of making them sing occupy the judge's attention, rather than the court decisions which the secretary is reading out for him to sign. Given such an intrusion of animals into the affairs of the court, it hardly seems surprising that a pig should rush in and, ignoring the *real* business of its occupants (the edible 'fruits' of their labours) should make off, not with a pie or a crust of bread, but with the petition of Ivan Nikiforovich. Such precipitate action on the part of an animal is in stark contrast to the customs of the court itself where non-action is the favourite legal procedure.

On one of those courtroom chests which have become the coffins for legal documents stands a symbol of the real values of officialdom: a cleaned and polished boot, and in a world where human beings are no more than their clothes, it is fitting that the deficiencies of the mayor should be characterised by a missing button. He lost it two years ago and his chief official concern still seems to be its recovery; for when the superintendent makes his daily report, the mayor never fails to ask whether his button has been found. Significantly, too, the mayor is introduced to the reader clothes first. Ivan Ivanovich is, as usual, lying under his awning, when: 'to his ineffable surprise he saw some sort of red object at the garden gate. It was the red cuff of the mayor which just like his collar had taken on a polish and at its edges had turned into patent leather' (II, 255). The clothes a man wears express his character completely, thus the bizarre inconsistency of Anton Prokofevich's nature is shown through his brown coat with light blue sleeves. This man of motley seems a strange choice for the role of 'diplomat', and as he sets off to persuade Ivan Nikiforovich to come to the mayor's assembly, his dignity seems even further reduced by the remarkable qualities of his trousers, which always attract the neighbourhood dogs to bite him. In this depiction of clothes suggesting the personalities of their wearers, Gogol is looking forward to the methods of psychological portrayal of 'The Overcoat': the personality of a character seems to reside in his clothes rather than in himself.

A similar effect is achieved through an obsessive concentration on one particular physical feature. Thus the judge is distinguished by his upper lip, which acts as an inbuilt snuffbox. When his nose inhales all the snuff from this natural shelf, it is a sign that he is very pleased. But such dominating physical features always threaten to assume a life of their own; and although the judge is far from happy to receive the complaint of Ivan Nikiforovich, nevertheless his nose: 'couldn't help taking a sniff from his upper lip, which formerly it usually did only as a mark of great pleasure. Such independence of action from his nose caused the judge even more annoyance. He took out a handkerchief and wiped all the snuff from his upper lip in order to punish its boldness' (II, 253). The independence of action of a nose looks forward to Gogol's story of that name. Moreover the way a nose is treated reveals social distinctions. Thus the judge makes use of a handkerchief, whereas the secretary blows his nose in his fingers, as, we are told, do all court secretaries.

The mayor's inefficiency is characterised not only through clothing (e.g. the missing button), it is also expressed through an autonomous part of his own body: 'His left leg had been shot in the last campaign, and therefore as he limped he would throw it so far to one side, that in doing so he destroyed almost all the effort of the right leg' (II, 256).

That 'other' Ivan Ivanovich at the mayor's reception seems to be totally characterised by his one eye. The insistence on one bizarre feature of a character is an essential element of Gogol's humour, and in the figure of Ivan Ivanovich it is almost as though he is 'laying bare' the device; for the character himself constantly uses his physical defect as his one source of humour, and when we read 'the one-eyed Ivan Ivanovich always spoke about himself ironically', we may suspect that the self-irony is also Gogol's: 'Everyone liked the one-eyed Ivan Ivanovich very much because he made jokes completely in the modern taste' (II, 265). One of Ivan Ivanovich's jokes is to wager his blind eye against the mayor's lame leg that Ivan Nikiforovich will not come to the mayor's reception. The humour associated with this wager is then taken a stage further and given concrete expression; for it is these two comic cripples who try to bring the two Ivans into physical proximity to effect a reconciliation:

Ivan Ivanovich, the one with only one eye, shoved Ivan Nikiforovich, a bit obliquely but nevertheless fairly successfully to the place where Ivan Ivanovich was standing; but the mayor's direction was too much to one side, because he was not at all able to cope with his wayward infantry, which on this occasion obeyed no command, and as though on purpose lurched out extremely far and in absolutely the opposite direction (which could have come about because there had been an extremely great number of liqueurs of all sorts with the meal) so that Ivan Ivanovich collided with a lady in a red dress, who out of curiosity had shoved herself into the very middle of it. Such an omen did not augur anything well. (II, 272)

The story is a wealth of absurd detail: the nakedness of Ivan Nikiforovich and his habit of having a table and a samovar in the water whilst bathing; his fat body getting stuck in the courtroom door; Ivan Ivanovich's house likened to a plate piled with pancakes or to layers of fungus on a tree; the mayor's reception with its weird roll-call of guests, who are responsible for such a quantity of wheels in the courtyard that it is like the inside of a clock; the absurd descriptions of the coaches themselves, and the bizarre food which is offered to the guests (one dish is even like boots boiled in kvass), all this shows Gogol at the height of his comic powers. Yet is the story just comedy or is there something in its very conception which justifies the undeniably gloomy ending: 'It is boring in this world, Gentlemen!'

It is illuminating to compare Gogol's story with Narezhny's *The Two Ivans or the Passion for Litigation*. The similarities are evident, yet they are superficial. Narezhny's work is also about two Ivans and an eternal feud, and the quarrel also begins with an incident involving a gun but it proceeds from one act of violence to another, the destruction of property, burning and beating, until finally it ends in litigation. In Gogol's story, by contrast, the only real act of destruction is the sawing down of Ivan Nikiforovich's goose house. The other allegations of arson, attempted murder etc. are all in the absurd imagination of the protagonists.

Real violence is carefully avoided by Gogol. Thus Ivan Nikiforovich keeps doves which he feeds with his own hands, but these symbols of peace are not brutally massacred as they are in Narezhny's novel, when Nikanor kills the doves of Pan Khariton for sport, as he despises such small game as quail (Gogol's Ivan Ivanovich is reputedly a hunter of quail and it is for this purpose he apparently wants the gun).

Gogol eschews overt manifestations of violence in order to present the quarrel in comically absurd terms. The comic is also Narezhny's intention, but his effects are crude and overdone and are ultimately undermined by the dominant strain of violence. Thus Narezhny's two Ivans fight with a goat at night, believing it to be a spirit (*domovoy*) and an animal is also mistaken for a spirit in Gogol's tale; for in sawing down his neighbour's goose-pen, Ivan Ivanovich is frightened by a goose which he takes for a ghost.[75] The incident is inherently no less absurd than Narezhny's, but Gogol by contrast shows real artistic economy in the brevity of its depiction, its lack of physical violence and its relevance to the central issue of the quarrel itself: Ivan Ivanovich's 'fear of the gander'.

Narezhny's subtitle is 'The Passion for Litigation', and his courts show the same crude violence in their operation that permeates the novel as a whole. Both sides in the feud lose to the established organs of justice they seek to invoke. Khariton is put in prison and loses all his property to the court officials he has insulted. The sotnik and his associates take over the House of Ivan the Elder; they beat him up and leave him in the street. It is Ivan the Elder who makes the outspoken social point: 'Oh Justice where are you?... There is justice somewhere, only there is none in our country.'[76] Similar criticism of the courts is implied in Gogol's story, but justice in Mirgorod is presented as incompetent and venal rather than aggressively acquisitive.

The subtitle: 'The Passion for Litigation' would, in fact, be more appropriate for Gogol's story, for here, unlike Narezhny, hostilities are channelled almost exclusively into the legal battle, and if Narezhny's novel is spattered with blood, Gogol's tale is soaked in ink.

The Mirgorod court consists of an antechamber and a room with a table decorated with ink blots. The table bears visible witness to the way business is conducted in the court itself; for after Ivan Ivanovich has deposited his complaint, the officials express their reaction in ink: 'The judge sat not uttering a word. The secretary took snuff, the clerks upset the piece of broken bottle which was used instead of an inkwell, and the judge himself absent-mindedly spread a pool of ink across the table with his finger' (II, 251). To draft his second complaint Ivan Nikiforovich makes use of a professional scribe who is described as 'an absolute official inkwell', but to no avail; for the whole affair is put away in a cupboard, which, appropriately, has become like marble from ink blots. The litigation would have remained entombed in 'marble', if the unfortunate attempt at reconciliation had not revived the legal corpse, and caused Ivan Ivanovich to dig into his ancestral hoard of silver roubles to put them 'into the stained hands of businessmen of ink'. It seems only fitting, in view of the 'literary' form the relationship of the two protagonists is to take, that letters of the alphabet should be used to characterise them. Ivan Ivanovich is described as having a mouth the shape of *izhitsa*[77] and in extreme anger at the insults he has received from his 'friend' this becomes stretched in an 'O'. On the clothes line of Ivan Nikiforovich are a strange pair of trousers in the shape of the Russian letter 'л'.

Bizarre surrealistic descriptions occur in Narezhny's work but not to the same extent as in Gogol and there is genuine naivety in his narrative whereas Gogol's narrator is disingenuously naive.[78] Nevertheless, at the end he suddenly adopts the serious tone of a man of common sense and sensitivity, almost as though he is assuming the role of the *raisonneur* figure who enters Narezhny's novel in the guise of the uncle. Such a character is not uncommon in Narezhny; many of his works have a strong element of didacticism, and the fact that there is explicit social criticism in *The Two Ivans or the Passion for Litigation* may lead the reader to suspect that his intentions encompass more than the writing of a mere comic tale.

It is perhaps significant that the narrative is set in history by reference to a political event. Thus Ivan the Younger begins his tale: 'I promised to tell you about the beginning and continuation of our litigation, so stubborn and implacable, the like of which no one in the locality can remember since the Union of little Russia with Great Russia, which took place over seventy years ago.'[79] There is concealed irony in the way Narezhny pointedly relates his account of personal dissension and the abuse of law to the legal union of two great nations. Their destinies were linked by hetman Khmelnitsky, as a political move in his struggle against the Poles, and the union was proclaimed in 1654. Narezhny is therefore pointing to a period a century before his novel was published (i.e. to about 1724), and Ivan the Younger states that the quarrel started some ten years earlier, it is obvious that the action must be set in the latter part of the reign of Peter I. This was an extremely low point in the relationship between the two nations; for, during the rebellion of Mazeppa, Peter's generals had razed the Zaporogian *Sech'* to the ground (1709) and in 1723 he had refused to allow the election of a Cossack hetman for the Ukraine. Thus at this period the Zaporogian Cossacks were being completely reduced as a military and political force. This oblique historical reference is not unlike Gogol's allusion to Catherine II's treatment of the Cossacks in 'Christmas Eve' (in 1755 Catherine II finished off the work of Peter I: she disbanded the Zaporogian Cossacks entirely).

Narezhny's novel is implicitly about Ukrainian military impotence. It describes how once-noble warriors are reduced to mere acts of petty violence and interminable litigation. In this 'warfare' they are ironically likened to such doughty knights of folk legend as Dobrynya and even, obliquely, to Don Quixote.

The feud begins as the Cossacks are sitting around listening to tales of the military exploits of Ivan the elder, and counting the fruit ripening on the trees (one may compare the theme of melons associated with the lying around of Gogol's Ivan Ivanovich). Shots ring out; but it is merely Pan Khariton shooting tame rabbits. From such an absurd incident of domestic violence a feud is born, but stories of past military valour are its ironical background.

A similar intrusion of the 'reality' of war occurs in the middle of Gogol's account of the quarrel over a gun, when, as if to change the subject, Ivan Ivanovich introduces the news that three kings have declared war on the tsar, and the two 'friends' can at least agree that their own side will win. Gogol's theme is the same as Narezhny's, but he takes it a stage further. His 'two Ivans' are not even capable of acts of physical violence: their feud is carried on entirely through the courts. Moreover, by simplifying Narezhny's plot, and presenting the feud as one which divides the two Ivans themselves (who in Narezhny's novel are comrades in this battle) Gogol is suggesting the degeneracy of *tovarishchestvo* itself: that ineffable bond of male comradeship extolled in 'Taras Bulba'.

Gogol's narrator reacts with mock incredulity at the news that two such 'friends' could ever quarrel: 'When I heard about it, it was as though I had been struck by thunder. For a long time I did not wish to believe it. Oh, righteous Lord! Ivan Ivanovich has quarrelled with Ivan Nikiforovich! Such worthy people! What then now is firm in this world?' (II, 239). It is not only the sense of a whole world having come to an end; the final phrase: 'What then now is firm in this world?' ('*Chto zh teper' prochno na etom svete*?') will be picked up and echoed in the famous last line of the story: '*Skuchno na etom svete, gospoda*!' ('It is boring in this world, Gentlemen!') Here is a key to that sudden, unexpected shift from comedy to melancholy, which occurs in the final section of the tale.

Gogol, like Narezhny before him, hints at the time that the action is supposed to take place. Typically, it is through an article of clothing, a *beshmet*: 'the light blue quilted Cossack overcoat which Ivan Nikiforovich had made some twenty years ago, when he was considering joining the volunteers, and had for a time let his moustaches grow' (II, 229). The volunteers in question are the *militsiya* formed to repel the French invasion of 1812,[80] and this gives us an approximate date of 1832 for the action of the story. Gogol himself ascribed the fictitious date of 1831 to his tale, and that date is significant: it was the year of a major Polish rebellion, and the fact that Ivan Ivanovich mentions the three kings who have declared war on the tsar, could well be a reference to Russian fears at the displeasure of both France and Britain at the suppression of Polish freedom, linked to the ever present threat from the Turks (peace with Turkey had been concluded only two years before the Polish uprising and Ivan Ivanovich suggests that the three kings wish to impose the Turkish faith on Russia). The events of 1830–1 could well evoke long Cossack memories; for the Poles in seeking national freedom were also laying claim to the old Poland of Rzecz Pospolita, which included the Ukraine.[81] Ivan Nikiforovich's Cossack *beshmet* hung out on a clothes line hints therefore not at one failure in times of national crisis but at two.

If the origins of a coat point to the abortive military career of Ivan Nikiforovich, the making of Ivan Ivanovich's famous *bekesha* is related to a figure absolutely inimical to Cossackdom (at least as it is presented in 'Taras Bulba') a violent woman:[82] 'He had it made at the time, when Agafiya Fedoseyevna did not yet travel into Kiev. You remember Agafiya Fedoseyevna, the one who bit off the tax-assessor's ear?' (II, 223).

Nevertheless, other items of Ivan Nikiforovich's wardrobe which are hung on the line seem to be compromised in a similar way: thus a frayed uniform embraces a female blouse, and a fancy waistcoat is soon to be covered by the old skirt of a dead grandmother (with pockets large enough to accommodate melons).

The emblem of Ivan Nikiforovich's nobility, his uniform with crested buttons, has a moth-eaten collar and former elegant trousers are stained and ridiculously shrunk, another pair is misshapen. The sun shining on all these oddments evokes an extended simile worthy of *Dead Souls* itself: the effect is likened to a Ukrainian puppet theatre (*vertep*). The aptness of the simile can only be appreciated when it is borne in mind that the chief character of the *vertep* was always 'the Cossack'. Although other stock figures are mentioned (Herod, Anton, the Gipsy) it is nevertheless the brightly coloured clothing of red and gold and the flashing sword which suggest 'the Cossack' himself:

> An indication of the important place of the Cossack in the imagination of the people is the fact that this puppet was generally considerably larger than the others. It is easy to recognise by its appearance and dress, which is colourful and flamboyant. He usually wears baggy trousers of scarlet or other brightly coloured material and a *zupan* (a loose upper garment worn by Ukrainians and Poles). In some cases the latter may even be decorated with gold lace for a more splendid effect.[83]

Sure enough, the items which the old woman next brings out are all Cossack accoutrements: an ancient saddle with torn stirrups and worn leather holsters for pistols, a once elegant but faded shabrack, the Cossack breeches (instead of Ivan Nikiforovich himself),[84] his hat and finally his gun. All these objects have seen better days; they are the broken-down accoutrements of a warrior reduced to a crude provincial caricature – a Cossack worthy of the *vertep*. As if to reinforce the suggestion of a peepshow, they are all seen again, inverted through the *camera obscura* formed in their owner's darkened room. There is inversion in the simile of the *vertep* too; for the hot sun of July which, playing on these objects, evokes the comparison is significantly replaced by a setting sun which also brings a strange coldness associated with the theme, inimical to Cossackdom, of female blandishments: 'But the sun is setting, and the fresh coldness of a southern night imperceptibly squeezes up ever more forcibly to the fresh shoulders and breasts of plump village girls' (II, 229).

The story provides further examples of military decrepitude. The soldier who keeps order in the courtroom: 'although he has only one eye and a somewhat damaged arm, nevertheless has abilities completely commensurate with driving out a pig and hitting it with a club' (II, 262). The mayor himself is an old soldier who has been crippled in warfare and the gulf between his martial past and his present grotesque ineffectuality is emphasised through the comic use of military vocabulary: 'The faster the mayor moved his infantry, the less he advanced.' Here 'infantry' (*pekhota*) refers to the mayor's feet, and the joke is further carried on when he is described as 'taking by storm' the porch of Ivan Ivanovich and quarrelling with his infantry in the process. He himself uses in a comically ambiguous way, the word *pokhod*, which in military terms is 'a campaign', but in an amorous context alludes to 'love exploits' and also seems, once more, to refer to the mayor's gait (cf. *pokhodka*).[85]

In 'Taras Bulba' militarism, comradeship and the Orthodox faith are all inseparably linked. These elements are parodied in the tale of the two Ivans:

On Sundays Ivan Ivanovich in his cloth coat, Ivan Nikiforovich in his short yellow brown Cossack coat would set out together for the church, almost arm in arm. And if Ivan Ivanovich, who had exceedingly sharp eyes, noticed first a puddle or something foul in the middle of the street, which sometimes occurs in Mirgorod, then he would always say to Ivan Nikiforovich, 'Take care, don't put your foot there, it's not nice.' Ivan Nikiforovich for his part also showed the most touching signs of friendship, and however far off he might be standing, would always hold out his hand with his snuff-horn to Ivan Ivanovich, saying, 'Do me the honour.' (II, 239)

There are differences here already apparent, and not only of behaviour but of dress. Ivan Ivanovich wears his *bekesha*, but the coat of Ivan Nikiforovich (*kazakin*) proclaims him as a Cossack.

For the Cossacks of 'Taras Bulba' Orthodoxy was a principle for which they were prepared to lay down their lives, but such self-sacrifice in the cause of the faith has been inverted in this last story into a petty self-centredness, most clearly seen in Ivan Ivanovich's smug tormenting of the beggars at the church door under the guise of charity. Such behaviour puts into perspective the often repeated statement of the archpriest Petr, that he knows no one who could fulfil his Christian duty like Ivan Ivanovich.

It is significant that at the end of the tale the narrator encounters the two antagonists in church, and that even here their immediate preoccupation is the next stage in their eternal litigation. This scene also provides a general comment on the state of the faith in Mirgorod as a whole; for in spite of the fact that it is a feast day, the church is nearly empty. This the narrator attributes to the weather and the mud, yet as he himself learns almost immediately, and much to his surprise, these conditions have not deterred Ivan Nikiforovich from undertaking a journey to Poltava to advance his litigation with his erstwhile friend.

It is the weather which communicates a pervasive air of melancholy to the ending. Thus there are tears in this church: 'The candles on a day that was dull, or better described as ill, were somehow strangely unpleasant, the dark side-chapels were sad, the oval windows with their round panes were streaming with rainy tears' (II, 275). The mood is in sharp contrast to the bright sunlit scenes which have gone before: eternal summer has been replaced by drab, cold autumn, as though in harmony with the two protagonists, who are now in the sad autumn of their own lives. They too have been transformed from figures of fun to poor old men worthy of pity, and with this change the atmosphere of the whole story has shifted from light-hearted playfulness to gloom and despondency, dramatically exemplified in the contrast between the opening, with its mock-ecstatic eulogy of Ivan Ivanovich's coat, and the words which conclude the tale: 'It is boring in this world, Gentlemen.' The tears have finally shown through Gogol's laughter.

The whole of this ending is one of inversion and there is no more striking change than that which has taken place in the narrator: he is no longer the naive, optimistic simpleton of the earlier chapters, but a thoughtful world-weary observer of human folly.

In discussing the genre of the 'tale' (*povest'*), Gogol concedes that it has great diversity, but asserts that if it describes an incident satirically: 'Then it becomes a significant creation in spite of the triviality of the incident it treats' (VIII, 482). These words aptly fit his own story of the two Ivans. In satirising a trivial quarrel between two friends, Gogol has extended its scope to imply a comment on contemporary Ukrainian life, and the final words leave us in no doubt that it is a sad comment.

There is satire too of local courts and administration which looks forward to the themes of the *Government Inspector* and *Dead Souls*. The language of legal documents is parodied; even the literary genre of the 'tale' itself is mocked. The very title is absurd: the length is self-defeating for its function as a title – it openly mocks eighteenth-century literary conventions.[86] The headings of individual chapters carry on the parody, reaching the height of absurdity in the heading for chapter 6: 'From which the reader may easily learn all that happens in it'. Nothing, alas, is ever so easy to learn in Gogol! Such humour derives from Sterne and Fielding and parody of the *povest'* form will be continued in later stories (notably in 'The Tale of Captain Kopeykin' in *Dead Souls*). Critics have pointed out the debt of Russian naturalism to 'The Tale of how Ivan Ivanovich quarrelled with Ivan Nikiforovich' and to the parody of it by Dostoevsky in *Poor Folk*, but its unexpected 'mood' ending seems to look forward to a writer later in the century. Chekhov in his stories was to bring the techniques of 'mood' to perfection.

Mirgorod *as a cycle*

The four stories of *Mirgorod* are set in different periods of historical (and non-historical) time, and may be seen as four distinct and contrasting genres: idyll, epic, fairy story, comic tale. Although each one may stand independently, it nevertheless gains from being read in the context of the others; for there is a mutual interpenetration of themes which gives greater unity to the collection than may at first be apparent.

The central themes of *Mirgorod* are: love, valour, the supernatural and spiritual inertia. Each theme is taken up by each story in turn and interpreted in the light of its own genre. Thus we have: love as idyll; valour as epic; the supernatural as fairy story; spiritual inertia as comedy. But such categorisation is too simplistic. Is the love of Pulkheriya Ivanovna and Afanasiy Ivanovich really an idyll? Are the acts of Taras Bulba motivated solely by valour? Is 'Viy' really about the supernatural and is it a genuine fairy-tale? Is the spiritual inertia of the two Ivans in essence comic? The ambiguity at the heart of each story stems in large measure from the presence within it of themes from the other stories, occurring as dissonant overtones to the dominant note.

Thus the first theme, love, is central to 'The Old World Landowners', but the ostensible presentation of their relationship as an idyll is undermined by the presence of the supernatural, spiritual inertia and even to some extent, military prowess. Love as a secondary theme in 'Taras Bulba' is even more negative. It is a constant threat to the dominant idea of military valour. But love as a demonic force reaches its apogee in 'Viy' where it subverts the theme of the supernatural by turning it into a metaphor for the 'unnatural'. In the final story love, in the shape of Agafiya Fedoseyevna, aids and abets the spiritual inertia of the two Ivans: it is she, more than anyone, who is responsible for the continuation of their quarrel and her unsolicited domination of the affairs of Ivan Nikiforovich evokes a personal comment from the narrator: 'I confess, I do not understand, why it has been so arranged that women seize us by the nose just as dexterously as if it were a teapot handle. Is it that their hands are created in such a way, or that our noses are not fit for anything else?' (II, 241).

The second theme of valour, or military prowess, central to 'Taras Bulba' is also present in 'The Old World Landowners' in Afanasiy's teasing that he will desert his wife and go to war. This is no longer a joke in 'Taras Bulba' itself, where Taras's desertion of his wife for the military life takes on a grim and poignant reality. In 'Viy' the Cossacks are lost to the military ethic; it has yielded to heavy drinking, which in 'Taras Bulba' was a surrogate for martial feats (Taras, we are told, considered it 'one of the chief virtues of the knighthood' II, 48). The Cossacks of 'Viy' have trained their coach-horses to stop at every pothouse on the way to their village, so in bringing back Khoma Brut they all get terribly drunk. In the village itself decoration on the doors of the outside storerooms clearly indicates what is seen as the chief thing in life. One depicts a Cossack on a barrel holding a tankard above his head, and has the inscription: 'I shall drink all up'; another with the motif of drinking vessels, a pipe and cards proclaims: 'Wine is the Cossacks' pleasure'. The Cossacks themselves seem far from young and the scars on their faces speak of warfare in the past. Certainly drums, trumpets and cannon in this village now appear to be merely the paraphernalia of revelry.[87]

Finally the two Cossacks of the last story do not even engage in heavy drinking. Their sedentary, vegetable life marks the ultimate degeneracy of the Cossack military ethic. The permanently naked Ivan Nikiforovich is symbolically divorced from his Cossack past, which is only occasionally brought out to air, on his clothes-line. The stout figure of Taras Bulba is parodied in his obesity and in contrast to the free-ranging warriors of the earlier story, Ivan Nikiforovich seldom leaves lhis house.[88] It is therefore apt that his Cossack breeches are only as wide as his own backyard, whereas those given to the sons of Taras on achieving manhood are as 'wide as the Black Sea' (II, 51). Even Cossack etiquette which demands that an elected leader should only accept the staff of office on the third time of asking is parodied in the way Ivan Nikiforovich accepts the offer of tea (II, 246–7). As the stories progress the theme of Cossack valour, like the first theme of love, becomes more and more negative.

Negative too is the third theme of the supernatural, which in its own story 'Viy' exhibits two aspects: the black magic of the witch opposed to the 'white magic' of the Orthodox faith. In 'The Old World Landowners' it is significant that the idyll contains no hint of church-going, and that it is destroyed by the intrusion of the supernatural in the form of folk belief. By contrast the warriors of 'Taras Bulba' are not prey to any folk superstition, yet the Orthodox faith and the Cossack military ethic are identified as one, and the supernatural intervenes in the form of angels carrying the souls of heroes killed in battle up to heaven (at the end of the first version of the story Taras actually appeared to undergo something akin to a crucifixion). In the final story the 'spiritual world' of the two Ivans is inert, as we see in the 'Christian' charity of Ivan Ivanovich and the fact that the last glimpse we have of these two uncharitable 'friends' is in church. By contrast the 'world of spirits' in the story is presented through comedy. So the ghost which frightens Ivan Ivanovich turns out to be a goose, and the narrator says of the rumours that Ivan Nikiforovich was born with a tail:

> But this piece of invention is so absurd and at the same time vile and unpleasant, that I do not even consider it necessary to refute it for educated readers, who without any doubt are aware that it is only witches, and very few at that, who have tails behind their backs, and these moreover appertain to the female sex rather than to the male one.[89] (II, 226)

The fourth theme, spiritual inertia, is closely linked to the concept of 'habit' (*privychka*), and it is this which the idyll of love in 'The Old World Landowners' turns out ultimately to be. At first sight Taras Bulba might seem to be untainted by habit and inertia. Yet this man of action is driven by one thing: a simple militant faith. Human values, his relationship with his wife, his affection for his sons, everything is sacrificed to this one spring of action. When he first brings his sons to the *Sech′*, and finds that the *Koshevoy* (a Cossack leader) is not prepared to mount an attack against the Turks, he is astounded: 'But they are heathen. Both God and Holy Scripture order us to fight the heathen' (II, 68). When the *Koshevoy* adamantly refuses, Taras asks a fundamental, and very revealing question: 'What, then, do we live for?' (II, 69). For Taras the meaning of existence consists in the uncritical acceptance of a traditional way of life,[90] and when a given button is pressed, it elicits a given response. Thus even when disguised as a foreign dignitary, on the dangerous mission of contacting his son in a Polish prison, he betrays himself with naive spontaneity at the first slighting reference to the Orthodox faith. Taras, therefore, acts from habit, even though it is presented epically as tradition. Inertia, too, conditions the behaviour of Khoma Brut; he cannot be shaken from the habits of a lifetime even by his terrifying encounters with the supernatural, and the story ends with Khalyava and a further restatement of the tyranny of 'habit': 'Moreover, in keeping with former habit, he did not forget to carry off the old sole of a boot which was lying about on the bench' (II, 218). The final story marks the ultimate triumph of spiritual inertia. The two Ivans are only 'friends' because of lifelong habit, and once they become enemies they are unable, for the same reason, to break this new relationship.

As we have seen, the tale of the two Ivans was written and published before the other stories of the collection, yet Gogol had an obvious artistic aim in placing it last: the story is the negative summation of all that has gone before. The heroic pretensions of the Cossacks of history have been reduced, via the good natured carousing of the Cossacks of 'Viy', to the mean-spirited philistinism (*obyvatel'shchina*) of the two Ivans; their militant Orthodoxy has sunk to Khoma Brut's ritualised incantations, and finally to the inverted Christian charity of Ivan Ivanovich and the very negation of the precept: 'love thy neighbour'. Even the poetic and terrifying supernatural elements of 'Viy' have become trivialised and turned into mere grotesque examples of the comic. A similar fate has overtaken the demonic theme of love whose mysteries, in the figures of Gapka and Agafiya Fedoseyevna, have been deflated to the level of banal, comic innuendo.

Yet, above all, it is with 'The Old World Landowners' that the tale of the two Ivans has most in common. There, this same life of habit had been projected in would-be positive terms, but whereas 'The Old World Landowners' opens with a statement of affection for this life: 'I very much love...', the tale of the two Ivans ends on a note of rejection: 'It is boring in this world, Gentlemen.'[91] Moreover, the despondent mood created by the rain and the view from a carriage seems to parody and invert a passage near the opening of 'The Old World Landowners', where the narrator likens their quiet idyll to the harmonious daydreams induced by the sound of falling rain or by a country-ride in a calash (II, 16). From the narrator figure who happily steps down from his carriage into the world of the Afanasiy Ivanovichs and the Pulkheriya Ivanovnas to the narrator who leaves in disgust in his carriage at the end of the tale of the two Ivans, the reader himself has been taken on a journey – back into history, into legend, folklore and a world of magic. Yet despite the exoticism of these travels, he has always been aware of them as a struggle with inertia, be it habit, tradition, or spiritual impotence. It is this inertia which finally triumphs in the world of vegetables, animals and objects which is the Mirgorod of the two Ivans.

No wonder Gogol in his first epigraph chose to describe Mirgorod as a place of things rather than people, but his second epigraph is even more revealing: 'Although in Mirgorod bread rings [*bubliki*] are baked from black dough, they are very tasty.' This weighty assertion is ascribed to the 'notes of a traveller',[92] and one wonders, whether he is not connected with those other travellers who begin and end the cycle. For *Mirgorod* is round in form: its end goes back on its beginning. It is like a bread ring, well-cooked and tasty, but the dough from which it is made, it must be confessed, is indeed black.

The pessimism which the reader ultimately takes away with him from the stories is the result of two deep-seated preoccupations of the author himself: one social – the fate of the Ukraine and the degeneration of a noble ideal; the other personal – a complex moral struggle in which fears about the nature of sexuality and the power of religion produce a spiritual inertia akin to impotence. Yet the social theme also has personal implications, in as much as Gogol's own social status was based on a bogus claim to be descended from a Cossack nobleman, whose name the family had adopted and which he had begun to use to the exclusion of his own.

These two areas of authorial concern, the sexual and the social, will surface again and again in Gogol's writing. Sometimes they are linked, sometimes they are separate, but in their many forms they are persistent motifs throughout his works.

2

The St Petersburg Tales

The tales as a group

Unlike *Mirgorod* the so called *St Petersburg Tales* do not constitute a cycle of stories as such. 'Nevsky Prospekt' and 'The Diary of a Madman' were first published in part II of the collection entitled *Arabesques* (1835). 'The Nose' first appeared in 1836 in Pushkin's journal *The Contemporary* (*Sovremennik*) and although 'The Portrait' had ante-dated the other stories, in that it had first come out in part I of *Arabesques* (*Arabeski*) 1835, it was nevertheless substantially reworked for a new version published in the *Contemporary* in 1842. In that same year Gogol's own edition of his collected works published the last of these St Petersburg stories, 'The Overcoat'.

The title 'St Petersburg Tales' is not Gogol's own, yet it makes sense to group these five stories under one heading; for just as *Mirgorod* is concerned with the Ukraine, so these St Petersburg stories constitute the anatomy of another locus: the capital city of the Russian Empire. Nevertheless the focus and the mood have changed; gone is the historical perspective which in 'Taras Bulba' Gogol had sought to provide for his depiction of the Ukraine (even though in his projection of St Petersburg, *The Bronze Horseman*, 1833, Pushkin had also felt the need for an historical perspective). Gone too, is the note of nostalgia, that sense of separation: historical in 'Taras Bulba' and 'Viy'; geographical in 'The Old World Landowners ' and the tale of the two Ivans. For Gogol the world of St Petersburg is the world of the present, both in space and time, yet it is a world permeated by the fantastic to no less a degree than the Ukraine of *Mirgorod.* However, this element of the fantastic is of a new kind; it is no longer that of a rural community steeped in tradition and folklore. It springs rather from the distorted vision of isolated individuals, driven in upon themselves by a city environment in which they feel themselves insecure. The fantastic in these stories is, in essence, the same as that of Pushkin's poem *The Bronze*

Horseman; it is the nightmarish unreality of a city and a society redolent of persecution. In Pushkin's poem the fantastic nature of the city induces madness. This is a theme which Gogol too explores, and in various ways, in the figures of Poprishchin, Piskarev and Chartkov. Pushkin's hero, the little man, the humble civil servant, is also Gogol's (Bashmachkin, Poprishchin) but Gogol introduces another element: the theme of art and the artist.[1] In this he reflects not only his own interest in painting and his association with artists in St Petersburg and later in Rome, but also the imprint of aesthetic ideas dominant in the Russia of the 1830s: the relationship between a transcendental idealism and base, everyday reality.

The theme of the artist is clearly in evidence in such stories as 'Nevsky Prospekt' and 'The Portrait', but it also has a submerged, shadow existence in the civil service 'writer' of 'The Diary of a Madman' and 'The Overcoat'; for related to this figure is a basic motif of all the St Petersburg tales; the relationship between surface and content. A theme which strongly suggests a sense of crisis in Gogol's own view of himself as an artist.

For Gogol the Ukraine is linked with 'origins'; St Petersburg with 'career'. The particular associations of these two *loci* are reflected in the differing obsessions of the 'authorial confession' submerged in each group of stories. It is a difference between *Heartland* and *Capital*, with all the linguistic and symbolic connotations that these two opposing concepts evoke.

'*The Nevsky Prospekt*'

The title indicates the ostensible subject of the story: the Nevsky Prospekt, the main artery of St Petersburg, yet its implications may be compared with those of that other title, *Mirgorod*; for implicit in the narrower concept of the Nevsky Prospekt is the whole of St Petersburg itself.The opening words of the story make this plain: 'There is nothing better than the Nevsky Prospekt, at least in St Petersburg; for that city it represents everything (i.e. *dlya nego on sostavlyayet vse*)' (III, 9). The street, we are further informed, brings people together from all parts of the city: 'The Nevsky Prospekt is St Petersburg's universal means of communication' (*Nevskiy prospekt est' vseobshchaya kommunikatsiya Peterburga*). Indeed the two central figures of the story pass along it to find adventures in other streets, the *Liteynaya* and the *Meshchanskaya*.

The title, therefore, hints at synecdoche – a device which permeates the whole of the story. In this respect it has something in common with the tale of the two Ivans (the only one actually to be set in Mirgorod and to some extent the 'kernel story' of that earlier cycle). In a similar manner 'Nevsky Prospekt' has nuclear importance for Gogol's other four tales of St Petersburg. Moreover the ending of the story shows that same reversal of the opening which can be seen, not only in the tale of the two Ivans, but in the whole sequence of Mirgorod stories, viewed as a cycle:

> There is nothing better than the Nevsky Prospekt...
>
> It lies at all times, that Nevsky Prospekt...

The germinal significance of 'Nevsky Prospekt' for the other four stories is striking. The theme of art, the artist and his attitude to good and evil (the story of Piskarev) becomes the central issue for Chartkov in 'The Portrait', and the confusion of dream with reality, so skilfully conveyed in Piskarev's story, assumes here a nightmarish quality. The comic fate of the overweening, self-satisfied officer portrayed in the second story of 'Nevsky Prospekt' (Pirogov) is further developed in the ludicrous adventure which befalls 'major' Kovalev in 'The Nose', and the civil servants who have the main walking on and off parts in 'Nevsky Prospekt' receive individual attention in 'The Diary of a Madman' and 'The Overcoat'. Thus the hero of this latter work seems almost to emerge as a particularised portrait of a whole group described by the narrator of 'Nevsky Prospekt':

> But old collegiate secretaries, titular and court councillors walk quickly with heads bent. Not for them to occupy themselves with examining the passers by. The have not yet fully torn themselves away from their cares; their heads are in a muddle with a whole archive of business begun and not yet finished, and instead of a shop sign for a long time they have before their eyes either the document box or the fat face of the office director. (III, 14)[2]

The condition of madness which afflicts Piskarev before his suicide[3] is also used as a thematic development in the portrayal of that other artist, Chartkov, in 'The Portrait', but it is explored with greater psychological subtlety and depth in the figure of Poprishchin ('The Diary of a Madman'). Above all, that very device of synecdoche, which so pervades the fabric of 'Nevsky Prospekt', seems to become particularised and to take on a life of its own in 'The Overcoat' and

'The Nose'. Thus, of one of the anonymous personages on the Nevsky Prospekt, the narrator observes: 'Do you think that this gentleman, who is strolling along in an excellently tailored little frock coat, is very rich? Not in the least: he entirely consists of his little frock coat' (III, 45). Here we might almost have the starting point for 'The Overcoat', with its interrelated themes of poverty and clothing, its overcoat which assumes the significance of a 'lady friend' for its owner, who himself only seems to awaken to some sort of life when he is wearing it.

In the attempt of the German tradesman Schiller to have his nose cut off, because it consumes too much snuff, we have the germinal idea of 'The Nose', where a nose which has 'got above itself' does indeed become detached from the face of its owner.[4]

After general, rapturous introductory remarks about the main thoroughfare of St Petersburg, the narrator gives a description of Nevsky Prospekt in all its moods, from early morning until night. It is a description which develops the idea of the street as a microcosm; for a typical day is broken up into six periods of unequal length to provide a sociological cross-section not only of the people on this thoroughfare itself, but of the life of the whole city. The street is used by all classes, from beggars and workmen to society ladies and men of rank. Each social group has its allotted period of the day, and the effect is not unlike the social cross-section afforded by one of the many-storied large houses of the city, with a basement (early morning) occupied by workmen, beggars and errand boys, the attics (night time) tenanted by prostitutes and their clients, whilst the intervening 'floors' are occupied by other classes each according to his social station. Thus the street almost becomes a 'table of ranks' in itself, and such a device seems to look forward to some of the more overtly 'sociological' writing that was to follow on from Gogol.[5] Nevertheless the treatment here is not primarily sociological, its idiosyncratic nature is obvious from the key words Gogol chooses for each category of his six-part scheme:

1. *Early morning until noon* – a 'means' (*sredstvo*) not an 'end' (*tsel'*)
2. *Midday until two o'clock* – 'pedagogical' (*pedagogicheskiy*)
3. *Two o'clock until three* – an 'exhibition' (*vystavka*)
4. *Three o'clock until four* – 'spring' (*vesna*)
5. *Four o'clock until dusk* – 'empty' (*pust*)
6. *Night time* – an 'end in itself' (*tsel'*)

Such categorisations are both fanciful and humorous, and these same qualities are present in the descriptions of the people who pass along the Nevsky Prospekt, each at his allotted time. For the most part they seem not to be human beings at all, but a garish mixture of clothes, accoutrements and prominent physical features. It is not people who throng the street, it appears, but shoes, boots, sleeves, moustaches, whiskers, swords. It is not merely that such objects characterise people: they have actually replaced them. Thus the story piles synecdoche on synecdoche; not only does the street stand for the capital itself, but even those who people it are merely represented by their salient parts.

The use of synecdoche says much about Gogol's attitude to characterisation: people in the story are presented in a purely external way; they are assessed by their exteriors. The narrator's imagination sees objects instead of human beings. The effect is dehumanising, and yet, at the same time, these objects in themselves are a further stimulus to the narrator's flights of fancy. His imagination, however, does not strive to penetrate; it does not treat the façade as a key to unlock the inner personality of the wearer of these clothes, these swords, these whiskers etc.,[6] quite the reverse: the narrator's imagination uses such externals as a starting point to move *outwards* towards fantasy, towards a view of the world which becomes increasingly more grotesque. It is a process in which the imagination is the vehicle for flight, away from any human content, towards a bizarre and ever increasingly dehumanised world of fantasy:

> And the ladies' sleeves that you meet on the Nevsky Prospekt! Oh, what enchantment. They are a little bit like two airborne balloons, so that a lady might suddenly rise up into the air, if she were not supported by a man, because a lady is just as easily and as pleasantly lifted into the air as is a glass filled with champagne, which one raises to one's lips. (III, 13)

Thus, in this imaginative 'flight' a lady is first characterised by her sleeves, which in turn become balloons, while she herself is in danger of becoming a glass of champagne.

In another such passage, men and women seem to undergo a metamorphosis almost worthy of Kafka: 'It seemed as though a whole sea of butterflies had suddenly risen from the grasses and was surging in a glittering cloud above black beetles of the male sex' (III, 12). Yet it is not that nature transforms the city, but rather the city which transforms and mocks the natural world: 'Spring suddenly comes to the Nevsky Prospekt: it is entirely covered by civil servants in green uniforms' (III, 14). According to such 'laws' it is only civil servants of the foreign office who have black beards: fate has decreed that those in all other departments should have ginger ones.

On the face of it, it is obvious why clothes and other human appurtenances should have ousted people themselves in these descriptions: such objects of vanity are the main reason why their owners disport themselves on the Nevsky Prospekt, particularly between the hours of two and three in the afternoon, which the narrator characterises as an 'exhibition'. Yet, at the same time, he disingenuously promises us that there are real personalities lurking behind all these objects on display, and claims to be impressed by the multiplicity of characters he observes: 'Here you will meet a thousand unfathomable characters and phenomena. Oh, Creator! What strange characters one meets on the Nevsky Prospekt' (III, 13). What follows, however, hardly provides the evidence for this statement: 'There is a host of such people, who on meeting you, will invariably look at your boots, and if you pass them, they will turn right round in order to take a look at your coat tails' (III, 13). He then explains that he took such people at first for shoemakers, but he knows they are not, since they all work in various departments of the civil service. The irony here is obvious: all that interests civil servants is clothing and finery. Nevertheless, at the same time, the expectations of the reader have been deceived: the 'thousand unfathomable characters and phenomena', he was promised, remain 'unfathomable' and, significantly, are still bracketed together with 'phenomena' in the narrator's further 'description' of them. Even worse, this multiplicity of characters has been reduced to a single type: a mere observer of clothing and outward appearance – just such a man as the narrator himself.

When an attempt is made to portray two individuals, the artist Piskarev and the lieutenant Pirogov, it is significant that both are introduced, in fact, as general types. The life of the St Petersburg artist is described in some detail, but this is not so much Piskarev's own life as the life of a whole class, as the opening words of the description make clear: 'This young man belonged to that class, which in our country represents a rather strange phenomenon' (III, 16). It is even, as the narrator seems to conclude, the life of a whole genus: 'To this genus the young man we have described belonged.'

When both Pirogov and Piskarev are attracted to different women on the Nevsky Prospekt, the behaviour of each is true to type: Pirogov reacts like a lieutenant, Piskarev like an artist.

Piskarev sees his girl as a painting; she is Perugino's 'Bianca'. Moreover he appears to regard her face from a technical viewpoint: 'And what eyes! Oh Lord, what eyes! the whole positioning, contour and setting of the face – marvellous' (i.e. *vse polozheniye i kontura i oklad litsa*) (III, 15). Piskarev in looking at the girl as at a painting is not seeing her as a human being but as an idealised object. Even worse, when his friend suggests that she might be a woman of easy virtue he defends her in terms of the only criteria which ever seem to be applied to people on the Nevsky Prospekt, her clothing: '"As though she could be one of those who walk at night on the Nevsky Prospekt! She must be a very well connected lady" – he continued with a sigh. "Her cloak alone is worth eighty roubles!"' (III, 15–16). Indeed, in Piskarev's pursuit of her, the girl herself becomes reduced to a mere cloak – a cloak which grows now lighter now darker as she moves along the lamplit street, and the pursuit itself is described with studied ambiguity. (Compare 'Secretly trembling he hastened after his object', i.e. *predmet*.) Thus the girl is an article of clothing, an object. She is dehumanised in the same manner as everyone who passes along Gogol's Nevsky Prospekt, and like all objects there she impels the imagination outwards towards fantasy:

The beautiful girl looked round, and it seemed to him as though a light smile flashed on her lips. He began to quiver all over and could not believe his eyes. No, it was the street lamp, with its deceptive light which had imparted to her face the semblance of a smile; no, it was his own dream which mocked him. But his breath stopped in his chest and everything within him was somehow set atremble. All his senses were on fire, and everything before him plunged into a mist. The pavement rushed beneath his feet, carriages with galloping horses seemed motionless, the bridge stretched itself out and broke at its arch. A house stood upside down on its roof, a sentry-box fell headlong to meet it, and the halberd of the sentry together with the gilded words of a shop sign and the drawing of a pair of scissors appeared to shine on the very lashes of his own eyes. And all this had been produced by one glance, by one turn of a beautiful head. (III, 18–19)

It is significant that the flight into fantasy is no longer now that of the narrator, it is that of Piskarev. Moreover in a world in which human life can be reduced to objects, objects themselves can assume qualities of life:

He did not even notice how a four-storied house *suddenly rose* before him. All four rows of windows, shining with light, *looked at* him at once, and the hand rail at the front door *opposed* him with an iron push. (III, 19) (my italics)

Piskarev enters this building after the girl and follows her up to the fourth floor (alas the least respectable part of the house):

The furniture, which was quite good, was covered in dust; a spider had covered a moulded cornice with its web. Through the unclosed door of the next room could be seen the shine of a jackboot with a spur and the red of the braid of a uniform. A loud male voice and female laughter rang out without any restraint. Oh, God! Where had he come to! At first he did not want to believe it, and began to scrutinise the objects which filled the room more closely. (III, 20)

Thus, typically, it is from *objects* and the synecdoche of 'jack boot' and 'braid' that Piskarev realises he is in a brothel, and it is to *objects* again that he turns in his desire not to believe.

An outward world of objects mocks an inner world of ideal and illusion. Yet Piskarev is the victim of his own naive faith in the values of this external world of objects; from the very beginning he had dismissed the idea that the girl was a prostitute, by pointing to the quality of her cloak. He is also the victim of his own imagination, and as an artist, he belongs to that class of people which: 'as much belongs to the citizens of St Petersburg, as a figure appearing in a dream belongs to the real world' (III, 16). To some extent Piskarev himself seems aware of the insubstantiality of his artistic world of dreams: 'No these were his own daydreams laughing at him!' 'But was all this not happening in a dream?' we read, as he pursues the girl along the Nevsky Prospekt. Nevertheless the painter's imagination of Piskarev, like the artistic imagination of the narrator himself, reduces human beings to objects, then flies from their surface into fantasy, rather than penetrate the essence within.

When confronted by a reality far different from that suggested by his imagination, Piskarev is deeply shocked. He returns to his garret in despair. There he has a dream, which is presented in the story as a real experience. It is a dream to which, significantly, Piskarev clings as being more meaningful than reality itself.

The girl he has followed sends a footman with a carriage to bring him to a society ball, at which she herself is the centre of attention. Piskarev's original feelings of unworthiness for the girl, which had been so cruelly shattered then later inverted, now, in this dream are reinstated in full measure. His new sense of inferiority is, typically, brought out and emphasised by external appearances. Everybody at the ball is in marvellous evening dress; Piskarev has come just as he is in his old paint-stained frock-coat. In spite of this the girl singles him out, shows him special attention, and tells him that he was mistaken about her visit to *that* house. Yet it is only a dream. Piskarev wakes up in his garret and exclaims: 'Oh, how disgusting reality is! What is it compared with a dream?' (III, 27). From now on dreams have more to offer him than reality. He dreams of the girl constantly, but begins to rely on opium to do so.

One such vision of her as a pure, simple, country girl returns him to his starting point – his painter's appreciation of her as a work of art rather than a human being:

> It would have been better if you did not exist at all, did not live in this world, but were merely the creation of an inspired artist. I would not leave the canvas, I would look at you for ever and kiss you. I would live and breathe you as a most beautiful dream, and I should then be happy. (III, 29–30)

This is the extreme artistic view of the human being as object; it completely ignores the human being as a subject in its own right. Piskarev wishes to reduce the girl to a mere surface on canvas.[7] It would be better if she 'did not exist at all', except of course to provide a stimulus for the aesthetic imagination of the beholder.

After another dream in which the girl is perceived as his wife and his artistic inspiration, he finally decides to sally forth into the real world to try to save her by offering her marriage. Yet what he attempts to save is, again, not a real woman, but something nearer to a beautiful picture: 'But my noble deed will not be unselfish, it might even be considered great. I shall return to the world its finest adornment' (III, 31). The prostitute does not take this offer of marriage seriously; he is mocked. Piskarev returns to his garret. His mind is unbalanced, and he cuts his throat.

The second story concerning Lieutenant Pirogov is obviously to be taken as an ironic comment on the sad tale of Piskarev. The narrator presents his second hero exactly as he had presented his first (and indeed as he does all the denizens of the Nevsky Prospekt) not so much as a character in his own right, but as a type. If Piskarev is the typical St Petersburg artist, then Pirogov is the typical St Petersburg lieutenant; both are introduced in the feigned 'sociological' manner which we see elsewhere in the story: 'But before we say who Lieutenant Pirogov was, it would not be harmful to relate something about the society to which Pirogov belonged' (III, 34). The 'sociological' method is, of course, entirely deceptive; it is merely a device of characterisation which substitutes the whole for the part. It is a reversal of the synecdoche, though, strangely enough, the effect is precisely the same; for the partial truth of the general is substituted for the fuller truth of the particular; the broader *surface* – for the deeper *content*. Yet even within this 'reversal' the synecdoche is reinstated: in the sort of society frequented by Pirogov an officer is reduced merely to an epaulette shining amidst other objects:

> Several pale daughters, absolutely pale like St Petersburg itself, one or two of whom were past their best, a little tea table, a pianoforte, dances at home – all this is usually inseparable from the light epaulette, which shines in the lamplight, between a well-behaved blonde and the black dress coat of a brother or an acquaintance of the house. (III, 34)

The parallel here with the 'sociological' portrait of Piskarev is preserved, for the paleness of St Petersburg is a conditioning factor in the artistic milieu, and is present in their very paintings: 'On almost everything they do there is always a grey, dull coloration – the indelible imprint of the north' (III, 17). Yet the epaulette of Pirogov's circle would be out of place among the artists frequented by Piskarev: 'They are in general very timid; a star and a fat epaulette make them so confused, that they inevitably lower the price of their works' (III, 17).

The feigned 'sociological' method in the portrayal of Pirogov is doubly effective; it not only reveals him as a man without any real character of his own, but shows that such people are met with quite commonly. Having ascribed to Pirogov certain qualities, which in effect are quite mundane and entirely unexceptional, the narrator ends his portrait with words that seem to echo his earlier ironic enthusiasm for the 'thousand unfathomable characters and phenomena' encountered on Nevsky Prospekt itself: 'But enough about the qualities of Pirogov. Man is such a wonderful being that it is never possible to enumerate all his merits, just like that, and the more closely one looks at him, the greater the number of new peculiarities which appear. The description of them would never end' (III, 36). The high opinion which the narrator holds of Pirogov is blatantly contradicted by the facts he chooses to present. But the reader is aware that the narrator's 'idealised' view of the hero is merely a reflection of that high regard in which Pirogov holds himself. He is nothing more than a brash and self-satisfied nonentity, and although the narrator pretends to present him as a man who, like Piskarev, has a passion for the beautiful, it extends no further than chasing after women and a desire to see his own 'manly face' depicted in the art of Piskarev.

Like Piskarev, Pirogov too pursues his woman into a house. He too gets a shock:

> He was amazed by an unusually strange sight. Sitting in front of him was Schiller, not the same Schiller who wrote *William Tell* and *The History of the Thirty Years War*, but the well known Schiller, the tinsmith of Meshchanskaya Street. Next to Schiller stood Hoffmann, not the writer Hoffmann, but a reasonably good shoemaker from Ofitserskaya Street, a great friend of Schiller. (III, 37)

Both are drunk, and Hoffmann, it seems, is about to cut off the nose of Schiller at the latter's request.

The fact that the blonde woman is Schiller's wife does not in the least deter Pirogov from pressing his attentions on her. He returns more than once on the pretext of placing various orders with her husband, but when he is caught kissing her foot he is given a thrashing at the hands of Schiller, Hoffmann and the carpenter Kunz – a physical humiliation which corresponds to the mental one experienced by Piskarev when he pressed his honourable advances too far.[8]

Nevertheless the outcome is not the same. As the narrator himself comments: 'But all this turned out rather strangely.' After the thrashing, Pirogov (whose own name is derived from *pirog*, a pie) calls in at a confectioner's, eats two puff pastries and reads the *Northern Bee*. Already he has begun to feel a little better and in the evening he goes to a party where he distinguishes himself by his masterful dancing of the mazurka.

As these two contrasting tales in themselves suggest, a central theme of 'Nevsky Prospekt' is incongruity. Piskarev in the first story complains of the 'eternal discord between dream and reality' (*vechnyy razdor mechty s sushchestvennost′ yu*). Yet the narrator himself, musing on both these stories as he walks along the Nevsky Prospekt, draws a moral in terms of desires: 'Do we ever get what we want? Do we ever achieve that for which it might appear our powers had been destined as though on purpose? Everything happens *vice versa*' (III, 45).

The examples of unrequited desires, with which the narrator further seeks to illustrate his theme of *vice versa*, seem grotesque in the context: a passion for horses and an appetite for food. Nevertheless the first example is merely the thwarted passion for the beautiful, which we see in Piskarev, brought down to a mundane and comic level, with horses, rather than women, as the exemplars of beauty: 'Fate has given one man the most beautiful horses, and he rides on them with indifference, not noticing their beauty at all, whereas another whose heart burns with horsey passion walks on foot and has to be contented with clicking his tongue whenever a trotter is led past him' (III, 45). The narrator's second illustration has relevance in a similar grotesque way for Pirogov, that lover of puff pastry: 'One man has an excellent cook, but unfortunately such a small mouth, that he just cannot get into it more than two pieces of food. Another has a mouth the size of the War Office Arch, but unfortunately he has to make do with any old German meal of potatoes. How strangely our fates play with us' (III, 45). Pirogov had 'a mouth as big as the War Office Arch', in as much as he wanted to complain to the War Office (*Glavnyy shtab*), but in the end he accommodated himself to the rough German 'hospitality' that had been meted out to him.[9]

By choosing two such grotesque pendants for his stories of Piskarev and Pirogov, the narrator is illustrating the theme of 'incongruity' in terms of the incongruous itself. No less incongruous is the juxtaposition of the two main stories themselves; for although one must obviously be taken as a comment on the other, their essential relationship is just as oblique and grotesque as the commentary provided by the narrator's two 'pendants'. They are a reflection of that eternal tension in Gogol's art between 'tears' (Piskarev) and 'laughter' (Pirogov). The story about the artist is in essence a sentimental tale about the hidden tears the world does not see;[10] the story of the lieutenant is permeated with a laughter which chastises overweening mediocrity more soundly than a physical drubbing.

Pirogov, the self-satisfied nonentity, is an absurd figure, yet no less so than the artist Piskarev: 'He was an artist. A strange phenomenon, do you not agree? A St Petersburg artist! An artist in the land of snow; an artist in the country of the Finns, where everything is wet, smooth, even, pale, grey and misty' (III, 16). In part, the incongruity which surrounds this Russian artist stems from the fact that he is really a figure taken from German Romantic literature. Gogol's first story about an artist, 'The Portrait', which had come out in part I of *Arabesques* (the first drafts of both 'Nevsky Prospekt' and 'The Portrait' were jumbled up in the same notebook) was criticised by Belinsky for being too derivative of E. T. A. Hoffmann,[11] and this presence can also be detected in 'Nevsky Prospekt'. Thus Piskarev's sudden fantastic perception of reality under the 'magical' influence of the young girl (a house upside down, a bridge breaking in the middle etc.) is strongly reminiscent of the grotesque and the magical which breaks into the real world in the stories of Hoffmann.

On the other hand Piskarev's idealism is reminiscent of Schiller; it has all the qualities of *rytsarstvo* (knightly chivalry):

> The trust which this defenceless but beautiful creature had shown him, this trust bound him with the strict obligations of a knight, the obligation to carry out slavishly her every behest. He only desired that these behests should be as difficult as they could be, that it should be virtually impossible to fulfil them, so that with a great concentration of effort he could fly off to overcome them. (III, 19–20)

If these two strands of German Romanticism, the Schilleresque and the Hoffmannesque, seem to condition Piskarev's state of mind as he enters the house in pursuit of the girl, with Pirogov the same two elements are given a comic twist: the house he enters is that of 'Schiller' who is entertaining his friend 'Hoffmann'. Moreover the carpenter Kunz, who takes part in his beating, may be related to C. F. Kunz, the publisher and friend of E. T. A. Hoffmann.

The parallel plots, in acting as a comment one for the other, further reveal the theme of incongruity. It is as though Piskarev and Pirogov had each gone to the wrong house; for had Pirogov's pursuit taken him to the brothel instead of the house of the German tinsmith, he would not have turned a hair, but would have become just another military uniform and boot glimpsed through an open door. If Piskarev, instead of entering a brothel had ended up in the abode of Schiller and Hoffmann, it would again have seemed more fitting, though, of course, he would still have been deceived; for Schiller is not 'that Schiller' nor is Hoffmann 'that Hoffmann'. Nothing is ever what it seems in this world of the 'Nevsky Prospekt'; the story's fabric, like the reality it purports to reflect, has been so cut up that its pieces never quite fit. It is analogous to the impression gained by

Piskarev himself during his dream of the society ball: 'It seemed to him as though some demon had crumbled up the whole of the world into a multitude of various pieces, and had mixed all these pieces together, without rhyme or reason' (III, 24). In the words which close the story the narrator too repeats this view that a demon is responsible for the bizarre incongruity of illusion and reality, the discrepancy between men's desires and their ability to satisfy them:

It lies at all times, that Nevsky Prospekt, but most of all when night settles its opaque mass upon it, and picks out the white and pale yellow walls of the houses; when the whole of the city is turned into thunder and glitter; myriads of coaches rush off the bridges; when postilions shout out and jog up and down on the horses, and when a demon himself lights the lamps in order to show everything not in its true aspect. (III, 46)

Piskarev's disillusionment at the beautiful prostitute is a revelation of how this demonic force seeks to destroy the harmony of the world:

She would have been looked on as a goddess in a crowded reception room, on a bright parquet floor with candles shining and amid the silent awe of a crowd of admirers whom she held in thrall; – but alas by some terrible will of a spirit of hell, which thirsted to destroy the harmony of life, she was thrown with jeering laughter into the abyss. (III, 22)

The dream, which follows, is merely a wish-fulfilment reversing this cry of despair; beauty is reinstated as 'divine' and the machinations of the demon 'crumbler up of the world' are allowed no further than the 'crowded reception room and the bright parquet floor'. Beauty herself is unassailable amidst a demonic chaos.[12]

'Nevsky Prospekt' poses two fundamental questions about beauty: is physical beauty necessarily identical with spiritual beauty; and if not, can physical beauty alone have the power to transcend moral failings? The dilemma implied in the first question is linked with Piskarev; the problem behind the second question – with Pirogov.

Thus in musing on the story of Piskarev the narrator asserts: 'Beauty, gentle beauty. In our thoughts it is fused only with innocence, with purity alone' (III, 22). But unfortunately for Piskarev, his feminine ideal of beauty is fused not only with vice, but with vulgarity (*poshlost'*) and with stupidity too: 'She opened her beautiful lips and began to say something, but it was all so stupid, so vulgarly trivial (*poshlo*), as though with the loss of innocence a person's wits also desert him' (III, 21).

By contrast the narrator's musings on Pirogov's feminine ideal seem to imply that stupidity, *poshlost'*, even vice can all be redeemed by physical beauty:

However, one must say that for all her attractiveness the wife of Schiller was very stupid. But stupidity constitutes a special charm in a beautiful wife. At least I have known many husbands who are in raptures over the stupidity of their wives and see in it all the signs of childish innocence. Beauty produces complete miracles of its own. All the spiritual failings of a beautiful woman, instead of evoking disgust, become, somehow or other, unusually attractive. In them vice itself is fair of face (*dyshit milovidnost'yu*). But should beauty disappear, then a woman needs to be twenty times cleverer than a man in order to win respect for herself, let alone love. (III, 40)

Transferred to the realm of art this whole dilemma is particularly revealing. There are two aesthetic ideals: that of Piskarev for whom beauty of form and content must be identical; and that of Pirogov for whom form alone is important and may even have the power to transcend content. Pirogov (the Philistine) is soundly thrashed for trying to attain his ideal (by Schiller, Hoffmann and Kunz) but can nevertheless shake it off and behave as though nothing had happened. The artist, on the other hand, has no way out but to commit suicide, when he realises ultimately that his harmonious ideal is unattainable, even though for a long time he had cherished the illusion, in dreams and under the stimulus of opium, that beauty of form could dictate beauty of content.

There is in these two stories something which goes to the very heart of the aesthetic dilemma facing the author himself, and it seems significant that Gogol chooses to examine the theme of the 'artist' through the figure of a painter both here and in 'The Portrait'.[13] It is for the visual artist, above all, that the relationship between façade and content is most crucial. The painter can only reproduce surfaces, can only put down on his canvases the exterior of things and people. Yet, at the same time, he must strive to go beyond this, as the words of the old artist to his son at the end of 'The Portrait' make clear: 'Subject everything to your brush, but know how to find in everything an inner significance' (III, 135).

Unfortunately, there is no evidence that Piskarev has this ability. He is presented as a typical St Petersburg artist who:

would always call to his room some old beggar woman, and would force her to sit six whole hours on end, in order to transpose her pitiful, insentient expression on to the canvas. He drew his room in perspective, in which there would appear all sorts of artist's rubbish (*vzdor*), plaster arms and legs, which had turned brown from time and dust, broken artist's easels, a palette which had been knocked over, a friend playing the guitar. (III, 17)

In this description the old beggar woman with her insentient expression' (*beschuvstvennaya mina*) is perceived more as an object, of the same status as those reified human parts, the plaster arms and legs; and the 'artist's rubbish' seems to have precedence over his friend playing the guitar.[14]

The narrator comments that such artists are often not without talent but they need the sun of Italy to make it flourish. Gogol, himself, certainly felt the need of Italy for his own art. Yet it is doubtful whether the sun of Italy would bring true illumination for Piskarev; artists, such as he, seem to have an inability to look, certainly to look deeply at other human beings: 'He would never look you straight in the eyes; but if he did look, then it would be in some opaque and vague fashion. He did not penetrate you with the hawk eye of an observer or the eagle gaze of a cavalry officer' (III, 17). Here the quality of sight which penetrates into the human being (*vonzayet v vas*) is ascribed to the 'observer' (but surely not the observer of clothing on the Nevsky Prospekt?) or to an officer (but surely not Lieutenant Pirogov?). Such suggestions lead us back to the incongruity of the world as perceived, not only by Piskarev, but by the narrator himself: they are further ill-assorted scraps in a demon's kaleidoscope. Indeed, it is this piecemeal world of things which gets in the way of Piskarev's vision, as the narrator goes on to explain:

This came about because at one and the same time he would see both your features and the features of some plaster Hercules or other, which stood in his room, or he would imagine a picture of his own, which he was still thinking of producing. Because of this he would frequently reply disjointedly and not to the point, and the objects jumbled in his head would increase his timidity even more. (III, 17–18)

The way the 'objects of art' dominate Piskarev's own pictures has already been seen, and they get in the way of his view of the young girl: he thinks of her as a painting; follows her as a cloak; pursues her as an 'object'. Moreover his imagination, like that of the narrator, flies outward into fantasy instead of striving inward to understand the true nature of what lies beneath the façade. No wonder such an artist feels cruelly deceived and complains of 'the eternal discord between dream and reality', and it is significant that in this formula 'dream' (*mechta*) is really 'daydream' (i.e. fantasy) whereas 'reality' (*sushschestvennost'*) suggests 'essence' (*sut'*).

Piskarev seeks to project what, at root, is a psychological dilemma on to a metaphysical plane: it is a demon who is responsible for the chaos of the world, and when God is invoked it is invariably in His role of Creator (*sozdatel'*). Moreover, in both these respects he is echoed by the narrator himself.[15]

It is fitting that the narrator should end the story on a personal note: 'Oh, do not believe this Nevsky Prospekt! I always wrap myself a little more tightly in my cloak, when I am walking along it and I try to avoid looking at the *objects* (*predmety*) one meets. Everything is deceit, everything is a *dream* (*mechta*), everything is not what it seems!' (III, 45) (my italics). He then lists a whole series of examples in which imagination suggests one thing about the being and the actions of those who stroll on the Nevsky Prospekt, and warns that the reality is quite different. But the experience of Piskarev is the one against which he most admonishes the readers, and against which he himself takes the most precautions: 'But Lord preserve you from peeping under ladies' hats. However much the cloak of a beautiful woman should flutter in the distance, not for anything would I go off after her and show my curiosity' (III, 46). Thus this strange story in which sociology passes into aesthetics, aesthetics into psychology, and psychology into metaphysics, also proclaims another Gogolian theme: the flight from sexuality. The narrator at many points seems close to the psychology of his hero Piskarev, but the most intriguing question is how close is the psychology of the narrator to that of the author himself?

The gulf between a sordid reality and a high ideal was very pertinent to the strivings of Russian intellectuals in the 1830s;[16] it can be seen particularly clearly in the soul-searching of the critic Belinsky when under the influence of German idealistic thought (e.g. Schelling and Schiller). Indeed the phrase 'the eternal discord between dream and reality' may be taken as the dilemma of a whole generation (A. N. Stankevich, M. Bakunin, V. Belinsky) caught between lofty idealism and the painful consciousness of base reality. The fact that ideal beauty is embodied in a woman is in itself of importance for future developments in Russian literature. Such symbolic weight placed on the female form looks forward to Dostoevsky's portrayal of women as the embodiment of ideals, and to a whole cult in Russian literature which apotheosised the eternal feminine: Vladimir Solovyev,[17] A. Blok, G. Chulkov. Piskarev's constant dreaming about the beautiful girl seems close to the obsessive quality of Blok's: *Verses about the Beautiful Lady* (*Stikhi o prekrasnoy dame*). (Piskarev has also been called the first decadent in Russian literature.)[18] The outcome of Blok's infatuation led to deep disillusionment.

It is with Dostoevsky that the theme of beauty finds its most profound treatment. The idea that beauty might be the 'ideal of Madonna' or the 'ideal of Sodom' is touched on in many of his novels, but more particularly in *The Brothers Karamazov*. It is a similar ambivalence of Madonna and Sodom which is adumbrated in Piskarev's vision of ideal beauty. In first perceiving her as Perugino's 'Bianca', he is perhaps identifying her as a madonna.[19] Certainly the idea of childlike innocence and holy iconographic inspiration is present in his attitude to her: 'All that remains from the memory of childhood, that induces daydream and quiet inspiration before a shining icon-lamp, all this, it seemed, was united, fused and was reflected in the harmony of her lips' (III, 18).[20] Such a holy ideal could redeem Piskarev's art: 'I would invoke you as a guardian angel before sleeping and waking, and I would wait for you, if I had to depict the godly and the holy' (III, 30). Yet the girl does not embody the ideal of 'madonna' but that of 'Sodom'. She lives in a den of vice; a mockery which Piskarev interprets as the work of a demon; with satanic laughter she has been 'cast into the abyss'.

If such a double view of beauty seems to look forward to Dmitri Karamazov's torment over the two poles of beauty, there are nevertheless other Dostoevskian themes hinted at in the work. Both Piskarev and the hero of *The Dream of the Comic Man* believe profoundly in the harmony they have experienced in a dream state; each is prepared to cling to his dream rather than to the reality of the waking world, and harmony in both cases is related to a picture.

Piskarev's attempt to rescue the prostitute is also not without its further reflection in *Notes from Underground*. The hero of Dostoevsky's work will also preach to Liza, and attempt to show her the fate which awaits her in much the same way as Piskarev. Although Dostoevsky's 'idealist' is soured he is no less tormented by the gulf between dream and reality, but with him the dilemma has taken another form.[21]

There is no doubt that 'Nevsky Prospekt' has left its mark on Russian literature, and not least of all in the way that subsequent writers have depicted St Petersburg, but the importance of the work in Gogol's own *oeuvre* chiefly resides in the questions it raises about the nature of his own art. This is an issue which must be taken further in discussing the next story 'The Portrait'.

'*The Portrait*'

'The Portrait' was originally published in part I of *Arabesques*, 1835, but it appears to have been conceived at the same time as 'Nevsky Prospekt',[22] and obviously has much in common with that work. The two stories share a common theme of the artist, and both have the form of a diptych. Yet the second part of this diptych is not only a commentary on the first, as in 'Nevsky Prospekt', it explains it in the sort of way that the second story of Petro in 'A Terrible Vengeance' explains the story of Katerina, and the original version of 'The Portrait' is very much in the uncomic, eschatological vein of 'A Terrible Vengeance', without having its poetry. Both works treat the theme of the perpetuation of the demonic, associated with a 'Petrine' originating figure (Petro in 'A Terrible Vengeance'; Petromikhali in 'The Portrait') but whereas the vehicle for such perpetuation in the first work is sexuality, in 'The Portrait' it is art. In the first part of the diptych a young artist, Chertkov (Chartkov in the later version) gains possession of a demonic picture which influences him to betray his talent. The second part of the diptych tells how this demonic portrait came to be painted in the first place.

The artistic problem of surface and content, raised by 'Nevsky Prospekt', is of crucial importance here. Thus it is significant that the first attack on Chertkov's talent occurs when the surface of the demonic portrait leaves its canvas in the middle of the night: 'He saw the surface of the old man detach itself and come down from the portrait, just as the upper scum is skimmed from a boiling liquid, it rose in the air and soared nearer and nearer to him, and finally drew close to his very bed' (III, 409). The 'superficial' old man advises him not to waste time in deepening the knowledge of his art, but to set about at once to paint portraits as fast as he can. Chertkov is miraculously provided with money and, no less inexplicably, with his first client, the daughter of a society lady.[23]

When he tries to paint this young girl with any depth, he is firmly discouraged by her mother. Yet we are told that the girl's 'almost expressionless face' does in fact express her inner attitudes and thoughts, and that if Chertkov had any knowledge of the heart, he would immediately have read her 'not very voluminous history' in her face. When the mother seizes on a portrait of Psyche as a remarkable likeness of her daughter, Chertkov submits to the deceit, and from then on is doomed to the superficial art expected of a society painter, without 'any knowledge of the heart, the passions or even the habits of man'. Chertkov receives a profound shock when in later life he is confronted with a picture by a contemporary who has spent his life studying painting in Italy. Try as he might, Chertkov cannot paint like him, he cannot cross the 'boundaries' which he has placed on himself: 'A simple, insignificant point of technique would cool the entire impulse and would stand as a threshold for the imagination, which could not be jumped over' (III, 423). The crossing of boundaries, or thresholds, is a recurrent image in the first version of 'The Portrait', and it has obvious connections with that theme of surface versus content, so central to 'Nevsky Prospekt'. Once Chertkov realises the irredeemable superficiality of his own art, his actions become almost a parable of the way profundity is destroyed by the superficial: he uses the money he has received for his own hack work to buy paintings of genius, which he then tears into shreds: 'And people, bearing within themselves a spark of godly knowledge, hungry for only that which is lofty, were pitilessly and inhumanly deprived of these holy and beautiful works, in which great art slightly raised the cover from heaven and showed man a part of his own inner world, full of sounds and holy secrets' (III, 424). In this view, the 'innerness' of art can reveal to man that part of his own inner self which is holy and divine, and the phraseology ('sounds and holy secrets') suggests not just painting but art as a whole. Yet in seeking to 'go beyond' the artist might also uncover 'disgusting man'; this idea had occurred to Chertkov when he first saw the demonic picture which was so to change his life:

> What a strange, incomprehensible problem! Could it be that for man there is a line to which he is drawn by higher knowledge, but once having stepped across it, he steals something which has not been created by human effort; he seizes something living from the life which animates the original? Why is crossing this line, placed as a boundary for the imagination, so terrible? Could it be that beyond imagination, beyond the impulse, there finally comes reality? That terrible reality at which imagination becomes unhinged by some external push; that terrible reality with which the person who thirsts for it, is faced when, wishing to understand man in his beauty, he arms himself with an anatomical knife, opens up his interior, and sees man in all his horror. (III, 405–6)

'Man in his beauty' is quite literally 'beautiful (good) man' (*prekrasnyy chelovek*) 'man in all his horror' is 'disgusting man' (*otvratitel'nyy chelovek*).

There is a line which it is dangerous for the artist to cross, a line (*cherta*) which Chertkov's own name suggests.[24] It is a boundary between imagination and inner reality: the very line which Gogol is not prepared to transgress in 'Nevsky Prospekt', where the narrator's imagination constantly flies out into fantasy rather than inwards towards the psychological reality behind the façade. We have seen that through this process a lady is in danger of becoming a champagne glass; a prostitute – a goddess, and it is significant that in 'The Portrait' the beginning of Chertkov's fall is marked by the presentation of a young society girl as Psyche rather than as herself. The allusion to Psyche is, in itself, suggestive: the mythological story points to the dangers of 'looking' at beauty,[25] and it is above all the eyes of the demonic portrait which are its most disturbing attribute. They are the only feature of the antichrist, which the artist actually finished. Eyes, and the danger of looking, had been a central theme of 'Viy', Khoma Brut was struck dead, when the Viy's eyelids were raised and he saw him, in spite of the impenetrability of the 'line' (*cherta*) which Khoma had drawn round himself. In 'Viy' the supernatural can be identified as psychology; in 'The Portrait' it is related to the theme of art, but there is also a psychological dimension to the 'reality' beyond the line. Much as these eyes suggest to Chertkov the physical opening up of a human being to reveal 'the disgusting man', in the second part of the diptych they seem psychologically to 'open up' the man who painted them and reveal 'disgusting man' once more:

> Everything that settles like a black sediment in the depths of man, which is destroyed and dispelled by education, noble deeds and the vision of beauty: all this he felt in ferment, constantly striving to come out to the surface, to develop in all its vicious perfection. The gloomy state of his soul was just such as to force him to seize on this dark side of man. (III, 438)

Chertkov himself dies tormented by nightmares of a room filled with portraits of eyes, and the doctor who attends him seems to be thinking of a psychological explanation, when he tries to uncover the 'secret link' between these dreams and the facts of Chertkov's life. Nevertheless if there is a black sediment in the human soul, there is also a part of man's inner world 'full of sounds and holy secrets'.

Chertkov in his flight from the 'disgusting man' in art has also denied himself the ability 'slightly to raise the cover of heaven'. The perception of this ability in his contemporary seems to turn Chertkov into that very demon who destroys harmony in 'Nevsky Prospekt'.[26]

In 'The Portrait', as in 'A Terrible Vengeance', 'Viy' and 'Nevsky Prospekt' itself, the psychological is projected into the metaphysical. Art can show man heaven – a heaven within himself, or it can show him hell. Boundaries here are no sure defence against the metaphysical, just as in 'Viy' a boundary is no proof against penetrating sight. When Chertkov seeks to hide the portrait under canvas, the eyes still appear to shine out at him from under their covering, and the painter of the second part of the diptych tells his son:

> But our earth is dust before the Creator. According to His laws it must be destroyed, and with each day the laws of nature will become weaker, and because of this the borders which hold back the supernatural will become more vulnerable. (III, 443)

Through the weakening of these borders antichrist can penetrate art and the affairs of man himself:

> In these disgustingly living eyes a diabolical feeling has been retained. Marvel, my son, at the terrible power of the devil. He attempts to penetrate into everything: into our affairs, into our thoughts, and even into the very inspiration of an artist. Countless will be the victims of this spirit of hell, living unseen without form on earth. It is that black spirit which breaks in on us even at moments of most pure and holy thoughts. (III, 443–4)

In the 'black sediment' within man, and the 'black spirit which breaks in at moments of most pure and holy thoughts', we catch a glimpse of a Dostoevskian world of underground psychology and 'double thoughts': a world which Gogol strives to keep within its bounds, for fear that its eruption could trouble the apparently innocent surfaces of his art. What is most disturbing about the genius who had painted the eyes is that 'he had far too audaciously stepped over the boundaries of man's will'.

The first version of 'The Portrait' contains a whole complex knot of attitudes to art. Thus the problem of 'realism' is strangely mixed up with the question of boundaries. The eyes are both supernatural and too natural. The shock of this paradox comes out even more starkly when Chertkov, immediately after his image of opening up a corpse, goes on to speculate: 'Or could it be that an excessively close imitation of nature is just as cloying as a dish which has an excessively sweet taste?' (III, 406). Yet the fact that 'penetration beyond the boundaries' and absolute realism should both be linked together in a negative sense, is not surprising; for in 'Nevsky Prospekt', as we have seen, imagination in refusing to go beyond surfaces does not create a 'real' world from external objects; it, rather, flies off into fantasy. The flight from the inner truth and the flight from absolute realism are thus part of the same process in Gogol's aesthetic universe. This point must be borne in mind when appraising the so-called realism of a story like 'The Overcoat'.

In this first version of 'The Portrait', Gogol seems concerned to make his story as 'unreal' as possible. Motivation is unexplained, except in terms of the fantastic and when a passage of traditional 'realistic' writing is introduced (i.e. the description of Kolomna) its effect is completely 'unreal', as a detail in a story related in a hushed auction room: 'literary' realism is merely used to destroy 'artistic' realism.

Two other strands in this aesthetic knot are the ability of money to destroy talent, and the possibility of art itself becoming a vehicle for evil.[27] All these themes are present in the second version, and it is instructive to see what different emphases they receive.

In revising 'The Portrait' for *The Contemporary* seven years later, Gogol eliminated many of the more overtly supernatural elements. Although the portrait still miraculously disappears at the very end of the tale, its inexplicable appearances in the apartments of both Chertkov and the original painter have gone, as also has the futile attempt to destroy the portrait by fire. The handing on of the picture from person to person has replaced the miraculous appearances, even though the trail of misery left behind is still much the same. Thus members of the narrator's family still die, but the lack of detail given is in sharp contrast to the description of the grotesquely spectacular deaths of the wife and the son in the first version.

More significantly the identification of the moneylender with antichrist is absent, while at the same time greater emphasis is placed on the corrupting power of money. Thus, as Mashkovtsev has pointed out, the acquisitive urge of Chertkov (now Chartkov), is suggested from the very beginning; he rummages among the pictures in the shop in the hope of finding a valuable old master.[28] In other respects too the development of Chartkov is psychologically more 'prepared'. His professor has already warned him against the danger of becoming a facile society painter, seeing a potential tendency towards this already present in his work. Thus there is now a strong hint that the seeds of Chartkov's destruction lie within himself:[29] a radically different motivation from the corruption by 'surface' of the first version. Moreover the aesthetic ideas of the second version show a corresponding inner shift: the 'disgusting man' revealed by the anatomical knife is no longer the terrible reality beyond the line 'placed as a boundary for the imagination', quite the reverse. It is produced when artistic sympathy is not capable of seeing an inner idea: 'Could it be that if you take an object impartially, without sensitivity, without sympathising with it, it will inevitably merely be presented solely in its terrible reality, unillumined by the light of some inscrutable idea which is concealed in everything' (III, 88). In the second version the substitution of artistic sympathy for imagination is revealing; for whereas imagination in Gogol's writing, as we have seen, represents a flight away from inner reality, artistic sympathy, by contrast, is an attempt to penetrate it and to understand it. Mere imitation is not art. In the first version the artistic effect of imitation was put forward as cloying: 'a dish which has an excessively sweet taste'. This idea is now recast in a more negative way: 'Or could it be that the slavish, literal imitation of nature is a fault, appearing like a loud dissonant cry' (III, 88).[30] It is precisely this effect that the eyes, which are too real, produce in the portrait: 'It was no longer art, it destroyed the whole harmony of the portrait itself' (III, 87).[31]

The realism of Leonardo da Vinci's *Mona Lisa* is quite different:

> The most finished part of all was the eyes, which his contemporaries marvelled at, even the smallest, scarcely visible, veins in them were not left out, but were put down on the canvas. (III, 87)

Here is a dilemma to which Chartkov returns:

> Why is it that, with one artist, simple, lowly nature appears in a certain light, and you feel no lowly impression? On the contrary, it seems as though you have experienced enjoyment, and after it everything around you flows and moves more quietly, more evenly. But why then, with another artist, does this very same nature seem lowly and squalid, and yet he has been just as faithful to nature? But no, there is nothing illuminating in it. It is just like a natural view, which, however marvellous it might be, nevertheless lacks something if there is no sun on you. (III, 88)[32]

The illumination here is obviously the same as 'the light of an inscrutable idea concealed in everything' which only artistic sympathy can reveal.

It is this quality, above all, which is evident in the artistic ability of the narrator's father at the end of his life: 'With a lofty inner instinct he sensed the presence of an idea in every object.' Yet in earlier life it was he who had painted the diabolical portrait, and in his own attitude towards this picture he seems at one with Chartkov: 'It was not a creation of art and therefore the feelings which possess everyone looking at it, are rebellious feelings, disturbed feelings, not the feelings of an artist; for an artist even in anxiety breathes peace' (III, 136). His account of how he painted it also supports the speculations of Chartkov on the need for artistic sympathy: 'I painted it with revulsion, I felt no love for my work at the time. I wished to overcome myself forcibly, and be faithful to nature, by suppressing everything in a soulless way' (III, 136). It is this *soulless* faithfulness to nature which is the death of art. Chartkov's contemporary who returns from Italy is a true artist because:

> It was obvious that everything which he had drawn from the external world, the artist had first locked away in his soul, and from there, from the fountain of his soul, he sent it out as one harmonious, triumphant song.[33] And even to the uninitiated it became obvious what a gulf there existed between creation and the simple copying from nature. (III, 112)

These aesthetic concepts: the inscrutable idea concealed in everything; the role of the artist as a creator rather than a copier of nature, are merely commonplaces of German Idealistic thought, and in the Russia of the late 1830s their most ardent champion was Belinsky.[34] He it was, who had criticised the first version of 'The Portrait', and Gogol, in rewriting his tale in 1841–2, did so, he said, because of these criticisms.[35] Between 1838 and 1840, Belinsky himself had fallen under the influence of a right-wing interpretation of Hegel, which saw reality as rational and sought reconciliation with the *status quo*. It is just such a reconciliation which is implied in Gogol's new interpretation of the terrible reality under the anatomist's knife, as something in which artistic sympathy can reveal a concealed idea. It is therefore reconciliation which the narrator's father puts forward as the true aim of art: 'For the high creation of art descends into the world to calm and reconcile everybody. It cannot implant discontent in the soul but strives eternally towards God in resounding prayer' (III, 136).

Thus the aesthetic shift we witness in the second version of 'The Portrait' not only follows, consciously or unconsciously, the final stages of Belinsky's passionate affaire with German Idealistic philosophy, it is also permeated by the religious attitude of Gogol's own later years.[36] Reconciliation with the *status quo* is Gogol's moralistic theme in the *Selected Passages from Correspondence with Friends*; it was also to have been his aim in the second and third parts of *Dead Souls*. Unfortunately for Gogol when *Selected Passages* appeared, Belinsky had already vehemently denounced his own earlier period of reconciliation with reality, and the violence of his rejection of *Selected Passages* in his famous letter to Gogol may in some measure be due to an anger directed against himself.

In his new view of art, and its relationship to reality, Gogol seems to be in a terrible trap of his own making. The parting words of advice to the narrator from his father make the task of the artist plain: 'Research and study everything that you see. Subject everything to your brush, but know how to find in everything an inner idea, and above all try to comprehend the lofty secret of creation' (III, 136). If Gogol sought to apply this precept to himself in his own great work *Dead Souls* (and there are indications that he did) then the difficulties before him were immense. To know how to find in everything an inner idea, would mean the complete reversal of his most fundamental artistic procedures; an outlook of comic dissatisfaction with the world as it is, would have to turn into a religious and political philosophy of reconciliation. The exhortation is to research and to study, and this Gogol did in preparation for the subsequent parts of *Dead Souls*, hence his incessant requests for material from friends and readers. Study must also be of the masters, and when he says that Chartkov's contemporary had reduced intensive study to Raphael alone, Gogol strikes what must surely be a personal note: 'Like a great artist-poet, who having read a great deal of all sorts of works full of much charm and great beauty, finally leaves only Homer's *Iliad* on his desk, having discovered that everything that you want is in it, and that there is nothing which has not already been reflected there in profound and noble perfection' (III, 111).

Nevertheless in spite of the deep studies of Chartkov's contemporary, it is emphasised that on their own they are not sufficient: 'but most powerful of all was the creative power, already contained in the soul of the poet himself'. The narrator's father also studies deeply but places most emphasis on the artist's soul as the refiner and purifier of reality. Thus the artist bears a heavy burden of moral responsibility: 'He who has talent within him must be purer in his soul than all others. Some may be forgiven much, but he will not be forgiven' (III, 136).[37] As Gogol worked on the continuation of *Dead Souls*, he became increasingly dissatisfied with what he had written, and the implications of such a theory of art could only be that his failure sprang from the lack of purity of his own soul: an artistic crisis became identified in a fundamental way with a spiritual crisis. The matter was not helped by the preachings of father Matvey Konstantinovsky on the sinful nature of his writing which seemed to support the antithetical argument on art in 'The Portrait', that it could also be the vehicle of the devil. It is not surprising that a writer with such ideas on the nature of his craft, should act in the way he did. He first burned his offending manuscript (cf. the attempt of the narrator's father to burn the diabolical portrait in the first version) then prepared himself spiritually by fasting so strictly during Lent to the point where he refused all food.

It is in much the same sort of way the narrator's father prepares himself in the monastery for the great work he has been asked to undertake:

> The Father Superior of the monastery learning of the art of his brush, demanded that he should paint the chief icon for the church. But the humble brother said bluntly, that he was unworthy to take up his brush, that it had been defiled, and that he must first purify his soul with labour and great sacrifices, in order to be worthy to begin such a work. They did not wish to force him. He himself increased the strictness of monastery life for himself as much as possible. Finally even this seemed inadequate and not strict enough for him. He went off, with the blessing of the Father Superior into the wilderness, to be entirely alone. (III, 133)[38]

Although the narrator's father is a figure whom Gogol in later life seems consciously to emulate, it is, nevertheless, to Chartkov that he attributes small marks of authorial self-identification.[39]

Unexpectedly finding himself rich with the gold from the picture frame, Chartkov does not heed the inner voice which tells him to spend it on study, but immediately goes off to buy fashionable clothes, eat well and show himself off. The words chosen to describe this change seem significant: *chertu ne brat. Proshelsya po trotuaru gogolem'* (literally: 'not brother to the devil. He went along the pavement like a golden-eye duck').

Chartkov is the hero of the story, in the sense that he alone of all the characters has a name, but it has been changed from the Chertkov of the first version to Chartkov, so in that sense he is 'not brother to the devil' (i.e. *chert* = devil) but in what sense is he like a gogol (a golden-eye) or even the *Gogol*? The phrase means 'to strut'. Chartkov is showing off his finery, and the whole of his behaviour after receiving the money could well be that of the young Gogol himself; he liked to dress fashionably, and eat large meals. On receiving money entrusted to him by his mother he went on an abortive spree to Germany.

Gogol may be consciously likening the superficial show of Chartkov to his own behaviour, but even more strange is the fact that he chooses the clothes of a dandy to exemplify the doctrine of the purity of the artist's soul:

> A man who has left his home in bright Sunday-best clothing only needs to be spattered with one splash of mud from a wheel, for everybody to surround him, point a finger at him and talk of his slovenliness, whereas the very same people do not notice the great number of stains on other passers by dressed in weekday clothing. For on weekday clothing stains are not noticed. (III, 136)

It is as though Gogol, in spite of his new aesthetic theory of the inner idea and spiritual purity, can still only interpret the values of the 'inner man' in terms of externals.[40]

Indicative too is the fact that he should still retain his simile of the terrible secrets of the corpse as his image for inner reality. Moreover the eyes of the portrait, for all their living quality, also seem to be associated with the anatomist's knife ('it seemed as though they had been cut out from a living human being and placed in here'). The hint of greater reality coming from something dead, which is implicit in both these images, may seem a paradox, but it is intimately connected with the artistic preoccupations of Gogol's later years. It is implied in the very title *Dead Souls*, and further reflected in the punning on 'dead' and 'alive' at the end of 'The Overcoat'. Moreover in this latter work the inner world of a 'living corpse' has been entirely replaced by an article of clothing.

Death is never far away from art in this strange story. It is not merely that the portrait itself is the bringer of death, but the description of the auction at the beginning of part two is full of funereal imagery (in both versions). Those who have come to bid for works of art like rapacious birds about to fall on carrion (III, 117); the auction itself reminds the author of a funeral procession (III, 118), and the auctioneer with his sepulchral voice, performs a funeral service on these examples of art with his gavel (III, 118). This imagery, of course, serves to reinforce the idea suggested elsewhere in the story that money spells death for true art, and in his own life Gogol strove to divorce the two. Thus he supported himself with 'loans' from his friends and subventions from the emperor himself,[41] whilst at the same time wishing to devote the royalties from his own works to poor students. Nevertheless the conjunction of art and death in this story is such as to suggest an even more fundamental relationship between the two.

'The Portrait', in both its versions contains images which recall *Dead Souls*. Thus the character of Chertkov/Chartkov's landlord, a retired officer, is described as 'just as difficult to define as the colour of a worn frock-coat' (III, 93). Later the 'ash-grey' inhabitants of Kolomna are described as people, who: 'with their clothes, their faces, their hair, their eyes have a sort of opaque ashy exterior, like a day when there is no storm or sun in the sky, but is simply neither one thing nor the other, there is a scattered mist and it takes all sharpness from things' (III, 119). Both these images of indeterminacy (faded soldier's clothing and the weather) fuse in chapter 2 of *Dead Souls* to form an introduction for the vague *ni to ni se* of Manilov.

Part I and part II both open with descriptions of a jumble of objects not unlike the setting in which Plyushkin lives. In part I the setting is the fleamarket (*Shchukin dvor*) to which Plyushkin's own courtyard is actually likened in *Dead Souls*; whereas of the auction which opens part II we are told: 'everything represented a sort of chaos of art': a phrase which seems to echo the theme of chaos and art described in Plyushkin's garden. There the knife (*rezets*) intrudes as the liberator – it is the cutting edge of nature itself; but in Chartkov's musings on the portrait, the knife (*anatomicheskiy nozh*) reveals for art a reality which is too terrible. Chartkov himself becomes a miser like Plyushkin and as a collector of art, he is also its destroyer (the idea of the miser who destroys what he hoards is also implicit in the figure of Plyushkin). Because of his love of money Chartkov is about to turn into a 'dead soul' like Plyushkin himself: 'one of these strange beings, of which there are many to be encountered in our world bereft of feelings, upon whom a man full of life and heart looks with horror, for they seem to him moving stone coffins with a corpse inside them instead of a heart' (III, 110).[42]

We have already seen the close affinities between 'The Portrait' and 'Nevsky Prospekt'. The interior of Chartkov's garret with its plaster limbs and assorted artistic *bric à brac* is very similar to that of Piskarev. Mashkovtsev sees similarities in their careers.[43] The need for a Russian artist to study in Italy is advanced in both works, and the German tradesman who loves to drink on Sundays and lives in Meshchanskaya Street also makes a fleeting appearance in 'The Portrait'.

The fact that Chartkov, as the destroyer of harmony, becomes a sort of demon is made more explicit in the second version: 'it seemed that in him there had become incarnate that terrible demon ideally depicted by Pushkin' (III, 115). Finally the gulf between desires and fulfilment is expressed in both works through food. Thus Chartkov in his vision of the old man's gold is likened to a child 'sitting in front of a sweet dish, his mouth watering as he sees it being eaten by others' (III, 92) – an allusion which is taken up again once he has the money: 'Now within his power was everything, on which he had looked up to now with envious eyes, which he had admired from afar with watering mouth' (III, 97).

The second version of 'The Portrait' contains more of the 'naturalistic' description that one associates with Gogol. The staircase of Chartkov's garret is not unlike the staircase in the house of Petrovich in 'The Overcoat'. The comic conversation with the policeman has a counterpart in 'The Nose', and Chartkov's dealings with a popular newspaper introduce a polemical note directed against Bulgarin's *Northern Bee* which recalls Kovalev's visit to a similar newspaper office.

In the second version of his story Gogol introduces a political note. Catherine the Great is quoted as saying that only under monarchies have great artists flourished. Yet this loyal championship of autocracy is in reality, a defence of artists (in particular 'artist–poets' – *poety khudozhniki*), it is they, it is argued, who justify monarchy: 'Scholars, poets and all producers of art are the pearls and diamonds in the imperial crown' (III, 123).

The paean to autocracy is but a launching pad for an oblique attack on censorship; for the empress's words are in censure of a courtier who changed from champion of the arts to their persecutor, after he had borrowed money from the old moneylender of Kolomna: 'Then, unfortunately, the French Revolution occurred. It immediately served him as a weapon for all kinds of disgusting things. He began to see a revolutionary tendency in everything; he saw hints in everything' (III, 123). These two passages; one of royal support for the artist; the other of suspicious and pernickety criticism, may be related to Gogol's attempts to get *Dead Souls* published.

The fact that 'The Portrait' is not one of Gogol's more popular works, and is generally felt to be flawed artistically, would seem to preclude the work's having had a great influence on subsequent Russian literature. Yet there are several aspects of the story which are strikingly close to Dostoevsky's *Crime and Punishment*. The experiences of Chartkov after he has bought the portrait, when dream and reality seem to fuse into one another in an eerie evocative way, are a foretaste of a similar technique which Dostoevsky would exploit for his hero Raskolnikov. There is moreover *The Landlady* which shows Dostoevsky's early interest in this whole side of Gogol's writing (i.e. 'A Terrible Vengeance', 'Nevsky Prospekt', 'The Portrait'). More significant is the figure of the old money-lender, living amid the abject squalor of a poor part of St Petersburg, who is identified as evil incarnate. The *Arabesques* version even seems to hint at the essential link between such 'capitalists' and the poverty around them. Here, then, in embryo is the social theme of the evil, exploiting pawnbroker, whom Raskolnikov can feel it is justified to eliminate, if only he 'can step over'. (The idea of crossing a boundary is a recurrent image in the first version of 'The Portrait'.)

Although 'The Portrait' is not in itself great art, its relevance to Gogol's aesthetic ideals is undeniable. It mirrors the hopes and the fears he had for his own writing, and in odd ways is disturbingly prophetic about the future course of his life.

'*The Diary of a Madman*'

In the figures of Piskarev and Chartkov in 'Nevsky Prospekt' and 'The Portrait' madness is presented as the outcome for an artist unable to realise his true ideal. Gogol's title for his story devoted to insanity itself had originally been 'Notes of a mad musician', but for this 'artistic' figure, he ultimately substituted a madman whose life depended on writing: a minor civil servant.

'The Diary of a Madman'[44] is Gogol's one work of sustained first-person narration: its hero is the only character whom the author 'gets inside'. In 'The Portrait' Gogol warns of the boundaries the artist crosses at his peril, but in portraying Poprishchin he himself has crossed the line separating imagination from inner reality; has stirred up the 'black sediment'. He himself has taken the 'anatomist's knife' and, for the first and only time, has opened up the inner man to reveal *otvratitel'nyy chelovek*: 'man in all his horror'.

This self-revelation of increasing madness is skilfully and convincingly handled, yet, for all the tragic seriousness of the theme, it bears the recognisable Gogolian stamp of 'laughter through tears'. Laughter, which treats madness as comic, is not that of a modern sensibility, but its cruelty is redeemed by pathos which is implicit throughout, and which rises to a poignant climax in the justly famous ending. Here the Gogolian formula is seen at its most striking. The sudden descent from the high note of genuine pathos to the grotesque inconsequentiality of: 'And do you know that the King of France has a lump right under his nose?' (III, 214)[45] is not 'laughter' which mocks the preceding 'tears', it is rather a sudden tension projected on to the mood of pathos, which heightens and sharpens its impact.

The story is usually translated as the 'diary' of a madman, but more accurately it should be 'notes' (*zapiski*). The fact that it purports to be a written self-revelation is important, since the concept of writing is central to the whole work. Poprishchin's madness is a crisis of identity, which reaches its climax in the delusion that he is the King of Spain, but the origin of his malaise lies in his sense of insecurity within the civil service hierarchy. He is a titular counsellor, a rank of ambiguous distinction, since it conferred the all important status of 'noble' (*blagorodnyy*) on the holder but not on his descendants (this could only be achieved through promotion to the next rank of collegiate assessor).[46] In real terms Poprishchin's status depends on his ability to write: he is 'noble' by virtue of his job as a copy clerk. More than once he himself points to the connection. Thus, in a moment of apparent lucidity at the opening, he writes: 'Yes, I admit, if it were not for the nobility of the service, I would long ago have left the department' (III, 194). And later in his reaction to the hallucination of reading the letters of a dog: 'May I never receive a salary:[47] I have never in all my life heard that dogs could write. Only a nobleman can write correctly' (III, 195).

Nevertheless, it is precisely his own ability to write correctly which is called in question; at the very outset he quotes the criticism to which he is subjected by the head of his section: 'Why, my lad, is there always such a jumble in your head? Sometimes you run around like a madcap and at times you so muddle up your work that Satan himself would not be able to make it out. You put a small letter in a title, and you don't put down either a date or a reference number' (III, 193). It seems likely that it is because of these shortcomings that he is often assigned to the more humble task of sharpening pens for the director.

Poprishchin seeks to counter his feelings of insecurity at work (so intimately connected with status) by one of Gogol's favourite devices – inversion: his menial task in the director's office is a mark of special favour; the criticisms of the head of section are occasioned not by dissatisfaction but by envy; civil servants, as noble and dashing fellows, are not a whit the inferior of any officer. His negative fears have all been turned into positive attributes and as his madness progresses inversion achieves its most glaring form: consciousness of himself as a complete nonentity becomes the conviction that he is the King of Spain.

Poprishchin's feelings of insecurity are clearly discernible in his opening entry. Not only is the criticism of his incompetence on his mind, it seems borne out in fact: he is late for the office and claims that he would not be going there at all were it not that he wanted an advance on his salary (later he admits that he knows these hopes to be vain). His confusion seems to be mirrored in his description of a 'brother' civil servant who precedes him along the street (the only other man of 'noble' status there). Poprishchin first describes him as 'trudging along', but immediately reinterprets his progress as 'hurrying', yet not to the office (like himself) but rather on some amorous pursuit. His speculation on the dashing way that civil servants, like himself, have with women is suddenly interrupted by an unexpected encounter with Sophie, the director's daughter, with whom he is secretly in love. In alarm he shrinks into the background, and his behaviour thus gives the lie to the brave words which have gone before.

Sophie sweeps into a shop without noticing him, and her lap-dog, Madgie, is also left unnoticed on the pavement. Therefore another and different parallel for Poprishchin's behaviour may also be drawn, and it is at this point that the reader first becomes aware that all is not well. Poprishchin claims that Madgie is addressed by another dog, significantly called Fidèle, who reproaches her for a breakdown in their relationship. This, though patently absurd, is nevertheless explicable in psychological terms; for just as Poprishchin had earlier projected his own desire for self-assertion on to the civil servant in the street, he now projects a re-awakened sense of his own inferiority on to the dogs: the 'faithful' dog reproaches the dog of his mistress with Poprishchin's own failure: that of communication. Such a substitution is not only a re-interpretation of a real situation, it also serves as a shield against it. When Poprishchin a second time resorts to its protection, this communication between dogs, significantly, takes the form of writing.

Working at close quarters with the director and seeing his daughter, Poprishchin is in the tantalising situation of being with them, but not of them. So deprived of any real entrée into their lives and thoughts, he finds it through the hallucination of discovering letters from Sophie's lap-dog to the dog Fidèle. From the condescending tone it is obvious that these missives are addressed to a social inferior, thus the gulf between Poprishchin and his masters, though bridged, is still maintained. The correspondence also puts the critic of his own writing skills in his place: 'The letter is written very correctly.[48] The punctuation and even the letter *yat'* is everywhere in its proper place. Yes, even our head of section simply cannot write like this, even though he makes out that he has studied somewhere or other at a university' (III, 202). The dog's letters are an hallucinatory device, the underlying purpose of which is to cope with the unpalatable truth of his own situation in the household, and the rumours of Sophie's impending marriage. They are a means of filtering reality, slowly and indirectly, into a consciousness, which is far too vulnerable.

The letters begin well, but every time they touch on the all important subject of Sophie, Poprishchin, as a reader, imposes his own veto: 'silence!' It is scarcely surprising that he finds them less and less satisfactory. Yet, significantly, a failure at the level of content he interprets as deficiency of form: 'An exceedingly uneven style. It is immediately obvious that they were not written by a man. It begins as it should, but ends in a doggy-fashion' (III, 203). The next letter he criticises for one of his own clerical shortcomings: it does not bear a date. It is this letter which broaches the central problem of Sophie's intended marriage and the reality of his own position, but it does so in terms of the dogs who are Madgie's suitors. One is an exceedingly coarse mongrel;[49] the other is the greatly admired Trésor, whose name is a phonetic echo of Treplov – the suitor of Sophie herself. Having moved one step nearer the truth, Poprishchin is pained, yet at the same time frustrated: 'Pah! Devil take it, what rubbish! How can one fill letters with such stupidities? Give me a human being! I want to see a human being. I demand food, such as will nourish and content my soul. But instead of that, what trifles!' (III, 204).

Poprishchin's plea for human, rather than canine, protagonists is granted in the next letter, but their intrusion is hardly food 'to nourish and content the soul'.

This next letter tells him what he must have known all along: Sophie is to marry Treplov, a gentleman of the royal bedchamber: Poprishchin, she regards merely as a clumsy, comic figure, who performs the function of a servant in her father's study. These two views of himself Poprishchin had already unwittingly recorded in his entry of 4 October, where he comments that Sophie had almost smirked as he picked up her handkerchief, and where he reveals his annoyance that the servants treat him in a familiar way, as though they are on equal terms with a 'nobleman'. Nor could the attentions of a highly-placed suitor have escaped the notice of one who watched Sophie's movements so assiduously. The letters have failed in helping him come to terms indirectly with the facts. Writing, originally seen as putting the head of section in his place, is now seen, after all, as having been inspired by him: 'As though I don't know whose tricks these are. These are the tricks of the head of the section. After all the man has sworn implacable hatred, and here he is causing harm, causing harm, at every step causing harm' (III, 205).

The next stage in the development of Poprishchin's madness marks his ultimate retreat from reality. The inescapable fact of Sophie's impending marriage to the gentleman of the bedchamber causes him to question the very nature of rank and what it means to be a titular counsellor. On the other hand the very 'nobility', which the rank of titular counsellor obviously confers, must somehow be a pledge of something greater:

> Perhaps I am some count or other, or a general, and only just seem to be a titular counsellor. Perhaps I myself do not know who I am. After all, how many examples are there, according to history: some simple fellow, nothing like a nobleman, but simply some petty tradesman or other, or even a peasant – and suddenly it is revealed that he is some kind of bigwig, and sometimes even a sovereign. If such a thing can sometimes become of a peasant, what then can become of a nobleman? (III, 206)

Poprishchin's crisis of identity is here at its most acute, and its solution is no less extreme: he claims a rank which enables him to look down on all those whom he considers to have injured him, Sophie included: he is none other than the missing King of Spain. Yet his megalomania is merely a refurbishing of his status as copy-clerk-titular-counsellor ('if such a thing can sometimes become of a peasant, what then can become of a nobleman') so he cuts up a new uniform to make his regal robes, and his shortcomings as a scribe are now boldly blazoned forth at the head of each new entry in the 'diary', in the form of fantastically jumbled dates. His belief that he is king of Spain, for example, starts on a day in the doubly chiliastic year 2000. The month, suffering from similar pretensions to grandeur, is recorded as 'April 43rd'. The confusion of dates grows ever more absurd until with the final entry it reaches its apogee of inversion and distortion. His muddling is no longer evidence of mere incompetence, it is the mark of ever-increasing insanity.

In the office, when he is given a document to sign, Poprishchin now puts the signature 'Ferdinand VIII' in the place reserved for the director, and the kingdom of Spain itself may be interpreted as the realm of scribal madness: 'I advise everybody purposely to write down Spain on paper, and China will come out' (III, 212). Jumbling the letters of *Ispaniya* (Spain) does not produce *Kitay* (China) but it could result in *pisaniya*[50] – the act of writing itself, that very activity on which his true status is based: a nobility which his own muddling had seemed to place in jeopardy. By a simple inversion of letters, scribal faults have turned 'writing' into 'Spain' and a 'nobleman writer' into its 'king'. A related discovery is that every cockerel has its Spain and that this is situated under its pens.[51]

Both the form and the progress of Poprishchin's madness clearly indicate its origin as a crisis of identity and of status. His very name suggests 'career' (i.e. *poprishche*[52] = 'career', 'arena of activity') but although he claims that he can gain promotion through service, and that he is capable of becoming a colonel, his incompetence as a copy clerk suggests quite the reverse. The gulf between his name and his actual position is borne in on him through the dog's letters: 'His surname is exceedingly strange. He always sits and sharpens pens....Papa always sends him on errands instead of the servants' (III, 205).

On the other hand, many commentators see the root of Poprishchin's problems to be sexual.[53] The erotic is undoubtedly an element in the story, nevertheless sexual anxiety is mixed with the more dominant concern about his social status. Thus Poprishchin is almost equally fascinated by the father as by Sophie herself; he is attracted by the power and prestige which she represents as the daughter of a general. Thus the embarrassment he feels, when alone with her in the same room, is not only sexual, it is excruciatingly social: '"Your excellency", I almost wanted to say, "will you not order my execution, and if you want to execute me, then execute me with your little general's hand"' (III, 196–7). When, shortly afterwards, she drops her handkerchief, he rushes to pick it up, but the fragrance it exudes is not sexual allurement, it is the attraction of status: 'Fragrance, absolute fragrance. It so smelled of general' (III, 197).

There are moments which are more openly erotic. Thus he thinks of her in her boudoir, having just risen from bed and putting on white stockings. Nevertheless, later, in his madness, when he does gain access to this forbidden boudoir, his designs are not explicitly erotic, he merely seeks to confront her with his new regal status.

The curious thing about Gogol's one attempt to go beyond the boundaries and penetrate the 'inner man' is that the world he discovers is just as absurd as the fantastic reality of appearance and surface which he describes in 'Nevsky Prospekt': madness, it seems, is the outer world's lack of harmony transferred to the inner realm. The anatomist's knife in revealing 'man in all his horror', strangely enough, has shown the reader nothing new; for the phenomena of Poprishchin's inner world are reminiscent of that bizarre kaleidoscope of objects which Gogol elsewhere seeks to present as outward reality. Poprishchin's inner self is compounded of random external phenomena – a civil servant in the street; encounters with dogs and their letters; events in Spain. In Gogol the external world is always to some degree 'psychological'. This is obviously true *a fortiori* when that outer world has become the inner one, and on the one occasion when it clearly has done so, the condition is identified as madness. In the next story 'The Nose' such madness will be placed back again in the external world itself.

'*The Nose*'

Major Kovalev had the habit of strolling every day along the Nevsky Prospekt. The collar of his shirt front was always extremely clean and starched. His side whiskers were of the sort that one can see even now on provincial and Ukrainian regional land surveyors, architects and regimental doctors, as well as those performing various police duties, and in general on all those men, who have full ruddy cheeks, and play boston whist very well. These whiskers go along the very middle of the cheek and stretch right up to the nose. (III, 53)

Thus major Kovalev appears to be one of the 'thousand unfathomable characters' of the Nevsky Prospekt. His chief attributes are a shirt front and masculine appendages which not only mark his social status (in the pseudo-sociological manner, reminiscent of 'Nevsky Prospekt' itself) but ominously 'stretch right up to the nose', an organ which is, in fact, the focus of Kovalev's anxiety about status; for in the course of the story it will leave his face and assume the guise of a civil servant of higher rank than he is himself. This fact alone is sufficient to suggest that the fantastic occurrences which befall Kovalev are similar in origin to those which afflict the hero of the 'Diary of a Madman'. Indeed the opening of each story is almost identical,[54] but in 'The Nose', Gogol has taken his treatment of psychology in terms of the fantastic a stage further; for although the fantastic happenings which Poprishchin records in his 'diary' can all be explained by the hero's madness, there is no attempt in 'The Nose' to provide any logical handle by which the reader might grasp the story's absurdity.

Nevertheless, Kovalev's search for an explanation of his plight recalls Poprishchin; initially both wonder whether they are drunk, though, significantly, Kovalev links his drunkenness to shaving; 'Perhaps somehow or other by mistake, instead of water, I drank the vodka, with which I rub my beard after shaving' (III, 65). Kovalev's other 'explanation' is to think that he is dreaming. This too is dismissed, but in the original manuscript version everything had been explained as a dream. Gogol removed this logical resolution when he sent the story to Pushkin's *Contemporary* (possibly because Bulgarin had criticised Pushkin's own story, 'The Undertaker', for a similar dénouement). The effect in the original version is certainly weak: 'but everything that is described here was seen by the major in a dream' (III, 399). Moreover it is unconvincing, since even in this version the 'dream' is recounted by a narrator who knows about the reality of Kovalev's life: his earlier career; his daily walks along the Nevsky Prospekt; his future hopes. Nevertheless, as Janko Lavrin has pointed out, the very title *Nos* (Nose) is merely the Russian word for 'dream' written backwards, and this observation suggests the story as a literary joke, though at the same time it recalls the inversion of words associated with Poprishchin's madness.[55] Whatever may have been Gogol's reason for eliminating overt explanation as a dream, the story certainly gains from being uncompromising in its absurdity.

The author himself is puzzled by his own story. He seems to be in a position similar to that of the postmaster in *Dead Souls* when he has narrated the incredible story of Captain Kopeykin. It is only after the story has been told, that he appears to realise just how absurd it really is: 'Now, after taking the whole of it into consideration, do we see that it contains much that is improbable' (III, 75). Then, pretending to discuss the various absurdities in his tale, Gogol mockingly points to the strangest thing of all:

> But what is the strangest, what is the most incomprehensible of all is how it is that authors can take such things as subjects. I admit it is completely incomprehensible, it is just...no, no, I don't understand it at all. In the first place there is absolutely no advantage to the fatherland, and in the second place...but in the second place there is again absolutely no advantage. I simply don't know what it... (III, 75)[56]

Thus the absurdity of the story is thrown back at the reader as something which defeats even the author himself, and he, disclaiming his story in this fashion, is in effect perpetrating a joke against the reader. 'The Nose' is the Gogolian equivalent of the 'shaggy dog story': the joke is not for the reader but against him. To this extent the term *shutka* (joke), used by Pushkin to describe 'The Nose', seems valid – at least on one level.

Absurdity is everywhere in this story. It inheres not merely in the subject itself, but also in the manner of narration. Thus, in effect, there is not one story of the disappearance and reappearance of a nose: there are at least two.

First of all the barber Ivan Yakovlevich finds a nose baked in a loaf of his wife's bread, and realises that it belongs to Major Kovalev, whom he shaves every Wednesday and Sunday. He disposes of his 'guilt' by throwing it from a bridge into the river Neva.

The second account concerns Major Kovalev himself, who wakes up one morning to find his nose has vanished from his face. However, he sees it in the street in the guise of a civil servant and pursues it into the Kazan Cathedral, where he accosts it, but his attention is distracted and the nose disappears.

Both these accounts open with their chief protagonists brought from sleep into the waking world by their noses: Ivan Yakovlevich by the smell of his wife's bread; Kovalev by his desire to see in the mirror whether a pimple has disappeared from the side of his nose. What they both wake to is a detached nose; in the first case an unwanted presence; in the second a mysterious absence. Yet these two stories are essentially different. In the barber's tale the nose is something thrice dead. It is first cut from a living face (he suspects, by himself), then baked in an oven by his wife, and finally drowned by the barber in the river. In Kovalev's story the nose is very much alive. It rides about in a carriage, talks, wears a uniform, makes visits, and prays in church.

Because of the accusations of his wife, and his own inability to remember the events of the previous day, Ivan Yakovlevich suspects himself of the deed. Kovalev, for his part, has no such suspicions:

> The barber Ivan Yakovlevich had shaved him on the Wednesday, and throughout the whole of Wednesday, and even the entire Thursday, his nose was intact. This he remembered, and knew very well. Moreover he would have felt pain and undoubtedly the wound could not have healed up so quickly and be smooth like a pancake. (III, 65)

The incongruity is therefore complete. The two stories touch at only one point: both protagonists recognise the nose as belonging to Kovalev.

It is as though Gogol is taking the structural device of the diptych, which he had used for the purposes of commentary in 'Nevsky Prospekt' and 'The Portrait', and now in this 'joke' is mocking his own procedures. Yet the central theme introduced by 'Nevsky Prospekt', and carried on in all the St Petersburg tales, is incongruity, and in the diptych of 'The Nose' incongruity has developed into a narrational perception of reality which is almost schizophrenic. Moreover the dichotomy reflects another obsessional theme: 'dead and alive', which points to the problem underlying Gogol's very methods of characterisation.

There is, however, yet a third narrative strand which attempts some form of reconciliation between the disparate plots. After disposing of the nose in the Neva, Ivan Yakovlevich is apprehended on the bridge by an officer of the law. It is this same officer who later returns the nose to Kovalev, but the nose he has seized was the living one, with the passport of a civil servant, sitting in a stage coach and on his way to Riga. Yet the nose he returns is wrapped up in a piece of paper, and is carried in his pocket: it is the 'dead' nose. When Kovalev attempts to put it back in place, he not only notices that it feels wooden, but it falls on the table with a strange sound like a cork. All his attempts to affix it fail, and it is only thirteen days after its appearance in the freshly baked bread of Ivan Yakovlevich that it unexpectedly returns to its rightful place on the face of Kovalev. Although all this appears to have little to do with the activities of the barber, it is nevertheless he, whom the policeman blames, though he manages to suggest that it is somehow more a case of drunkenness and theft. These jumbled narrative lines are further complicated by fresh rumours of the nose taking a regular stroll along the Nevsky Prospekt at three o'clock (the hour for civil servants according to the narrator of 'Nevsky Prospekt'), or being seen in a fashionable shop there, or even in the Taurida Gardens.

In this narrative cause and effect are completely disconnected. The whole story seems merely a series of logical dislocations, even in its minor details. Thus, on first discovering the loss of his nose, Kovalev's first response is to go to the police rather than to seek medical advice, and despite the fact that the police officer, who brings the nose back, roundly accuses the barber for its loss, Kovalev still prefers to think it was really the work of a female acquaintance Podtochina, whose name is connected with *podtochit'* – 'to undermine' (e.g. of a person's health or powers). He writes her an absurd letter of accusation, which from the threat of legal action passes directly to:

> But with complete respect for you, I have the honour to be
> Your humble servant,
> Platon Kovalev (III, 70)

At the end of the story when the nose is miraculously restored to Kovalev's face, its reappearance is followed almost immediately by the usual professional visit of Ivan Yakovlevich. Yet Kovalev allows himself to be shaved by the very barber accused of its loss without a word of reproach. His only fears are not about the clumsiness of the barber's hands, but about their cleanliness. Such psychological dislocations are everywhere apparent: the discovery of a nose in his wife's bread is not a cause for Ivan Yakovlevich to scold her, but rather for her to scold him; and when Kovalev returns home to find his servant spitting at the ceiling[57] he reproves him not because the habit is disgusting, but because it is foolish.

The closing words constitute a 'tongue in cheek' justification of the story's absurdities: 'and well then, where are there no absurdities? All the same, if you think a bit about it, it is true there is in all this something or other. Whatever anybody says similar occurrences do happen on this earth, seldom, but they do happen' (III, 75). The incongruities in the story can be justified by reference to the absurdities of the real world; they are not the faithful reflection of such incongruities, but rather their imaginative projection in art. Thus synecdoche in art parallels synecdochal values in Russian society where, as in the story itself, one 'member' can represent the entire 'body': 'But Russia is such a land of miracles,[58] that if you say anything about one collegiate assessor, then all the collegiate assessors, from Riga to Kamchatka, will invariably take it as referring to themselves. And the same goes for all titles and ranks' (III, 53). Kovalev himself exemplifies these values; for him the titular 'part' is greater than the human 'whole': 'He could forgive everything that might be said about himself, but just could not forgive anything which referred to his rank and title' (III, 64). It is in such a world that a nose can be of higher rank than its owner.

Alogism and dislocation are often used to make a social point, to mirror a discrepancy between private interest and public duty. Thus when the policeman who brings back the nose suddenly breaks off his official business to discuss his private life, the dislocation is intended as a 'jolt' to remind Kovalev that money is called for.

The efficiency of this policeman may be further judged by his 'short-sightedness', which is such as to prevent his seeing the very two features which the 'culprit' has removed from the face of the 'victim': 'If you were to stand in front of me, I can see only that you have a face, but neither your nose nor your beard. I don't notice anything at all' (III, 66). The bribe-taking of yet another policeman is presented as an eccentric passion for sugar: 'In his home the whole of the entrance hall, as well as the dining room were heaped round with blocks of sugar, which merchants had brought to him out of friendship' (III, 63).

The fact that Kovalev regards the loss of a nose as a police rather than a medical matter is an absurdity with its own social implications. A doctor actually lives in the same house, but he is the last person Kovalev turns to for help; for although the doctor takes good care of his own health, he is unable, even unwilling, to help Kovalev. He claims it would be worse for his patient if he were to fix the nose back in its place,[59] and seems more interested in acquiring it as an object to exhibit for money. Although he himself disclaims any interest in money: 'I never cure people for profit, it is against my rules and my profession' (III, 69), he nevertheless takes care to add: 'It is true I take money for visits, but solely in order not to give offence by refusing' (III, 69). This, no doubt, explains why he can afford to live in one of the best apartments in the house. Through the doctor's interest in acquiring the nose for exhibition Gogol seems to suggest a certain connection between the medical profession of his day and the role of mountebank.

The central incident with the nose is the most absurd of all the logical disconnections in the story. It may be taken on one level, as a joke against the reader, but there also lies behind it a more serious significance. A key word throughout the whole story is *mesto* – (place, position, job). Thus *mesto* is Kovalev's sole reason for being in St Petersburg: 'Major Kovalev had come to St Petersburg on necessary business, to be precise to look for a position fitting to his title' (i.e. *iskat' prilichnogo svoyemu zvaniyu mesta*) (III, 54). Kovalev is very conscious of his title, the civil service rank of collegiate assessor: 'He had only had this title two years, and therefore could not forget it for one moment' (III, 53). Yet his way of 'not forgetting it for one moment' exhibits a striking dislocation of logic: 'But in order to give himself a bit more nobility and weight, he never called himself collegiate assessor, but always major' (II, 53).[60] Kovalev is a civil servant masquerading as a military man, and he is not even sure of his status as a collegiate assessor, as the text slyly hints:

> But meanwhile it is necessary to say something about Kovalev, so that the reader can see what sort of collegiate assessor he was. One cannot in any way compare collegiate assessors who receive this title with the help of diplomas of learning, with those collegiate assessors who are made in the Caucasus. They are two types completely on their own. (III, 53)

Thus there are 'educated' (*uchennyy*) collegiate assessors and 'Caucasian' collegiate assessors. Kovalev belongs to the latter. It is implied that he has gained this title by virtue of having served in a distant outpost of the empire, but that he lacks the educational qualifications to achieve the rank in the capital. Yet it is precisely to St Petersburg that he has now come in search of a position, and is trying to cover up his true title by calling himself major.

The phrase 'a position fitting to his title', therefore, has an ironic ambiguity, and this is reflected in the two posts he has in mind: either that of a vice-governor (ridiculously ambitious), or the job of *ekzekutor* (more fitting to his rank).[61] Instead of either of these 'places', however, Kovalev wakes up one morning to find 'a very stupid, even and smooth place' (*preglupoye, rovnoye i gladkoye mesto*): the place, in fact, that was once occupied by his nose. When Kovalev pursues his nose into the Kazan Cathedral, 'place' again is uppermost in his mind: 'It seems strange to me, dear sir, I think you ought to know your place' (III, 55). The use of the word *mesto* here is ambiguous: the nose should know its 'place' to be on Kovalev's face,[62] and not in the Kazan Cathedral praying; but the nose should also know its social 'place'. It is, after all, dressed up as a state counsellor, a rank three 'places' above Kovalev himself, and one more fitting for his own ambition to be a vice-governor. Kovalev seems to feel that without a nose he cannot further his career but he breaks off without mentioning the 'place' he hopes to receive, asserting instead that he mixes in company of equal rank to the nose (i.e. a state counsellor's wife – Chekhtyreva). The nose in reply claims independence, and in words which not only have physical but social and psychological ambiguity: 'there can be no close relationships between us'. He appears to mean that they each work in different departments, yet the statement that he himself serves in education is phrased in terms of an 'educated part' (*ya zhe po uchenoy chasti*,[63] which could also be interpreted: 'whereas I – according to an educated part'). The 'Caucasian' nature of the collegiate assessor is thus mocked by the superiority of his 'educated' part, and the irony is further strengthened by the connotations of foolishness associated with 'nose' in Russian.

Apart from differences of rank and education the superiority of the 'part' to the 'whole' is emphasised throughout. Thus Kovalev has to walk because he cannot get a cab: the nose is riding around in its own carriage. In the cathedral the nose is absorbed in prayer: the less spiritual Kovalev is distracted by thoughts of an amorous adventure. So that there is obvious irony in the subsequent statement: 'One could already see from the nose's own replies, that for this man there was nothing holy' (III, 58).[64] The nose seems to represent all Kovalev's own pretensions, all his efforts to reach beyond himself. It is his most prominent external feature,[65] but it seems to assume significance for his inner world: the baseless psychological projection of his own character becomes identified, through fantasy, with a detachable physical protuberance. Thus the loss of the nose he equates directly with the loss of career prospects and the inability to make an advantageous marriage, whereas its sudden appearance as a civil servant in its own right mocks him in the form of a 'double' which is in every sense his better, and yet can have no connections with him.

For Kovalev, as for Poprishchin in 'The Diary of a Madman', status seems to be linked with amorous aims. The statement about his ambition to become a vice-governor or an *ekzekutor* is followed immediately by another possibility: 'Major Kovalev was not against getting married even, but only on condition that his bride should have two hundred thousand in capital behind her' (III, 54). As we have seen he does not finish his sentence to the nose about his hopes for preferment, but goes on to mention his acquaintance with Chekhtyreva and other ladies. When visiting the newspaper office his eye lights on the name of a pretty actress in a theatre announcement, and once more a sexual response seems intimately connected with the question of status; 'staff officers in the opinion of Kovalev ought to sit in the orchestra stalls'.

On the other hand women seem, somehow, to be connected with the loss of his nose. In spite of everything Kovalev is convinced that its disappearance is the work of Podtochina, and when, in the Kazan Cathedral, he allows himself to be distracted by a pretty girl his nose 'disappears' a second time.

The fact that the loss of the nose both springs from, and further inhibits, Kovalev's relations with women seems to suggest that the protuberance might be equated with a more obviously masculine organ. Such an identification has good literary antecedents, and the story is a happy hunting ground for critics of a Freudian bent.[66]

Nevertheless Freudian insights are not limited to sexual matters alone. Indeed it is interesting to note the 'Freudian slips' in Gogol's first full draft of the story. Here, when discussing the difference between 'educated' collegiate assessors and 'Caucasian' ones, the term 'collegiate professor' occurs twice instead of 'collegiate assessor' (III, 385). The writing of 'The Nose' coincides with Gogol's own abortive career as a university lecturer with the official title of '*adyunkt-professor*', but like his hero Kovalev he was of the 'Caucasian' rather than the 'educated' variety; for he had achieved the position without the aid of any real qualifications. The post was obviously beyond him, and it is tempting to see in this 'history on account of my nose'[67] an artistic reworking of the author's anxieties connected with his own *mesto* as a 'professor' of history.

The other element of Gogol's academic title has a vaguely military ring (*adyunkt* suggests adjutant) – a fact which was exploited by Gogol and his friends as they returned from the Ukraine in the summer of 1835. They succeeded in conveying to the postmasters along the route that the title *adyunkt-professor* in Gogol's passport meant he was a very important person, perhaps even a government inspector. Thus the Kovalev who is a collegiate assessor/'professor', who passes himself off as a military man, and whose alienated 'superior' self is serving in education (and making a fool of him) could well have oblique autobiographical relevance for Gogol himself.[68]

The story ends happily for Kovalev. With the restoration of his nose we witness the restoration of Kovalev himself. He is shaved as usual by Ivan Yakovlevich, as though nothing had happened, and his actions on its return seem to recreate in a positive sense his behaviour on first discovering its loss. He now orders a cab (there was none available on the first occasion); goes into a pastrycook's and is served (previously he was not); he looks into the mirror and reassures himself about the nose's presence (it was not there when he looked in the pastrycook's mirror before). Moreover, the nose seems now to establish his 'military' superiority: 'He turned round quite happy and with a satirical expression, slightly closing one eye, he looked at two military men, one of whom had a nose not a whit larger than a waistcoat button' (III, 74). At the end both his overweening ambition and his amorous proclivities seem to have been reinstated in full vigour: 'After this Major Kovalev was to be seen always in a good mood, smiling, determinedly pursuing all pretty ladies and even once stopping in front of a stall in the *Gostinyy dvor* and buying a ribbon for some decoration or other, why is unknown because he himself was not a knight of any order at all' (III, 75).

Word-play is important for the story. Gogol exploits the idea of 'nose', not only conceptually as a kind of metaphor, but also verbally, much as he does that other key concept 'place'. Thus Podtochina, in her reply to Kovalev's strange letter, thinks that his references to the nose are allusions to the Russian idiom *ostat'sya s nosom* – 'to be duped' (literally: 'to remain with a nose') a verbal ambiguity already anticipated in Kovalev's complaint to the doctor; 'How can I remain without a nose?' (*Kak zhe mne ostavat'sya bez nosa*?) There is also the frequent identification of noses with buttons.[69]

Such elements help to reinforce the view of the story as a joke, yet, at the same time, they may be taken as devices of ambiguity pointing to a serious psychological undertone. The story may be interpreted as a joke, or, in spite of Gogol's suppression of the original ending, it may be seen as the fantasy of dream. There are other tentative straws of explanation at which the reader might also clutch. Thus it could be related to silly rumours, garbled in the salons of St Petersburg: 'And all these events were extremely gratefully received by all those society gentlemen, the indispensable visitors at evening gatherings, who loved to make the ladies laugh, and whose store at that time had been completely exhausted' (III, 72). Again it might all be a form of hypnotic illusion: 'It was precisely at that time that everybody's mind had been turned to exceptional things. It was not long before that experiments on the effects of magnetism had been the talk of the town' (III, 71). Indeed the doctor, who refuses to put back Kovalev's nose, has this quality of magnetism in his voice.

There is the possibility, again, of taking the story as an allegory. The clerk in the newspaper office refuses to print Kovalev's advertisement for his nose, from fear that it might have a hidden meaning.[70] He quotes the case of an advertisement about a runaway, black-haired poodle, which turned out to be an attack on the treasurer of some institution. Kovalev's reaction to this is, in itself, revealing: 'But, after all, I am not making an announcement to you about a poodle, but about my very own nose: therefore it is almost the same thing as about myself' (III, 61).

'The Nose' is indeed a sort of allegory 'almost about Kovalev himself', which at the same time has overtones of authorial self-confession. On the surface it can be read as a joke: a bizarre story which proceeds by verbal associations and logical dislocations rather than by the cause and effect of the everyday world.[71] To this extent it looks forward to the next story about St Petersburg, 'The Overcoat' in which another civil servant makes vain efforts to retrieve a lost synecdoche – a coat (with overtones of a human being) which will only be restored to him, as in the case of Kovalev, by supernatural means.

As a piece of psychological writing, 'The Nose' is the forerunner of Dostoevsky's short novel *The Double*. There are many points of similarity. Both Kovalev and Dostoevsky's hero, Golyadkin, enter their respective works by waking up, and then looking in a mirror (mirrors, in fact, figure prominently in both stories). For both heroes marital ambitions and career ambitions seem irretrievably mixed; both feel basically insecure about their status, and their fears take the form of an encounter with a 'double', who seems to possess all the qualities envied by the hero. The fact that in Gogol's story the double is also the hero's nose gives added piquancy to his dilemma by suggesting that, psychologically, the part can be greater than the whole. Nevertheless in Dostoevsky's work there is a revealing moment, when Golyadkin wishes that his double could be removed in exchange for his own little finger.[72]

Dostoevsky deepens Gogol's theme, gives it a tragic dimension, and in assigning to Golyadkin's double an unequivocally human identification, he is humanising a Gogolian theme in much the same way as he had done in *Poor Folk*.

'*The Overcoat*'

'The Overcoat' has long been held up as a key work in the Russian realist tradition, but in the twentieth century the view that the story is 'realistic' has been strongly challenged.[73] The opening paragraph, in itself, should act as an *avis au lecteur*. It is little more than a verbal arabesque which at its end returns the reader to the very point of its opening: 'a certain department'. The intervening verbiage has mocked the reader for his social susceptibilities in literature and established an authorial tone of playful mystification. Moreover, since the whole impetus behind the arabesque has been provided by the one word 'department', the reader should be warned that here is a story in which words have a wayward dynamism all their own: they are more capable of retarding or advancing the plot than mere actions.

This opening prepares us, not for realism, but for the sort of incongruous world already encountered in a story like 'The Nose'. The absurdity is carried on in the depiction of the central character, where for realistic description Gogol substitutes the verbal formula: Akakiy Akakiyevich is 'a little bit pockmarked, a little bit red-haired, a little bit blind in appearance'.[74] Two other verbal formulae take the place of real biographical detail; for at birth the hero pulls a face which suggests he senses himself as a future titular counsellor: later when people see him in the office they think that he must have been born 'ready made' complete with uniform and bald patch. Moreover his long years of service are reduced to a bureaucrat's *bon mot*: 'He had earned a buckle in his button hole and haemorrhoids in his crutch' (III, 144). The nature of this service has entirely swamped his private and inner world. As he walks along the street, he sees only his own handwriting on everything, and if he is suddenly brought to his senses by bumping into a horse: 'Only then would he notice that he was not in the middle of a line, but rather in the middle of the street' (III, 145).

Such verbal play detracts from any serious, realistic presentation of the hero and through visual effects he is reduced to the grotesque. Thus his neck is compared to that of a wagging plaster kitten; things permanently adhere to his clothing because of an unfortunate gift of always managing to be under a window whenever rubbish is thrown out; he eats his food without noticing either the taste or the dead flies, and only realises that he has had enough when he sees that his stomach has swelled.

The realist approach to the story stresses the social theme of humble destitution, but it is difficult for the reader to understand Akakiy Akakiyevich's poverty. He has no dependants, no extravagances, not even any amusements; he has a very careful system of saving money,[75] is not at the very bottom of the civil service hierarchy and has been in his position for longer than anyone can tell, yet he appears to be unable to afford such a basic necessity as a winter overcoat to keep out the St Petersburg frost. The description of his meagre possessions and of the methods he employs to save wear and tear to his clothing and boots is comic. The poverty of Akakiy Akakiyevich, in real terms, is absurd: it is presented hyperbolically.

The coat, too, is presented with hyperbole, not merely as regards its material quality, but also in respect of the effect it has on its wearer. Under its influence he becomes a new man; he experiences something akin to an awakening of the senses. The coat replaces his obsession with copying and in its turn dominates his existence, whilst at the same time offering a pledge for a new and fuller life. At this point it is as though Gogol has taken up one of the 'myriad characters' on the Nevsky Prospekt, a man who consists entirely of his clothing, and devoted a whole study to him. Yet his analysis is not pursued by going inside the character, as in 'The Diary of a Madman', the psychological world of Akakiy Akakiyevich, such as it is, is projected through externals: the whole tale is a finely spun cocoon which houses a 'dead soul'.

Almost everything in the tale can be seen as 'psychological'. The poverty of Akakiy Akakiyevich is presented in the same grotesque way as is the central character himself. The narrator's verbal onslaught, in the enormous sentence which contrasts the life of other minor civil servants with that of his hero, suggests (in spite of certain verbal flourishes) that he is deprived of all amusements through the dearth of inner resources rather than a lack of financial ones.[76] He is a man with one obsession – copying; his work, humdrum though it may be, has become his private pleasure, and he is happy with his inner world of stereotyped creativity, unable to communicate with others and little interested in them.

The outward poverty of Akakiy Akakiyevich is a metaphor of his spiritual indigence. The coat, too, is lined with metaphor: his outward wrapping is identified as a 'lifelong lady friend', and on acquiring it, it is 'as though he has got married'. Having put it on he assumes a new personality, or, at the very least, a new frame of mind. The coat seems to open up a whole new possible life of conviviality, drinking, even amorous adventure. He goes to the apartment of the assistant chief clerk and is forced to drink champagne; on his way there he had chuckled at an erotic picture in a shop window; on his way back he almost chases after a woman in the street.

These outward and return journeys must in themselves be taken as metaphors of inner movement. The outward journey is from the darkness and meanness of his own quarter of the city towards the growing light and bustle of his convivial destination: the way home is the same spiritual journey in reverse. Thus the streets of St Petersburg, which in 'Nevsky Prospekt' were both a sociological metaphor and a catalyst for human folly, here assume a psychological function. Setting forth he had increasingly been opening his eyes and seeing – for the first time; returning to his old life, he closes his eyes, and is robbed of his coat. The thieves are men with large moustaches (a recurring symbol of male sexuality in Gogol)[77] and the phrase of expropriation is significant: 'but the coat is mine'.

Akakiy Akakiyevich is deprived of something that was never really fully his. The awakening of his senses, which he experienced under the influence of the coat, was merely a wraith-like potential, which was never fully convincing. After his embryonic erotic experiences on the streets of St Petersburg, Akakiy Akakiyevich is now thrown back on his seventy-year-old landlady, about whom his fellow clerks used to tease him, pouring paper 'snow' on his head, and asking when he was going to marry her. Now when he returns covered in real snow, his reception by his landlady seems to recreate in ironic terms the essential features of the erotic picture, which had first stirred something unknown within his breast: a man in a doorway looking at a woman with only one shoe on her foot (the erotic irony is underlined by the fact that the landlady has just jumped out of bed and is holding her nightshirt to her chest 'out of modesty').

The ostensible plot of the story is, of course, the acquisition and loss of an object – the overcoat, but in some strange way this gets mixed up with psychological awakening and eroticism: a confusion which may be observed even in the reaction of the policeman to whom Akakiy Akakiyevich first turns for help: 'The district superintendent received the story of the theft of the coat in an exceedingly strange way. Instead of turning his attention to the main point of the matter, he began to question Akakiy Akakiyevich on why it was that he was returning home so late, and hadn't he called off and been in some disorderly house or other?' (III, 163).

The police prove entirely unhelpful. The policeman (*budochnik*)[78] who witnesses the theft is not prepared to act, and Akakiy Akakiyevich is told by his landlady that it will be useless to go to the local police officer (*kvartal'nyy*). She advises him to apply directly to the district superintendent, who, as we have seen, has his own oblique view of the matter. As the normal channels seem so perverse, the pursuit of the coat takes its own obliquity: Akakiy Akakiyevich seeks to recover it through the intercession of a person of significance. His exact office is unknown, it is sufficient that he is a 'significant person'; but just as the coat had been seized by aggressive men with moustaches, so now the insignificance of Akakiy Akakiyevich quails before the 'significance' of this man, and he is robbed of his life by a verbal bully.

The story assumes its final obliquity in the account of Akakiy Akakiyevich's vengeance. He returns to the streets of St Petersburg as a ghost, and poetic justice is done, when he takes the overcoat of the significant person in circumstances which seem to reflect the symbolic potential of Akakiy Akakiyevich's own coat. The significant person has just been to a party; he too has drunk two glasses of champagne, and instead of returning home is entertaining thoughts of an erotic encounter. At this point his coat is seized from his back with the words: 'Your coat is the one I want.' With its loss the 'significant person' becomes a different man, and the ghost itself disappears. The only sighting reported later is of an 'apparition', which turns out to be a figure strikingly like the original coat thief.

The plot of this story is scarcely less oblique than that of 'The Nose': 'titular' poverty forces a titular counsellor to make sacrifices to acquire a coat, which is somehow more than mere clothing. It is stolen by robbers and when he tries to retrieve it through civil-service channels he is put so firmly in his place that he dies. He returns as a ghost, but exacts retribution for his stolen coat not from the thieves but from the 'significant person'. The obliquity is reinforced on a verbal level. The hero is a clerk who cannot use words, but yet is obsessed by their calligraphic reproduction. He is at the mercy of the verbal effects of the tailor Petrovich, and, more devastatingly, those of the 'significant person'. An automaton, to whom a coat has brought the pledge of feelings, is devastated by one who is: 'absolutely delighted by the thought that a word from him could even deprive a man of his feelings' (III, 167). Akakiy's awakening had been the development of feelings. Formerly copying had engulfed his life in entirety: 'It is not enough to say that he worked with zeal. No, he worked with love' (III, 144). This 'love' was transferred to the coat and from this, in turn, there stems a dimly awakened interest in such erotic objects as the picture of the woman with the shoe, and the woman in the street whose body is full of movement.

Gogol presents his theme through verbal play and literary joke, gently mocking in turn his hero's surname, Christian name and rank. The narrator himself calls attention to the verbal undercurrents of the story when he claims that the hero's name has been derived from a shoe (an object, which, as an erotic symbol, is a motif both for his outward journey and for his return). The disingenuous narrator finds it strange that the name could be derived from a shoe, since all his relations wore boots. Amongst the relatives listed is a 'brother-in-law' (*shurin*), who could not be a 'real Bashmachkin', as this is a relationship by marriage, but even more perplexing is the fact that the relationship is very precise: *shurin* is 'one's wife's brother'. With the gratuitious introduction of this brother-in-law, Gogol is again pointing to the sexual theme; for if Akakiy Akakiyevich ever had a *shurin*, he must also have had a wife.

The choosing of the hero's Christian name is treated comically. The description begins with a pun on the word *izyskannyy* (recherché) then develops in detail quite disproportionate to the treatment accorded to the rest of his life. The emphasis placed on choosing the correct name has strong overtones of one of the literary jokes in *Tristram Shandy*, and this, taken together with the verbal formula linking his birth to the rank of titular counsellor, and vice versa, indicates that the name he bears is of more importance for his personality and career than the formative experiences of childhood and youth. The name Akakiy, it has been pointed out, has comic associations, suggesting a children's word for excrement – *kak*.[79] On a more elevated plane, some commentators see his life as reflecting that of St Akakiy.[80]

Akakiy Akakiyevich has the rank of titular counsellor, and the narrator pretends to disapprove of writers who poke fun at those who bear it (Gogol's own story 'The Diary of a Madman' might be a case in point). Nevertheless, his own treatment of his hero is scarcely less mocking than that of Akakiy Akakiyevich's colleagues in the office. The ambiguous distinction of the rank of titular counsellor has already been noted, but it seemed anomalous in yet another way. All the senior grades in the hierarchy (rank one excepted) were various degrees of 'counsellor' (ranks two to seven inclusive); the titular counsellor, however, was separated from these 'real' counsellors by the career threshold of rank eight, the collegiate assessor.[81] He was thus a 'counsellor' only in name. At the very end of the section introducing his hero, the narrator plays with the words 'counsellor' and 'counsel'. He talks of the misfortunes which bestrew the path not only of titular counsellors, but of privy, actual, court and all counsellors 'even those who give no one counsel, nor take it from anyone else'. As a 'counsellor' Akakiy Akakiyevich is obviously in the latter category: he is incapable of performing any duty other than routine copying.

The official responsible for the death of Akakiy Akakiyevich must be a true counsellor (probably actual state counsellor) as he has recently attained the rank of general, nevertheless he is always referred to as the 'significant person', *znachitel'noye litso* (literally – 'significant face'). It is through this formula that further word-play is possible, suggesting the essential link between this verbal tyrant and his victim.

The introduction of this new figure is accompanied by extended punning on the significance of the word 'significant'. His post is significant, but not as significant as some, and in order to uphold his significance he has to resort to well-tried authoritarian formulae, while at the same time 'looking very significantly into the face of the person to whom he spoke' (i.e. *smotrel ochen' znachitel'no v litso tomu, kotoromu govoril*). There is here a play on both *znachitel'noye* (significant) and *litso* (person, face). The suggestion is that the general is little more than a 'significant face'; for we learn that he has had to practise his expressions before a mirror.

By contrast 'significance' is a quality which, in both its senses, Akakiy Akakiyevich completely lacks. He is so insignificant, the narrator tells us, on his death, that he would not have attracted even the attention of an entymologist.[82] Significance, in yet another respect, is foreign to him: he copies words without understanding them, and his own speech is incoherent and lacks meaning: 'It must be explained that Akakiy Akakiyevich expressed himself, for the most part, in prepositions, adverbs and ultimately in particles which had absolutely no meaning [i.e. *znacheniye*] whatsoever' (III, 149). His favourite all-purpose phrase is *togo* – 'and that...' and when confronted by the general, he is so overwhelmed by his 'significance' that he uses more of this semantic debris than normal. Ironically, he is annihilated by formulae of significance which are little more than the practised copying of stereotyped phrases: the exercise to which Akakiy Akakiyevich has devoted his own life.

The final section of the story contains the ultimate identification of the hero as a 'dead man/civil servant' (*chinovnik-mertvets*). Akakiy Akakiyevich returns as a ghost (*mertvets* = literally 'corpse') and the whole of this ludicrous sequence is permeated by punning on the concept 'dead and alive'. Such verbal play goes to the root of Akakiy Akakiyevich's character; for, paradoxically, when he was alive he seemed one of the walking dead, whereas after death he shows more 'life' in his behaviour as a ghost.

Verbal play, as we have seen, runs all through the story. Although it adds to the humour, its chief contribution lies elsewhere: it is intimately connected with definitions, with names, titles, states of being. Its function is to suggest another meaning below the level of the blandly smiling surface of a joke, and as such it may be compared to the device of a 'coat', which is not a coat, and 'poverty', which is not poverty, or even the naive narrator, who is really the sophisticated author himself.

The tale may be related to the genre of the *skaz*. The story is filtered through the unsophisticated consciousness of an inept narrator, who places unusual emphases on unimportant areas of his narrative, whilst neglecting others altogether. A desire to be accurate about dates and street names obsesses him when it is least called for, and deserts him on other occasions. His naive incomprehension of the psychological motivation of his characters is almost as great as the innocence of Akakiy Akakiyevich himself. The focus is one of distortion: Petrovich's big toe and his snuff box loom larger than the man himself; Akakiy Akakiyevich's baptism is described with mock seriousness. The relative positions of mother, godfather and godmother are recorded with fastidious accuracy, yet the conventional hierarchy of virtues is inverted (the mother is described merely as 'a very good woman', while the godfather is 'a most excellent man', and the godmother is a 'woman of rare virtues').

Behind his simpleton–narrator lurks the wily author himself, who laughs at his narrator, at his heroes, but above all at his readers. Mockery of the reader is present, as we have seen, in the very opening of the tale, and one of the ironies of the genre is that a tale told by an 'inept' narrator posits the need for a sophisticated reader.

The fact that the author also laughs at his hero, would seem to undermine the traditional view, that in 'The Overcoat' Gogol is the champion of the underdog: the little man persecuted by authority. It was this view that Eykhenbaum and others attacked, interpreting the 'humanitarian' passage of the awakening of a conscience in a fellow clerk as a mere artistic device.[83] It cannot, however, be denied that there is both 'laughter' and 'tears' in the presentation of Gogol's 'little man', but unlike Karamzin he does not seek to redeem the sufferings of his central character through the sympathetic tears of his readers; there is only a nod in the direction of Sentimentalism. On the other hand the 'medieval' morality demands strict recompense: a justice which is both supernatural and of this earth. It is this that Gogol has given us in the ghost who steal overcoats.

The ghost sequence is no less absurd than the fantastic world of 'The Nose', or the hallucinations of Poprishchin. Indeed 'The Overcoat' has much in common with 'The Diary of a Madman'. Both heroes are titular counsellors, for whom the copying out of documents is intimately connected with their self-regard. One, whose writing is perfect, lacks imagination and any inner life other than that provided by his passion for copying; the other, whose writing is full of aberrations, falls prey to imagination and an inner aberration which swamps his sense of reality. Poprishchin, to achieve a new identity cuts up his uniform, and becomes the King of Spain; clothing brings the promise of a new personality to Akakiy Akakiyevich. For Poprishchin status is mixed with eroticism, and the 'new self' of Akakiy Akakiyevich, as we have seen, also has its erotic overtones.

Yet in one thing the stories are radically different: Poprishchin, through his diary, is seen from the inside; the narrator of 'The Overcoat' refuses categorically to get inside his characters. He states this at two crucial points in the psychological development of his hero: once, when Akakiy Akakiyevich, on his way to the party, is confronted by the titillating picture, and a second time when the situation is reversed, and he returns to his landlady without the coat. Just as the narrator refuses to speculate about the arousal of his hero: 'For it is impossible to get into the soul of a man and learn all that he is thinking' (III, 159), by the same token he leaves the psychology of defeat to the empathy of his readers: 'and how he spent the night there, can be left to the judgement of him, who can to any extent imagine the situation of another' (III, 162).[84]

'The Overcoat' is probably the most famous story in the Russian language. Its germinal significance for later writers seems to be enshrined in the apocryphal remark attributed to Dostoevsky: 'We have all come out of Gogol's *Overcoat*'.[85] For Dostoevsky himself this is largely true. He began his career by rewriting Gogol and earned overnight acclaim with *Poor Folk*, which is a conscious attempt to humanise and psychologise Gogol's story of a poor clerk. It is interesting that for this purpose Dostoevsky goes back to the earlier, and sentimental, form of the novel in letters, in order to do what Gogol refuses to do: 'get into the soul of a man'. Dostoevsky's novel is more openly sentimental, and he presents psychology directly and analytically, rather than in the devious and oblique method of Gogol. The promise of a saving relationship in Dostoevsky's work is not with a coat, but with a girl; correspondingly the hero's name, Devushkin, is not 'derived from a shoe' but from the word for a girl *devushka*. Devushkin is not a clerk obsessed by mere copying, writing has real significance in his life. He communicates through letters and even tries his hand at *belles lettres*. His interest in literature leads him to read 'The Overcoat', which he severely censures, finding Akakiy Akakiyevich unconvincing.

It is Dostoevsky, not Gogol, who brings realism to the depiction of poverty and the theme of the downtrodden clerk.[86] Yet one of the chief differences between them lies in their treatment of psychology. Gogol, as we have seen, uses external poverty as a psychological metaphor. Dostoevsky's method is the very reverse of this: outward poverty is not used to hint at an inner state of mind, it is rather psychology which is used to explore poverty as a physical state. In polemicising with Gogol, Dostoevsky shows a great perspicuity and subtlety. He understands Gogol fully but disagrees with his methods.

One of Gogol's chief devices, the use of clothing to suggest a state of mind, was not new in Russian literature. Pushkin had coined the phrase: 'a Muscovite in a Harold cloak' to describe the assumed Byronism of Onegin, but here the 'cloak' is only metaphorical. An actual greatcoat had been used by Lermontov in *Hero of Our Time* to clothe Grushnitsky in a sentimentally heroic guise, that had certain erotic pretensions, as it was the chief prop in his intrigue to win Princess Mary. Nevertheless it is the use of clothing as a substitute for character which is essentially Gogolian; the device can be seen throughout his work, whether it be in the fashion parade of the Nevsky Prospekt or the *bekesha* of Ivan Ivanovich.

In later literature, clothing as a key to mental attitudes is used by Turgenev in *Fathers and Children*, where Bazarov's carefully calculated smock contrasts with the English attire of Pavel Petrovich. The most striking example, however, is in Goncharov's novel *Oblomov*. The hero's *khalat* (dressing gown) comes to symbolise a whole attitude to life, and is ceremoniously donned or discarded according to altering circumstances and the hero's state of mind.

In contrast to Dostoevsky, Chekhov seized on the comic aspects of the plot of a humble civil servant annihilated by pompous authority, and took the black humour a stage further in his story *The Death of a Civil Servant*. The fact that a situation, which has death as its dénouement, can be given an uncompromisingly comic treatment raises the question of Chekhov's conception of comedy, and although this is an early story, it has a distinct bearing on the misunderstandings which surrounded his later plays, particularly *The Cherry Orchard*. Behind Chekhov's view of the comic lies the great legacy of Gogol.

3

Theatre

The Government Inspector: *characters and themes*

Gogol's father had written Ukrainian comedies, and his son showed an interest in acting from his school days. On arriving in St Petersburg, he failed to be accepted as an actor, but went on to conquer the Russian stage with his play *The Government Inspector*. Work on this masterpiece dates from 1835, the fertile period of his *St Petersburg Tales*. It was first performed at the Aleksandrinsky Theatre in St Petersburg on 19 April 1836 in the presence of the tsar. Although Gogol was not pleased either by its performance or its reception the play rapidly became a classic of Russian and, later, world theatre.

The Government Inspector is a play of great originality, yet at first sight it appears to be in a conventional mould. Its plot is built entirely round the well-worn comic device of mistaken identity; a comedy of situation is used as a stock peg for a comedy of manners. But we have only to look at the precursors in this field to realise the extent of Gogol's innovatory talent, and why this play is in a class of its own.

The nearest in theme to *The Government Inspector* is a play by Gogol's fellow countryman Grigoriy Kvitka (Osnov′′yanenko), *The Visitor from the Capital or Turmoil in a District Town* (*Priezzhiy iz stolitsy ili sumatokha v uyezdnom gorode*). Despite the fact that this play was not published until some four years after the first production of *The Government Inspector*, it is nevertheless difficult to escape the conclusion that Gogol knew the play in some detail (it was actually written in 1827 and copies were circulated in manuscript), and that Kvitka stands in the same relationship to Gogol's theatre, as his other fellow countryman, Narezhny, stands in relation to *Mirgorod*.[1]

In essence the two plots are the same: in both a civil servant from St Petersburg is mistaken by the officials of a small provincial town for a government inspector; he gets money from the mayor (*gorodnichiy*) and arranges to marry his daughter/niece; his arrival has been prepared by the receipt of one letter, and the fraud is disclosed at the end by the receipt of another; the final disclosure takes place in public with all the elements of a scandal scene. The *dramatis personae* of Kvitka's officialdom would seem quite familiar to readers of *The Government Inspector*; they are: the mayor, the local judge, the school superintendent, a post official and a comic policeman. But given such similarities it is nevertheless the differences which are striking. Kvitka's comedy is, in every sense, more conventional; thus it has positive characters (three in all).[2] Gogol's play has none. The device of mistaken identity is used by Kvitka twice: once in the main plot (the 'government inspector' and the officials) and again in the subplot (to thwart designs against the course of true love). It is here that we see Gogol's originality; he has pared down Kvitka's play to its bare essentials: to its central plot, with the love interest as merely one of the stages of its development. The play, therefore, is almost 'classical' in its simplicity, but it is a Ukrainian simplicity and hides a lot of guile; for *The Government Inspector* gains added comic energy from the fact that it is a parody of the conventional comedy of errors with its obligatory subplot of lovers' intrigue.

Gogol provides no evidence to make the mistaken identity credible; indeed, quite the reverse: he strives to make his audience realise how utterly incongruous it is that Khlestakov should be taken for a high-ranking official. If this is what the Formalists call 'laying bare the device', then his treatment of the conventional love interest shows the same merciless drive towards parodying exposure; for behind Khlestakov's amorous advances can clearly be seen a purely glandular response to any female. Thus he instantly pursues both mother and daughter, changing from one to the other indiscriminately according to circumstance, and his letter to Tryapichkin makes clear what his real aims are: 'Only I haven't made up my mind with which one to begin. I think first with the mother, because she seems prepared to provide all services' (IV, 90).[3]

The two ladies, for their part, seem bent on deflating any romantic element in Khlestakov's advances. Anna Andreyevna advises him to get up off his knees as the floors are dirty, and her daughter in embarrassment looks out of the window, pretending to be interested in a bird. Thus the indissoluble sugary residue of 'true romance', to be found in traditional comedies from Molière on, has itself been turned into the subject of comedy in Gogol's play.

Russian comedies of the eighteenth century (Fonvizin, Kapnist etc.) have characters whose names clearly label their characteristics. This convention still lives on in Kvitka's play: Spalkin is the judge who sleeps (cf. *on spal* = he slept); Uchenosvetov is the superintendent of local schools (*uchenny svet* = the world of learning); Pustolobov is the villain (*pustoy lob* = empty forehead); Milov is the hero (*miliy* = nice). Gogol breaks away from this convention by giving his main characters names which are comic without being crudely explicit. Thus Skvoznik-Dmukhanovsky in its first component suggests 'draught'; in its second – a tartar ancestry (hinting at the town's remote situation). The names Bobchinsky and Dobchinsky are comic through their phonetic parallelism; Khlestakov's name hints at 'a slap'.[4] In the minor characters, however, the older convention still subsists, thus there are two policemen called 'Mugholder' (Derzhimorda) and 'Eartwister' (Ukhovertov).

Another shift of emphasis is towards criticism which is more explicitly social than moral (although Gogol himself would later challenge this view). Nevertheless Kvitka's comedy hinges on the foolishness of the civil servants rather than on their corrupt practices, whereas in *The Government Inspector* corruption is very much to the fore. In this shift Gogol is closer in spirit to Kapnist's *Malicious Litigation* (*Yabeda*).

The character, around whom the whole play revolves, Khlestakov, is certainly not a hero in any accepted sense, but he is not a villain either. Gogol makes this clear in his own directions to the actors. He is the sort of self-satisfied nonentity we have already met in Lieutenant Pirogov. Indeed there is something genuine about Khlestakov, even if it is only that he is a genuine fool: 'The more the person playing this role shows frankness and simplicity the more effective will he be' (IV, 9). These are characteristics which link him with another kind of 'dubious hero', the type of Chistyakov, the picaresque hero of Narezhny's novel *The Russian Gil Blas*. Both Chistyakov and Khlestakov have a certain naivety and childlike quality which does not prevent them from deceiving when necessary.[5]

Khlestakov seeks only enjoyment in life; his most significant statements show a concern only for his own well-being. Thus he likes respect:

> I could not demand anything more than just show me loyalty and respect, respect and loyalty. (IV, 37)

He likes food:

I like to have a good meal. Well that's what one lives for, to pluck the blooms of pleasure. (IV, 45)

He likes to travel in comfort:

And I, I confess, absolutely abominate depriving myself of anything when travelling, and why should one? Isn't that so? (IV, 61)

Khlestakov wants to have everything provided for him (like the professional child);[6] he instinctively feels this as a natural right, and in this, if this alone, his assumptions are the same as those of a true government inspector. He is so sure that the world owes him a living that the thought does not cross his mind (not, at least, until later) that all this hospitality might be offered for any reason other than that his hosts are as enamoured of him as he is of himself:

I like hospitality, and, I confess, I prefer it, if people are obliging to me from pureness of heart, and not because of interest. (IV, 59)[7]

Nevertheless, by the middle of act IV, even Khlestakov is aware that this reverential treatment is due to his being considered more important than he really is: 'It seems to me, however, that they are taking me for a statesman. Indeed, I did show off to them yesterday. What idiots' (IV, 67). Even though he has obviously profited as much as he can from the situation by asking for loans of money with increasing brusqueness and effrontery, he is, nevertheless, too stupid to realise the true nature of the mistake; it is his servant Osip who has to point out the dangers: 'Why get mixed up with them for long? Don't give a fig for them! At any moment another could arrive' (IV, 68). Even in amassing his 'loans' Khlestakov reveals himself not so much a rogue as a fool; for his aim seems to be to find the cardsharp who beat him at Stoss: 'Well, now then, Captain, now then, just you meet me now! We'll see who beats whom!' He appears to be interested only in money, as 'loans'. When the merchants bring him goods (sugar and wine) he claims to regard such offerings as bribes, and declares himself unable to accept them. Osip, however, has no such scruples, and easily persuades his master to take them. Between 'righteous' master and 'practical' servant the merchants are robbed twice; for Khlestakov has already received a 'loan' of money from them in lieu of the sugar and wine.

For all Khlestakov's genuine naivety, the suspicion remains that there could be some element of calculation behind his actions – a suspicion not dispelled by his letter to Tryapichkin:

You remember how you and I lived in poverty, and got our meals by fraud, how once a pastrycook almost seized me by the collar in respect of pies eaten on the account of the King of England's revenues. Now things have taken quite a different turn. Everyone lends me as much money as I want. They're terrible eccentrics. (IV, 90–1)

The mixture of fool and rogue is present in each of the town's officials, but in most of them the rogue is uppermost. Corruption for the mayor is not only his second nature, he even seems to view it as part of the natural order: 'And strange to say: there is no man who does not have to his account some sins or other. It has been arranged like this by God himself, and it is no good the Voltaireans speaking out against it' (IV, 14).[8] Here, then, is a comic 'theological' justification of sin as a necessary element in God's world. For the mayor corruption is almost holy; it must be a comforting doctrine for one who has appropriated the funds destined for the building of a church. The mayor knows he has much to answer for, but God may still be placated: 'Oh, akh, ah, hh! I have sinned. I have sinned a great deal...May God grant that I get away with it as soon as possible, and then I will dedicate such a candle as no one has ever dedicated' (IV, 23). This candle will indeed be unlike all other such votive offerings. Extortion is such an unquestionable way of life that it even seems proper in a thank-offering to God; for the mayor promises: 'I will impose an obligation on every wretched merchant to provide 108 lb of wax per man' (IV, 23).

In a world in which sins are seen as part of God's natural order, the merchants have to admit that to expose the mayor is to be guided by the devil: 'We are guilty before God, Anton Antonovich! The Evil One confounded us. We swear never to complain in future' (IV, 84). The religious consciousness of the mayor himself is medieval: it is more important to observe ritual than the dictates of conscience. Thus he parries the excuses of the judge on the innocent nature of his own bribe-taking, by more fundamental criticism: 'What does it matter that you take your bribes in borzoy puppies? You don't, on the other hand, believe in God; you never go to church. I, at least, am strong in the faith, and am at church every Sunday' (IV, 14). Yet it is more with spirit than form that he tries to impress Khlestakov, when he claims that it is not mere duty but Christian humanitarianism, which prompts him to accord a good reception to every stranger. Given such hypocrisy it is not surprising that the mayor regards lying as just as natural and essential in life as extortion.

The mayor is king of his little domain, and like any self-respecting sovereign he has two birthdays a year (at least according to the merchants who are expected to provide him with presents on both occasions). He may be their scourge but he also reminds them that he has helped them in their own corrupt practices. He, himself, is answerable to the governor, but he has no fear from this quarter, boasting that, in his time, he has deceived three governors.

If the mayor reproaches the judge for being a man without God, he has no such reservations about the judge's office: 'it's such an enviable post, that it has the protection of God Himself'. This is a view also shared by the judge:

As regards that, I'm not worried. Who indeed would call in at the district court? And if he should take a peep at some document or other, he would soon feel sorry. I have been sitting in the judge's seat for fifteen years and as soon as I look at a report, I have had enough. Solomon himself would not be able to decide what is right in it and what is wrong. (IV, 21)

Here Gogol is more explicit in his social criticism than Kvitka: 'Only the judge is not worried, in spite of the fact that the government inspector is round everyone's necks, he sleeps very secure, and you can't distrub him.'[9]

Lyapkin-Tyapkin is the very reverse of the stock comedy figure of the judge (such as Kvitka's Spalkin) who does nothing but sleep. He is, by contrast, a lively sportsman, profiting from the litigation of the local squires to hunt over their land. In this respect Lyapkin-Tyapkin is more like Atuyev in Kapnist's comedy *Malicious Litigation* – a great hunter of hares: 'with him and a pack of good hounds one could hunt down even Justice herself descended from the heavens'.[10] Gogol makes much the same comment about justice, but with greater subtlety: in Lyapkin-Tyapkin's courtroom a whip hangs over the document cabinet.

The judge has another passion; if the tale-teller Zemlyanika is to be believed, he is having an affair with Dobchinsky's wife.[11] Indeed Zemlyanika characterises his behaviour as 'most reprehensible' (*povedeniya samogo predosuditel'nogo*) an adjective which puns on the words for 'court' and 'judge' (*sud* and *sud'ya*).

Lyapkin-Tyapkin is the only one of the major characters to bear a name in the older comic tradition, which designates moral qualities (*lyapat'* = 'to bungle'; *tyapat'* = 'to steal'; the phrase: *tyap lyap* means 'anyhow', 'in a slipshod way'). These slipshod ways are in evidence in his courtroom, which has more the appearance of a farmyard. The presence of livestock where there are petitioners, is a comic detail in the tale of the two Ivans, where it is suggested that poultry thrives on the spilling of corn brought by the litigants as bribes.

On the whole the officials of the town look up to the judge, almost as an intellectual; they admire his ability to speak about the Tower of Babel. This view, however, is not shared by the mayor, who not only regards his initial reaction to the news of the inspector's arrival as stupid, but seems to think of him as a dangerous freethinker who does not go to church and has suspect views of the creation of the world. This aspect of Lyapkin-Tyapkin seems to be confirmed when he himself quotes the authority of *The Acts of John Mason*, an enigmatic title suggestive of Freemasonry.[12] The Masonic lodges in Russia played a large part in moulding the opinions of the officers who in 1825 staged the Decembrist uprising. But it is only in the remotest of provincial backwaters that a hunting judge could be considered a dangerous liberal, and in reality 1825 was the year in which Lyapkin-Tyapkin received the order of St Vladimir, fourth class, 'with approval on the part of the authorities'.[13] Nevertheless, given such a reputation, it is perhaps significant that he should interpret the strange arrival of the government inspector as 'political': that he is coming *incognito* to sniff out treachery to the state.

The postmaster, too, has a similar view: the advent of the inspector can only mean that Russia is going to war with Turkey. In the reactions of both these officials, Gogol is exploiting the device of 'microcosm' to comic effect: a threat to the stability of this provincial town is interpreted as a threat to the security of Russia herself. As we have already seen, the concept of the 'microcosm' lurks behind much of Gogol's writing, and although the author himself later gave conflicting interpretations of his play, at least one of them sees the town as a concentration of Russia's evils:

> In *The Government Inspector* I made up my mind to gather together into one pile all that in Russia was bad, such as I then knew it, all the injustices, such as are done in those places and on those occasions, where most of all justice is demanded, and in one go to laugh at everything. (VIII, 440)

In his directions to the actors Gogol characterises Shpekin as 'a man who is simple to the point of being naive', and in this respect he obviously has much in common with Gogol's other postmaster in *Dead Souls*, *Shprekhen zi deytsh.* Through the postmaster we learn that this 'microcosm' of the Russian State carries out its own form of censorship and spying. Shpekin opens letters out of curiosity, and has even kept back one of the more amusing ones, for the sake of its diverting contents. It is this habit, which not only leads to the play's dénouement, but also reveals an unwelcome personal criticism: Khlestakov suspects that he is a heavy drinker.

The curator of the charitable institutions bears the comic name Zemlyanika (i.e. 'Strawberry') a name which like Yaichnitsa 'omelette' in *Marriage* is comic, not in the 'congruous' eighteenth-century manner but in the incongruous manner adopted by Gogol.[14]

In act I the mayor had wondered whether the inspector was coming because someone had denounced him; an idea repeated by Dobchinsky in act III: 'They have now driven off to inspect the charitable institutions...For, I confess, Anton Antonovich was already wondering whether there might not have been a secret denunciation' (IV, 42). This link between the charitable institutions and denunciation is perhaps not fortuitous; for act IV reveals Zemlyanika as the Judas, only too eager to tell the 'inspector' all the misdeeds of his colleagues: the postmaster, the school superintendent, even the private life of Dobchinsky and Lyapkin-Tyapkin: 'Of course, I must do this for the good of the fatherland, even though he is related to me and is a friend' (IV, 64). These words have a sinister ring. Zemlyanika is the comic embodiment of the informer, a figure common enough in the Russia of Nicholas I. This is not just tale-bearing; for Zemlyanika himself suggests that he should set it all down on paper and thus make a more formal report.

It is characteristic that the most glaring example of corruption, but at the same time the most powerful figure of authority in the town, the mayor, is not included amongst those whom Zemlyanika denounces. It is the same instinct for cautious self-advancement which we see in act V, where, although he gives vent to his true feelings of annoyance and envy at the mayor's sudden apparent good fortune, he nevertheless, in an aside, assesses the possibility that the mayor might indeed become a general, and therefore seeks to exploit what benefit he can, with the plea: 'Don't forget us then Anton Antonovich'.

The theme of the town as a microcosm is further developed through Zemlyanika, when with his informer's caution he suggests the 'correct' way to bribe Khlestakov:

Listen, these matters are not done like this in a well-ordered state. Why have a whole squadron of us? We must present ourselves singly, and the thing done in private, as it should be, so that no ears can hear. That's how it's done in a well-ordered society. (IV, 58)

In Khlestakov's letter Zemlyanika is characterised as 'a pig in a skull-cap'. The reference to the Jewish head-dress *yermolka* (skull-cap) seems to indicate Khlestakov's opinion of him as a Judas. Zemlyanika tries to justify himself to the audience: 'It's not even witty, wherever is a pig to be found in a skull-cap?' The incongruity of this image, with its strong implications of an anti-Jewish jibe, is further deepened by the fact that Zemlyanika occupies the very 'Christian' post of Curator of the Charitable Institutions. The doctor there is certainly 'Christian', if only in name: Christian Ivanovich is a German who cannot speak a single word of Russian. Indeed he seems like a man with no language at all, only capable of emitting a sound 'partly like i and partly like e'. In this figure Gogol has reduced the un-Russian speech of the stock German character of earlier comedy (cf. Vralman in Denis Fonvizin's *Nedorosl'* (*The Minor*)) to its most grotesque minimum essentials.[15]

In act I we learn of the dirt and bad food in the hospital. There is even a suggestion that the patients die 'like flies'.[16] The treatment applied is a 'natural' one. Man, after all, is very straightforward, if he is going to die he will die, if he is going to live he will get better. Towards the end of act I Zemlyanika, having learned of the inspector's arrival, rushes back to the hospital, because the patients have been given gruel, and all the corridors reek of cabbage. Yet it is precisely here that Khlestakov, shortly afterwards, is taken for a good meal with plenty of wine – an incongruity, which, in itself, suggests a social comment.

The Superintendent of Schools, Luka Lukich Khlopov, is extremely shy, and easily embarrassed. He admits that his own education and upbringing have instilled in him undue veneration for authority. Nevertheless Zemlyanika denounces him for being worse than a Jacobin and for inculcating free-thinking into his pupils. The mayor levels a similar charge against one of the teachers, although his only fault is the habit of grimacing. The local Marshal of the Nobility happened to walk into a class as the teacher was pulling a face, so Khlopov himself received the reprimand: 'Why are free-thinking ideas being instilled into the young people?'

Yet another of Khlopov's teachers is accused of causing the town funds unnecessary expense, because he breaks chairs in his zeal for the teaching of history. In this obscurantist backwater of provincial Russia, education is regarded as a potential threat to the *status quo*. Luka Lukich complains of the vulnerability of his profession: 'God preserve anyone from serving in education! You're frightened of everything; everyone interferes, everybody wants to show that he too is an educated man' (IV, 15–16). In his letter, Khlestakov merely sees Luka Lukich as comic, saying that he reeks of onions (obviously punning on his Christian name and patronymic and their similarity to the word for onion – *luk*).

Open denunciation of the mayor, which Zemlyanika avoided, is left to the merchants; but when the tables are turned, and the mayor believes that Khlestakov is about to become his son-in-law, he reminds them of their own corrupt practices: 'Complain would you? And who helped you to cheat, when you built a bridge and put down the timber as twenty thousand, when there wasn't even a hundred roubles worth of it? I helped you, you goat's beard' (IV, 84). These portraits of the civil servants and the merchants add up to a striking condemnation of the corruption of the town. That other social class – the landed gentry, in its two representatives Bobchinsky and Dobchinsky, is merely depicted as stupid.

Bobchinsky and Dobchinsky are obvious comic characters with surnames which are differentiated by but one letter, and an identical Christian name and patronymic – Petr Ivanovich. In his remarks for the actors, Gogol stresses their similarity, and also singles out their common characteristic of inquisitiveness. It is because of their foolish nosiness that Khlestakov first becomes identified as the government inspector; indeed, Bobchinsky and Dobchinsky have an important role to play in the development of the plot as a whole.

As comic characters they are distinguished by three main features: a constant vying with one another (like a perpetual argument between Siamese twins); an inveterate nosiness; and a fussy obsequiousness. These three features are exploited verbally at their first appearance (act I, scene iii). They have what they think is important news to tell, yet because of these three comic characteristics, its communication takes far longer than necessary. The tale is held up because of their constant interruption of one another, and when Bobchinsky objects that Dobchinsky lacks the style to communicate such important news, and accordingly begins his own narration with 'style', what he intends as ingratiating politeness to the mayor turns out, in effect, to be the very reverse: 'As soon as I had the pleasure of leaving you, after you had deigned to get upset at the letter you had received' (IV, 18).

On the other hand, Dobchinsky objects that his *alter ego* will not remember all the details, and indeed between the two of them their account proves to have more detail than point. It seems constantly in danger of following irrelevant sidetracks created by their all-consuming curiosity.

The nosiness and obsequiousness of these two characters, who are constantly vying with one another is given visual expression. Thus Bobchinsky's inquisitiveness leads to his falling on to the stage through the door at which he has been listening (act II, scene x) and at the very point that his twinly rival is being entrusted with an important errand by the mayor. In act V, scene v their haste to congratulate Anna Andreyevna leads to their bumping their heads together.

The formula, 'laughter through tears', is nevertheless evident behind the portrayal of these two characters. Thus, according to Zemlyanika, not one of Dobchinsky's children is his own: they have been fathered by the judge Lyapkin-Tyapkin. Furthermore Dobchinsky himself tells Khlestakov that his eldest child was born out of wedlock, and does not bear his name; although (as if in refutation of Zemlyanika's slander) he explains: 'he was given birth by me just as completely as if in wedlock'.[17]

Dobchinsky petitions Khlestakov that he be allowed to legitimise his son, so that he may assume the name Dobchinsky.[18] Thus from the remarks of Zemlyanika and from the nature of his own request it would seem that Dobchinsky, the hereditary nobleman (*potomstvenny dvoryanin*) is doubly deceived in his *potomstvo*, his heirs.

There is no indication that Bobchinsky has any children at all, but the question of 'heirs' seems to obsess him too, though at a remove. In his absurd account of the discovery of the government inspector (act I, scene iii) he seems in danger of transferring his attention to the baby born to the innkeeper Vlas: 'Three weeks ago his wife had a baby, and it is such a very lively boy, he will keep an inn just like his father' (IV, 19). Again in wishing Marya Antonovna happiness (act V, scene v) he sees a son and heir, however grotesque his conception of it, as the greatest blessing: 'May God grant you every kind of wealth, money and a little son, such a small one, look, like this (he indicates with his hand), so that you could place it on the palm of your hand, yes. And the little boy would cry all the time: wa! wa! wa!' (IV, 86).

The shared personality of Bobchinsky and Dobchinsky may be a comic device, but their lack of individual heirs seems to point in another direction – to a pathetic dead end. Moreover, the denial of individual personality, implied in the comic double, has its serious side. Bobchinsky seems to suffer from the sense of a lack of identity. We see this as his instinctive reaction in act I, scene iv, when the mayor says: 'Well, Petr Ivanovich, let's go'; for there is no indication which of the two who bear this name he has in mind, but Bobchinsky immediately cries: 'Me too, me too, allow me to come as well, Anton Antonovich'. The mayor refuses his request, so he runs behind the coach, whilst his namesake rides in state, and at the interview which follows Dobchinsky is an actual participant, whereas Bobchinsky is reduced to the role of eavesdropper. The theme of a man deprived of his personality by the existence of an *alter ego* (later to be developed by Dostoevsky in *The Double*) takes on an almost tragic dimension, when Bobchinsky makes his request to Khlestakov:

BOBCHINSKY. I beg you most humbly, when you go to St Petersburg tell all the various important people there, senators and admirals, that, you know, Your Excellency, in such and such a town there lives Petr Ivanovich Bobchinsky. Just say: lives Petr Ivanovich Bobchinsky.

KHLESTAKOV. Very well.

BOBCHINSKY. Yes, and if you happen to see the monarch, then tell the tsar, that Your Imperial Majesty, in such and such a town there lives Petr Ivanovich Bobchinsky. (IV, 66–7)

The two requests to Khlestakov, on the part of Dobchinsky to allow his son and heir to bear his name, and on the part of Bobchinsky to corroborate his very existence, merely serve to emphasise the fragility of the identity each feels within the shared personality. The pair, though comic, are at the same time a serious expression of the theme of identity so central to the conception of the play and its plot.

In the portrayal of the female characters it is stupidity which here, as elsewhere, is stressed by Gogol. Anna Andreyevna and her daughter spend their time squabbling over such feminine preoccupations as fashions and male attention (i.e. Khlestakov). At the opening of act III they are still squabbling at the window, just as they had been at the end of act I. Emotion (much as it had confused her husband in act II) seems to interfere with Anna Andreyevna's perception of identity. She hotly disputes that the man she first sees through the window is Dobchinsky – until she realises her mistake, then scolds her daughter for daring to argue with her. Later both mother and daughter just as easily deceive themselves about the identity and intentions of Khlestakov. Indeed, the mother is so flattered by his offer of marriage that she even begins to waver in her attitude to her own status: 'But allow me to remark: I am in some way...I am married' (IV, 76).

In act V she has assumed yet another *persona*: the mother-in-law of an important man in St Petersburg. Correspondingly, she has a different view of her friends and acquaintances, whom she now insults as 'small fry' (*melyuzga*) and complains of the 'country air' of the town itself, when compared with St Petersburg. Thus in the weathervane shifts of Anna Andreyevna's views of herself and of others we have yet another facet of the central theme of 'identity'.

Marya Antonovna, who is told to take her example from her mother by Anna Andreyevna herself, is indeed merely her younger version. Her preoccupation with love owes something to literature and when Khlestakov's compliments become a little too explicit, she askes him to write some verses in her album instead. (She at least, unlike her mother, can identify the author of the novel *Yuriy Miloslavsky*.) In Gogol's treatment of the love theme there is an element of mockery at the cult of feelings. The sentimentalists' proposition that love knows no laws, no social boundaries, is used by Khlestakov to justify his amorous assault on a married woman: 'That is nothing. For love there are no distinctions, and Karamzin has said "the laws condemn". We will go off alone under the shade of streams' (IV, 76).

Female foolishness and envy are further reflected in the minor characters who appear in act V: the wives of Korobkin and Khlopov. But the women who represent the lower orders, the locksmith's wife and the NCO's wife, are both victims of the mayor's abuse of power. The NCO's wife has been flogged by mistake, and she is obviously on the mayor's mind. He recalls this incident with horror, when he learns how long the 'inspector' has been in town. Later he gives Khlestakov the unlikely explanation that she flogged herself. The locksmith's wife has a legitimate complaint about the mayor's abuse of the system of recruitment, but her cursing of him is so bizarre and violent that it alienates sympathy from her case and turns her into a comic character. The curse, like that placed on Petro in 'A Terrible Vengeance' and that of Pulkheriya Ivanovna in 'The Old World

Landowners', has a 'medieval' flavour: it recognises not the guilt of a mere individual, but that of a whole tribe, visiting the sins of the fathers on the children (and even aunts and uncles):

God send him every evil. May neither his children, nor he the rogue, nor his uncles nor his aunts, have any profit from anything...God strike him in this world and the next. May he, and if he has an aunt then may the aunt also, have everything vile, and his father, if he is alive, may he, the villain, drop dead, or choke eternally, the rogue!...The rogue. I am a weak person you scoundrel! May all your relatives never get to see the light of God and if there is a mother-in-law, then may the mother-in-law... (IV, 71–2)

As with Dobchinsky and his heirs, the individual is seen in the context of his line.

The psychological theme of 'identity' and the social theme of 'microcosm' both find formalised expression in the structure of ranks. The civil servants of the town are very conscious of *chin* (rank). From their individual interviews with Khlestakov we learn the rank of each one of them, and it is on this occasion that the supposed 'rank' of Khlestakov himself is uppermost in their minds. Thus Luka Lukich confesses that he becomes tongue-tied if he is addressed by someone who is only one grade above him in the hierarchy and his behaviour during the interview confirms this: 'I am timid, Your Hon...Gra...High...(aside) My accursed tongue has betrayed me, betrayed me' (IV, 62). Here Luka Lukich unwittingly begins to address Khlestakov by what in fact is the modest title (*Vashe blagorodiye*) fitting to his true status of collegiate registrator (the lowest grade in the hierarchy). He himself, as a titular counsellor, is five ranks above Khlestakov. However, he becomes confused and changes to an ecclesiastical title *Vashe preosvyashchenstvo* (Your grace), then to a princely one – *Vashe siyatel' stvo* (Your highness).

Dobchinsky, too, is prone to such fear, even though he has no connection with the civil service:

ANNA ANDREYEVNA. What have you got to fear? You're not in the service, after all.

DOBCHINSKY. Well I just am. When an important official speaks, you know, one does feel fear. (IV, 42)

Although we do not know the rank of the mayor,[19] he is addressed by a policeman in act V as 'Your high honour' (*Vashe vysheblagorodiye*) which suggests he must be between ranks six and eight. He could, therefore, be a collegiate assessor like Lyapkin Tyapkin (rank eight) – or even a grade above, a court counsellor.

The mayor is the most conscious of rank of all the civil servants in the town. At the beginning of act v he thinks gleefully of the promotion he might achieve in St Petersburg because of his son-in-law. He talks of 'wangling a big rank', and concludes he might become a general (i.e. at least rank four). At the end of the act, when his hopes are cruelly dashed, he appears to be incensed just as much at a possible insult to *chin* as at an attack on his person. As for many another Gogolian character, identity inheres in rank: 'As if that weren't enough you will be turned into a laughing stock. Some scribbler and penscraper will come along and put you into a comedy. That's what's insulting. He will not spare your rank or your title, and everyone will grin and clap their hands' (IV, 94).[20] In act I, we see that the level of bribery and corruption permissible is linked in the mind of the mayor to the degree of one's rank. He scolds one of his policemen for overstepping the bounds: 'What did you do to the merchant Chernyayev – um? He gave you almost one and a half metres of cloth for a tunic, and you grabbed the whole lot. Watch it! You are not taking according to your rank. Off you go' (IV, 22). A similar idea may be encountered in Kapnist's *Malicious Litigation* in Dobrov's advice to Pryamikov (act I, scene i) to preserve the dignity of ranks by the gradation of bribes.[21]

The absurd stories, which in act III Khlestakov tells about his life in St Petersburg, reduce the mayor to the sort of tongue-tied confusion more in keeping with Luka Lukich:

MAYOR (*approaching and shaking with all his body; he makes an effort to pronounce*). But yo- yo- yo . . . yo.

KHLESTAKOV (*in a rapid jerky voice*). What is it?

MAYOR. But yo- yo- yo . . . yo.

KHLESTAKOV (*in the same voice*). I can't make anything out, it's all nonsense.

MAYOR. Yo- yo- yo . . . urency, excellency. Do you not command that you should rest. (IV, 50–1)

By addressing Khlestakov as 'Your excellency' (or at least attempting to do so) the mayor must consider him to be a general of at least rank four or even three. But it is incredible that he is taken in quite in the way he is; for in the same act Khlestakov has already made a significant admission:

KHLESTAKOV . . . they even wanted to make me a collegiate assessor, but I thought; what's the point. Even the porter rushes after me on the staircase with a brush; 'Allow me, Ivan Aleksandrovich,' he says, 'I will clean your boots.' (*To the mayor.*) Why are you standing, gentlemen? Please sit down.

Together {
MAYOR. The rank is such, one can still stand.
ARTEMIY FILIPPOVICH. We will stand.
LUKA LUKICH. Pray do not trouble yourself about it! (IV, 48)

Unless the mayor is referring to his own rank (and the meaning is not absolutely clear) the rank which requires him to stand is that of collegiate assessor. Moreover, this is not Khlestakov's actual rank, but one, which, as the word 'even' suggests, might be conferred on him as an honour. The judge Lyapkin-Tyapkin is a collegiate assessor and the mayor, as we have already seen, must be of that rank, at least.[22] The veneration for Khlestakov's rank is patently absurd, and in the continuation of this scene, when Khlestakov insists that they sit, his words: 'No ranks. I pray you be seated' (*Bez chinov. Proshu sadit'sya*) seem like an echo of *The Visitor from the Capital.* In Kvitka's play the same phrase: 'no ranks' (*bez chinov*) is used by the false inspector (Pustolobov) to discourage the mayor's curiosity about his status.[23] He parries a direct question on the subject by saying: 'Please, no ranks with me' (*Pozhaluysta, so mnoy bez chinov*) then adds that if they wish to know: 'I have already attained that degree, higher than which people like me do not rise' – a fine phrase which leads his hearers to believe that they should address him as 'excellency' (i.e. through the play on words: *ne voskhodyat/prevoz-khoditel'stvo*).[24] What is significant in this comparison is that Kvitka seeks to make the deception credible, whereas Gogol, with the same devices at his disposal, chooses rather to parody and flout them, in order to make the deception as incredible as possible.

The civil servants feel called upon to stand again when Khlestakov boasts of counts and princes crowding his hallway: 'and at times the minister too...(*the mayor and the others timorously get up from their chairs*). Even on the packets they write "Your excellency" to me' (IV, 50). The *chinovniki* are easily impressed by all this, in spite of the word 'even', and in spite of the fact that Khlestakov has inadvertently revealed his true social position immediately before. Indeed his grand talk of princes and ministers is designed to cover up this chink of unflattering reality: 'When you run up the staircase to your own place on the third floor, and just say to the cook, "Here, you are, Mavrushka, my overcoat..." What nonsense I am talking I have even forgotten that I live on the *bel étage*' (IV, 49). Thus in reality Khlestakov lives on an unfashionable floor of a St Petersburg house, and has only a cook, who acts as a general servant.[25]

This scene ends with Khlestakov retiring, overcome with drink, and solicitously accompanied by the mayor, leaving Bobchinsky and Dobchinsky in the next scene to speculate about the 'inspector's' rank. What he has just heard induces Dobchinsky to alter his earlier opinion (expressed to Anna Andreyevna at the beginning of the act) that Khlestakov was not a general, but not a general's inferior in education and behaviour; now he thinks of him as a 'generalissimus'.

Strangely the mayor, for all his apparent concern for status, is remarkably incurious about the rank of the man he has accepted as a government inspector. In act III scene ix, filled with apprehension, he sees in Khlestakov the man he wishes to see – an important man of state; his wife, however, also sees in him the man *she* wishes to see – a captivating man of society:

ANNA ANDREYEVNA. But I felt absolutely no timidity at all: I simply saw in him an educated, society man of the top drawer, but as regards his ranks, they don't bother me. (IV, 52)

The mayor reproaches her for her lack of seriousness on such an important issue. Yet in the very next scene, when they both have an opportunity to cross-question Osip about his master, it is Anna Andreyevna, not her husband, who is concerned to find out the rank of Khlestakov:

ANNA ANDREYEVNA. And what rank does your master have?
OSIP. The usual sort of rank.
MAYOR. Oh! Good Lord, you go on all the time with your stupid questions! You don't allow anyone to say a word about real business. Well, now my friend, what is your master like? Is he strict? Does he like to give people a dressing down or not? (IV, 54)

Thus for the mayor, the establishment of Khlestakov's true status, the all important question of his rank, is after all not 'real business' (*delo*) what is more important is to find out how he will behave. This 'oversight' is all the more remarkable, since in the first rough draft of the play the question about Khlestakov's rank was actually asked by the mayor and not his wife;[26] there he had received the answer that it was 'no less than a colonel, if not yet greater'. In the final version Osip's parrying answer: 'The usual sort of rank' arouses neither curiosity nor suspicion in the mind of the mayor.

Earlier (act III scene iv) Osip had given a similar enigmatic reply to the mayor's servant Mishka, claiming his master was a general, 'only the other way round', but now in his interrogation by the mayor and his wife he refers to his master as 'Your high honour' (*Vashe vysokoblagorodiye*) implying that he is at least a collegiate assessor (rank eight) and could be as high as rank six (a collegiate counsellor): Osip, too, is seeking to impress.

Even more remarkable is the end of act IV, where Khlestakov, as a future son-in-law, is taking his leave of the mayor. Khlestakov is addressed correctly by Osip as 'Your honour' (*Vashe blagorodiye*) – implying that he cannot be above rank nine, yet, in spite of this the mayor persists in calling him 'Your excellency' (*Vashe prevoskhoditel'stvo*) implying that Khlestakov is at least rank three:

The voice of OSIP...Now get in, Your honour.
The voice of KHLESTAKOV. Goodbye, Anton Antonovich.
The voice of the MAYOR. Goodbye, Your excellency. (IV, 80)

Confusing, too, is the suggestion in act I scene V, that the person the mayor is expecting as the government inspector is of a low rank anyway; for in rehearsing his police force in the answers they should give, he expects them to address the inspector as 'Your honour' – (*Vashe blagorodiye*):

MAYOR...and if the visiting civil servant should ask you about your service, and whether you are happy, then you must say, 'We are happy with everything Your honour'. Anyone who is not happy, I'll give him afterwards such unhappiness... (IV, 23)

It may well be that the mayor wishes to preserve the incognito of an inspector, whom he might suspect will announce himself as of low rank, but certainly the townsfolk would not be impressed by somebody who was addressed as 'Your honour', even though he did come from St Petersburg. This much is evident from the way Gogol motivated the opening of Khlestakov's letter to Tryapichkin in earlier versions:

POSTMASTER...On the envelope is written 'To his honour Arkadiy Ivanovich Tryapichkin'. I confess this drove me on even more; if it were to some important person, then, I confess, perhaps I would have been scared, but as soon as I saw that it was to Your honour, I became so very curious, about what such an important person was writing to such a simple Your honour, that I simply couldn't hold myself back from unsealing it. (IV, 222)

It seems significant that Gogol removed this explanation from the final version, yet retained the other references which identified Khlestakov himself as a 'simple your honour'. Through such incongruities he throws into even starker relief the degree of self-deception in the mayor's attitude to Khlestakov.

The *chinovniki*, as this very name itself suggests, should know all about *chin* (rank). It is not, as it might be for the town's merchants, a hierarchy of prestige, which is not fully understood. Thus the complaint which the merchant Abdulin hands to Khlestakov is addressed: 'To his most honourable Highness Mr Finansov' (IV, 69). It elicits the response from Khlestakov: 'Devil knows what it is, there isn't even such a rank.' Apart from the misconception in the name 'Mr Finance', the style of address muddles middle-ranking civil service and princely titles (i.e. *Vysokoblagorodnomu svetlosti*).

In the minds of the merchants *chin* seems synonymous with the abuse of power, as can be seen from the use of the verb *chinit'* when complaining about the mayor: *takiye obidy chinit* (he executes such insults) (act IV, scene X).

For the mayor, on the other hand, the linguistic root *chin* has a completely different resonance: it is contained in the concept of *blagochiniye* ('decorum') by which he seeks to recommend himself to the authorities. 'But one can say that here there is no other thought than that of earning the respect of the authorities by decorum and watchfulness' (IV, 45).

Blagochiniye has a more ominous ring than its translation as 'decorum' would suggest: *Uprava blagochiniya* was a department of the police in the Russia of Nicholas I.[27] Thus in itself the word links two related concepts which recur throughout the play: *chin* (rank) and *poryadok* (order). The mayor's view of 'decorum' rests heavily on 'order': 'When in the town there is order in everything, the streets are swept, the prisoners are well looked after, there are few drunks...then what more do I want' (IV, 46).[28] Yet as we have already seen in act I all these instances of *poryadok* are duties for which the mayor has had no concern at all until the advent of the government inspector.

It is instructive to see how the representatives of law and order (the police) interpret *poryadok* themselves. Thus in spite of the mayor's boast that there are few drunks in the town, Prokhorov, a policeman, has himself got drunk, and in the very execution of *poryadok*:

'Yesterday a fight happened out of town, he went there for the sake of order, and returned drunk' (IV, 23).

The mayor feels that another policeman, Derzhimorda, must be restrained in his zeal for *poryadok*: 'For the sake of order he gives everybody black eyes, both the innocent and the guilty' (IV, 24). Those other bastions of 'order', the soldiers, seem rather the representatives of disarray, as the mayor points out at the end of the same scene: 'And do not let the soldiers out on to the streets without anything on. That worthless garrison will put only a tunic on over a shirt, and down below there's nothing at all' (IV, 24).

Soldiers play a large part in the mayor's own misrule. He not only has the power to billet them on merchants who go against his wishes (act IV scene X), but also the power of recruitment as a weapon in establishing his 'order'. The wife of the locksmith claims that her husband has been illegally conscripted because those who should have gone have bribed their way out. The mayor's justification, again, seems to be in the interests of 'order', at least as it is reported by the locksmith's wife: 'He, he says, is a thief, although he hasn't stolen anything now, all the same, he says, he will steal, and he would, therefore, in any case be conscripted next year' (IV, 72). At the beginning of act IV the judge, whose immediate reaction to the news of the inspector in act I had been to give it political and military significance, now seeks to save the *chinovniki* by resorting to the values of order and military discipline:

AMMOS FEDOROVICH (*arranges everybody in a semicircle*). For God's sake, gentlemen, get quickly into a circle, and a bit more order! Damn it. He visits the palace, and tells the State Council off. Arrange yourselves in military fashion. In military fashion, without fail! (IV, 57)

The association of Khlestakov's visits to the palace with the need for military order is revealing: not for nothing was the Russia of Nicholas I designated 'the barrack room regime'. It is ominous, too, that it is the judge with the whip in his courtroom who makes this connection between military values and *poryadok*.

There is a story, probably apocryphal, that the tsar's reaction to Gogol's play was that he had 'caught it' more than anybody. The play's constant use of *poryadok* as an ethical principle, linked as it is here to military values and to the palace, as well as the overriding sense of the town as a microcosm – all this seems to suggest that this story, whatever the facts, may have its own truth. Nevertheless the *poryadok* of the 'barrack room regime' was a sham, which the Crimean War was to reveal in all its inefficiency and corruption. This too is the reality of *poryadok* in Gogol's town: the soldiers are not properly clad; the police force is extortionate, drunk and brutal; legal procedure is a muddle, which even the judge cannot fathom – everywhere bribery, inefficiency and corruption flourish under the name of 'order'. Yet in this society everybody knows that *poryadok* is the only word necessary to earn official approval.

Thus the mayor, faced with Khlestakov's apparent failure to appreciate his suggestion about inspecting various institutions, jogs his understanding with the vital word *poryadok*:

MAYOR. Would you not like now to inspect one or two of the establishments in our town, such as the charitable ones and others?

KHLESTAKOV. Why do you say that?

MAYOR. Oh just, so you will have a look at how things go with us...what order there is. (IV, 37–8)

'Order' is a virtue which the mayor wishes to ascribe to each one of the town's institutions:

MAYOR. Also, if it is your wish, to go from there to the district school, to inspect the order with which we teach the sciences. (IV, 38)

It reigns supreme in the hospital. When Khlestakov comments on the small number of patients Zemlyanika replies:

About ten of them have remained, no more. All the others have got better. It has already been arranged like this, that is order. (IV, 45)

It has, indeed, been arranged like this, for the mayor had advised him in act I to reduce their number, in case a hospital full of patients was interpreted as a sign of medical incompetence. Zemlyanika's reply about the 'natural' method of cure employed in the hospital is now reinterpreted in act III in terms of *poryadok* for the benefit of the 'inspector':

No sooner does a patient come into the hospital, than straight away he is well, and not so much by medicine as by honesty and order. (IV, 45)[29]

Nevertheless for the merchants, who are outside the hierarchy of *chin*, but subject to the workings of *poryadok*, such 'order' has a different connotation, as they make plain in their complaints about the mayor:

I swear to God! It isn't as though we haven't tried to humour him at all, we always fulfil the requirements of order. We don't refuse what is expected of us for the dresses of his wife and his daughter. (IV, 70)

The servant, Osip, is quick to seize on the central issue of *poryadok*, when the mayor, for some reason, has avoided asking about *chin*:

MAYOR... Well, now my friend, what is your master like? Is he strict? Does he like to give people a dressing down or not?
OSIP. Yes he likes order. He must have everything as it should be. (IV, 54)

In fact, of course, Khlestakov is the least concerned about *poryadok* of anyone in the play. The only time he uses the word is obliquely and to express satisfaction with the drunken sleep he has had: *ya kazhetsya vskhryapnul poryadkom* ('I have had a pretty good snore') (IV, 59).

The women, too, whose interests, as always in Gogol, are different from those of the men, are not interested in *poryadok* as such, though Anna Andreyevna uses the adjective derived from it: *poryadochnyy* ('decent'). At the beginning of act V the mayor is still amazed at landing such an influential son-in-law, and his wife comments: 'It's a wonder to you because you're a simple fellow, you have never seen decent people' (IV, 81). To which her husband replies, not without a certain ambiguous justice; 'I myself ma'am, am a decent man' (i.e. 'man of order' *poryadochnyy chelovek*).

With the non civil servants, Bobchinsky and Dobchinsky, the word assumes a comic function, as they insist on retailing their encounter with Khlestakov with great consequentiality and detail:

BOBCHINSKY. Allow me, allow me, I will tell everything in order. (IV, 18)

It is the faithfulness of Bobchinsky and Dobchinsky to their own interpretation of the need for *poryadok*, which, through Gogolian irony, becomes the deceptive maze leading the *chinovniki* into their greatest confusion, and to the exposure of their own values of *poryadok*.

A secondary, but important, theme in the play is the conflict between the values of St Petersburg and those of the provinces; it is the central clash implied in Kvitka's play: *The Visitor from the Capital or Turmoil in a District Town*. The first real introduction of the theme is in the opening speech of act II, Osip's monologue, in which the differences between life in St Petersburg and the country are discussed from a servant's viewpoint. Khlestakov himself is very much a man of the capital. He says he cannot live without it; yet his father has summoned him home to the provinces and he speculates on the fine figure he would cut with provincial society, if he were to arrive in a coach of St Petersburg make. Despite this lack, he manages to succeed admirably, both with the two ladies of the house and with the mayor himself, precisely because of his St Petersburg clothes and manner. At least this is how he explains his success to Tryapichkin: 'When suddenly, by my St Petersburg physiognomy and suit, the whole town took me for a governor general' (IV, 90).

Life in St Petersburg, as described by Khlestakov, is pure fantasy. Yet the more extravagant the details, the more these poor provincials are impressed. In his own eyes Khlestakov is presenting himself, not so much as a man of power, as a man of society. He condescends to his hosts because he despises provincial life, and this air of condescension is an important element in his success. When the mayor and his wife think that they have caught him as a son-in-law, they too (more particularly Anna Andreyevna) begin to look down on local society, and think that a move to St Petersburg is inevitable. Even the country squire Bobchinsky, as we have seen, feels the need for his name to be known in St Petersburg. The play ends with the imminent intrusion of the real St Petersburg: the government inspector himself.

A more minor theme is the gulf between generations, Khlestakov and Marya Antonovna are the only young people in the play; all the other characters are elderly or middle-aged. Marya Antonovna is at odds with her mother, just as Khlestakov seems to be at odds with his father, and constantly to be quarrelling with his elderly servant Osip (even though he allows himself to be guided by him).

The mayor thinks he can deal more easily with the 'inspector', when he learns of his youth, but after Khlestakov's drunken ramblings he feels perplexed about the new sort of man in power. His bitterness when he learns the truth at the end of the play is directed as much against himself, as an old fool, as against such young whippersnappers who get the better of him. This comic antagonism between generations links the play with the cruder humour of *Evenings in a village near Dikanka.*

Nevertheless the central dramatic theme of *The Government Inspector* is identity. It seems utterly improbable that Khlestakov could ever be mistaken for an important civil servant by the hardbitten *chinovniki* of the town, yet rather than provide Khlestakov with plausibility for this role, Gogol appears to make the mistake as incongruous as possible.

At the first confrontation in the inn Khlestakov blurts out the truth about himself, but perversely the mayor regards these naive confessions as a clever evasion of truth. In Gogol's world naivety is often a mask for cleverness, and the mayor is caught in this trap; for in his naivety he thinks he is being clever in interpreting Khlestakov's foolishness as guile. Lying is second nature for the mayor; it is impossible for him to believe that anyone can tell the truth, as he says later about Khlestakov: 'Of course he lied a bit, but after all no speech is ever uttered without lying a bit' (IV, 52). For all his much vaunted astuteness, the mayor during this first encounter reveals himself as doubly naive; not only does he misinterpret what Khlestakov says, but he himself blurts out excuses which implicate him as a taker of bribes and conniver at police violence. Thus the two characters confront one another, each frankly revealing himself for what he is, but neither listening to what the other is actually saying. It seems as though the audience is witnessing, not so much the naivety of the characters, as the ineptitude of the playright. Yet, of course, such authorial simplicity is merely the vehicle for cleverness. Gogol in choosing to deal with mistaken identity in this superficially obvious way is in reality underscoring a psychological truth. Mistaken identity is not just a mistake, it is a conception of someone which differs from the facts, and in their first encounter each of the protagonists has a view of the other, which he seems compelled to have, and which persists in the face of contrary evidence. According to Belinsky this comes about through fear,[30] and Gogol's stage directions would seem to support him: '*The mayor having entered, stops. Both in fright look at one another for several minutes goggle-eyed*' (IV, 33). If the instruction 'for several minutes' is taken literally, it must result in a dumb sequence far longer than the final tableau scene itself, for which the directions merely read: '*The petrified group keeps the same position for almost one and a half minutes*' (IV, 95). In this alone the mayor's first encounter with the pseudo-inspector is marked out as a pendant, to the town's final confrontation with the real one. Both 'dumb shows' are an expression of fright, yet the fear of the mayor at his first encounter with Khlestakov does not lead him to proceed with timidity and act with caution – quite the reverse: he only too readily confesses his misdeeds. There is some other force behind the fear.

In Gogol's later interpretation of his play the government inspector is seen as representing conscience, whereas Khlestakov represents a false, pseudo-conscience which can be readily bribed. Although it is easy to reject this interpretation as a fanciful afterthought by an author who had undergone a radical change of heart, the view, nevertheless, recommends itself both on formal and on psychological grounds. At the confrontation in the inn, Khlestakov and the mayor are motivated principally by guilt: each believes that he sees retribution personified in the figure of the other. Guilt in Gogol is a persistent theme, and it is more than once developed through the device of an 'external phantom'. There is the ghostly figure of Nemesis in 'A Terrible Vengeance', and in 'Viy' external phantoms are an expression of inner guilt; moreover the petrified act of retribution in that story is a close analogy of the final dumb scene of *The Government Inspector*. In *Dead Souls* sudden doubts about the identity of Chichikov, the purchaser of 'dead souls', not only conjure forth all manner of phantom-like people, but also set the consciences of the *chinovniki* to work, so that they remember all their past misdeeds.

At this first meeting the mayor persists in his view of Khlestakov, because he has projected on to him a psychological role, which corresponds to an inner need and it is for the same reason that he takes so long to be convinced about Khlestakov's desire to marry his daughter in act IV scene XV – a scene which seems the very reverse of the encounter at the inn. But his willingness to believe in act II, and his unwillingness to do so in act IV both tend in the same direction: to preserve Khlestakov as an awful figure of retribution. It is because of this that the many incongruities which Gogol flaunts before his audience: the attitude of the mayor to Khlestakov's rank; the belief in his incredible stories, and the failure to comprehend his lapses of self-exposure – all these spring from an essential psychological truth: the mayor and the *chinovniki* need to believe in Khlestakov, because for them his 'reality' does not come from outside facts, but from something within themselves – conscience goaded by fear.[31]

The process of the inner world seizing on the phantom is given dramatic expression at the end of act I scene ii:

> MAYOR. I have that accursed incognito sitting in my head. You just expect that now the door will open and suddenly... (IV, 17)

The door at that moment does open and Bobchinsky and Dobchinsky rush in with news of the 'phantom' inspector: the incognito in the head has been dramatically identified in the world outside.

Here, as elsewhere in the play, Bobchinsky and Dobchinsky play a role of go-between linking the inner and outer reality. Thus Dobchinsky's account to Anna Andreyevna of the confrontation at the inn makes the mayor's mistake seem quite plausible. It is a view of events as they should have taken place, not as they did in reality:

At first he seemed to receive Anton Antonovich somewhat sternly, yes, he was angry and said that everything about the hotel was bad, and that he would not go to see him, and that he did not wish to be put in prison on his account, but then as soon as he had realised the innocence of Anton Antonovich, and got talking to him on more intimate terms, he immediately changed his ideas, and, God be praised, everything started to go well. (IV, 41–2)

Speculation on the actual rank of Khlestakov, in which inexplicably the mayor shows so little interest, is left to Bobchinsky and Dobchinsky, who assess him as at least a general if not a generalissimus (act III, scene vii). It is on them, as false interpreters, that the wrath of the assembled *chinovniki* is about to fall at the end of the play, just as the arrival of the true inspector is announced.

He is the one character, whom the play puts forward as, in any sense, positive, yet we never see him.[32] For the audience he is less substantial than the inspector wrought in the imagination of the townsfolk out of the improbable figure of Khlestakov. The play has no tangible, positive characters. Unlike the comedies of Denis Fonvizin, Grigoriy Kvitka, Vasily Kapnist, there is no *raisonneur* figure to point the moral, no active evidence of justice being done, and yet the play achieves its moral end, by the operation of a formula which is typically Gogolian: a minus cancels a minus to give a plus. Thus the negative character Khlestakov is the undoing of characters who are even more negative: the corrupt *chinovniki* of the town, much as in the play *The Gamblers* one set of card-sharpers gets the better of another professional cheat. Yet Khlestakov is more fool than rogue and, although he does appear to come off unscathed, he is too foolish to be allowed to enjoy his dubiously acquired gains for long. Perhaps he will meet the captain he is anxious to beat at Stoss (and if so, how does the captain himself gain his come-uppance?) or perhaps his father will teach him a final lesson, will, in the words of Osip 'lift up his shirt' and give him a drubbing (IV, 27).

All this speculation is, of course, vain. Most significant of all, the Khlestakov who leaves the town at the end of act IV with his 'flying' horses, is very like the Chichikov who leaves the town of N. at the end of part I of *Dead Souls*: there the horses become a symbol for Russia herself.

The Government Inspector: *comedy, construction, devices*

The Government Inspector is quintessentially the comedy of situation. Everything, including the traditional element of amorous intrigue, is ultimately reducible to the one denominator of 'mistaken identity'. In itself the central situation is doubly one of mistaken identity: the townspeople deceive themselves about Khlestakov, and he, in turn, misinterprets their hospitality. By pushing this theme to its extreme, Gogol is able to extract its full potential for bizarre comedy. Thus 'identity', the core of Gogol's comedy of situation, also lurks behind his presentation of the comedy of character. The comic treatment of character has long relied on the notion of 'identity': it is the discrepancy between the two faces of a Falstaff or of a Tartuffe which evokes the audience's laughter, and the same holds true for the characters of *The Government Inspector*, with one important difference: it is the mistaken view the townspeople have of Khlestakov which forces each one to reveal his own hidden face. In this sense Gogol's comic portrayal of character is an integral extension of the comedy of situation.

The mayor's ostensible identity is a rogue of great experience and cunning. Yet the advent of Khlestakov reveals him as a naive and easily duped fool, whereas, in his wife, it uncovers the duality of matriarch and coquette. The confrontation with Khlestakov shows us that Zemlyanika, the curator of the charitable institutions, is in reality the least charitable of men, and the judge with the reputation of a free-thinking liberal reacts by wishing to impress with military values, nor does the anti-authoritarianism attributed to the schools accord with the timidity of their superintendent before the 'authority' of Khlestakov. Duality of identity is presented at its most patently comic in the twin figures of Bobchinsky and Dobchinsky, yet, as we have seen, it is also portrayed here with pathos.

Given the sort of ambiguity which lurks behind each of these figures, it is surprising that often the initial impression is of the clear-cut lines of caricature. Gogol himself was most explicit in his directions to the actors, that they should above all not fall into a caricature of their parts,[33] and for all the bold and exaggerated features of the play's characters, they have a greater depth than is perhaps at first obvious. A case in point is Khlestakov himself. A superficial acquaintance with the play often leads to the view that Khlestakov is a conscious deceiver, indeed the producer Meyerhold strove to create this very effect. Nothing could be further from Gogol's intentions, and yet he himself implants this idea towards the end of the play, through the reminiscences of conscious knavery in Khlestakov's letter to Tryapichkin.

Khlestakov is a striking example of Gogol's ability to make something out of nothing: a somebody out of a nonentity. This, of course, is the very substance of the play; but the trivial endowed with importance lies at the very centre of Gogol's artistic universe, be it in his detailed descriptions, or his methods of characterisation. Shponka, Pirogov, Bashmachkin, Kovalev are all nonentities whom the author persuades us to take seriously. Khlestakov could be a typical hero from the St Petersburg collection of stories, yet, in a sense, he is more than this: his role in the play is the thematic embodiment of Gogol's own procedures of characterisation.

The impression of caricature may in part stem from the need to exploit the dramatic potential in situation rather than the detail of comic characterisation; an emphasis more vital for a play than for a novel. The first part of *Dead Souls* has a similar structure, in as much as a central nonentity (Chichikov) poses the question of identity, and ultimately of conscience, for the representatives of a provincial society; but more specifically, the sequence of interviews between Khlestakov and the local citizenry in act IV of *The Government Inspector* can be expanded in the novel into five chapters of successive confrontations between Chichikov and the local landowners. In the play the last ounce of comedy is wrung out of situation, whereas in the novel the lack of an overall need for dramatic concision allows Gogol to expand the comic possibilities of more detailed characterisation. Such detail is, in any case, less essential for a play; for characters can be given greater depth through performance by living actors. Nevertheless Gogol did not find this state of affairs satisfactory, as his many directions and exhortations to actors and interpreters volubly attest.

Another feature of Gogol's methods suggesting caricature is the boldness of his strokes which at times verges on the grotesque. This can be seen in the twin characters Bobchinsky and Dobchinsky and in the apparently obtuse desire of the mayor to be deceived by

Khlestakov. But there are odd moments when the grotesque seems to enter the play as a rococo grace note, as when Khlestakov suggests to Zemlyanika (act IV scene vi) that the day before he had been smaller in height, and receives the reply: 'Very probably.' A similar bizarre distortion of size conditions Bobchinsky's idea of a baby, which can be placed in the palm of the hand. Grotesque, too, is the moment of 'reality' at the end of the play, expressed in a tableau of petrified poses.

The play offers a wealth of bizarre and improbable detail, whether it be the product of Khlestakov's extravagant imagination: his banal conversation with Pushkin; the soup direct from Paris which arrives in St Petersburg still steaming; the water melon worth 700 roubles; the game of whist for five people (act III, scene vi) or the equally absurd suggestion by the mayor that the beating of the NCO's wife was carried out by herself.

Similar 'grace notes' are provided by a secondary cast of non-appearing characters. We are aware of such shadowy grotesques from the very opening scene when the mayor reads out his letter: 'My sister Anna Kirillovna has come to us along with her husband. Ivan Kirillovich has grown very fat and still plays the violin' (IV, 12). In the same act we learn of the policeman Prokhorov who has become drunk through the execution of his duties, and of the assessor in the local court who smells of vodka because his wet nurse bruised him as a child.

Such bizarre detail easily passes over into elements of genuine slapstick: Bobchinsky falling on to the stage in act II, and his clash of heads with Dobchinsky in act V, or the policemen colliding with one another in act III, scene v, as they rush to pick up a piece of paper (only shortly before, the mayor's own servant has thrown rubbish out of the door). At the end of act I, scene iii, the various town functionaries take their leave of the mayor and collide at the door with an entering policeman. A similar crush in a doorway takes place at the end of act IV, scene i. Indeed much of the visual comedy is connected with doors (through which rubbish is thrown, or characters fall, or where they collide and trample on one another).[34] Although such elements bring the play near to farce, they are nevertheless valid as a visual expression of the confusion inspired by the threatened visit of a government inspector. A case in point is the absurd behaviour of the mayor (act I, scene v) in putting the hatbox on his head instead of the hat itself. All this flurry of activity is evoked by the presence in the town of the false inspector, Khlestakov. Significantly, when faced with the real inspector, the reaction of the townsfolk is complete immobility.

The comedy is also verbal; characters reveal their essential ambiguity through words which betray their intentions. Thus when Zemlyanika tells Khlestakov that his patients 'recover like flies' (act III, scene v) he is really suggesting the way they die. The dubious nature of Khlestakov's chivalry is sensed from the start, at his being introduced to the mayor's wife, when, instead of claiming the pleasure 'in his own turn', he replies: 'How happy I am, madam, that I, in my own fashion, have the pleasure of seeing you' (IV, 47). Similarly, the bearer of false tidings, Bobchinsky, allows his 'style' in act I, scene iii to offer the mayor an insult in the guise of a compliment.

Another type of comic device unites the verbal with the visual, in a kind of formulaic comedy. We see it at its clearest in act IV, scene xii, in the repeated verbal advance and retreat, expressed in question and answer between Khlestakov and Marya Antonovna, which is accompanied by a corresponding movement of chairs:

KHLESTAKOV...It would be better for me, instead of this, to represent to you my love, which from your glance...(*moving up his chair*).

MARYA ANTONOVNA. Love! I don't understand love, I have never even known, what sort of love...(*moves away her chair*).

KHLESTAKOV (*moving up his chair*). Why are you moving your chair away? It would be better for us to sit near to one another.

MARYA ANTONOVNA (*moving away*). Why near? It's just as good further away.

KHLESTAKOV (*moving up*). Why further off? It's just as good near.

MARYA ANTONOVNA (*moving away*). What's the point?

KHLESTAKOV (*moves up*). Well, you see, it only seems to you as though it's near, but just you imagine that it's far away. How happy I should be, dear lady, if I could squeeze you in my embrace. (IV, 74–5)

Here the stylised nature of Khlestakov's advances not only aptly conveys the superficial nature of his feelings, but the whole pattern of the verbal interchange, accompanied by the movement of chairs, imparts a rhythm to the scene which underscores its humour as well as adding to the movement of the play itself.

A similar humour of formula is achieved in act V, scene viii through the public reading of Khlestakov's letter. As it passes from the postmaster to Zemlyanika and from Zemlyanika to Korobkin, its flow is broken by attempts to veto passages by those whom the letter defames.

The Government Inspector is a remarkably well-constructed play; it is almost classical in its concentration of space and time and its unity of action. It works like a well-oiled machine with everything in its place. The first act not only winds up the central spring with the letter and the wild surmises of Bobchinsky and Dobchinsky, but this same act also primes the release mechanism by which this spring will suddenly be uncoiled: the mayor's instructions to the postmaster to open up and read all letters. Thus the action of the play is initiated by a letter and concluded by a letter. When the arrival of the real government inspector is announced no further 'action' is possible; the characters await their fate like the motionless figures of a run-down clock, whose time has suddenly run out.[35]

Letters are important not merely for the first and final acts: no act passes without the writing or the reading of a missive. In act II the mayor writes a note to his wife on Khlestakov's bill; in act III this message is read and the mayor's wife in turn writes a note for the merchant Abdulin; whilst in act IV, Khlestakov writes his ill-starred letter to Tryapichkin. The mayor's note to his wife, read out in the third and middle act of the play, is important in a formal sense, as an uncoiling of comic bathos between the hammer blows of the opening and concluding letters. In itself it is indicative of that other element required to make the play work – foolish confusion: 'my condition was a very sorry one, but, hoping in God's mercy, for two salted gherkins on their own and a half portion of caviare twenty roubles five copecks' (IV, 42).

It is perhaps through the formal mechanism of the plot, which functions with such a sense of rightness, that Gogol manages to allay the incredulity his audience must feel about the many absurdities of the play itself. Here, as elsewhere in Gogol, form has a strange ascendancy over content.

The play is extremely tight. The opening words plunge us straight into the central issue: 'I have invited you here, gentlemen, in order to inform you of an extremely unpleasant piece of news. A government inspector is coming to visit us' (IV, 11). Not a word is wasted. Everything is clear: the reason for this gathering of middle-aged civil servants which the opening curtain discloses; the sense of foreboding connected with the word 'government inspector' (*revizor*), an unknown figure who, as yet, is merely identified with bad news; the sense of collective involvement, yet the authority within that group of the speaker himself. From these opening words the plot develops quite naturally without deviation or complicating subplot; each act is impelled forward by its own internal logic on the premiss of what has gone before.

In act I the fear engendered by the one word '*revizor*' is sufficient for the tale told by the gossipmongers Bobchinsky and Dobchinsky to be accepted. Through them this fear gains momentum so that, when in act II Khlestakov tells the truth, he is not believed, but he is believed in act III when he tells lies. In act IV he reaps full benefit from the situation, almost unconsciously, and leaves at the end of the act having set up the mayor for a great fall. In act V the mayor feels he has turned what might have been disaster into complete triumph, but the end of the act converts his exultation into even greater defeat. The play has come full circle: it returns the people of the town even more dramatically to the position they were in at the opening of the play. For them the three central acts in which Khlestakov appears, like some deceptively irridescent bubble, have merely been a costly aberration. The bubble has been inflated by the townsfolk themselves but it has floated away: it is not it, but they who collapse.

The penultimate act of a five-act play often marks the low point of audience receptivity. It is here that Gogol shows great artistic skill; of all the acts the fourth is the busiest. It develops Khlestakov's activity in the town in crescendo yet it begins on a quiet subdued note with the civil servants waiting in hushed apprehension for Khlestakov to wake from his slumbers. He then interviews them one after the other and accepts their bribes as 'loans', yet it is only at the end of this sequence that he appears to have some inkling of the true situation. He commits his experience to paper in a letter to Tryapichkin and, on the advice of Osip, orders horses to be prepared for his departure. A second sequence of interviews follows: first the merchants, from whom he takes both money and goods, then the two female petitioners. Towards the end of the act he makes amorous advances to both the mother and the daughter of the household, and gains the hand of the daughter; hence more money and presents to speed him on his way. He leaves in triumph in the final scene with the coachman shouting encouragement to his swift steeds. It is from two of Khlestakov's actions in act IV that the whole dénouement of the final act is developed: his proposal to Marya Antonovna and the letter he writes to Tryapichkin. The one creates an overweening confidence and sense of euphoria in the mayor and his wife throughout most of act v: the other deflates it most cruelly and dramatically.

For all the tightness of the plot[36] there is one tendency which seems to work in a contrary direction – Gogol's love of minor, episodic characters. They are many: policemen, servants, coachmen, merchants, female petitioners, townsfolk – characters who appear only in one act or even in one scene. Gogol is not economic in his use of *dramatis personae*, and it falls to his producer to be more so through the judicious doubling of parts.

Nevertheless the pace of the play is helped by the clever use of rhythm, climax and mood. Early in act I the mayor becomes more and more agitated at the very thought of the government inspector, and, as we have seen, a climax is turned to bathos by the dramatic entry not, as he fears, of the government inspector, but of Bobchinsky and Dobchinsky. The way their news is told, with one constantly interrupting the other, sets up a rhythm of frustration, a sense of long-winded urgency, which adds even more to the mayor's confusion. These same qualities of foolish urgency, frustration and confusion all come together at the end of the act in the words and behaviour of the mayor's wife. The curtain falls with her still shouting: 'Quicker, quicker, quicker, quicker!'

In act II the mayor's painful meeting with Khlestakov is given a certain comic rhythm by the constantly repeated appearance of Bobchinsky's face peering in at the door, until the climax is reached at the end of the act when he falls through on to the stage.

In act I the curtain falls with the mayor's wife and daughter standing at the window; act III opens with the stage directions: '*Anna Andreyevna and Marya Antonovna are standing at the window in the same positions.*' The continuity of the action is thus established. The act works up to its climax in scene vi, where Khlestakov, under the influence of drink, becomes more and more carried away with his fantastic boasting about the life he leads in St Petersburg, until he almost falls on the floor, but the act ends on a quiet note, with everybody walking about on tiptoe to the mayor's repeated admonition of 'shush'. This subdued note is in direct contrast to the confusion and shouting with which act I had ended, and the mood is carried on into act IV, where the stage directions for the first scene read: '*the whole scene takes place in hushed voices*'. This mood of anticlimax is necessary as a contrast for the crescendo of events which is to follow.

In act IV the rhythm of Khlestakov's successive interviews with the town's functionaries and worthies is given ever increasing pace through the treatment of the element common to them all: his request for money. The request begins almost by accident in his conversation with the judge; occurs to Khlestakov as an idea in his interview with the postmaster; and becomes firmly established with the advent of the superintendent of schools. By the time he has reached Zemlyanika, Khlestakov is almost *blasé*; he calls Zemlyanika back rudely to ask for the money, and the sum has now risen from 300 to 400 roubles. With Bobchinsky and Dobchinsky the amount requested becomes a thousand roubles (even more ridiculous in view of the fact that the pair are private citizens and have no need to bribe an inspector). With them Khlestakov's tone is even more rude and abrupt, as the stage directions make clear.

The later interviews with the merchant petitioners and the two women are an obvious pendant giving balance to the fourth act, but the interview with the locksmith's wife sets up its own comic rhythm through the repetition of her complicated formulaic curse. Towards the end of the act a parodying rhythm is established in the love scene with the chairs, which has a further echo in Khlestakov's advances to mother and daughter in turn (expressed visually through repeated kneeling, and verbally through the reiterated phrase: 'What a pass!' – *kakoy passazh*).

In act IV, scene XV, the mayor's unwillingness to believe his good luck is a pendant for his extreme readiness to be deceived throughout acts II and III. The scene is marked by a rhythm of obtuseness (cf. the mayor's repeated assertions 'I cannot believe it' – *ne mogu verit'*, varied at one point to 'I dare not believe' – *ne smeyu verit'*). Once this reluctance to accept what he is told has been overcome, the way is paved, in a stroke of irony, for his downfall in act V.

In scene ii of the final act the motif of undoing all that has gone before is inaugurated by the mayor's confrontation with the merchants: an obvious reverse echo of Khlestakov's interview with them in act IV, scene X.

Scenes iii to vi of act V are characterised by a pattern of 'congratulations', as each of the guests in turn comes up to compliment the newly betrothed daughter and her parents. Scene vii also provides a comic commentary on 'congratulations', when the mayor repeatedly sneezes (it is the Russian custom to wish the sneezer well). On the first occasion the stage directions read: '*the congratulations merge into a single roar*'. On the second occasion, however, we are told that some voices are more distinct than others. Some of these are far from wishing him well:

ARTEMIY FILIPPOVICH. May you get lost!
KOROBKIN'S WIFE. Devil take you!

The mayor for his part gives both well-wishers and critics their due:

I humbly thank you, and I wish you the same. (IV, 88)

Later in the act the reading of the letter provides its own rhythm, as well as providing a parallel to the letter received in act I. The final dumb scene is the halting of all movement, but its differentiated frozen postures may be taken as a kind of petrified rhythm. It is the visual accompaniment of the arrival of the real government inspector, and invites comparison with the departure of the false inspector at the end of act IV, which takes place unseen, off-stage and is entirely auditory.

In *The Government Inspector* Gogol shows himself a playwright with what, to some extent, is a modern outlook on the theatre: a desire to get beyond the physical confines of the stage. There is a constant feeling throughout the play that the boundary between on-stage and off-stage is in danger of being eroded. The effect is achieved in a variety of ways. Firstly, the audience is aware of a whole 'ghostly' cast of non-appearing characters, whose existence is not in doubt, yet who never set foot on stage. Secondly the three walls of the set are penetrated by doors and windows, which communicate directly with an off-stage world. Thirdly, this world's reality is further substantiated by innumerable off-stage sounds and conversations, and finally the putative 'fourth wall' is openly breached when actors address their remarks directly to, and at, the audience.

Act I (and the plot) begins with the reading of a letter from a certain Andrey Ivanovich Chmykhov, who never appears on stage. The act ends with Anna Andreyevna shouting instructions through the window to Avdotya, a servant (again mentioned in act III) whom we never see. At the beginning of act II we hear from Osip of the critical attitude of Khlestakov's father to his son, and later we learn much the same from Khlestakov himself, but this father is not a character who will unexpectedly enter the plot to exert his parental control as he might in an eighteenth-century comedy. Again, in scene ii we learn of the hostile and threatening behaviour of the innkeeper, but his only representative on stage is the waiter. Moreover, Bobchinsky's constant peeping round the door throughout much of this act reinforces the impression of off-stage characters threatening to irrupt on stage.

At the beginning of act III it is Dobchinsky who is now off-stage. Anna Andreyevna and Marya Antonovna, still looking out through their window, have an argument about his identity. In act IV the window is again used as a link between on-stage and off-stage; it is through a window (scene ix) that Osip receives a complaint from the merchants.

Act IV which, as we have seen, is the busiest act, is also remarkable for its extended use of off-stage conversations, sounds and characters. Act III had ended with Khlestakov asleep in another room (he can be heard coughing off-stage). Act IV begins with the sounds of Khlestakov (still off-stage) waking up. These sounds frighten the civil servants and they flee, leaving the stage to the now fully wakened Khlestakov. Then follows the sequence of their individual interviews, but these confrontations greatly concern the civil servants as a group, and their presence can be sensed just outside the door. Thus the entry of Khlopov is marked by the stage directions '*Behind him a voice can be heard almost audibly saying*: "What are you scared of?"' Words can also fly in the other direction; after the departure of Zemlyanika, Khlestakov opens the door and shouts for him to return.

Just as Khlestakov is sealing his letter to the non-appearing Tryapichkin, there are sounds behind the scenes of Derzhimorda restraining the merchants: 'Where are you off to, big beard? You have been told, the orders are not to let anybody in' (IV, 69). The off-stage noise, however, grows. Khlestakov speaks to the merchants through the window before letting them in. The same pattern is repeated with the two women petitioners. They are heard protesting to Derzhimorda off-stage, then Khlestakov speaks to them through the window, before allowing them in to see him.

The sense of a great wave of complaint and protest behind the door is communicated in scene xi by the numerous hands which thrust petitions through the window and by the remarks of both Khlestakov and Osip addressed back at them. Then the door itself opens to exhibit: 'some sort of figure in a frieze overcoat, unshaven, with a swollen lip and a bandage round his cheek. Behind him, in the distance, several others show themselves' (IV, 73). The precision of detail for such a minor figure may seem remarkable, but he is typical of the human oddities which flit in and out of all Gogol's writing. In the play, however, he and his like are not even allowed on stage: 'Osip shoves against the stomach of the first one with his hands and pushes out with him into the entrance hall, banging the door behind him' (IV, 73). Even more remarkable, the act ends on an empty stage. As Khlestakov prepares to leave, everybody exits, and the action is continued off-stage through the voices of Khlestakov, the mayor, the coach driver, Osip and the ladies. The curtain falls on the off-stage sound of carriage bells.

If this is a kind of dramatic limbo for Khlestakov before his final disappearance from the play, he is nevertheless just as influential in his new status as an off-stage character. The dénouement in act V is entirely dependent on two non-appearing figures: Khlestakov and the real government inspector. Khlestakov is still a presence on stage through his letter, and as a concept 'the government inspector' has never left the minds of the townsfolk. A double moment of truth bursts in from off-stage: in act V the blows are delivered from the 'wings'.

Act IV marks the culminating penetration of the three walls of the conventional set, but act V is remarkable for the growing tendency to break down the invisible 'fourth' wall separating the actors from the audience. The process begins in scene iv, when Lyulyukov congratulates, first Anna Andreyevna, then Marya Antonovna; in both cases the stage directions indicate that afterwards he turns to the audience, and clicks his tongue with a bold expression. A rhythm is thus established which will be developed fully in the climactic build up of scene viii; for as Khlestakov's criticisms of the civil servants are read out, each character in turn appeals to the audience with a comment or an attempt at self-justification. First the postmaster, then the curator of the charitable institutions, finally the superintendent of schools – each, one after the other, turns to the audience in protest. All this serves to prepare for the famous remark of the mayor which by tradition is directed at the audience: 'What are you laughing at? You are laughing at yourselves' (IV, 94). This comic device goes back at least as far as Molière (Harpagon in *L'Avare*),[37] but it is typical of Gogol that he should treat his audience as he treats the readers of his short stories; for the remark is not so much directed at them as against them. The impression is reinforced by the epigraph which Gogol later chose for his play: 'It's no good complaining at the mirror, if it's your mug that's awry.'

Despite the play's tendency to reach out beyond all four walls of the set, it is not really suited to 'theatre in the round'. Gogol's little world is bounded by walls, and although these are breached by doors and windows, which communicate with a world beyond, this must never be allowed to come on stage. Gogol's stage is a visible expression of that constantly recurring concept: the microcosm which hints at a larger world outside. The play's very title is that of an influential off-stage figure who never appears. A representative of the Russian State itself, he is the most important of the illusory characters hovering in the wings.

Gogol was not the first to make use of a *dramatis personae* of allusion; Aleksandr Griboyedov had done so before in *Woe from Wit*. The device was later brought to perfection by Chekhov in *Three Sisters*, and it is obvious that Chekhov must have learned a great deal from *The Government Inspector*.[38] Particularly Chekhovian is the use of sounds off, such as the carriage bells which end act IV.

Another noticeable feature of the play is mimicry. In act I scene vi Anna Andreyevna shows her impatience with her daughter by mocking her: '"I'll just fix a pin, just a headscarf", and, "Mummy, mummy, wait. I'll pin my headscarf at the back. I'll come immediately"' (IV, 24). As this mimicry takes place before Marya Antonovna herself has spoken on stage, the effect is a comic introduction, presenting the daughter in caricature, and conditioning the audience's reaction to her in advance.

The same device is used at the beginning of act II to introduce Khlestakov. Osip in his long opening monologue mimics his master before he has even appeared on stage: 'Heigh, Osip, off you go and look out a room, the best one, and order a meal too, the very best. I need the best of dinners' (IV, 26). There is almost a ventriloquial[39] suggestion in both cases, and Marya Antonovna and Khlestakov (the only young people in the play) are in fact more like recalcitrant dolls manipulated by their mocking guardians.

Once a character has appeared on stage further mimicry of him may add a new element of comic distortion. Thus in act III scene ii Dobchinsky's portrayal of Khlestakov to Anna Andreyevna casts him as far different from the flibbertigibbet young man of Osip's verbal parody:

A young, young man, about twenty three; but he speaks exactly like an old man: 'If you like', he says, 'I will go there and there...' (*waves his arms about*). So it's all marvellous. 'I', he says, 'I like both to read and write a bit, but I am hindered, because the room', he says, 'is a bit dark.' (IV, 42)

Through their respective dramatisations of Khlestakov's words both Osip and Dobchinsky reveal their different views of his character: the one inspired by familiarity, the other by fear. Between these two representations lies that wide gulf from which most of the play's comedy springs.

Anna Andreyevna, for her part, uses a similar dramatic rendering of Khlestakov's words to present him in yet another light: the romantic admirer (of herself rather than of her daughter):

He says: 'out of respect for your qualities alone, Anna Andreyevna, I'...

...'For me, do you believe me Anna Andreyevna? For me life is worth a mere copeck; I am saying this only because I respect your rare qualities.'...

...'I am astonished Anna Andreyevna...'

...'Anna Andreyevna, do not make me unhappy! Agree to respond to my feelings, otherwise I shall end my life by death.' (IV, 87)

Here Anna Andreyevna is reporting, not so much a real conversation, as one which her own imagination has dramatically heightened. The effect is close to her attempt in act III scene viii, to explain why Khlestakov might have been looking at her daughter instead of at her:

'But', he says to himself, 'let's just take a look at her!' (IV, 52)

Such filling out of mere hypothesis by dramatic 'substance' comes near to the central idea of the play itself. Thus in act I the government inspector already has a dramatised mimic existence in the mind and mouth of the mayor:

He will suddenly look in: 'So you are here, my dear fellows! and who', he will say, 'is the judge here?' 'Lyapkin Tyapkin.' 'Then let me have Lyapkin Tyapkin here! And who is the curator of the charitable institutions?' 'Zemlyanika' 'Then let me have Zemlyanika here!' (IV, 16)

It only needs the foolishly dramatised account in scene V of Bobchinsky's and Dobchinsky's encounter with Khlestakov for mimicry itself to be accepted as a genuine original.

Khlestakov's own use of mimicry reveals his true character. It is an essential element in the 'dramatisation' of his life, such as his unbridled imagination suggests it should be. Thus in act II scene V, Khlestakov, left alone, begins to imagine the impression he might make, if he were to visit some rural landowner. He mimics the household's surprise, the words of the footman who meets him, and his own words to the landowner's daughter. This is an anticipation of the extravagant self-dramatisation in act III scene vi when he describes his 'life' in St Petersburg with many snippets of mimic conversation, from the supposed words of Pushkin to his own exhortations to his cook. Here is a young man whose life is all mimicry and acting; it is full of absurdities and inconsistencies, yet such self-dramatisation can be believed by those who, through fear, have already dramatised his very existence.

The tendency towards self-parody can be seen in other characters who resort to mimicry and dramatisation. In act V scene vi the wife of Luka Lukich expresses her delight at Marya Antonovna's betrothal by reproducing a dialogue between her husband and herself. It is a dramatisation of the trivial and the banal which reveals the emptiness of her own character (in much the same way as the Pleasant Lady's report of her conversation with her maid in chapter 9 of *Dead Souls*).

A similar effect is created in act V scene viii when the postmaster gives dramatic expression to the conflict he felt within himself on the question whether or not he should open the letter of Khlestakov.

The mimic voice, of course, is a device which is comic in its own right. In act III scene xi the mayor mocks his subordinate Derzhimorda for shouting 'as though bellowing in a barrel' when everybody is trying to be as quiet as possible. Mimicry need not be auditory: in act I scene i the mayor apes the face pulled by the teacher of whose behaviour he is complaining; or if it is auditory it may have no verbal content: in act V scene v Bobchinsky mimics the cry of a baby with comic effect.

From the stage directions it is obvious that many non-verbal sounds are there to be exploited for comedy. There is the noise of stamping (by Derzhimorda in the quiet scene, act III scene xi; and by the mayor in anger, act V scene viii). There is the coughing of Khlestakov off-stage in act III scene x, and again in act IV scene viii. In act V scene vii the mayor sneezes twice, and in act II scene iii Khlestakov whistles on stage (a sound conjuring up the spectre of bad luck – in Russia one whistles up the devil). Moreover a distinguishing feature of Dobchinsky, so his comic double tells him, is a tooth which causes him to whistle as he speaks. Stuttering, too, produces a comic auditory effect. The mayor's: 'But yo-yo-yo. yo'

(*A va-va-va. va*) in act III scene vi, is repeated three times, and its effect is even more ludicrous than the confused stuttering of Luka Lukich (act IV scene v). Most bizarre of all, however, is the sound between 'i' and 'e' produced by Christian Ivanovich instead of speech (act I, scene i).

The sounds of conventional expletives also take on a comic function: the oft-repeated 'Sh!' (*Chsh*!) in act III, scenes ix, x, xi; the thrice repeated 'Wo!' (*Tpr'*) uttered off-stage by the coachman at the end of act IV (this together with the bells also helps to create the illusion of the waiting horse and carriage); the sounds of distress 'Ay! Ay!', which escape from the townsfolk as they stumble over one another at the end of act IV, scene i; Osip's expletive: 'Phoo, phoo, phoo', in act II, scene i, which seems to indicate a mixture of amusement and disapproval. Gogol's ear for such sounds looks forward to Chekhov's approach to the theatre; but auditory effects in Gogol are principally used for comedy, whereas in Chekhov, for the most part, they assume symbolic force.

Gogol's ear is correspondingly matched by his eye for comic visual detail. The civil servants express their awe and fear of Khlestakov by repeatedly standing (act II, scene viii and act III, scene vi) or visibly quaking, whereas Khlestakov for his part totters and nearly falls flat on the floor. All this imparts a certain stylisation to an already 'improbable' scene (act III, scene vi). Bobchinsky, of course, does fall at the end of act II, and from then on wears a plaster on his nose as a visible sign of his accident. In Gogol figures with bandages and plasters are always comic, moreover they seem connected with the theme of scandal (one may compare the figure with the swollen lip and bandaged cheek who appears in the doorway, act IV, scene xi, and similar figures in *Dead Souls* and the tale of the two Ivans).

At the end of act III, and again at the beginning of act IV, there is much play with the need to walk on tiptoe. At the same time the judge feels constrained to put his colleagues on what he calls 'a military footing' by arranging them in a semicircle. In the interviews which follow, objects or parts of the body are given a certain prominence to indicate the character's confusion (a visual emphasis typical of Gogol's procedures in his short stories). Thus, in act IV, scene iii, the stage directions make plain that the judge must thrust forward his fist (it has a bribe in it and when questioned by Khlestakov, the judge in his confusion will drop it on the floor). Here is a simple visual effect, which a skilful actor can make the most of.

The same is true of Luka Lukich's inept handling of the cigar given to him by Khlestakov (act IV, scene V). The play contains a great deal of stage 'business' of this nature: letters are written on stage (by Khlestakov, the mayor and his wife), Khlestakov eats on stage; he falls to his knees twice;[40] he moves his chair forward as Marya Antonovna moves her chair back.

Gogol attempts to make his play as visually comic and as visually interesting as possible. Indeed, the visual has a strange ascendancy in the play: the mayor does not fully listen to the St Petersburg fop whose appearance so confuses him; and in act IV he still does not trust his ears – it takes a kiss before his very eyes to convince him that Khlestakov has proposed to his daughter. Gogol himself at the end of the play trusts entirely to the visual: the curtain comes down on a dumb scene in which all the motion, all the mimicry, all the sound, have suddenly become frozen – the audience is left with the purely visual effect of the *tableau vivant*.

Marriage: a completely improbable event in two acts

'It's no good complaining at the mirror, if it's your mug that's awry.'
Epigraph to *The Government Inspector*

PODKOLESIN...I know these other mirrors. It shows you older by a full ten years, and your mug comes out awry.
Marriage, act I, scene X

Although conceived as early as 1833, *Marriage* was not published until 1841. It received its first performance in St Petersburg on 9 December 1842. The plot is simple: Podkolesin, a reluctant suitor, is almost bullied into marrying a merchant's daughter by his friend Kochkarev, who disposes of the professional matchmaker, Fekla, and a bevy of rival suitors, only to be thwarted at the end by Podkolesin's escape through a window.

It is a lighthearted play, which both in length and weight is less substantial than *The Government Inspector*, yet the comic pace is kept up throughout the two acts, and it is successful largely because of its fresh and vivid language. Gogol's ear for dialogue is at its most acute; it is above all through their speech that the characters are individualised and made comic.

It would, however, be unjust to dismiss *Marriage* as a mere farce. As with much of Gogol's writing the comedian's mask conceals a worried face; indeed the central comic theme is anxiety, that same irrational fear which Gogol had already turned to comic account in 'Ivan Fedorovich Shponka and his Aunty': the middle-aged bachelor's dread of marriage. Like Shponka, Podkolesin is being bullied into taking a wife by a forceful character, though not by an aunt who should have had jackboots and military moustaches, but by a blustering male friend. Unlike the earlier story the play is not named after its principal characters, and Gogol abandoned the titles of earlier versions which emphasised protagonists: *Suitors* (*Zhenikhi*) and *Provincial Suitors* (*Provintsial'nyye zhenikhi*) in favour of the institution itself. It is marriage – *zhenit'ba*: the taking on of a wife, which is the real subject of the play, and which Gogol presents through the symbols and devices that are the hallmark of his literary manner. Marriage is clothing; social status; an inventory of objects; its carnality is suggested through synecdoche; it is food; it is words.

Clothing and marriage are associated elsewhere in Gogol's writing. Ivan Shponka's nightmare identifies a wife with woollen material which the tailor rejects because of its quality, and the garment sewn by the tailor Petrovich in 'The Overcoat' almost assumes the status of a wife for its wearer. In *Marriage* Podkolesin's first two questions to his servant Stepan are: 'Has the matchmaker been?' and 'Did you go to the tailor?' Podkolesin wishes to know the state of readiness of his new tailcoat, but Stepan's reply that the tailor 'has already begun buttonholing' is confusing, and Podkolesin asks him to repeat it. The phrase *petli metat'* ('to work buttonholes') literally means 'to cast nooses': an ominous expression in the context of marriage. Indeed, Podkolesin is at once anxious to know whether the tailor associates the tailcoat with a forthcoming marriage; he feels that the quality of the cloth might arouse his suspicions.

The master calls his servant back a second time to ask about the polish he has bought for his boots. He wonders whether the shopkeeper entertained suspicions that such a purchase might mean a marriage (later in scene xi an uncleaned boot is seen by Kochkarev as a sign of Podkolesin's unorganised, bachelor status). Just as the tailor 'has begun casting nooses', so the bootmaker, he feels, could be creating corns. He summons Stepan back yet again for reassurance on this score.

Podkolesin cannot step into wedlock as easily as into his boots. In scene viii he says to that other symbolic figure, the matchmaker: 'But you think, no doubt, that marriage is just the same as: "Hey,

Stepan, give me my boots", you pull them on your feet, and off you go?' (v, 14). A similar link of footwear to a sexual theme occurs in 'The Overcoat', where a shoe (*bashmak*) is associated with the name of the bachelor hero, his aged landlady and a titillating picture. In the play Podkolesin is called 'an old, womanish shoe' (*staryy babiy bashmak*) by an angry Kochkarev, who despairs of his getting married.

Marriage is a threat to Podkolesin's very identity. An inner sense of insecurity is expressed through an obsession with outward appearance, particularly clothes, and the idea of marriage as a state which can be put on like a new tailcoat or a pair of boots is both reassuring and alarming in a psychological world of outer form. Podkolesin's insecurity, like that of Kovalev, drives him to look in mirrors. When Fekla tries to spur him into action, by claiming that his hair is already turning grey, Podkolesin rushes out to look at himself in a mirror. Kochkarev causes him to drop it and break it, but the arguments, which he then uses, as a matchmaker, present Podkolesin with more substantial images of himself: if he gets married he will be surrounded by children who will look exactly like him. At first Podkolesin objects to the 'otherness' of children, then suddenly sees them as forms of the self: 'Yes, it's amusing, all right, devil take it. Such a little dumpling, such a puppy, and already he looks like you' (v, 18).[41] At this point he agrees to go with Kochkarev to visit his proposed bride, but getting dressed before a full-length mirror he perceives that a sexual liaison has caused a blemish to his image: his collars are not properly ironed because the laundress has been spending time with her lover. Imperfections in clothing are thus a pretext for avoiding marriage itself – he is, once more, reluctant to go with Kochkarev.

The sartorial and the sexual are symbolically associated with the route to the proposed bride. Agafya Tikhonovna's house, according to Fekla, stands behind that of a seamstress who used to live with an over-secretary of the Senate. Fekla's directions even appear to warn against calling in there (*ty k shveye ne zakhodi*) (v, 16).

In act II clothes again delay the reluctant suitor. Although he arrives at Agafya Tikhonovna's house at the end of scene iv, he does not actually appear until scene xii, giving as his excuse the need to adjust a strap on his trouser-leg. Kochkarev thinks he can exploit this sartorial fastidiousness, and keep Podkolesin in the house right up to the wedding, by removing his hat, but Podkolesin's fear of marriage is such that he is prepared to jump out of a first-floor window, and even face the world without his hat. When Kochkarev and Fekla each trade insults about the suitors championed by the other, it is done principally in terms of clothing. Those of Fekla are: 'threadbare kaftans', 'a hole in each pocket'; whereas Podkolesin, ironically, is reduced to 'a hat worth a rouble' (act I, scene xvii).

For Agafya Tikhonovna, too, sexual shyness can also be translated into a sense of sartorial inadequacy. When the suitors are announced (act I, scene xiii) she suddenly feels that she has nothing on more than a shirt.

The rival suitor, Zhevakin, is Podkolesin's opposite; he seems full of confidence not only sartorially, but sexually. Indeed, of all the suitors, he is the only one to show a genuinely amorous interest in the opposite sex, even though his description of a Sicilian beauty seems to place its emphasis on what she wore. These two elements are presented to us at his first entry (act I, scene xvi) in his attitude to the maid Dunyasha. He asks her to brush him down, whilst he himself praises the durable quality of the cloth from which his coat is made; he compliments her, kisses her hand, then goes to admire himself in the mirror. Later he seems to ascribe his rejection by Agafya Tihkonovna to a failure of clothing, pleading that a black tailcoat would make his face look whiter.

Clothes and social status are closely associated in Gogol. Podkolesin is no exception even though he cannot formulate it precisely:

> I am of the opinion that a black tailcoat is somehow more solid. Coloured ones are more suitable for secretaries, titular counsellors and other such small fry. It's a bit callow. Those who are a bit higher in rank, ought to observe more, as it's called, that... now, I have forgotten the word. It's a good word, too, but I've forgotten it. Yes, sir, from whatever end you look at it, a court counsellor is no different from a colonel, only perhaps he has no epaulettes on his uniform. (V, 10)[42]

There is a parallel here with 'major' Kovalev in 'The Nose'. He, too, is contemplating marriage and is very conscious of his own status, which he links to a military rank. Like Kovalev, who seems to be fascinated by the status of staff officer, Podkolesin seeks military rank in a wife. He asks Fekla whether the proposed bride is of staff-officer status, claiming he needs to know, because he is, himself, a court counsellor.[43]

The theme of marriage for social status is treated both in 'The Nose' and in 'The Diary of a Madman'. Here its chief embodiment is Anuchkin, another suitor, whose social pretensions are fixed on a wife who can speak French, even though he himself cannot understand a word of the language. His sense of social insecurity is exposed in act I, scene xix, when he takes Kochkarev's championship of Podkolesin, as a man in charge of a civil service department, almost as a personal slight. Again the military theme is dominant: 'Why the prejudice? Why do you wish to show contempt for a man, who, of course, although he served in the infantry, knows how to value the manners of high society' (v, 33). The identification of social pretensions with a knowledge of French is a comic theme in Fonvizin's play *The Brigadier*; it is also mocked in *Dead Souls*. Anuchkin's unquestioning acceptance of the notion that the native language of Sicily is French puts his pretensions in their true perspective, as does his absurd demand for this aristocratic accomplishment in a merchant's daughter – all the more absurd, given that Agafya Tikhonovna, for her part, is also seeking 'to better herself'. She insists that all her suitors should be 'noble' and is pointedly rude to Starikov, the one suitor from her own class.

The relative merits of merchants and noblemen are heatedly contested in act I, scene xiii by Arina Panteleymonovna (the bride's aunt) and Fekla. After Podkolesin's strange behaviour at the end of the play, Arina Panteleymonovna thinks her opinions have been vindicated, and her final words condemn Podkolesin, not so much as an individual, as the representative of a class: 'I am a peasant woman, and I would not do that. And a nobleman to boot! It's obvious that your nobility is only good for foul deeds and roguery!' (v, 61).

In Gogol's fictional world objects have strange ascendancy; marriage itself has the status of 'thing' for Podkolesin. In act I, scene vii he is musing on the 'troublesome thing', as the matchmaker is shown in: 'Yes, it's a thing...a thing, not the sort of...a difficult thing' (v, 12). Such reification easily passes into a view of marriage as the mere acquisition of objects, so before Podkolesin thinks of asking Fekla to describe his prospective bride, he wants to know, yet again, all the details of her dowry.

The chief representative of this view of marriage is Yaichnitsa. He is reported as saying: 'Don't you talk to me about trifles, that the bride is like this, or like that. Tell me straight out, how much she brings in movables and immovables' (v, 22). On arriving at the house, Yaichnitsa's first concern is to examine the inventory of the dowry, to check it against what he can see for himself. At the first confrontation of prospective bride and suitors (act I, scene xix) Yaichnitsa comes straight to the point, but his phraseology is the language of reification: if she had to choose an 'object' (*predmet*) whom would she choose? Agafya Tikhonovna flees in confusion, and, typically, Yaichnitsa profits from her absence to look round the outside of the house and the yard.

When Kochkarev contrives to present Agafya Tikhonovna as suffering from congenital feeblemindedness, Yaichnitsa is not deterred 'provided the additional items are in good order', and it is only when Kochkarev manages to cast doubt on these, that he loses interest in the match. Zhevakin is the only suitor to persist. His apartment completely lacks furniture, and although the dowry may not be what it seems, he is prepared to settle for what he sees in the room.

The folk tradition of courtship and marriage was very ritualised. Not only were such figures as the matchmaker important, but the pretext for the visit of a matchmaker or a suitor was often given as the acquisition of goods.[44] Thus Yaichnitsa claims he has called to negotiate for timber, Zhevakin adduces a similar, though vaguer reason, whilst the merchant Starikov announces that he has come to buy wool. As he is not a favoured suitor he receives the rebuke: 'It is not a merchant's store here.'

A more physical attitude to marriage is expressed through parts of the body. 'To ask for the hand' of someone is an idiom common to both English and Russian (i.e. *trebovat' ruki*, act II, scene xii). The phrase is an example of Gogol's favourite device – the synecdoche, but he uses it in the play as more than a courtly euphemism.

Thus in act I, scene xi, Kochkarev leads Podkolesin on to the thought of marriage by conjuring up visions of the female 'hand':

KOCHKAREV ...and imagine, you are sitting on a sofa, and suddenly a nice little woman sits down close to you, a pretty one, and with her hand...

PODKOLESIN. What the devil, when you come to think about it, it's true, indeed what hands there are. You know, brother, just like milk.

KOCHKAREV. What are you on about! As though it was only hands that they have. They've got, brother, well what is there to say, they've got, brother, simply, the devil knows what they haven't got. (V, 17)

Later in act II, scene xix, when Podkolesin kisses Agafya Tikhonovna and takes her hand, it is this part of her anatomy which suddenly seems to banish his reluctance; he wishes to marry her straightaway.

Kochkarev also turns his attention to Agafya Tikhonovna, trying to persuade her to show off her 'parts' to greater effect:

So give your eyebrows a screw in some way, or lower your eyes and suddenly pierce him, the rogue; or present him, somehow or other with your shoulder, and let the scoundrel have a look. It's a pity, however, that you did not put on a dress with short sleeves, but, never mind, that's all right. (v, 50)

What are euphemistically referred to as her 'shoulders' must be one of Agafya Tikhonovna's most attractive features. In act II, scene ii, Yaichnitsa looks at them and says in an aside: 'Oh, she isn't the same as thin German women are. She has something' (v, 40).

Agafya Tikhonovna, on her own account, is interested in the various 'parts' of her suitors (act I, scene xiii). She asks about the hair of Zhevakin. Fekla assures her it is good. (When Zhevakin approaches the mirror, in act I, scene xvi, he slightly ruffles his hair; but later, in act II, scene X, he thinks that baldness might have counted against him.) When Agafy Tikhonovna asks about Zhevakin's nose, Fekla again reassures here: 'Ah, the nose, too, is a good one. Everything is in its place' (v, 23). The various charms of her suitors so confuse Agafya Tikhonovna that she feels a composite of their best parts might be the ideal: the lips of Anuchkin added to the nose of Podkolesin, and the corpulence of Yaichnitsa added to the free and easy manner of Zhevakin. Podkolesin's nose is seen as desirable for such a farrago, but her own nose is not thought to be her best feature. Yaichnitsa dismisses it as too big. On the other hand Kochkarev calls attention to it in his eulogy of her 'parts':

Just you have a good look at her eyes; they're devil knows what sort of eyes: they speak, they breathe. And her nose? I don't know what sort of nose it is! Her whiteness is alabaster! Yes, and not every kind of alabaster can compare with it. You have a good look yourself. (v, 36)

Noses in Gogol have their own prominence and assume their own metaphorical overtones. When Zhevakin leaves as a disappointed suitor, Kochkarev comments: 'Did you see what a long nose he went out with?' (v, 49).

We have already seen in 'The Old World Landowners' that food can have a metaphorical significance for marriage. This is implicit in Podkolesin's opening soliloquy, where he regrets that a period of the church calendar, when marriage is possible, has passed once more and he has taken no advantage of it. This period, between Christmas and Shrovetide, when the eating of meat is sanctioned, is known in Russian as *Myasoyed* (it might be translated literally as 'Meat-eat'). Thus from the very beginning food and marriage are obliquely linked:

Later (scene viii) Fekla presents to him the charms of Agafya Tikhonovna as some strange gastronomic concoction: 'Like refined sugar! Pale and full-complexioned, like blood and milk; such sweetness, that it's impossible to tell you, but you will be satisfied right up to here (*pointing to her throat*)' (v, 13).

When Fekla is asked to describe the suitors to Agafya Tikhonovna, she calls the lips of Anuchkin: 'raspberries, absolute raspberries', and then reveals that one of the suitors is actually called 'Omelette' (Yaichnitsa). This leads to a ridiculous misunderstanding as the suitors gather before their meeting with the prospective bride. Zhevakin (whose name hints at chewing – cf. *zhevat'*: to chew – and who has just referred to a Sicilian beauty as 'a tasty morsel') mistakes Yaichnitsa's introduction as a statement about omelettes. When the confrontation with the bride comes to nothing, and the suitors are invited to come again to take tea, Yaichnitsa sees the whole process as some minor gastronomic exercise, in which suitors are perpetually fobbed off with tea.

For the amateur matchmaker, Kochkarev, marriage is a major gastronomic exercise. Once he thinks his friend has 'bitten',[45] his first thought is of the wedding breakfast. He promises Podkolesin a feast after which 'you just won't be able to get up', and in act II, scene xii, he reveals that these arrangements are under way even before the proposal itself has taken place. In scene xvi Podkolesin talks of putting the wedding off for a month, but is told that if he is not prepared to get married for himself, he ought to get married for the sake of Kochkarev: the wedding breakfast is already ordered.

Kochkarev's words can achieve everything in the play except bring Podkolesin ultimately to say 'the word'. Yet words are something the reluctant suitor seeks from marriage. He easily falls for Kochkarev's lies about Agafya Tikhonovna's endearments:

PODKOLESIN (*with a self-satisfied smirk*). Yes, indeed. A woman, if she wants, what words won't she say. You wouldn't think of them in a hundred years: 'dear little mug', 'dear little cockroach', 'blackie'.

KOCHKAREV. What words are they! As soon as you get married, you will see what words will flow during the first two months. You will just simply melt, brother. (v, 49)

The abortive proposal scene (act II, scene xiv) shows Podkolesin struggling for words. He asks Agafya Tikhonovna, whether she likes boating (is this to be an invitation to an outing?). He says no one knows what the summer will be like, and Agafya Tikhonovna hopes it will be good (both are considering the prospects of the immediate future!). Podkolesin asks her what flowers she likes, and concludes that flowers suit ladies very much (flowers! A step nearer weddings?). Agafya Tikhonovna then asks him which church he went to last Sunday (churches! A further step towards weddings?). Both of them then set to work to calculate a date in the future with exaggerated concern (it is, unfortunately, only a public holiday). Podkolesin then surprises Agafya Tikhonovna by exclaiming how bold the Russian people are (Kochkarev's last words to him before leaving them alone had been 'more boldly, more boldly!') but all Podkolesin has in mind is the bravery of Russian workmen who apply stucco to the upper storeys of houses.

At this point our hero thinks it fitting to take his leave. The conversation has been apparently random and inconsequential, yet in its subtext an invitation to a pleasurable outing has been extended; flowers of the lady's choice have been offered; a church has been named and a date carefully calculated; Podkolesin has concluded by congratulating himself on his boldness. None of this, of course, has actually happened: it has not even been put into words.[46]

In this play the concept of marriage is reflected and refracted through many symbols typical of Gogol's writing; there is yet another – the carriage, which appears to have a negative force for the hero himself. His very name is derived from 'wheels' (i.e. *kolesa*) and an earlier version of the play links 'wheels' quite specifically to marriage. Thus in *Suitors* (*Zhenikhi*) Yaichnitsa says: 'A wife without a husband is just a cart without wheels; to drive without wheels, as you know, is impossible' (v, 251).

Nevertheless the particle *pod* (under) which prefixes the hero's name suggests misfortune:[47] that he is in some sense a 'man under a wheel', and a motif linking vehicles, marriage and misfortune can be traced throughout the play. Thus in act I scene xviii Agafya Tikhonovna tells Kochkarev that a supposed mutual acquaintance has been involved in some incident. Kochkarev's response is: 'What has she got married?', but it turns out that she has broken a leg, because her drunken coachman toppled her out of her droshky. Later Kochkarev himself seems consciously to be refurbishing these details in his curse on Podkolesin for his adamant refusal to get married: 'Off you go, off you go, and may you immediately break your leg. From my very heart I send you a wish that a drunken cabby will drive his shafts into you, right into your very throat!' (v, 54). When, at last, Kochkarev thinks he has got Podkolesin to commit himself, he seeks to dissociate marriage from the image of the cab: 'Marriage is such a matter...It is not the same as if you have taken a cab and gone off somewhere or other. It is duty. Just at the moment, however, I haven't the time, but later I will tell you what sort of duty it is' (v, 57). Yet Kochkarev has already invited the guests and ordered the carriage to take the bridegroom to church. Left on his own, Podkolesin suddenly feels the need to escape from this waiting carriage: 'In another minute I'll be at the ceremony. It will be impossible even to get away. The carriage is already there, and everything stands in readiness' (v, 59). He jumps through a window, hires a cab, and thus makes his exit like those other Gogolian heroes Khlestakov and Chichikov, riding off out of trouble. In so doing he neatly inverts the ominous symbolism of carriages, and underscores the words of Kochkarev himself that: 'marriage is not the same as hiring a cab and going off somewhere'.

Marriage could almost be the dramatisation of a short story. Its absurd theme suggests this, as well as its imagery, which manages to cover nearly the full range of Gogolian symbol found in the stories. Nevertheless it did not suffer the fate of *St Vladimir of the Third Grade*: it remains a play.

In construction and dramatic devices *Marriage* bears a distinct relationship to *The Government Inspector*. The symmetry which characterises the five-act play is here also in evidence. Indeed, because of its division into two acts, effects of balance are more obvious. Thus the behaviour of prospective bride and groom is contrasted in a patterned way. Towards the beginning of act I, Kochkarev bullies Podkolesin; towards the beginning of act II he bullies Agafya Tikhonovna. Near the end of act I Agafya Tikhonovna makes her escape from the suitors, while towards the end of act II it is Podkolesin who takes an even less ceremonious exit.

Although this may be formally satisfying (like the letter scenes which open and end *The Government Inspector*) the division into two acts is, nevertheless, contrived. Scene xii of act I involves a complete shift of location: from the house of Podkolesin to that of Agafya Tikhonovna. The act thus falls more naturally into two distinct halves. The sense of this scene's initiating a new act is further strengthened by the fact that both here and at the beginning of act II, Agafya Tikhonovna is engaged in a ritualised form of choice (cards in act I, scene xii and names on scraps of paper in act II, scene i). She is trying to determine her future husband, as she is already in love, but she does not know with whom!

Rhythm is just as important for comic effect as in *The Government Inspector*. The very opening of the play, with the repeated summoning and dismissing of Stepan establishes this from the outset. Act II, scene i has another such rhythm, though less protracted: the covering and uncovering of Agafya Tikhonovna's face with her hands to the accompaniment of a sharp cry. The second half of act I also has its own comic parallelism: at the end of scene xiii Agafya Tikhonovna and the ladies look through the keyhole at the first of the suitors; whilst in scene xvii Kochkarev and the suitors try to look through the keyhole at Agafya Tikhonovna herself.

Movements, too, are comic: in act I, scene vi Zhevakin acts out the scenes of his gallantry to the ladies of Sicily chiefly through gestures, and later in the same scene he explains that it is possible to communicate with foreigners entirely by signs. Innuendo may be served by gesture. In act I, scene xiv Yaichnitsa reads the inventory of the dowry, and when he comes to the item: 'four big feather beds and two small', the stage directions read '*purses his lips significantly*'.

The comic device of the double which Gogol exploits in Bobchinsky and Dobchinsky, is not given full dramatic expression in *Marriage*, but is endowed with verbal existence. Thus Zhevakin introduces himself to the ladies in act I, scene xviii:

> Lieutenant of the naval service, retired, Baltazar Baltazarov Zhevakin the second. We had yet another Zhevakin, but he retired before me: he was wounded, lady, below the knee, and the bullet passed through in such a strange way, that it did not touch the knee itself, it went along a tendon, sewed it up as though with a needle, so that whenever you were standing with him, it seemed all the time as if he wanted to give you a blow from behind with his knee. (V, 31)

Such absurd digression, typical of Dobchinsky and Bobchinsky themselves, is even more in evidence in the speeches of the garrulous matchmaker, Fekla.

The comic curse of the locksmith's wife in *The Government Inspector* has its counterpart in Kochkarev's cursing of Podkolesin (act II, scene xvi). Nevertheless, it is not as elaborate, and seems, rather, to look forward to the way Nozdrev will express himself in *Dead Souls* (a character with whom Kochkarev has much in common). There is a clear echo of *The Government Inspector* when

Kochkarev, in cursing himself, turns to the audience: 'Well, tell me please, I am now appealing to all of you. Well am I not a blockhead, am I not stupid? etc. etc.' (v, 54). The 'four walls' of the stage are penetrated, as in *The Government Inspector*, by devices such as this. Both Agafya Tikhonovna and Kochkarev look off-stage through keyholes. (Agafya Tikhonovna reports that what she sees is a very fat man; whereas Kochkarev, hoping to catch a glimpse of the prospective bride getting dressed, says he can see something white, but he is not sure whether it is a woman or a cushion.) In act II, scene ix Zhevakin pushes his head round the door to overhear Kochkarev denigrate him and not praise him, as he expects. In act II, scene xvi, Kochkarev opens a door and shouts 'fool' after Podkolesin who has just left the stage, whilst, in act II, scene xix, Podkolesin is pushed through a door, back on to the stage to make his proposal.

Yet it is the window which provides the most dramatic link between on-stage and off-stage. When Podkolesin makes his famous escape through a window in act II, scene xxi, his jump is followed by an off-stage conversation with a cab driver and by the sounds of a departing droshky strongly reminiscent of the off-stage departure of Khlestakov at the end of act IV in *The Government Inspector*.

Earlier his arrival in act II had also taken the form of an off-stage conversation, thus providing a parallelism which makes its own dramatic point about the character of Podkolesin; for the reluctant suitor is, in a metaphorical sense, an 'off-stage person': a hero escaping from the action. Even when he is 'on stage' he is always threatening to leave, and does in fact walk off.

In scope *Marriage* is obviously less broad than *The Government Inspector*. It is as though Gogol has taken the parody of a lovers' subplot in act IV of *The Government Inspector*, and inverted it: Podkolesin is the reverse of a hero ready to press his attentions on any woman to hand, nor is it he who is faced with choice, but the heroine. The parody of a proposal, with Khlestakov on his knees to both mother and daughter, is in itself parodied in *Marriage*. In act II, scene xvi, the man on his knees is Kochkarev, beseeching the suitor himself, 'out of love' to get married, and using extravagant endearments. In scene xx, they actually kiss.[48]

Nevertheless scene xvi, in spite of the wheedling endearments, shows a rapid change of mood. Kochkarev, annoyed at his inability to persuade Podkolesin, suddenly becomes angry and begins to curse him. Similar comic inversions can be seen in the soliloquies of both

Agafya Tikhonovna (act II, scene xviii) and Podkolesin (act II, scene xxi) when each is musing on marriage.

Gogol's play has had an influence on writers who came later. The comedy of the merchant milieu was taken up by A. N. Ostrovsky and developed in numerous plays. Moreover the whole situation of a lazy hero who likes to sit at home in his dressing-gown, smoking his pipe, and who has to be bullied by an enterprising and dominant friend, in order to go out into the world is the basic plot of Ivan Goncharov's novel *Oblomov*. In both works the friend brings the hero into contact with an eligible young woman, for whom the hero develops a wavering affection, yet cannot bring himself to marry. The opening of *Marriage* with its dialogue between master and servant, from which Podkolesin tries to elicit what curiosity there is among the lower orders about his forthcoming marriage, must have been in Goncharov's mind when he wrote part III, chapter IV of his novel. The relationship of master and boot-cleaning manservant has also something in common with Goncharov's earlier novel *A Usual Story*.

Podkolesin's non-declaration of love (act II, scene xiv) is a dramatised reworking of a similar incident in 'Ivan Fedorovich Shponka and his Aunty'. It seems to look forward to a similar scene between Koznyshev and Varenka in Tolstoy's *Anna Karenina*,[49] as well as to Lopakhin's failure to propose to Varya in Chekhov's play *The Cherry Orchard.* Indeed with its numerous embarrassed silences, punctuated by Podkolesin's fingers drumming on the table, the scene could almost have been written by Chekhov himself. Chekhovian, too, is the 'subtext' of a suggested proposal, which lurks behind this apparently random conversation. Nevertheless, in both Tolstoy and Chekhov, even though comic elements are present, the overriding mood, surrounding the failure to propose, is pathos.

The rest of Gogol's dramatic output is not impressive. There are the two play-like postscripts to *The Government Inspector*: 'Leaving the Theatre after the Performance of a New Comedy' and 'The Dénouement of *The Government Inspector*', neither of which is truly dramatic. They are tedious attempts to justify and explain his intentions, and reveal a neurotic urge to be author, critic and director of his own play (even its actors and its audience). It would, however, be unfair to dismiss all Gogol's theorising on this subject. His article

'A Forewarning for those who would like to play *The Government Inspector* as it should be played' shows a concern for dramatic realism and for the methods by which this might be achieved, which is not only well in advance of his time, but even looks forward to the theory and practice of Stanislavsky.

The one-act comedy *The Gamblers* is interesting principally in that it is constructed on a typically Gogolian double negative: a card-sharper is himself deceived by a band of card-sharps. A second Gogolian feature is that an inanimate object, a specially prepared pack of cards, is given the name of a woman (Adelaida Ivanovna). There is an unfinished play on Alfred the Great, and fragments connected with the projected play *St Vladimir of the Third Grade*. Several other disparate fragments have survived. Gogol's reputation as a playwright rests securely on his masterpiece *The Government Inspector* and only to a lesser extent on *Marriage*.

4

The Carriage and *Rome*

The Carriage (Calash)

CLOWN. What is the opinion of Pythagoras concerning wild-fowl?
MALVOLIO. That the soul of our grandam might haply inhabit a bird.
CLOWN. What thinkest thou of his opinion?
MALVOLIO. I think nobly of the soul, and no way approve of his opinion.
Twelfth Night, act IV, scene ii

What is man
If his chief good and market of his time
Be but to sleep and feed? a beast no more.
Hamlet, act IV, scene iv

The Carriage (*Kolyaska*), written in 1835, appears at first sight to be a story on its own. It is Gogol's only short story about provincial Russia (as opposed to the provincial Ukraine) and was written at a time when he appeared to have turned his attention to St Petersburg as the theme for his short stories. Yet the isolation of this story is deceptive; the provincial Russian town forms the setting both for his play *The Government Inspector*, which dates from the same time, as well as for his later novel, *Dead Souls*. Moreover, in a sense, we have already been here before: the Ukrainian town of Mirgorod, depicted in the tale of the two Ivans, has many features in common with 'the little town of B.' The town might even be Ukrainian; it is at least 'southern' ('the roofs for the most part were covered by reeds, as is usually the case in our southern towns').

Nevertheless it is consonant with the St Petersburg setting of Gogol's other stories of this period that the anecdote on which *The Carriage* is reputedly based, should belong not only to the capital, but to the highest echelons of St Petersburg society. Count M. Yu. Vielgorsky (one of Gogol's influential friends and patrons) was well known for his absent-mindedness, and on one occasion he invited the diplomatic dignitaries of St Petersburg to a banquet at his house, but promptly forgot about it. When the foreign diplomats arrived in full dress, wearing all their decorations, they found neither host nor meal.[1] It is significant that Gogol has transferred the basic material of this anecdote from the highest reaches of St Petersburg society to the lowly level of the Russian provincial backwater, an area in which his talent as a writer was more at home. Significantly, too, the absent-minded count has been replaced by a typically Gogolian figure: a nonentity with social pretensions, whose empty boasting and weakness of character lead to his final disgrace in the dénouement.

Pifagor Pifagorovich Chertokutsky is the only person in the story to bear a name; every other figure is designated by rank, class, social function or relationship. Reticence about names is apparent from the opening sentence: 'The little town of B. brightened up a lot when the *** cavalry regiment began to be stationed there' (III, 177). Such authorial caution was the practice of the age, yet it does set an immediate tone of anonymity which will largely be maintained throughout the story. Strangely enough, there is another name apart from that of the hero. It is given not to a human being but to a horse, and this animal, Agrafena Ivanovna, is even described as: 'strong and wild like a southern beauty'.

Before the arrival of the regiment the town had seemed to be populated principally by animals:

> You wouldn't meet a soul on the streets, except for the occasional cockerel crossing the roadway, which was as soft as a pillow from the inches of dust lying on it, and at the slightest rain it would turn to mud, and then the streets of the little town of B. would be filled with those corpulent animals which the local mayor calls Frenchmen. Shoving their serious snouts out of their bath, they would set up such a squealing that there was nothing for it for anyone driving through but to urge on his horses as fast as possible. Though, in the town of B., it would be difficult to find anyone driving through. (III, 177)

There is irony in the mayor's equation of Frenchmen and pigs, but the irony is turned back to him, when we learn of his own animal existence: 'An intelligent man, but who slept the whole day – from lunch until evening and from evening until lunch' (III, 179).

Here then is a town, where horses are given human names, where pigs are called Frenchmen by the town's chief dignitary who himself lives as 'a beast no more', and where before the advent of the cavalry not a 'soul' was to be seen, except perhaps a cockerel. Given such an ironic 'transmigration of souls', it is even more piquant that the central character should be called Pythagoras son of Pythagoras (Pifagor Pifagorovich) and that his surname, Chertokutsky (i.e. 'dock-tailed devil') should contain a further hint of the 'animal' and the 'supernatural'.[2]

Chertokutsky's sense of his own worth is based on an erstwhile military association with the horse; he is an ex-cavalry man, and to prove it he still wears spurs; sports cavalry moustaches; and refers slightingly to the infantry as '*pekhtura*' and '*pekhontariya*'. Unfortunately, some obscure incident in the regiment has caused him to retire and he is now a landowner living on his estate. Towards the end of the story, the somnolent affection he offers his wife is described in farmyard imagery as a calf reaching for its mother's udder.

Despite the predominance of animals in the story, the title gives sole prominence to an inanimate object: a carriage; and in this town it is often difficult to distinguish human beings from things: 'In the middle of the square are the smallest of little shops. In them one could always observe a string of bread rings, a peasant woman in a red head-scarf, a pood of soap, several pounds of bitter almonds, shot for shooting, cheap cotton cloth, and two shop assistants playing quoits near the doors at all times' (III, 178). Through the Gogolian process of synecdoche the newly arrived soldiers, in their turn, become reduced to their cavalry moustaches: 'These moustaches could be seen in all places. If townswomen gathered at the market with their pails, then, without doubt, moustaches would be peeping out from behind their backs' (III, 178). The local squires, whose heads up to then 'have been flustered with the sowing of crops, their wives' errands and hares' are represented at the general's banquet by one of their number who not only 'thinks' crops, but is physically crop-like himself: 'One extremely stout landowner with short arms, rather like two sprouting potatoes, listened with an unusually sweet expression on his face, and only from time to time attempted to get his short little arm behind his broad back, in order to drag out his snuff box' (III, 184).

The moral and spiritual sloth of local society seems to be epitomised, not only in the mayor who sleeps all day, but also in the judge who is living with the wife of a church deacon. This society, we are told, is 'animated' by the newly arrived officers (*ofitsery ozhivili obshchestvo*), yet their values are scarcely more impressive. As cavalry men their prestige is founded on the horse, and the general's one comment on the town is to curse it for its lack of good stables.

As he causes Agrafena Ivanovna to be paraded before his admiring guests, his pompous self-satisfaction is conveyed not only in his words, but through the repeated 'puff, puff' of his pipe, which interrupts their flow, and whose results even engulf him physically, as when he tells Chertokutsky where the horse was broken in: '– Puff, puff, pu... pu... pu... u... u... ff, here – Having said this the general disappeared entirely in smoke' (III, 181).

It is admiration of the horse which marks the beginning of Chertokutsky's downfall. Anxious to impress, he asks the general various would-be intelligent and interested questions: has he had the horse long? Where did he break her in? He inspects her from her rear and asks how she moves. Then he makes his first stupid mistake, which glaringly reveals what he knows about horses: 'She is very fine, but have you, your excellency, a carriage to match?' The general is obviously amazed: 'A carriage?...But it's a riding horse' (III, 182). Chertokutsky saves the situation by claiming he meant a carriage to match his other horses, and the general replies that he has considered getting one of these 'modern calashes'. It then turns out that Chertokutsky himself has a calash of which he can be proud, but the general again expresses surprise: 'What, the one in which you arrived?' (III, 182). Chertokutsky assures him he means another, which he has left at home (though it is not explained why a man as vain as Chertokutsky should come in his second-best carriage to a banquet, at which he wishes to impress).

The excellence of Chertokutsky's calash has all the marks of a hastily improvised and face-saving boast – an impression further strengthened by his explanation of its acquisition. First he tells the general that he paid the impressive sum of four thousand roubles for it (we have already learned that he received several thousand roubles as dowry from his wife, but that this has been spent on 'six really fine horses, gilded locks for the doors, a tame monkey for the house and a French butler'). Next, however, he says that he acquired the calash at second hand, having won it at cards from his best friend.

There is something inherently incongruous about Chertokutsky's attempt to impress the general by the excellence of a carriage, particularly as he appears to be vying, in some sense, with the general's horse. To real cavalry men carriages are of secondary importance, as can be seen from their attitude to the droshky, which is called 'regimental' because ownership passes so easily from one member of the regiment to another. It is a permanent stake at cards, and as such invites comparison with Chertokutsky's own calash which he also claims to have won at cards. He incautiously invites the general to lunch the following day to inspect the calash, but it is made clear to him that the general cannot go alone, so, perforce, he extends the invitation to all the officers.

Chertokutsky is a typical Gogolian nonentity, a man motivated by the immediacy of the moment, with little thought either for past or future. He is about to leave to make arrangements for the meal, when the appearance of card tables lures him to stay. He drinks punch, because he finds a glass before him, and its effect leads him to assert himself as a cavalry man once more. He constantly interrupts a conversation on drill, and asks questions which have no relevance to the discussion.

Supper then follows. Once again Chertokutsky is the prisoner of the moment: 'It goes without saying that there was no lack of wines, and that Chertokutsky almost involuntarily had to fill his glass, because there stood a bottle on the right as well as on the left of him' (III, 185). The evening is very lively and pleasant, but such animation produces inanimate guests: 'The coachmen had to take several personages into their arms, as though bundles of purchases' (III, 185). Even Chertokutsky, 'despite all his aristocratic ways', ends up with a burr sticking to that very symbol of cavalry glory – his moustaches.

After midday on the following day he is still in bed, blissfully unaware that he has invited the officers of the regiment to lunch, but has failed to make provision for them. When his wife wakes him to announce the officers' approach, his first thought is to hide, but rather than stay safely in bed, he chooses the strange hiding-place of his own calash.

The general, annoyed that he and his officers have come out to no purpose, feels that he might as well see the carriage which has been so praised. The groom wheels it out (there is no indication that there might be a second one in the shed) and, needless to say, the general and his officers are far from impressed. The general concludes that it is not worth two thousand roubles, let alone four. Then, unfastening the calash to see if there is anything more impressive inside, the officers discover the crouched up figure of the owner himself. The calash, as the last refuge for Chertokutsky's social inadequacy before the real gentlemen of the cavalry, has thus been glaringly, and symbolically revealed for what it is.

Like the 'philosopher' Khoma Brut, Pythagoras son of Pythagoras is the least thinking of heroes, and this is part of Gogol's joke. Yet, in an odd way, he does represent a 'transmigration' of human values; for just as in another story the personal life of Akakiy Akakiyevich becomes identified with a coat, so here the self-esteem of Pifagor Pifagorovich is enshrined in a carriage. When this 'vehicle' of his bogus pretensions is shown up for what it is, it is more than fitting that Chertokutsky should be discovered skulking inside.[3]

Rome

Rome is really only a fragment (though a long one) from a projected novel *Annunziata*. It was published in 1842 in Pogodin's *Moskvityanin* (*The Muscovite*) and earned the censure of Belinsky, both for its anti-French sentiments and for its language, which reminded the critic of the stilted prose of Marlinsky.[4] Its central theme is the spiritual development of a young Italian prince, his early education, his experiences in Paris and finally his return to his native land with rekindled love and admiration for its beauty and its glorious past.

The prince's thoughts obviously reflect Gogol's own attitude to Rome and to Italian culture. The role of the visual arts: painting, sculpture, architecture looms large as it did for Gogol during his stay in Rome. Nevertheless behind the prince's response to Italy can be sensed something of the author's own attitude to his native land (the Ukraine). In a strangely Russian way Italy is opposed to Europe; its people have not been contaminated by European enlightenment; Italy is not free, and the prince cherishes vague (but apparently non-political) dreams of re-establishing his country's former glory; like Gogol himself, the prince's stay abroad has allowed him to see his native land with greater clarity.

Belinsky pointed to the untypicality of Gogol's style in *Rome*, and the writing is certainly ornate and heavy, but the matter goes deeper than this. Elements of the grotesque so abundant in Gogol's other tales, are here reduced to a minimum and, when they do occur, are employed with a restrained skill which results in some of the livelier passages in the story (e.g. the description of Peppe and the Roman street scenes). In many respects this fragment suggests a new departure both in subject matter and in treatment. The external method of characterisation has been replaced by a more conventional psychological method – as though the Western theme has dictated a more 'Western' form.

In replying to Belinsky Gogol defended the idea of his work, claiming that he intended to contrast living nations with a nation that had had its day, but one that had declined with beauty.[5] Death and art are thus once more associated, as they are in their different ways in 'Nevsky Prospekt' and 'The Portrait', and there are passage and ideas which link *Rome* to both these works.

Admittedly the description of the heroine's beauty is not entirely convincing, and the fragment is far too wordy, but what is striking is the tenacity with which Gogol pursues the thoughts, feelings and inner experiences of his central hero. Had he been able to finish *Annunziata* and perfect this new psychological technique, we might yet have seen another facet of his many-sided talent: Gogol the conventional novelist. This, however, is a problem which relates directly to his work on part II of *Dead Souls*.

5
Dead Souls

The gallery of portraits

In the so-called 'Author's Confession' Gogol records that he read a short scene from his works to Pushkin and that the poet, deeply affected, said to him: 'With this ability to understand a human being and to present him in entirety in a few strokes as a living man, with such a gift, how can you refuse to start on a great work. It is a sin' (VIII, 439). According to this story Pushkin then gave Gogol the theme for *Dead Souls*, which, he said, he would have given to no one else.

The 'Author's Confession' is a document of self-justification and its veracity is often in doubt. Nevertheless, the assertion of Gogol's ability to project a character in a few strokes reveals much about his methods in *Dead Souls*. The landowners as they are presented in chapters 2 to 6 of part I form a 'gallery of portraits', depicted by the half-dozen strokes of a master. In almost formulaic manner the character of each is revealed by:

(1) Physical appearance.
(2) Style of speech.
(3) Ambience (house, estate, etc.).
(4) Family relationships.
(5) Hospitality (especially food).
(6) Reaction to Chichikov's strange proposition.

From these six lines are formed the contours of each individual landowner, though the emphasis on each stroke varies from portrait to portrait. We are introduced to Manilov, Nozdrev and Sobakevich in chapter I, but the 'gallery' proper begins in chapter 2, and subsequent appearances merely confirm the lines of portraiture exhibited there.

The first portrait in the gallery is Manilov. He is the embodiment of insubstantial, yet exalted, 'niceness' (*prekrasnodushiye*) yet his very pleasantness is somehow a deficiency: it is 'neither one thing nor the other'.

In accordance with Gogol's procedures, Manilov's physical attributes betray the inner man: his essential insipidity – through his colouring, blond hair and light blue eyes; his excessive sweetness – by his features which, although not lacking in charm, are really too sugary. His smile is 'engaging', and yet this word (*zamanchivo*) suggests 'alluring', 'enticing', and seems to echo his very name. It even appears to correspond to some confusion in Chichikov's own mind; for when trying to reach Manilov's estate he asks for Zamanilovka instead of Manilovka: there is something not quite right about such alluring charm.[1]

His style of speech reveals over-zealous niceness: he begs his guest 'to allow him not to allow it' when Chichikov seeks to sit on an ordinary chair instead of the armchair assigned to visitors; nor can he permit 'such a pleasant and educated guest' to enter a room behind him (as a result he and Chichikov both get stuck in the door). The tenor of his speech is always bland: 'You would never expect to hear any brisk or even high-handed word from him, such as you could hear from anyone else if you touched on a subject painful to him' (VI, 24). Manilov even addresses Chichikov's servant in the polite form '*vy*' at least once, and he uses such phrases of sentimentalist vocabulary as: 'birthday of the heart', and 'magnetism of the soul'.

Manilov's surroundings are those of the impractical sentimentalist. His garden is in the English style (cf. the cult of nature which became confused with Sterne and Russian Sentimentalism). There is an attempt at a lawn, and clumps of bushes, trees and a pond, also a summerhouse named the 'Temple of Solitary Contemplation'. Yet such 'English' Sentimentalism does not extend to the peasants from whose huts nature seems to be excluded: 'Nowhere between them was there a growing sapling or anything green. Everywhere it was just logs that could be seen' (VI, 23). The only representatives of this village encountered by Chichikov, are two brawling women. Here is a temperament the very reverse of that of their master, and such details may be read as a realistic gloss on the Sentimentalism of Manilov and on the Karamzinian view of the idealised peasant.

Inside, the house is pleasant, even elegant, but we are told that there is always something just missing. Thus the drawing-room has beautiful furniture. The chairs are covered with an expensive silk material, with the exception of two armchairs which are covered with oilcloth. For years Manilov has been warning guests not to sit in them, as they are not yet ready. Yet another room has no furniture at all. The same marred elegance typifies Manilov's study; it is really quite pleasantly decorated, except that there is tobacco everywhere, and small piles of ash from his pipe are arranged in patterns on the window-sills.

Manilov's family life carries on the cloying sentimentalist theme. He and his wife constantly prepare little presents and surprises for one another, and indulge in extended kissing. His children bear fanciful names not unlike the Greek names favoured by such novelists as Karamzin and Narezhny.[2] Manilov is complacently proud of the very mediocre talents of Femistoklyus and seems to think that because the boy knows that Paris is in France, St Petersburg and Moscow are in Russia, and he is curious about insects, he possesses the qualities to make him an ambassador.

Food, which plays such a part in the hospitality of other landowners, is scarcely mentioned in the portrayal of Manilov. What we chiefly learn is that in the evening an elegant candlestick is 'served'[3] at table (its companion is of cheap copper, lopsided and dirty). When offering dinner to Chichikov, Manilov does speak somewhat rhetorically of cabbage soup in the Russian fashion, but Gogol has already warned us that the sentimental preoccupations of the masters blind them to 'lowly questions': the abuses and mismanagement of the servants. Among these he mentions that food was badly prepared in the kitchen. Certainly when the hostess comments that Chichikov is not eating very much, that normally hearty trencherman thanks her and says, 'I am satisfied, a pleasant conversation is better than any dish.' The food like the master, it would appear, is neither one thing nor the other.

Rather than food Manilov seems to prefer the less substantial oral intake of smoke; except at meal-times his pipe seems to be constantly in his mouth. Even so he speaks with admiration of a lieutenant in his regiment who did smoke at table, 'and even in all other places, if I may be permitted to say so'. Manilov has to lay aside his pipe to kiss his wife. Yet even this oral solace is measured in smoke:

> and very frequently sitting on the settee, suddenly for no apparent reason at all, the one leaving his pipe and the other her work, if she happened to have some in her hands at the time, they would imprint such a long, languorous kiss on one another, that throughout its course one could easily smoke a small straw cigar. (VI, 26)

The final trait of Manilov's characterisation is his reaction to Chichikov's strange request for dead souls. In confusion he falls back on his pipe. Smoke becomes a substitute for thought. He lets it out of his mouth then out of his nose, and at one stage he sucks so hard that the pipe wheezes like a bassoon; it seems as though he is trying to draw an opinion from it about what he has just heard. Of course he does not know how many peasants have died, and can only think of Chichikov's request as something which in some sense must be lofty: 'Perhaps you wished to express yourself thus for the beauty of the style?' (VI, 35). Prepared to think the highest of everybody, he is easily persuaded by Chichikov, and actually gives his 'souls' away. For this he is paid by Chichikov's effusive gratitude, which pleases him more than anything else, so that after his guest's departure he indulges in sentimental day-dreams about friendship with Chichikov. Such exalted feelings are even rewarded with rank in the impractical world of sentimental fantasy; for he dreams that the tsar on learning of their friendship, makes them into generals. In spite of these flights of fancy, he is still perplexed at Chichikov's request, and we leave him at the end of the chapter, smoking his pipe and trying to understand it.

Later, when Chichikov meets Manilov in the town, many of these traits are underscored with greater emphasis. Thus the sense of something missing because of excessive niceness is given physical expression: 'Because of his joy, Manilov's face was left with only a nose and lips. His eyes completely vanished' (VI, 140). (In chapter 2 this trait had been merely the screwing up of his eyes, 'like a cat tickled behind the ear by a finger') (VI, 28). Similarly his friendly effusions now verge on pain: 'The kisses on both sides were so energetic, that for the whole day the front teeth of both of them almost ached' (VI, 140). Moreover the ingratiating nature of Manilov's style of address has now become so exaggerated, that he pays Chichikov the sort of compliment, which it is only fitting to make to a young girl at a dance.

The supportive role of his wife is also evident. Earlier she had made a little beaded sheath for Manilov's toothpick, and now she has fashioned a special border for the list of dead souls which Manilov is to give to his 'friend'. Such attentions show Manilov's reconciliation to Chichikov's strange request. The enterprise is fully endorsed by his presence at the legal transactions and, later, when questioned by the civil servants about Chichikov's activities, he defends him with all the vigour of sentimental loyalty.

Korobochka is one of the landowners whom Chichikov visits by accident. She is a simple, superstitious country woman, absorbed in the narrow world of running her estate, selling her produce and making sure she is not cheated. She is another old world landowner: a Pulkheriya Ivanovna, who has outlived her Afanasiy Ivanovich. The same half-a-dozen strokes are used to depict her.

Her physical appearance is stressed the least: clothes are more important than features. When Chichikov knocks her up at night she has hastily put on the mob-cap she wears in her bedroom and has some flannel round her neck, yet in the digression which follows Gogol seems to suggest that clothes are regarded by old women like Korobochka as possessions to be locked away rather than worn (her name means 'little box'). The following day she is better attired in a dark dress, and without her night-cap, but there is still something fastened round her neck. Korobochka is characterised through her speech.[4] Her simple religious temperament and superstitiousness express themselves in constant references to God and fear of the devil. She addresses Chichikov in a familiar folksy way, revealing values and attitudes close to those of her peasants. She is blunt: 'Oh, dear, my old lad! Your back and side are all covered in mud, like a hog! Where have you managed to get so filthy?' (VI, 46). Not only does her farmyard comparison imply that Chichikov is a dirty pig, but she has trouble in keeping to the polite form of address: *vy*. Constantly, as here, she reverts to the familiar: *ty*. In this and other respects Korobochka is in direct contrast to Manilov, and just as Manilov is aloof from the everyday matters of his estate, so Korobochka is completely immersed in them.

This emerges from the details of her surroundings. Here the dominant motif is birds. They colour Chichikov's first impressions of the décor. The following day it is almost with surprise that: 'Casting a glance round the room, he now noticed that the pictures were not all of birds.' (VI, 47).

After Chichikov has finished dressing he is startled by a turkey-cock looking in at the window; it gobbles at him when he sneezes. His room looks out on to a hen-run with countless hens and turkeys; a pig inadvertently devours a chicken as it roots for food. Beyond the hen-run is a vegetable garden, and here too birds are felt as a presence; the fruit trees are covered with nets to protect them from the attentions of magpies and sparrows, 'of which the latter transferred themselves from one place to another in whole slanting clouds'. Several scarecrows have also been erected; one of these wears a mob-cap of the owner herself so that later, when Korobochka wonders whether dead souls might have some use on the estate, there seems added piquancy in Chichikov's reply: 'Do you think they will scare sparrows at night in your vegetable garden then?' (VI, 54). Just as the economy of Korobochka's estate is heavily dependent, in one way or another, on birds, so too is the old-fashioned comfort of her house. A featherbed is prepared for Chichikov which is nearly as high as the ceiling: 'When, having brought up a chair, he climbed on to the bed, it went down beneath him almost to the very floor, and the feathers squeezed out of the edges flew into all corners of the room' (VI, 47).

In the morning there is something else flying about the room – and here is another detail reminiscent of the house of Pulkheriya Ivanovna – flies. They have been sleeping on the ceiling and walls all night, but now they turn their attention to Chichikov. Korobochka lives surrounded by animals and animal noises: her choir of dogs announces Chichikov's arrival at night; her clock, which hisses like snakes, startles him once he is in the house; her flies torment him in the morning; her turkey-cock gobbles at him when he is dressing. Above all birds dominate the household, and this is suggestive, for the owner herself is like a clucking old hen.

Korobochka has no immediate family; she is a childless widow, but her servants seem almost her replicas. All we learn of her husband was his inability to sleep without first having his heels scratched. It is suggested that Chichikov might require this service himself: an indication of quaint rural ways which colour Korobochka's view of hospitality.

The chief form of hospitality is, nevertheless, food and in this too Korobochka reveals her character. She serves Chichikov plain, wholesome, Russian fare: pancakes, pies, dumplings. As Smirnova-Chikina points out, all her delicacies are made from flour;[5] there is a complete absence of meat (yet another feature she shares with Pulkheriya Ivanovna) but if there is no meat, as such, her chief pride derives from a bird: egg-pie.

The final revealing trait, her attitude to Chichikov's strange request, is compounded of superstitious fear, stubbornness and cupidity. At first she takes him literally and asks if he means to dig up her dead peasants. Gradually this fear yields to a different apprehension: she might be cheated in such a sale. Cupidity finally overcomes when Chichikov promises to return and buy other more conventional goods. Typically, she wonders whether he would be interested in feathers.

When we next encounter Korobochka (at the end of chapter 8) her fear of being cheated has got the better of her, and she drives into town to ask the going price for dead souls. The coach in which she drives seems to be the epitome of her housekeeping: it is melon shaped, and not only does it contain cushions of all shapes and sizes, it is also stuffed with food – pies, buns and many of the pastry products on which she fed Chichikov. This strange coach finally comes to rest in a narrow courtyard where, quite fittingly, there are hen-coops and all sorts of cages. Korobochka travels late at night and her arrival is greeted by dogs. Such details suggest that Korobochka has come to undo the earlier visit Chichikov paid to her.

Chichikov's next encounter, with Nozdrev, also occurs by chance. It is these two unplanned visits which ultimately lead to his downfall.

Nozdrev's physical appearance expresses his boisterous, yet absurd, nature. He is well-built, of fresh complexion, with white teeth and black hair. His whole being exudes health, but the fact that on one side of his face his whiskers are thinner than on the other suggests a lack of balance to an otherwise ideal picture of male vigour. Moreover Gogol deliberately makes this detail appear absurd. Nozdrev tells Chichikov that he has lost everything at cards, even his watch and chain: 'Chichikov looked and saw that indeed he was wearing neither watch nor chain. It even seemed to him that one of his side whiskers was less and not so thick as the other' (VI, 64). To lose facial hair at cards, as well as possessions, seems preposterous until we learn that Nozdrev often has his whiskers pulled for cheating. This asymmetrical physical detail is thus both the result of his behaviour and a visible expression of his character.

Nozdrev's style of speech is boisterous and insultingly familiar. As in the previous two portraits, the use of *vy/ty* is indicative; but whereas Korobochka's ambivalence to Chichikov is expressed through wavering between *ty* and *vy*, for Nozdrev it is the ambivalence of *ty* itself which is striking and suggests the inconsistencies of his character. In chapter I when Nozdrev is first introduced to Chichikov, he begins to call him *ty* (thou) almost at once: 'Nozdrev also called the police chief and the public prosecutor *thou* and treated them in a friendly way. But when they sat down to play cards the police chief and the public prosecutor examined the cards he took extremely attentively, and kept a watch on almost every card he led' (VI, 17).

Nozdrev's 'thou' which apparently shows friendship and familiarity is also the expression of contempt and hostility: 'the person who became more intimate with him would be spited soonest of all?' He is quite capable of offering undying affection and unpardonable insult in the same breath. The inconsistency of the two aspects of 'thou' permeates Nozdrev's dealings with Chichikov as it does with others:

'Well, look, I know *thee*, thou art a great rogue. Let me tell thee this as a friend. If I were thy master I would hang thee on the first tree'...

...'I swear I would hang thee', Nozdrev repeated. 'I tell thee this frankly, not to offend thee, I simply say it as a friend.' (VI, 79)

Nozdrev's very colourful speech is full of disparate elements, from the jargon employed by card-sharpers to the technical vocabulary of dog-fanciers and the names given to dogs. He makes use of not fully comprehended foreign phrases when talking of women, as well as such comic sounding euphemisms as: 'to take advantage of the strawberries'.[6]

Nozdrev's house and estate carry on the theme of riotous and jumbled inconsistency, which is the hallmark of the character himself. When Chichikov, Mizhuyev and Nozdrev arrive at the house there is no sign of preparation for their coming. On the contrary, two peasants are working on a trestle in the middle of the dining-room, whitewashing it and covering the floor in splashes. While dinner is being prepared, Nozdrev takes his guests to look round the estate.

It seems significant that although they inspect 'every single thing in the village' nowhere is there any description of Nozdrev's peasants and their houses. This omission is in marked contrast to the other four portraits of landowners in part I and is all the more striking given Chichikov's usual curiosity about such matters.[7] Instead of peasants Nozdrev shows him horses, a wolf-cub and a watermill which lacks a basic part so that the impression is created of spinning activity – yet all to no effect: it is like a symbol of Nozdrev himself.

In boasting about the extent of his estate, Nozdrev reveals a characteristic psychological trait: '"Here is the boundary!" said Nozdrev, "All that you see on this side, all that is mine, and even on the other side, all that wood showing over there, and all that beyond the wood, all that is mine"' (VI, 74). Such is Nozdrev's concept of a boundary; his is a character which knows no limits. Later when he says that Chichikov should be hanged, Chichikov has to tell him: 'there are limits to everything'.

Nozdrev's study, unlike other studies, has no books or papers, instead it has sabres and two guns (the description of which is limited to their value in roubles). There are pipes of all sizes and types and Turkish knives, which on inspection prove not to be Turkish at all. Among all these bizarre objects the barrel-organ bears most clearly the characteristics of its owner:

> The barrel-organ played not unpleasantly, but something appeared to happen in the middle; for the mazurka ended in the song *Malbrough s'en va-t-en guerre*, and *Malbrough s'en va-t-en guerre* finished unexpectedly in some well-known waltz or other. Nozdrev had long since stopped turning the handle, but there was one flute in the barrel-organ which was very lively. It did not wish to calm down, and for a long time afterwards it was still whistling on its own. (VI, 75)

This behaviour is that of Nozdrev himself, whose liveliness (the mazurka) very easily passes into aggressiveness (*Malbrough s'en va-t-en guerre*) mixed with a more intimate familiarity (the well-known waltz) and there is within him a persistent note of disharmony which just will not calm down.

The contradictions of Nozdrev's character are further revealed through family relationships. His brother-in-law, Mizhuyev, acts as a foil by contradicting everything he says. He not only points to the truth behind Nozdrev's boasting, but at the same time prompts him into even wilder assertions. Mizhuyev is also, in a sense, a double: an embodiment of Nozdrev's own 'hostility of intimacy' (the ambivalence of 'thou'). Nozdrev himself is only too ready to quarrel with his brother-in-law and in the process abuse his own sister (Mizhuyev's wife) with a word which cannot be printed: 'To...with her! Your wife! Important business, indeed, you'll get up to with her' (VI, 76). Nozdrev's own wife has died and left him with two children, but rather slyly Gogol mentions that he has a pretty nurse to look after them; the muddled unconventionality of his family life is consistent with the house he lives in and with the character himself.

The touchstone of hospitality (in particular food) is further revealing:

> Dinner, it was obvious, was not the chief thing in life for Nozdrev. Food

played no role; some things were burned, others not properly cooked. It was obvious that the cook was ruled by a sort of inspiration, and put in the first thing that came to hand. If pepper were nearby he would sprinkle pepper or if cabbage came to hand he stuffed in cabbage – he shoved in milk, ham, peas, as though without rhyme or reason. As long as it was hot, it didn't matter, a taste of some sort would undoubtedly emerge. On the other hand Nozdrev put great store on drink. (VI, 75)

Earlier at the inn Nozdrev had declined food, ordering a glass of vodka instead. Yet although he undoubtedly sees hospitality in terms of alcohol, the drink he offers is more remarkable for its quantity and bizarre strength than for its quality. Like his own character his drinks seem to be composed of the most disparate elements. Madeira laced with rum and even aqua-regia; a wine which is both burgundy and champagne; a rowanberry vodka which is supposed to taste like cream, but instead reeks of raw spirit; and finally a drink which Nozdrev keeps calling by completely different names.

Such hospitality does not have as its aim the well-being of the guests and Chichikov wisely does not drink everything he is offered. The aggressive element in Nozdrev's hospitality is further brought out when he refuses to wish Chichikov a good night, and gives orders that his horses be deprived of oats.

It is typical of Nozdrev that, when Chichikov makes his unusual business proposition, he should abuse him, not believe his reasons for wanting dead souls and only be prepared to let Chichikov have them if something else is included in the deal, or they can be gambled for or bartered, rather than sold direct. As Chichikov refuses these suggestions Nozdrev's counterproposals become more and more complicated. Finally Chichikov agrees to play draughts for them. Almost immediately he detects Nozdrev in cheating, and when he refuses to play any more, Nozdrev threatens him with the physical violence, into which his jovial familiarity is always about to erupt (at the inn he had forcibly bent Chichikov's head down to see his carriage nearly banging it against the window-frame).

Chichikov next meets Nozdrev at the governor's ball, and as with Manilov, his characteristic traits, on this third occasion, seem even more pronounced. His 'hostile intimacy' is glaringly revealed when in a 'half sober' speech Nozdrev publicly protests that he wishes to kiss Chichikov, that Chichikov is dearer to him than his own father, while at the same time denouncing him for buying dead souls and asserting before the governor and the assembled company that he would hang him. Finally his behaviour is too antisocial to be tolerated further: he sits on the ballroom floor and grabs at the clothing of the dancers.

We see Nozdrev on a fourth occasion when he is summoned (from the serious enterprise of inventing an infallible system for cheating at cards) to appear before the civil servants who are anxious to find out the truth about Chichikov. To all their questions Nozdrev gives them more than they bargained for: Chichikov has bought dead souls; he is a spy; he also forges money; he was planning to carry off the governor's daughter. Nozdrev claims he can tell them all these facts because he is intimate with Chichikov, he knew him as a schoolboy, and was himself taking an active part in the plan to abduct the governor's daughter. Once Nozdrev starts on all this nonsense he cannot stop. The more hesitant the questions of the civil servants, the bolder and firmer are his replies. Lying gets the better of him. Thus he says that after being beaten up for tale-telling at school Chichikov had 240 leeches applied to his temples: 'That is to say he wanted to say 40 – but 200 somehow inserted itself' (VI, 208). In retailing all the 'details' of the abduction of the governor's daughter, Nozdrev realises that he is implicating himself quite considerably but he cannot stop: 'because of their own accord such interesting details presented themselves that it was impossible to renounce them'. Finally when he is asked about Napoleon he utters such nonsense that nobody can understand him, not even the police chief who persists longer than the others. Nozdrev enters the work on a fifth occasion when he calls round to see Chichikov in his hotel room. Again he professes friendship but imputes to him all the crimes about which he himself has borne false witness.

In the portrait of Sobakevich physical description predominates. He is nothing but body:

> It seemed as if in this body there were no soul at all, or that he had one but it certainly was not where it should have been. Like that of the immortal Koshchey[8] it was somewhere over the hills, and was covered with such a thick shell, that everything that moved down below produced absolutely no shock on the surface. (VI, 101)

The body itself is extremely crude:

> It is well known that there are many people in the world whom nature has not exercised herself greatly to finish off, has not used any fine instruments such as files and gimlets etc., but has simply hewn with all her might. One stroke of the axe and a nose appears; a second blow, and you have the lips;

with a great auger she has gouged out the eyes; and unplaned has sent it out into the world saying: 'it lives'. Such a solid and astonishingly cobbled form had Sobakevich. (VI, 94–5)

It is almost as if Gogol is equating this character with some crudely made peasant puppet. Certainly he seems incapable of moving his head and therefore seldom looks at the person to whom he is talking. Sobakevich is little more than a big clumsy frame, and with his heavy, random tread he constantly steps on other people's feet: his own legs are compared by Chichikov to cast-iron bollards.

Nevertheless it is another part of the body which seems to express his essence. He is a 'man-fist' (*chelovek-kulak*). *Kulak* – 'a fist' is also widely used to mean 'a greedy person', so here is a dead metaphor for a 'dead soul', to which Gogol then gives dubious life: 'He who is already a fist will never uncurl into a hand' (VI, 106).

Images for Sobakevich are chiefly drawn from the animal and vegetable kingdoms. The constant comparison is to a bear: 'A bear! a complete bear! and what a strange coincidence he was even called Mikhail Semenych' (VI, 95). Misha, the diminutive of Mikhail, was the name commonly given to a bear.[9] Indeed, Chichikov later uses this name when comparing Sobakevich to a tame bear performing tricks. Yet Sobakevich, the 'bear', has a name suggesting a dog (*sobaka*) and there is something rather 'doggish' about the way in which he attacks his friends and acquaintances behind their backs (he even calls Plyushkin 'a dog'). Nevertheless it is the very reverse of such misanthropy, which Sobakevich himself sees as his animal weakness: 'I have such a doggish nature, I cannot help giving pleasure to my fellow beings' (VI, 105).

Sobakevich's speech habits typify his heavy nature. They contrast with those of Manilov. Where the latter is effusive Sobakevich maintains ponderous silence. Manilov is full of praise for the officials of the town, Sobakevich has nothing but abuse. Manilov is fond of diminutives, Sobakevich prefers augmentatives, particularly when he is putting flesh on his dead peasants.[10]

In the description of Sobakevich's surroundings we have the most explicit statement of the link between a character and his setting. Sobakevich's house seems to show the result of a battle between the architect's ideas of symmetry and the owner's concept of comfort. The effect is one of clumsiness: all the windows on one side have been boarded up, and the porch is not in the centre of the house, because one of the four columns has been taken out. It has the air of a building for military settlements, or for German colonists. Everything is very solid. The courtyard is surrounded by a heavy wooden fence. The barns, the outhouses, the well, the peasants' houses – everything is built of heavy timber: 'The landowner, it seemed, was greatly concerned with solidity' (VI, 94).

Inside, the pictures on the walls carry on the theme of military heaviness and foreign solidity: they depict Greek military leaders of hefty proportions. There is also a picture of the Greek heroine Bobelina, whose leg alone seems the size of a man's body: 'The host himself being a strong healthy man, it appeared, wanted his drawing-room also to be decorated with strong healthy people' (VI, 95). The one exception is a portrait of the thin, Russian general Bagration.

Near the portrait of Bobelina is a cage with a thrush which actually looks like Sobakevich. In fact, all the furniture reminds us of the owner. Not only is there a pot-bellied desk which is 'a complete bear', but: 'The table, the armchairs, the chairs, everything was of the heaviest and most uncomfortable nature. In a word, every object, every chair seemed to say "and I too, am Sobakevich", or "and I too am very like Sobakevich"' (VI, 96).

If Sobakevich's surroundings reflect the man, his family, on the other hand, provides supportive contrast. When Chichikov first approaches the house he is aware of two faces peering out of the window. One, long and thin, is likened to a cucumber, it is the face of Sobakevich's wife. The other, round and broad like a Moldavian pumpkin, is that of Sobakevich himself. These vegetable associations are continued in the wife; when she enters the drawing-room, she is likened to a palm-tree, and Chichikov, on being presented to her, is aware that her hands smell of cucumber pickle. She shares with her husband the doubtful distinction of being compared to an animal for, if she enters the drawing room as a palm-tree, she leaves it 'like a stately goose'. Just as there is a hint of the peasant puppet about Sobakevich's rough-hewn person, his wife by contrast gives herself the airs of a live actress: 'Feoduliya Ivanovna requested him to be seated saying, "I beg you" and making a movement with her head like actresses representing queens' (VI, 96).

What follows, however, is pure dumb show. She sits absolutely still not moving either eye, eyebrow, or nose: Chichikov and his hosts are quiet for almost five minutes. Nevertheless, the theatrical performance seems to Chichikov to come later when he is haggling with Sobakevich over the price of his dead peasants: 'I find it very strange

It is as though some theatrical show or comedy is taking place between us. I can't explain it in any other way' (VI, 103–4).

In her silence, and her stiffness Feoduliya Ivanovna seems a fitting wife for Sobakevich. It is only in girth that she seems at variance, like the thin Bagration who sets off the amplitude of Sobakevich's other pictures. It is interesting too that Sobakevich's wife is given a name and patronymic, and that we also learn that Sobakevich is called Mikhail Semenovich; for they are the only characters in the whole of the 'portrait gallery' to bear Christian names and patronymics:[11] a mark, perhaps, of their presence and substantiality.

The vegetable imagery for the couple at the window is developed into one of Gogol's extended similes – Sobakevich's face is as round and broad:

As are Moldavian pumpkins, called *gorlyanki*, from which balalaikas are made in Russia, light, two stringed balalaikas, the beauty and joy of a nimble twenty-year old lad, an ogling dandy, who winks and whistles at white-breasted, white-necked maidens gathering to hear his soft stringed strumming. Having peered out both faces disappeared at the same time. (VI, 94)

By the peculiar focus of a Gogolian simile a middle-aged man and his wife are linked to the dashing sexual exploits of the young – through vegetables.[12] Here is a hint about the 'physicality' of Sobakevich's portrait which takes up another suggestive passage at the end of chapter 1:

Even Sobakevich himself, who rarely spoke well of anybody, having arrived back fairly late from the town, and having got completely undressed and lain down on the bed beside his thin wife, said to her, 'I have been at an evening party at the governor's, darling, dined with the chief of police and I have become acquainted with Pavel Ivanovich Chichikov, a collegiate counsellor and a very pleasant man!' To which his wife replied, 'Hm!' and jogged him with her leg. (VI, 18)

In view of this Sobakevich's remark, when Chichikov is buying souls, does not seem out of character. Sobakevich asks:

'Do you want any of the female sex?'

'No thank you.'

'I wouldn't take much for them. Since we are acquainted, a rouble per item?'

'No, I have no need of the female sex.'

'Well, when you have no need, there's nothing to be said. There's no law for tastes. One man loves the priest, another the priest's wife, as the proverb says.' (VI, 107)

There is yet another member of the household, who only appears at table – a woman, about thirty, of indeterminate status:

There are people who exist in the world not as an object, but as foreign spots or marks on an object. They sit in the same place, always hold their heads in the same way. One is almost prepared to take them for furniture and to think that since birth no word has come from such lips, but somewhere or other in the maids' quarters or the storeroom there will simply be an oh – oh! (VI, 98)

Thus in contrast to the objects of the house, each of which proclaims itself a Sobakevich, this human being cannot even aspire to the status of thing. Yet the 'Oh – Oh!' uttered in the maids' quarters or the storeroom seems slyly suggestive, and we immediately learn that the master of the house is himself partial to 'nurse': '"The cabbage-soup, my dear,[13] is very good today!" said Sobakevich having supped at the soup and having pulled off for himself from the dish an enormous piece of nurse' (VI, 107). This nurse (*nyanya*) is not of the same genus as the one (*smazlivaya nyan'ka*) who looks after Nozdrev's children. It is kind of haggis, as Gogol is quick to explain.[14]

There is the suggestion of something almost cannibalistic about this great devourer of flesh, and, certainly, everything consumed by Sobakevich is meat (with the exception of the cheesecakes too big for the plate) in complete contrast to the fare offered by Korobochka. Sobakevich's attitude to food had already been outlined by the landlady at the inn where Chichikov had fortified himself with roast sucking pig after the farinaceous fare of Korobochka. He had been told that whereas Manilov would order many things: 'Sobakevich would only ask for one thing, but on the other hand would eat everything up, and would ask for a second helping for the same price' (VI, 63).

This heavy, crudely built man is a lover of unadorned and heavy dishes which he eats crudely:

'In my house when it's pork – then let's have the whole pig on the table; if mutton, then bring the whole sheep; a goose, then the whole goose. It is better I eat two dishes, but eat sufficiently[15] as the soul demands.'

Sobakevich supported this by deed. He rolled over on to his own plate a half of sheep's side, and ate up the lot gnawing and sucking it to the last bone. (VI, 99)

These are the table manners of a *kulak* and Chichikov will encounter this inability to let anything go without 'gnawing and sucking it to the last bone', when he later tries to buy dead peasants from him.

Sobakevich also reveals his doggish nature in his scathing criticism of the food of others. His remarks are hardly suitable at table and his wife, reproaching him, suggests this is his normal table conversation. Such delicacies as oysters and frogs' legs are revolting to the crude palate of Sobakevich, and the idea of diet is incomprehensible: he describes it as curing people by hunger. As a man obsessed by solid flesh, he can think of nothing more worthless than a steamed turnip.[16] Haggling with Chichikov over the sale of dead souls he comments: 'In truth, with you a human soul is just the same as a steamed turnip' (VI, 105).

His reaction to Chichikov's offer to buy dead souls is characteristic: he shows no surprise and immediately fixes his price high. This fleshy lover of solidity gives flesh and solidity to non-existent beings; for in spite of Chichikov's objection that all that has remained of these peasants is a sound imperceptible to the senses, these are, nevertheless names which evoke in Sobakevich real creatures of flesh and blood whose peculiarities and virtues he knows by heart.

When Chichikov points out that he can buy dead souls from anybody for almost nothing, Sobakevich hints that he would be prepared to report a matter like this, which doesn't seem quite legal. Chichikov finds it difficult to budge such a solid man. Sobakevich is the only landowner to demand an advance payment (on receiving it he complains that one of the notes is old) and he gives visible proof that he is a 'fist' by firmly placing his left hand on Chichikov's money, as he makes out the receipt with his right. When the deal is concluded Chichikov has the worst of the bargain. Sobakevich had wanted to sell him female serfs and he even manages this; for when Chichikov looks closely at the list he sees that it contains at least one female serf masquerading as a man. The list is so detailed that once again the illusion is created that these peasants have real life.

Chichikov meets Sobakevich a third time back in the town. Once more the characteristics of the 'portrait' are reinforced. The theme of 'the bear' re-emerges when he praises the physique of his father, who used to go hunting bears alone, and the 'doggish' habit of criticising others is now turned on himself. He compares his constitution unfavourably with that of his father, and even regards his own robust health as a bad sign: he will have to pay one day for his never having been ill. Boasting about the sterling qualities of the peasants sold to Chichikov almost leads him into trouble. When the chairman of the court remembers that one of them has died; Sobakevich unflinchingly brazens it out.

The consumer of flesh is again to the fore. At the dinner given by the chief of police (courtesy of the town's merchants) Sobakevich makes for the one big solid item, a whole sturgeon, and finishes it off before the others can turn their attention to it. This sturgeon is obviously the *pièce de résistance* of the meal:

> When the police chief remembered about it and saying 'What do you think of this product of nature, gentlemen?' approached it with a fork along with the others, he saw that of this 'product of nature' there remained only the tail; but Sobakevich slid away, as though he had nothing to do with it, and approaching a plate that was further away than the others, he kept sticking his fork into small smoked fish of some sort. (VI, 150–1)

Afterwards when Sobakevich is questioned by the civil servants he maintains that his peasants were alive when he sold them, but he cannot vouch for what might happen later.

Plyushkin is the last portrait in the 'gallery'. Miserliness has so disfigured him that Chichikov takes him at first, not for the master, but for a servant, and for a woman rather than a man. He thinks he is the housekeeper (or more accurately 'key-woman' – *klyuchnitsa*). The keys on his belt indicate his hoarding instincts – his desire to lock everything away, even his own life. Once inside the house, Chichikov realises, from the stubble on his chin, that he is a man, but is greatly surprised to learn that he is the master: his appearance is that of a beggar, yet he is a man of wealth. This changing into opposites: man into woman; master into servant; rich man into beggar, is a dominant feature of Plyushkin's physical appearance, and it expresses the very nature of his miserliness; for the one result of his hoarding is inversion: he is a Russian Midas who turns all he touches to dust.

His clothing carries on this theme. 'Accumulation' changes its basic nature: 'It was not possible by any effort or by any means at all to fathom what his dressing-gown was concocted of: the sleeves and upper parts of the skirts had become so greasy and shiny, that they resembled Russian leather, used for boots' (VI, 116). His tie has also lost its true characteristics; it could be a sock or a suspender. His back is stained with flour, and lower down there is a large rent, which later seems to assume the force of a metaphor for Plyushkin himself: 'everything became rot and rent, and he himself finally turned into a sort of rent on humanity' (VI, 119). His chin seems to lend itself to an expression of self-contempt against which he has to take precautions: 'only his chin jutted very far out so that he had to cover it every time with a handkerchief in order not to spit all over it' (VI, 116). Certain features of his face, too, seem to have lost their human characteristics. His eyes are like mice peering out of their holes and suspiciously sniffing the air. Yet in his younger days he had a keen glance which made him seem more like a spider: 'The sharp glance of the master penetrated into everything and everywhere, and like an industrious spider he would run, bustling but adroitly from end to end of his economic web' (VI, 118). It is later after his wife's death that he becomes a miser, a development which actually seems to be aided by a physical feature – grey hair: 'The true friend of miserliness, the grey sparkling in his wiry hair, helped it to develop even more' (VI, 118).

Plyushkin is not generous with words, and his brusque speech is consonant with an apparent reversal of social position. Chichikov concludes he must be a housekeeper partly on the evidence of his abusive words to a peasant. In a later exchange with his servant Mavra we see that his speech habits are those of Mavra herself, only sharper and more abusive. It is clear too that God is on the side of misers; Plyushkin threatens Mavra in some detail with roasting in hell at the last judgement for having stolen a sheet of her master's paper. Bribe-taking also arouses his religious wrath.

Plyushkin is scarcely more polite to Chichikov. He easily takes offence, and expresses himself in such pithy folk phrases as: 'you can't put condolence in your pocket' (VI, 122). His tone changes however when he senses an advantageous deal: 'How then, begging your pardon and not wishing to annoy you, are you going to take on payment for them, for every year then?' (VI, 123). Nevertheless it is again the language of a peasant, but one trying to placate an exacting master.

Chichikov receives a 'shock' when he first enters Plyushkin's domain. It is a physical shock because of the state of his log road, which moves up and down like a piano keyboard, constantly throwing Chichikov against the roof and sides of his *brichka*. The roadway is in direct contrast to the solidity of Sobakevich's estate, and it gives dramatic expression to the destructive nature of miserliness. Chichikov finds himself in the middle of a large village but it is in total disrepair; some of the houses even lack roofs. Most telling, as a symbol of self-defeating miserliness, are the mounds of grain which the landowner has hoarded only to rot and form a rich manure for the growth of weeds, and bushes.

Plyushkin's own house is dilapidated; it looks like some broken-down invalid. Everything man-made suffers from neglect; it is nature alone which is not marred by lack of attention: Plyushkin's overgrown garden is the only picturesque part of his estate. But the confusion of the garden is carried on indoors in a less attractive way. There are heaps of furniture and piles of rubbish, including such objects as a shrivelled lemon the size of a nut and an ancient toothpick. Gogol speculates that Plyushkin might have picked his teeth with this before the Napoleonic invasion of Russia, and the fact that time has stopped in this household is shown by the motionless pendulum to which a spider[17] has attached its web. Chichikov enters this room through a hall which has all the coldness of a cellar (i.e. *pogreb* suggesting *pogrebeniye* – 'burial' and death).

Everywhere there is dust. The scene is not unlike Miss Haversham's room in *Great Expectations* or Krook's shop in *Bleak House*. In both these cases the surroundings have symbolic value for the occupants,[18] and the same can be sensed here. In typical Gogolian fashion the owner is indicated by an item of clothing: 'It would have been absolutely impossible to say that a living creature inhabited this room, if its presence were not announced by an old well-worn night-cap' (VI, 115). This item of head gear (*kolpak*) can also mean a lampshade, and the statement seems to pick up a simile which shortly preceded it: 'From the centre of the ceiling hung a chandelier in a canvas bag, which from dust had become like a silken cocoon in which there sits a worm' (VI, 115). Plyushkin himself is like some caddis-larva, cocooning himself against the outside world with every bit of rubbish that comes to hand. He scavenges his estate, and in the process often robs his peasants of useful objects, to add to his pile in the yard which the author compares to the fleamarket in Moscow.

Plyushkin's pictures of a battle scene and an enormous *nature morte* of flowers, fruit, sliced melon, boar's head and suspended duck, serve to carry on the sense of confusion and destruction. The soldiers in their three-cornered hats might almost be Napoleonic, and thus date from the same time as the owner's toothpick.

Plyushkin prefers objects to human beings; his life has been a process of gaining things as he loses people. On the death of his wife his careful and thrifty running of the estate takes a new turn: 'a share of the keys, and of petty cares along with them, was transferred to him'. This is the beginning of the process which has turned him into the 'housekeeper'. His miserliness intensifies after his elder daughter runs away to marry an officer; all he sends her is a curse. The son angers his father by choosing a military career instead of the civil service, and when he gets in debt through gambling, Plyushkin sends him his parental curse and is no longer interested whether he is alive or dead. Finally his younger daughter dies; Plyushkin is left alone as 'the guard, the custodian, the owner of his wealth'.

Formerly there had been a full household with a tutor and a governess, but one by one all are dispersed; formerly, 'all the windows in the house were open', but now the windows are boarded up one by one; formerly merchants came to buy his produce, but his haggling drove them away, and he was left with his goods to rot. His elder daughter Aleksandra came to see him twice with her children. On the first visit Plyushkin forgave her: 'and even gave his little grandson some button or other which was lying on the table to play with, but he gave no money' (VI, 120). On the second occasion it is Aleksandra who gives – a dressing-gown (*khalat*) and some sweet-cake (*kulich*). Now the only memory that remains of his daughter and her young family is this stale and crumbling sweetcake. A neighbour, too, tries to arouse feelings in him by calling him 'uncle'. Plyushkin rejects such advances: he is at home only with things.

Given such behaviour, it might be thought that the 'stroke' of hospitality would be the least emphasised of Plyushkin's traits, yet it has its own bizarre prominence. Plyushkin appears to welcome Chichikov by mumbling some curse to himself. Then Gogol comments ironically: 'But as hospitality is in such vogue with us that even a skinflint is unable to transgress its laws, he added at once, and a little more audibly, "Please be seated"' (VI, 121). Nozdrev had deprived Chichikov's horses of oats and let them eat only hay, but Plyushkin is not prepared to let them have even that, claiming that he has not a wisp of hay on his estate.

Nevertheless, when he realises that Chichikov is prepared to relieve him of a tax liability for his dead souls, his gratitude is expressed in true miser's hospitality. He gives orders to serve the dried remains of his daughter's sweetcake but at the same time carefully instructs the servant to scrape off the top bit which has gone bad, and give it to the hens. The liqueur he is about to offer is of the same quality; for Plyushkin explains that the bottle has been left unstoppered, and that he has had to take out flies and all sorts of other filth. When Chichikov politely declines such hospitality, saying he has already eaten and drunk, Plyushkin is even more delighted with his guest, who 'doesn't need to eat to be full' (*on i ne yest a syt*). Yet, typically, Plyushkin is the only one of the five hosts to anticipate Chichikov's desire to leave once the deal is concluded: '"But what, are you getting ready to go already", he said, noticing the slight movement which Chichikov made in order merely to get a handkerchief out of his pocket' (VI, 129). Plyushkin is, in reality, the self-invited 'guest' of his own servants. After Chichikov has gone, he visits the kitchen, and pretending to make sure that the servants are eating well, he takes his fill of their cabbage soup and buckwheat porridge. As he does so he curses them for their thieving and their bad behaviour.

Plyushkin's reaction to Chichikov's proposal, which is to relieve him of a tax burden, is one of delight. He hails Chichikov as his benefactor, yet his joy is not unmixed with bouts of suspicion. His chief concern is to know the actual financial arrangements which Chichikov proposes to make: will he pay tax for the dead peasants every year; will the payment be to him or to the state? He is less happy about a sale because of the costs, but is relieved when Chichikov offers to pay these himself. He even sells Chichikov some runaway serfs. Although he attempts to get a better price by trying to evoke sympathy for his poverty, Plyushkin is very pleased with Chichikov's 'magnanimity' and even toys with the idea of giving him his silver pocket watch, which needless to say is broken. Yet he rejects the impulse: he can always leave it in his will.

Unlike the other characters in the portrait gallery, we see Plyushkin only once,[19] but by way of compensation we are told more about him. We learn of his previous life and see the process which has made him into a miser. The other landowners are presented 'ready made': there is no hint of the forces that have formed them or of any development in their lives. Thus when Chichikov had tried to speculate, about Sobakevich's becoming a bear, he could only conclude that he must have been born to his condition. Plyushkin is different, in him we not only see development of character, but through the contrast between past and present, he is presented with more than a hint of pathos.

This fifth portrait finishes the round of the 'gallery'. We have come from Manilov, who values human relationships above objects and his estate, to Plyushkin, who sacrifices human beings to 'housekeeping' and to things: in one we have open 'laughter' at the sentimentalist, in the other the 'tears' which lie behind a stock figure of comedy.

Negative types: positive ideals

Gogol's methods of characterisation reveal a strange tension between general and particular. If behind his idiosyncratic depiction of the landowners lurk broad strokes akin to a common grid, there is also something general about them in another sense; for in nearly every case Gogol seeks to stress typicality. Thus of Manilov he says: 'There is a type of person known under the name of "people who are not too bad" neither one thing nor the other, "neither flesh, fowl nor good red herring" in the words of the proverb. Perhaps Manilov ought to be included among them' (VI, 24). More specifically, however, Manilov may be taken as a caricatured portrait of the type of the Russian sentimentalist.

There is a similar attribution of typicality to Korobochka, who is introduced as: 'One of those old ladies and small landowners who lament bad harvests and losses, and hold their heads a little to one side, but at the same time are accumulating a bit of money little by little in small, coarse coloured cotton bags distributed throughout the drawers of a tallboy' (VI, 45). Gogol even seeks to extend the significance of this portrait by suggesting that her characteristics are to be found not solely in the country but also in fashionable St Petersburg. This parallel is unexpected, but it must be taken in a moral sense; women in *Dead Souls* form a broad and largely undifferentiated category.

Nozdrev, too, is described as a well-known type: 'The figure of Nozdrev is, undoubtedly, already to some extent known to the reader. Everyone must have come across quite a few of such people' (VI, 70), and he concludes: 'It will be a long time before Nozdrev is extinct in this world. He is amongst us everywhere, and is walking about, perhaps, only in a different kaftan' (VI, 72). In Kochkarev in *Marriage* Gogol has already given us Nozdrev 'in a different kaftan', and provided yet another in Chertokutsky (*The Carriage*) the idle, feckless boaster who has the same love of bartering, card-playing and fairs.

Pereverzev has suggested a forerunner for Nozdrev in Silvester, a landowner in Narezhny's novel *Aristion: or Re-education.*[20] Even closer is the figure of Glazdurin in Bulgarin's novel *Ivan Vyzhigin*, with his violence and his interest in dogs, pretty women, cards and drink. Such details as the settling of an argument over the rival qualities of two dogs by a game of cards, or the meal prepared by a drunken cook who jumbles everything up, seem to look forward to similar elements in Gogol's depiction of Nozdrev.[21] Moreover there is something approaching this figure in Griboyedov's portrayal of Repetilov (*Woe from Wit*) and the real-life figure of 'Tolstoy the American' to whom Repetilov himself refers. Herzen, too, discusses Tolstoy the American, and comments, in much the same terms as Gogol, on the undoubted continuity of the type.[22]

There is also a general aspect to the portrayal of Sobakevich. He is *kulak* – grasping fist, and Gogol speculates how this type would behave in St Petersburg, much as earlier he had sought to link Korobochka with her sisters in the capital. However, Gogol makes no overt attempt to project the last of his portraits as a general type. Perhaps there is no need to do so; Plyushkin is instantly recognisable as the universal figure of the miser, met with throughout literature be it in Molière's Harpagon or Pushkin's *The Covetous Knight*. In his more specific guise of the Russian landowner, Plyushkin may, as Pereverzev suggests, have a prototype in Narezhny's Tarakh (*Aristion: or Re-education*).[23] A further development of this character (especially that side which depicts relations with his family) may be seen in Saltykov-Shchedrin's portrayal of the 'hypocrite' Iudushka in *The Golovlyov Family* (*Gospoda Golovlevy*).

Gogol's love of depicting people in broad general categories is seen at its most extreme in chapter 1, when he describes the gathering of local society at the governor's residence. 'Here as everywhere' the men are divided into two groups: the thin and the fat. The thin men are interested in the ladies, whereas the fat men move away, and seem rather to be looking for the appearance of a card-table. Thus physical appearance seems to place actual physical distance between them; they naturally form two distinct groups, and this in its turn reflects not merely a difference of interests but even of character and career prospects. The social implications of this are made even more general as Gogol (as he will later do with Korobochka and Sobakevich) links some of the thin men to St Petersburg society.

A similar division of local society emerges in response to the rumours circulating about Chichikov. The men incline to a political interpretation of Chichikov's activities, but the women, because they are women, see his intentions as entirely amorous. Thus the town is divided into two distinct camps purely on the basis of sex. Admittedly some men are won over to the view that the rumour about 'dead souls' is pure fiction (presumably these renegades are 'thin') and they are ridiculed for such ideas by their fellow men.

The sexual division is visibly demonstrated at the funeral of the public prosecutor: the men are on foot whereas the women ride in coaches, and although both groups appear to have the advent of the governor general on their minds, the men are silent and inward looking, whereas the women are lively and talkative, no doubt thinking of the balls he will give and what the fashions will be.

Amongst the fat men with whom Chichikov had associated at the governor's reception were such pillars of local society as the public prosecutor and the postmaster. These two characters are to some extent individualised, but on the whole the civil servants are depicted only in a more general way, and here Gogol's technique of characterisation differs markedly from his portrayal of the landowners.

In chapter I Chichikov visits many homes and on his return to the town he goes to a ball at the governor's and has lunch with the chief of police. Yet these interiors are barely mentioned; there is no attempt to describe a home environment which reveals 'the animal which lives in the shell'. Nor, again, is food important, except in the case of the police chief, and that more from the point of view of the methods he used to acquire it and as a further example of Sobakevich's gluttony. The families of the various town functionaries, with the exception of the governor, are passed over in silence, as is, of course, that ticklish question of the purchase of dead souls. If the portraits of the landowners have certain features of a plan then the depiction of the civil servants gives more the impression of a sketch.

Yet there is one building in the town which reflects the nature of its inhabitants – the court building itself: 'all white, like chalk, probably to depict the cleanliness of the souls of those functionaries housed within it' (VI, 141). The irony of this comparison is given added piquancy, when Chichikov and Manilov enter only to find that everything inside is dirty: 'Themis just as she was, in negligé and dressing-gown, received her guests' (VI, 141). The reference to the Greek goddess of justice, Themis, heightens the bathos, but the chairman of this court, as we learn in chapter I, also receives guests at home in his dressing-gown, and is himself referred to as Homer's Zeus. We learn little else about him except that he is 'reasonable and nice', knows by heart Zhukovsky's poem *Lyudmila*, was the childhood friend of Plyushkin, and is prepared to charge Chichikov only half the amount he has incurred for the legal transactions.

The governor is one of those who is 'not too thin and not too fat', and his rank is 'not too high and not too low', but this is virtually all we know of him, except that a certain effeminacy is suggested by the fact that he does embroidery and sews purses; also at the ball he is carrying a lap-dog and drops the verse from a sweet-wrapper.[24] Nevertheless we do see something of his family; his daughter remarkable for her ovoid beauty, and his wife who speaks like a heroine in a society novel.

About the chief of police we learn even less. Only that he is the 'father and benefactor of the town', treating the merchants' shops as his own storehouses, and that he has managed to get twice as much income as his predecessor. The public prosecutor is characterised by his thick, black eyebrows and slightly winking left eye which gives the impression of saying: 'Let's go, dear chap, into another room, there I will tell you something.' Sobakevich says he is lazy and that his clerk does all his work for him. His death is treated by Gogol as having more importance than his life.

Slightly more detail is given in the portrayal of the postmaster. He is known by the ridiculous title of *Shprekhen zi deytsh* (*Sprechen Sie Deutsch*) and is in the habit of larding his speech with various meaningless Russian phrases, while screwing up one eye for special effect. He opens his snuffbox only half-way, so that it will not tempt the dirty fingers of others. He is called a wit and a philosopher, and reads Young's *Night Thoughts* and Eckartshausen's *Key to the mysteries of Nature*. Nevertheless his story about Captain Kopeykin reveals far more about his intelligence than his alleged reading.

The depiction of minor civil servants is reduced virtually to one trait. Thus the clerk Ivan Antonovich is remarkable in that the whole middle of his face seems to develop into his nose. He is, therefore, referred to throughout as 'pitcher snout' (*kuvshinoye rylo*). Another clerk has given such service to Themis, that his sleeves have burst at the elbows letting out the lining. For this, we are told, he has received the rank of collegiate registrator. The other clerks are reduced to 'broad backs of heads', 'dress coats' and 'frock coats', but Gogol's use of synecdoche reaches its extreme in the jacket seen writing away on its own, with its head on one side, nearly touching the paper.

The portrayal of women is almost equally idiosyncratic. In chapter 8 Gogol ironically warns his readers that he finds it difficult to describe the ladies of the town and can only do so superficially. In chapter 2 he had avoided saying much about the wife of Manilov, claiming that he was frightened of speaking about ladies, and, in effect Mrs Manilov is really only an appendage of Manilov himself, a detail in his characterisation. Even the governor's daughter, the ostensible heroine of part I, is presented with comic reticence: her name is not given; she does not even speak, and her beauty is reduced to the grotesque image of a freshly laid egg held up to the light in the hands of a housekeeper. Moreover the two ladies of the town of N., who take up chapter 9, are mere parodies of the female sex, comically referred to as 'the lady pleasant in all respects' and 'the simply pleasant lady'.

But what of the central figure himself? He is not too fat, not too thin: it is a stroke of genius that Gogol has made an eternally memorable character out of such a nonentity. Chichikov is a figure of mystery for the reader, from the very moment of his entry into the town. Everything about him is oblique.[25] The reader only learns his name when Chichikov has committed it to a scrap of paper, and it is read out syllable by syllable by a semi-literate servant of the inn. The method chosen to introduce the hero seems ironically symbolic, in view of his own later activities in the town; for he himself will be collecting names on paper – dead souls. The introduction of Chichikov through registration conceals more than a suggestion that he himself is merely one of that number: a great nonentity – who only exists on paper.

While the servant is still trying to make out the hero's name and rank, Chichikov himself has already gone off to look round the town. Here he collects another piece of paper with a list of names. It announces the performance of a play; Chichikov tears it down from a post, to peruse its contents at more leisure. Back in the inn he reads it thoroughly, right down to the name of the printer, then folds it away in his box 'where he had the habit of tucking away everything he chanced upon'. His chief characteristic as a 'snapper up of unconsidered (paper) trifles' is thus established.

Immediately after taking down the poster, Chichikov gazes at a woman 'of pleasing exterior', who is accompanied by a little boy. The second of Chichikov's interests is thus obliquely established: his pursuit of the fair sex (later to be represented in the figure of the governor's daughter), and, perhaps more importantly, his desire for descendants – *potomstvo*.

Nothing which Chichikov does is direct. When introducing himself to the dignatories of the town in chapter I, he seems to be defensively oblique: 'The new arrival, it seemed, avoided saying much about himself. If he did say anything, then it was in generalities of one sort or another' (VI, 13). This hero, who is not too fat and not too thin, not too old and not too young, is himself one great generalisation; there is no firm centre, just a lack of extremes. His tone and manner of speech alter according to the character of the person with whom he is dealing, and when he visits Korobochka we are told: 'The reader, I think, will already have noticed that Chichikov in spite of his tender expression was nevertheless taking more liberties in his speech than he had done with Manilov, and did not at all stand on ceremony' (VI, 49). Chichikov is all things to all men, he is the ultimate incarnation of Gogol's fictional and psychological world: a character without character. Although he has certain physical idiosyncrasies (the way he holds his head, and a tendency to express pleasure through jumping, jogging and dancing) we are nevertheless not deceived, there is only an emptiness contained between those circumscribing negatives which deny his existence to be in any way extreme.

Gogol manages to sustain the enigma of Chichikov through the various shifts of his behaviour, and to suggest different things about him by the range of contacts he makes. Thus his dealings with Manilov project him as terribly 'nice', whereas the simple superstitious nature of Korobochka contrives to endow him with an aura of the demonic. It is not until the final chapter of part I that we are given Chichikov's biography and also the real reasons for his strange behaviour. We can see how formative were the years of his childhood; his father instilling into him that money was more reliable than human beings; his teacher emphasising behaviour rather than knowledge – both these influences come together to produce in Chichikov a desire to please as a means towards the accumulation of wealth.

Having been given biographical detail to an extent unprecedented for a Gogolian hero, the reader ought to feel that at last he has 'got inside' Chichikov, but, alas, he is aware only of a resounding emptiness occupied by a shrivelled up object, not unlike a dead soul. Yet the author for his part, tries to persuade the reader that at last he has brought the trick off, that he has indeed penetrated the depths of Chichikov's psychology, and that if the reader doesn't like what he sees, it must somehow be the reader's own fault:

It is true there is something repulsive in such a character, and the very same reader who on the road of life would be friendly with such a man, would share hospitality with him and spend an agreeable time, will look askance at him, if he should turn up as the hero of a drama or a poem. Yet wise is he who does not disdain any character, but fixing him with a testing stare explores him to his very roots. (VI, 242)[26]

Wise indeed, the critic is tempted to comment; for such a reader would then have achieved more than the author. Yet penetration into the innermost depths of Chichikov's psyche, if not already accomplished, is at least held out as a promise for the future:

Were the author not to look a little more deeply into his soul, were he not to stir up on the bottom that which slips away and hides from the light, were he not to uncover the most treasured of thoughts which a man will not entrust to anyone else, but rather were he to show him just as he appeared to all the town, to Manilov and to the other people, then everybody would be happy and would accept him as an interesting man. (VI, 242–3)

It is perhaps significant that Gogol phrases his conditional clauses ('were he not to look'; 'were he not to stir', etc.) in the stylistic form of prohibitions ('*ne zaglyani*'; '*ne shevel'ni*'); for it is difficult to believe in Gogol's desire (even ability) to look deep into Chichikov's soul, to stir what is hidden from the light, to uncover his most treasured thoughts, and a secret fear that neither author nor hero can measure up to such demands seems to spill out as spleen against the reader.

If there is no real stirring of Chichikov's soul, there is, admittedly, a growing self-consciousness. The reader is first aware of it in the latter half of part I, after Chichikov has returned to the town. In chapter 7 he feels called upon to condemn the younger generation for their liberalism, but the author comments: 'Yet it was remarkable that in his words there was, all the same, a certain lack of sureness, as though at that very moment he had said to himself: "Oh, lad, you're telling lies, and what's more, big ones"' (VI, 146). He dare not look at the faces of Manilov and Sobakevich, but when he goes on to describe his supposed estate he glances at them by accident, and although he sees that Sobakevich's face is as expressionless as always, he nevertheless feels that he can read there: 'Oh, you're lying! I bet there isn't a river or a pond, nor even any land.'

Such moments of self-consciousness are, as might be expected, more in evidence in what we have of part II. Thus, having lied to General Betrishchev about the book which Tentetnikov is writing: 'Chichikov got completely muddled and became confused, he himself almost spat [from disgust] and inwardly said to himself, "Lord, what rubbish I'm talking!"' (VII, 40).

The self-consciousness of the hero reflects a similar process within the author. The second half of part I is marked by an ever increasing tendency towards authorial introspection and self-justification, and in part II when Chichikov visits Kostanzhoglo the reasons for his curiosity are not only made more explicit than would have been the case in part I, but at the same time Gogol also 'lays bare' the device of characterisation through surroundings which he had employed so consistently in his earlier portrait gallery of landowners: 'With curiosity Chichikov examined the dwelling of this unusual man who received two hundred thousand, thinking to find out the characteristics of the owner himself, as one can draw conclusions from a discarded shell about the oyster or snail, which had once been inside, and left its imprint' (VII, 58–9).

In part I Chichikov in his *brichka* had entered the '*poema*' through the gates of a provincial inn. His entry in part II is much more grand. 'In the gates appeared steeds, exactly as they are moulded or drawn on triumphal arches, one muzzle to the right, one muzzle to the left and a muzzle in the centre' (VII, 26). The horses of Chichikov's *brichka* have now not only become 'steeds' (*koni*), they are the steeds of a triumphal arch and accordingly the reader is prepared for the entry of a real hero, a noble conqueror, but unfortunately the deeds of Chichikov in part II are anything but noble. Far from being morally better, there is a marked deterioration: our hero is involved in acts which are even more base. In part I he was merely engaged in the dubious activity of buying dead souls, but in part II, while carrying on such purchases, he also forges a will to his own advantage, and buys an estate with borrowed money he does not intend to repay. Given these facts, the hope for Chichikov's spiritual regeneration in part II seems doubtful in the extreme. All the more so if its chief agent is to be the tax-farmer Murazov.

At the end of part I Gogol had used the following argument to refute the charge that his hero is a rogue: 'It would be most just of all to call him an owner (*khozyain*), an acquirer (*priobretatel'*). Acquisition is to blame for everything. It is because of acquisition that affairs have been conducted, which the world will call "not very clean"' (VI, 241–2). Yet in the tax-farmer Murazov we have acquisition (*priobretatel'stvo*) elevated to the highest degree. Not only is he a millionaire (*millionshchik*) – that alluring word, the mere rumour of which attracted the townspeople of N. to Chichikov himself – but he is also *khozyain* (owner, boss) and in a most ominous way. Kostanzhoglo estimates that he has amassed over forty million roubles, and that 'soon half of Russia will be in his hands'. A tax-farmer in Russia was synonymous with corruption, but Kostanzhoglo assures Chichikov that Murazov's huge fortune was acquired 'in the most irreproachable way, and by the most just of means'. In chapter I part I Chichikov had visited a tax-farmer as a member of the powerful 'establishment' of the town of N. This character is in no way developed, yet those on this 'visiting list' who are portrayed more fully later are all given negative characteristics.

A far less flattering view of a tax-farmer is given by Narezhny in his *Russian Gil Blas*. Kuroumov (the name suggests 'hen brain') has turned himself into a landowner, and having heard that important people punish their peasants for the slightest misdemeanour, he has had his hall hung with birches and whips: 'Mr Kuroumov wanted to prove that he was a landowner, although a recent one, and his house echoed to groans.'[27]

Another 'positive' character in part II is Kostanzhoglo. He is presented as the ideal landowner, for whom the peasants of his neighbours would be only to pleased to work. Everything is turned to account on Kostanzhoglo's estate, but his crops are traditional (no sugar, no tobacco). He is against the values of the West and Western industrialisation, yet he is not averse to opening a factory himself, if, for example, local fishermen dump large quantities of fish-scales on his land, and he can turn this to account by making glue.

Vasiliy Platonov (brother of the bored, lazy-bones Platon Platonov) is yet another 'positive' character in part II. He is in effect a pale shadow of Kostanzhoglo, but, if anything, the anti-Western, anti-St Petersburg, pro-Slavophile tendencies are in him even more pronounced. He is the guardian of peasant customs, and his phrase: '*Dlya menya obychay – svyataya veshch*' ('for me custom is a holy thing') suggests that he is a traditionalist and arch-conservative.[28]

It must be admitted that none of these characters is in the least convincing. They share with the 'negative' hero Chichikov an overruling passion for acquisition, and are positive only in as much as they are *successful* 'acquirers' and have built up a self-justifying philosophy of acquisition. Indeed, Kostanzhoglo's basic precept: 'every bit of rubbish yields a profit' (*vsyakaya dryan′ daet dokhod*) merely reveals him as a rational Plyushkin, or for that matter, a more scrupulous version of Chichikov himself; for in collecting worthless scraps of paper to turn eventually into money has not Chichikov himself been acting in accordance with this precept? The refurbishing of the negative motivation of Chichikov in part I as the positive message in part II glaringly reveals the intellectual and spiritual poverty of the whole enterprise as Gogol had at that point conceived it.

The precept of Kostanzhoglo is implicit in the values of Murazov himself; for here is a man who had begun with nothing and has ended up a millionaire. (Chichikov sees a certain hopeful parallel with himself as a man who is constantly having to start from scratch.) Of course, it could be argued that Gogol deliberately chose such positive acquirers as Kostanzhoglo and Murazov, as people with the only philosophy likely to impress Chichikov, so that once their influence was established, the authority of wealth and success could become a firm base for exercising real moral authority. It is certainly true that Murazov has a religious message for Chichikov, but his exhortation to give up worldly wealth relies on precept rather than example.

Chichikov, as he is presented in part II, still seems an unworthy vessel for such ideas, and the role of 'resurrected dead soul' appears almost to be passing away from him to Khlobuyev, a feckless landowner whose estate Chichikov buys, and whom he cheats of an inheritance. Khlobuyev is ordered by Murazov to go on a tour of Russia, not to collect dead souls like Chichikov, but to save his own living one by collecting money to build a church. Here then is the reworking in a positive sense of the theme of travel which lies behind the original comic conception of the work, and if the ideal of 'regeneration' is to any extent achieved in part II, it is only at the much lower level of the reworking of situations, themes and types.

Several of the characters in part II can be seen as more positive versions of types already encountered in part I. Thus Tentetnikov has much in common with Manilov. Both do absolutely nothing; both are dreamers and pipe-smokers (indeed for Tentetnikov Gogol coins the phrase: 'smoker up of heaven' – *koptitel′ neba*). There is in Tentetnikov, too, a sentimental strain; he cries over his childhood, and seems incapable of reprimanding his servants. Respect for the feelings of the lower social orders was a marked feature of Russian sentimentalism, yet if Manilov was even prepared to address Chichikov's coachman Selifan in the polite form of 'you' (*vy*), Tentetnikov, for his part, will not suffer being addressed by General Betrishchev in the intimate, condescending form 'thou' (*ty*). In his daydreams Manilov had thought that the rank of general might even be conferred on Chichikov and himself by virtue of their ideal friendship; Tentetnikov, however, is prepared to sacrifice his own ideal of love if it involves being patronised by a general.[29] There is, in fact, much more edge to the character of Tentetnikov; he is a man of principle and lacks the saccharine spinelessness of Manilov. Unlike the latter Tentetnikov actually reads books, and his daydreaming has a more serious character; he plans to write a huge work on Russia.

The physique and the gluttony of Petukh in part II recall Sobakevich,[30] and both characters have names derived from domestic animals (*petukh* – 'a cockerel'). Nevertheless, unlike Sobakevich he is a genial and generous man, but these more positive qualities, are, unfortunately, leading to his downfall. Through generosity, and hospitality Petukh is ruining himself.

Kostanzhoglo, as we have seen, is merely Plyushkin with a positive face. He admits that his neighbours call him a 'skinflint and a first rate miser' but believes that he is imitating God: 'It is precisely here that man imitates God. God granted himself the act of creation, as the greatest pleasure of all, and he demands from man also that he should be a similar creator of well-being around him. And they call this a boring matter!' (VII, 73). Plyushkin, too, believes that he has God on his side in his own labour of acquisition, and that He will punish those who thwart his miserliness.

The transmogrification of Plyushkin into Kostanzhoglo is as convincing as the sudden elevation of Chichikov's *troyka* into Russia itself. It does, however, help to explain why Plyushkin alone of all the characters of part I is allowed to evoke the reader's compassion. He is the very epitome of *priobretatel'stvo* (in its negative form admittedly) yet before this turned into miserliness, he was a careful landowner, not unlike Kostanzhoglo himself.

In view of the championship of *priobretatel'stvo* in part II, it is not surprising that there is implied censure of those who dissipate their wealth: Khlobuyev, Petukh; or those who need no longer strive to accumulate: Platon Platonov – his brother does this for him. No wonder Chichikov finds it hard to accept Murazov's teaching that to get rid of his possessions will lead him to salvation: it is contradicted by the evidence of all around him, including Murazov himself.

Negatively portrayed, too, are those imbued with civil-service values. Koshkarev runs his estate in imitation of the bureaucratic state machinery of St Petersburg, so that if Chichikov wants fodder for his horses he will have to make a written application, which will then be dealt with by the appropriate office, and the fodder will arrive – on the following day. Bureaucrats are just as much the butts for satire as they had been in part I. Indeed what is referred to as the 'Concluding Chapter' (*Zaklyuchitel'naya glava*)[31] is not unlike the end of part I in its description of the confusion generated by civil servants around the activities of Chichikov. This time, however, the confusion is intentional, and is the work of one of the most negative characters in part II, Samosvitov. At the close of part I (much like the end of *The Government Inspector*) Chichikov had left the civil servants fearfully anticipating the possible advent of the governor general. In part II Gogol seems to have projected the inevitable sequel: a governor general does in fact appear to sort out all the bureaucratic malpractices. Authority and the ways of the government are thus vindicated.

The didacticism of part II is disappointingly trite. Kostanzhoglo is strongly reminiscent of Rossianinov, the 'positive' hero (his name alone casts him as an emblematic Russian, consonant with official nationalist doctrine) of *Ivan Vyzhigin*, the novel by that paid apologist of the regime and apparent enemy of Gogol, Faddey Bulgarin. The ideas of Kostanzhoglo are at root obscurantist: he is against education and schools, and in his condemnation of enlightenment he has a forerunner in Sobakevich. The portraits of both Kostanzhoglo and Vasiliy Platonov are clearly influenced by Slavophile ideas which were hostile to Western influence and in favour of a return to the simple patriarchal ways of the past. In Koshkarev this tendency has taken a polemical turn. The way Koshkarev runs his estate reads like a Slavophile mockery at the Westernisers and the reforms of Peter I: 'He vouchsafed with his head, that if one were only to dress half the Russian peasants in German trousers, then the level of the sciences would rise, trade would pick up, and the Golden Age would come to Russia' (VII, 63). Here again Gogol comes close to Bulgarin; for in *Ivan Vyzhigin* the positive figure Milovidin ridicules landowners who try to build German houses for their peasants, and demand from them the same cleanliness as in Germany.[32]

Bulgarin sees the destiny of Russia to lie in the attitudes of the landowning class: 'The entire happiness of his villagers depends on the landowner, their morals, enlightenment and well-being, consequently the morals, enlightenment and well-being of the whole of Russia depends on the landowning nobility taken as a whole.'[33] These are ideas close to the ruling sentiments of Gogol's *Selected Passages from Correspondence with Friends* as well as those of part II of *Dead Souls*: the salvation of Russia lies with the landowners, who should cease mortgaging their estates and hanging about the capitals, employed as civil servants. They should instead return to the land and resume a life of thrift, bringing up their peasants to work hard and to fear God.

The unsatisfactory nature of part II is essentially a failure at the level of ideas – not merely their quality but an inability to clothe them in an artistically satisfying form. The old Gogol is still there, though cramped and harassed by the preacher. In particular the portrait of Petukh has all the vividness of detail and raciness of expression which characterise the portraits of part I (his hospitality by numbers; his story of the mayor in church; the ordering of the next day's menu overheard by a Chichikov full to bursting). Then there is the blustering, but essentially good-natured General Betrishchev, even the bizarre Koshkarev – all these recall the old Gogol.

Nevertheless, there is also the birth of a new Gogol; the figure of Tentetnikov marks a significant departure. Not only is he given biographical depth far more convincingly than either Plyushkin or Chichikov, but he himself is portrayed without caricature and comic distortion and in a way which looks forward to the future development of Russian prose fiction. Indeed part II, for all its sense of failure, is pregnant with the future. In essence it is an attempt to turn *Dead Souls* into a novel of resurrection: a theme which was to become a major obsession with Gogol's successors Dostoevsky, Tolstoy and, perhaps in a more direct sense, Ivan Goncharov.

Goncharov's hero, Oblomov, has much in common with Tentetnikov, a fact first pointed out by Dobrolyubov.[34] Like Oblomov, Tentetnikov does nothing all day long, yet he dreams of achieving great things. Gogol speculates that the reasons for such lethargy might be the lack of an external influence (after the death of his mentor): 'that there was now nobody in the whole world who would be capable of raising up his energies, shattered through perpetual lack of decision, and a will, impotent and lacking resilience. One who might shout, in an arousing cry to the soul, that inspiriting word: forward!' (VII, 23). Thus it seems that Tentetnikov, like Oblomov, is in need of a Shtolts, and 'forward' is an important concept for Goncharov's novel too.[35] Moreover, just as Goncharov makes his hero in some sense a representative of a whole area of Russian society (this is certainly the view of Dobrolyubov), so Gogol before him sees a general need for the word 'forward': 'Which is thirsted for by Russians of whatever degree, of every condition, calling and trade' (VII, 23).

In part II chapter 4 a similar idea is echoed by Khlobuyev, another of Gogol's feckless characters, who is a forerunner of Chekhov's Gayev in the *Cherry Orchard*: 'A Russian, I can see from myself, can do nothing without someone to urge him on, otherwise he will fall asleep, otherwise he will get soft' (VII, 83). There is perhaps something both in Russian mythology (the legend of Ilya Muromets) and in Russian history (the figure of Peter the Great) which was sensed equally by Gogol and Goncharov and which led both to see Russian life as 'a sleep and an awakening'.[36]

For Tentetnikov and Oblomov alike this awakening is nearly brought about by love. Yet in both cases the romance flags. Chichikov, the 'man of affairs', who is constantly travelling, sets out (like an embryo Shtolts), to patch up the misunderstanding for his friend. He leaves Tentetnikov at the end of chapter I, trying to think and not to think, but 'ends and tails of thoughts' come involuntarily into his head. It is in much the same situation that we find Oblomov at the beginning of Goncharov's novel, with thought hovering round his face like a bird.

Chichikov also plans to act as an 'urger on' (*ponukatel'*) for another Oblomov-like character, Platon Platonov, whose lethargy is defined by his brother as 'spiritual hibernation' (*dushevnaya spyachka*) resulting from a lack of 'vivid impressions and sensations' and much as Shtolts will urge Oblomov to travel with him abroad, so Chichikov plans to take Platonov with him on his journeys – to wake him up.

Chichikov, of course, is the bogus man of affairs. Nevertheless both Gogol and Goncharov seem to agree on the need for truly practical men, with common sense, who will show Russia the right way 'ahead'. Gogol sees this ideal, not in Chichikov, but in Kostanzhoglo, a character, who unfortunately is no more credible than is Goncharov's Shtolts. Strangely enough both authors seem diffident about presenting their positive men of affairs as wholly Russian. Shtolts is half German, and Kostanzhoglo, we are told, has southern blood: 'He was not entirely Russian. He himself did not know where his ancestors had come from. He did not occupy himself with his genealogy, finding it did not add up to anything and was superfluous to his farming. He was even completely convinced that he was Russian, and he certainly knew no other language, but Russian' (VII, 61). For Kostanzhoglo to have been half German would certainly have been unthinkable given the strong Slavophile ethos of part II. Nevertheless, given this ethos it is remarkable that Gogol conceived him as a character of such mixed racial origins.[37]

The overall plan for *Dead Souls* was of a work in three parts. Goncharov, too, spoke of his three novels: *A Usual Story*, *Oblomov*, *The Precipice* as but three parts of one work, and if part II of *Dead Souls* refurbishes characteristics of types found in part I, Goncharov could make a similar claim for his writing: 'Look into *Oblomov*. Olga is the reincarnation of Nadenka in the next epoch.'[38] Moreover, in Gogol's description of Tentetnikov's youthful flirtation with the civil service in St Petersburg, there lies in embryo much of Goncharov's first novel, *A Usual Story*. In both there is the contrast between the youthful idealism of the hero and the cynicism of his experienced uncle, which develops into an antithesis between the capital and the rural provinces.

Yet there is another author who also springs to mind. The young Tentetnikov's restless search for real activity, be it in the civil service, in intellectual circles (the so-called 'embittered people – *ogorchennyye lyudi*) or on his own estates, and his discovery everywhere of 'falseness' (*lozh'*) suggests that he is a hero almost in a Tolstoyan mould. Indeed his attempts to introduce reforms on his estate, and the suspicion and lack of co-operation with which these are greeted by his peasants, seem to look forward to the experiences of Nekhlyudov in *Resurrection*. The Tolstoyan solution for the problems of these restless searchers after truth, had actually been pronounced before Tolstoy, by Gogol's Kostanzhoglo: 'God grant that everyone be a tiller of the soil': 'It is said: Till the earth in the sweat of thy brow. It's no good splitting hairs. It has already been proved by centuries of experience, that man as an agriculturalist is more moral, more pure, more noble, more lofty' (VII, 69).[39] In his wrath at the way Khlobuyev has let his estate go to ruin, Kostanzhoglo tells him that he should have taken a spade into his own hands and have made his wife and children dig too.

Tolstoy is not alone among later writers in suggesting physical work on the land as the salvation for the gentry hero. It is seen as a remedy for Dmitri in Dostoevsky's *The Brothers Karamazov*, and in *The Devils* the same solution is suggested to Stavrogin by Shatov.[40] Nevertheless the idea that the criminal could be resurrected into a being of great value seems peculiarly Dostoevskian, yet the idea is already adumbrated in the second part of *Dead Souls*. Just as Porfiriy in *Crime and Punishment* tells Raskolnikov that he must be a sun for all to see,[41] so Murazov tells Chichikov: 'Your appointed role is to be a great man, and you have got yourself lost and ruined yourself' (VII, 112). It is chiefly Chichikov's strength of will which Murazov appears to see as the attribute of his greatness: 'You, it seems to me, might have been a doughty knight, for now people lack will, they are all weak' (VII, 114).

The problems of crime, the will and moral resurrection are all very Dostoevskian themes. In his plans for the future development of *Dead Souls* Gogol was moving out of the area of his own competence, but in so doing he was showing the way ahead. The allure of the didactic novel would obsess both Tolstoy and Dostoevsky. Nevertheless their solutions to its problems would not only be different, they would be more successful.

The poem in prose

When Gogol finally managed to have his 'poema' passed by the censors in St Petersburg, it was on the understanding that the title should be: 'The Adventures of Chichikov' (*Pokhozhdeniya Chichikova*) and that the controversial and enigmatic 'Dead Souls' should be allowed only as a secondary title (*ili Mertvyye dushi*). Gogol however designed his own cover, and although he kept to the prescribed formula, he contrived by typographic means to diminish the importance of the censor's title and to focus attention on his own.[42] 'Dead Souls' is boldly prominent on Gogol's cover, but there is another title which stands out even more boldly: *Poema*. If the prominence of the subtitle is a typographical 'thumbing of the nose' at the censor, the designation 'poema' is no less provocative as a challenge to the reader. *Poema* in Russian indicates a long narrative poem, such as an epic. Some critics seek to interpret this title in the light of Gogol's own pronouncements on genre, relating the concept to his definition of the smaller epic (*malaya epopeya*).[43] Yet, even if this is accepted, a sense of unease must remain. 'Epic poem' suggests Homer and Vergil, the sort of heroic poetry which affords a mythological basis for national self-consciousness. Indeed, Konstantin Aksakov made a brave attempt to interpret it in this way, comparing *Dead Souls* to Homer's *Odyssey*. But the work, as we have it, is a great comic masterpiece, so that if its designation as 'poema' is to be taken in the sense of 'national epic', then the very juxtaposition of *Dead Souls*: 'national epic' suggests a satire on Russia itself, a view which could be justified on the evidence of part one. Nevertheless a poem, be it epic or not, is written in verse, Gogol's *poema* is written in prose. The question remains: why did he not call it a novel?[44] This after all, is what it is.

As we have seen, Gogol himself claimed that this theme for a major work had been given him by Pushkin, and it is interesting that Pushkin's own major work, *Eugene Onegin* is not called *poema* (which is what it is) but 'a novel in verse'. It may well be that in choosing the designation '*poema*' Gogol had the perverseness of Pushkin's example in mind;[45] for in broad terms his poem in prose is not unlike a comic counterpart of Pushkin's 'novel in verse'.

Eugene Onegin is remarkable for its many digressions; indeed in developing his plot, Pushkin seems less interested in progression than digression. Much the same can be said of *Dead Souls* (particularly the latter half of part I), and like Pushkin, Gogol also plays both with his reader and with the literary conventions.

Gogol is particularly fond of suspending the action while he develops a simile often at such length that it is in danger of becoming a tale in its own right. The reader's first encounter with the device is the description of black tailcoats at the governor's reception in chapter I: 'Black tailcoats flitted and moved about separately and in clusters here and there, as flies move about on shining, white, lump sugar' (VI, 14). In any other writer the comparison would have ended here, and there are examples of short effective similes in *Dead Souls*.[46] Pushkin, in *Eugene Onegin* uses a comparable image to describe the black tailcoats of men gathered round ladies as pretty as pictures:

И темной рамою мужчин
Вкруг дам, как около картин.

(And the dark frame of men
Round the ladies as though around pictures.)

Yet for all the superficial resemblance between these similes, the difference is significant. Pushkin's is a drawing-room image – a picture; Gogol's is one of the kitchen. Whereas Pushkin's simile serves to enforce the dignity of the scene, Gogol's debases it, reducing it not merely to the comic, but to something even approaching the revolting: flies on sugar[47] suggest the corruption of purity. Pushkin's image is gracefully static; Gogol's is full of bustle and lumpiness (*nosilis′ vrozn′ i kuchami*). Yet the movement and comic vigour of Gogol's opening loses its effect in the heavy, involved sentences which follow, as the comparison takes on more precise, but apparently superfluous, detail: it is a hot July day; an old housekeeper is hacking sugar into dazzling lumps before an open window; children are watching her with curiosity; flies come in through the open window in swarms, profiting from the bad eyesight of the housekeeper and the fact that the strong sunlight makes her squint; the flies are sated with all the food of the summer and have only come to the sugar for social reasons and to perform their flies' toilet. The simile is remarkable for its supernumeraries: the old housekeeper, the children, even summer itself is personified. To add to the confusion the principal actors themselves, the flies, are not attracted to the sugar for the simple, ostensible reason of feeding.

The function of a simile is to generalise and broaden the action or object described by relating it to another context. Gogol, however, adds so much detail to his simile that in effect he narrows its impact through making it more and more specific, and the more detail he adds, the more the point of comparison recedes; the result is the destruction of the simile, as a simile. The 'tenor'[48] of the comparison (which, it might be added, is in itself a synecdoche): 'Black tailcoats flitted and moved separately and in clusters', is linked to a 'vehicle' which is so heavy, both in detail and in mode of expression, that all balance is lost. Indeed it would make more sense if the simile were inverted and the tenor became the vehicle, so that the movements of the flies were compared quite simply to tailcoats, rather than tailcoats given a complicated comparison with flies. This, the first extended simile of *Dead Souls*, is truly Gogolian; it bears the characteristic hallmarks of his style: synecdoche and inversion. Such similes are often referred to as 'Homeric', but they might equally well be termed 'inverted'. Moreover, such 'inverted similes' have a curious affinity to a synecdochal construction; for like Kovalev's nose, the appendage suddenly assumes greater importance than the whole – it runs away and assumes an independent life of its own, an existence which denies and even contradicts its origins, so that such inverted similes are also 'similes of subversion'.

There may, of course, be a comic parallelism intended between the toilet of the flies and that of Chichikov himself, described shortly before, which also consists of 'rubbing' of various sorts (i.e. with soap and towel), and the simile is comic in its own right: it reduces the elevated to the status of the lowly. Nevertheless the accumulation of detail destroys the initial comic impact and substitutes for it a mockery of the simile itself; thus comedy 'by comparison' develops into comedy 'at the expense of comparison'. Gogol, like Sterne, is parodying his own devices.

The simile of the flies is in an introductory position; it prefaces Chichikov's entry into the governor's drawing-room, where he himself will be introduced to some of these same tailcoats, and on the strength of invitations from two of them, will begin his round of visits, taking him from the 'sugar'[49] of Manilov to the old 'housekeeper' Plyushkin. The most striking of Gogol's extended similes are found in similar introductory positions: the comparison of the weather to the colour of soldier's greatcoats precedes Chichikov's entrance into the courtyard of Manilov; his arrival at the house of Korobochka is announced by dogs whose barking develops into a detailed comparison with a church choir; the encounter with the governor's daughter introduces her as a freshly laid egg held up to the light in the arms of the housekeeper; Chichikov's arrival at the house of Sobakevich is prefaced by an extended simile with pumpkins, which in their turn become musical instruments; and the comparison of Plyushkin's eyes to mice occurs at the beginning of their meeting, when Chichikov first sets foot in the house.

The only character in the 'portrait gallery' not to have his introductory simile is Nozdrev, and yet one of the most revealing uses of the device is associated with him. The simile occurs, not as an introduction, but at a dramatic point of farewell. Nozdrev, with the support of his peasants, is about to strike Chichikov, and at this dramatic moment Gogol suspends the action to compare Nozdrev with a giddy young lieutenant about to attack an impregnable fortress. The fortress is described with hyperbole worthy of Nozdrev himself. Thus its walls are lost in the clouds and *millions* (*sic*) of gun-barrels are pointing from its embrasures. The lieutenant gives not a thought: 'that his powerless company of men will be puffed up into the air like down, and that a fatal bullet was already whistling through the air to stop his raucous throat' (VI, 87). Not only is there here a simile within a simile ('puffed up into the air like down') but the device of the extended simile itself is at its most absurd: the vehicle does not expand and generalise the action of the tenor – it contradicts and subverts it. Thus it is contrary to the sense of the scene to describe Nozdrev and his men as about to be puffed up into the air like down or struck silent by a bullet. Such ideas would be more fitting for the situation of Chichikov. Moreover, Gogol, having developed his analogy in some detail suddenly renounces it and points himself to its inherent absurdity:

> But if Nozdrev represented a desperate lieutenant, who had got carried away, storming a fortress, then the fortress he was attacking, was not at all like an impregnable one. On the contrary the fortress felt such fear, that its soul sank to its very boots (VI, 87).

In such an absurd, self-defeating simile there is something akin to the patently self-contradictory 'Tale of Captain Kopeykin', and it is not only the simile which Gogol mocks in his *poema*, but that other literary convention, the 'tale within a tale'. On the other hand such an absurd simile is not without its own artistic logic. In suggesting the behaviour of Nozdrev it conveys a sense of his swaggering, violent nature, and its very absurdity mirrors the essential incongruity of the man: it is the verbal parallel of the barrel-organ which begins in one way and ends in another.

Much the same can be said of the introductory similes: they all serve in some measure to hint at the character which is to follow. Thus the indeterminate weather, likened to the colour of soldiers' greatcoats, serves as an introduction to the indeterminate nature of Manilov himself. Korobochka's church choir of dogs hints at her 'churchiness' and simple superstitious faith (for her the ambiguous phrase 'dead souls' at first takes on religious and metaphysical overtones, and it is to the house of her friend, the arch-priest's wife, that she drives, when she suspects that she might have been cheated).

The comparison with an egg emphasises the blank, unreal beauty of the governor's daughter – a beauty, which is un-Russian; for in an aside which seems to echo Pushkin's famous digression on women's feet, Gogol comments on the rarity of such a face in a country where everything is broad and on a grand scale. The egg simile has the same effect as that of the flies: it reduces society elegance to the level of the kitchen, and once more a housekeeper makes her appearance. She is checking the soundness of the egg by holding it up to the light.

The pumpkin simile used to introduce Sobakevich, which unexpectedly develops into an amorous vignette of village life, hints, as we have seen, at vegetable carnality, and Plyushkin's eyes likened to mice not only serve to suggest his furtiveness, but carry on the idea of his house as a cluttered cellar. In imagery, Plyushkin, as in other matters is treated more richly than his predecessors. His courtyard is likened, in some detail, to the fleamarket in Moscow, and the suspicion of a feeling appearing on his face is compared to the last appearance of a drowning man on the surface. Most striking of all is that Chichikov's visit is prefaced with a long and intricate description of Plyushkin's garden, which, although not an extended simile, conveys, nevertheless, the feeling of an extended metaphor.

However one strives to see these extended similes as 'fitting' for the characters they introduce, the overriding impression remains one of incongruity, and this is compounded by the fact that the images seem 'out of place' in yet another way. Thus the flyridden sugar of chapter 1 would be equally appropriate in chapter 2 as an image for the flyblown sweetness of Manilov. Manilov's own introductory simile is embellished with a cockerel ('to fill out the picture there was no lack of a cockerel, the herald of changeable weather'), a detail appropriate for the next landowner, Korobochka, who lives surrounded by poultry and pictures of birds. By the same token the introductory simile for Korobochka herself, the dogs' choir, would seem more fitting for the next portrait, that of the dog-fancier Nozdrev. The extended simile associated with Nozdrev which is entirely military, and mentions the Russian general Suvorov, seems to look forward to the next landowner, Sobakevich, who surrounds himself with portraits of generals and military heroes. Moreover the first extended simile of chapter 5 – the egg held in the hands of the housekeeper, might seem more relevant for chapter 6, where Plyushkin is first mistaken by Chichikov for just such a housekeeper. The absurdity of Gogol's extended similes is, therefore, even more contrived than may at first appear; they are not only 'out of place', they are actually, in significant respects, out of phase.

We have seen that Gogol himself questions the appropriateness of comparing Chichikov with a fortress, and he subverts a comparison again in a much shorter simile for civil servants: 'who were similar to industrious bees scattered through a honeycomb, if only a honeycomb could be compared with civil service business' (VI, 145).

The simile of the lieutenant and the fortress is remarkable not merely because it 'lays bare' the device of incongruity; it is unusual, too, in occupying a 'valedictory' position, but there is yet a further displacement. In chapter 9, 'the simply pleasant lady' is unexpectedly compared to a Russian huntsman with his dogs, who suddenly freezes and waits for a hare to be driven out of a wood. The comparison is curious. The Russian landowner, the great hunter and lover of dogs, suggests Nozdrev (specialised hunting vocabulary is used, similar to that employed by Nozdrev in chapter 4). Yet even more curious: the imagery is quite close, in essential features, to Nozdrev's own valedictory simile. Thus 'the simply pleasant lady' and Nozdrev are both compared to down about to be blown into the air, and in both there is the same sudden suspension of action and freezing into a threatening pose. The image of the huntsman, so out of place in the drawing-room of 'the lady pleasant in every respect', would be far more fitting as a simile for Nozdrev than his comparison to a giddy young lieutenant.

The incongruity of the provincial world of *Dead Souls* is reminiscent of the dislocated reality described in 'Nevsky Prospekt', in which a demon has crumbled up the pieces of the world and mixed them up without rhyme or reason. The lack of 'fit' of Gogol's similes is but a part of the total absurdity of the *poema*. There is a logic in this world, yet it mirrors a social order which reduces human beings to objects, whilst elevating them to 'souls', whose laws can be adapted to the smiling face of things ('even the chairman gave orders that only half of the tax should be taken from him, and the other half, by some unknown means, was put on the account of some other supplicant'); the 'realism' of whose reasoning makes justice itself absurd ('But Drobyazhkin was a man who was dead, therefore there would be little advantage for him, even if he were to win the case, but the peasants were still alive, therefore, for them, a decision in their favour was extremely important.')

Much that appears inconsequential in the *poema* is really not so when seen in the light of such all-pervading oblique logic. Thus the peasants' conversation about Chichikov's wheel at the opening of the work, not only sets the theme of peasants and journeying, it even hints at ultimate failure ('it won't get as far as Kazan'[50]) and Chichikov's enigmatic actions on arrival have significance for his character and intentions, as we saw in the last chapter.

The entry of Chichikov's coach is witnessed by yet another character: a young man, whose dress is described in such detail, that the reader could easily take him to be a person destined to play a part in later events – someone, perhaps, even more important than the 'nonentity' sitting in the coach; but the young man merely holds his cap to prevent it being blown off by the wind, and goes 'his own way', never to be seen again. The building up of detail round a character of such transitory importance achieves a distortion similar to that effected by the excessive detail of the extended simile. There are many such episodic characters who flit in and out of the *poema*. Most of chapter 9 is taken over by 'the simply pleasant lady' and 'the lady pleasant in every respect', whom Gogol introduces as ostensible narrators. Their real function, however, is to suspend, rather than advance, the narration. Another such pair, Kifa Mokiyevich and Mokiy Kifofich, are brought in to make a polemical point, but many of these episodic characters appear to have no function at all. There is, for example, the lieutenant from Ryazan, who is first mentioned by the hotel waiter at the end of chapter 6 in a short piece of absurdly banal conversation which seems to look forward to such writers as Ionesco and Pinter:

'You have been off a long time, sir', said the waiter, lighting up the staircase.
'Yes', said Chichikov, when he got on to the staircase. 'Well, and what about you?'
'Praise God', replied the waiter bowing, 'yesterday, some sort of military lieutenant arrived, and took room sixteen.'
'A lieutenant?'
'I don't know what sort, from Ryazan, bay horses.'
'Good, good, behave well in the future too!' said Chichikov and went into his room... (VI, 131)

The lieutenant reappears at the end of chapter 7, where he is described as the only one awake in the hotel; he has ordered five pairs of new boots and can't get to sleep for admiring them. This is the last we see or hear of him.

Why does Gogol bring this non-protagonist into his *poema*,

endowed, as he is, with such apparent significance? In the popular fiction of the day lieutenants were equated with love for society heroines (yet, typically, the love of Gogol's lieutenant is for boots).[51] Nevertheless, there is in the introduction of this figure the covert hint of a rival to Chichikov for the affections of the governor's daughter. If this is so, it is a false trail, but, as such, it provides a clue to Gogol's use of episodic characters in his *poema*: the false trails they suggest serve to add to the mystery of the central line of the plot. Chichikov's own activities are enigmatic, his true motives are not revealed until the last chapter of part I, and it is significant that after the governor's ball, when his intentions are seen at their most controversial, episodic characters should flood the plot: the two 'pleasant' ladies; the crippled Captain Kopeykin; Sysoy Pafnut′evich, Makdonal′d Karlovich and all the weird people who emerge because of the rumours.

The fact that the fabric of *Dead Souls* is composed of such bizarre detail, raises the question of Gogol's view of reality. At the beginning of chapter 6 there are two attitudes to reality put forward as the author's own. One is the view of his youth, when, as he claims, he delighted in visiting any new place, and: 'every building, everything that merely bore the imprint of any noticeable peculiarity, everything would make me stop in wonder' (VI, 110). His imagination, he says, would be stirred into flight by the mass of everyday objects he saw; he would invent a whole life for any passer-by, and the house of any landowner would present him with: 'then alas, an exterior which was far from vulgar'; but now, claims Gogol: 'Now it is with indifference I drive up to any unknown village, and with indifference I look at its vulgar exterior' (VI, 111). The view of his youth, therefore, picks out a mass of idiosyncratic detail, which feeds the artistic imagination (a process typical of Gogol's methods, as in 'Nevsky Prospekt'). The other view merely presents a 'vulgar exterior' to his cold and indifferent glance (and here, in the artistic problem of the exterior and of surface, we are reminded of the central theme of 'The Portrait').

The tone of authorial self-pity, in regretting his long lost youth, should not deceive us. The same imaginative eye for idiosyncratic detail, which the author claims to have lost, is everywhere in evidence, and nowhere more strikingly so than at the end of chapter 6 itself:

It was already deep twilight when they drove up to the town. Light and shadow were completely mixed, and it seemed that objects themselves had

> become mixed too. The multi-coloured toll-bar took on a nondescript colour; the moustaches of the soldier on guard seemed to be on his forehead and much higher than his eyes, and it was as though he had no nose at all. (VI, 130)

Not only is this reminiscent of the fantasy experienced by Piskarev, but the world of this twilight scene, with its strolling civil servants, coarse women, and the young man who 'has visited Schiller', reads like a minor restatement of 'Nevsky Prospekt'. Once more we have the gulf between reality and the world of the imagination, but is that gulf all it seems?

It is not merely 'shade and light' which is jumbled up in this strange scene: imaginative fantasy is mixed with vulgar reality. The end of chapter 6, therefore, returns us to the theme of its opening, and serves to remind us that if Gogol has not lost the imaginative view of his youth, that other view, of the vulgar exterior of reality, is equally valid. Indeed, throughout *Dead Souls* there is a sense in which all the extravagant detail builds up merely to present a vulgar exterior. Nowhere is this more true than in the description of Plyushkin's house, for which this authorial confession serves as introduction, and although one may have reservations about Gogol's wish to identify one view with his youth, the other with his middle age, nevertheless, in terms of the artistic process itself this progression from one to the other is perfectly valid.

Shorn of emotional ballast Gogol's first view of reality may be called the 'particular', his second – the 'general'; the interaction between the two permeates the whole *poema*. On the one hand, as we have seen, Gogol seeks to ascribe general significance to his landowners, while, on the other, each is particularised even as a type; all are drawn from common strokes, yet the detail is idiosyncratic to a degree. His portraits are thus generalised in their idiosyncracies and individualised in their typicality. At the centre stands that 'man for all occasions', Chichikov himself, who is introduced as an enormous generalisation: 'not too fat and not too thin, not too old and not too young', but, nevertheless, is engaged in the most bizarre of particular business – the purchase of 'dead souls'.

It is significant that the very chapter which introduces this theme of particular and general views of reality (and concludes Chichikov's journeying with particularities reminiscent of 'Nevsky Prospekt') should also dwell on the garden of that arch hoarder of bizarre detail – Plyushkin himself. The garden is presented in a way that reads like a metaphor: a statement of the author's own views on art. It is a riot of overgrown vegetation described in that wealth of particular detail, so typical of Gogol's own hoarding proclivities as an artist. The ultimate effect is of a romantic theory of aesthetics:[52]

> In a word everything was such a wilderness of beauty, as neither nature nor art could invent, but which only happens when they are joined together; when nature passes its final blade along the labour of man, heaped up, often without sense, lightening the heavy masses, destroying a coarsely-felt sense of order and beggars' rents, where the bare, unconcealed plan peeps through, giving a wonderful warmth to everything that had been created in cool, restrained purity and neatness. (VI, 113)

The passage is strangely self-contradictory: the work of man is planned, restrained and neat, yet 'heaped up without sense' in 'heavy masses'; nature appears to destroy the bare plan with its prolixity, but its instrument is one of shaping and excision, the blade – the tool of man himself.

Such contradictions which tend to obscure the meaning taken at its face value, are resolved if the passage is seen as a metaphor of the interrelationship of the conscious (art) and the unconscious (nature) in the artistic process itself; for in its interaction with the conscious mind the unconscious both excises and embellishes: it 'frees' the pressure of 'the heavy masses', the labour piled up to the detriment of artistic sense, and at the same time it adds 'warm' detail to the bare plan.[53] It is in such a manner that the scheme behind the characterisation of the landowners in part I loses all 'coarsely-felt sense of order', and that the wayward force of the unconscious sabotages the conscious plan for the work as a whole. Plyushkin's overgrown garden is a symbol for the *poema* itself. Nevertheless, it is the opening of the next chapter (chapter 7) which discusses the question of art, and more particularly *Dead Souls* itself. Once more the instrument is the blade (*rezets*) and there is a distant, yet obvious, connection between the imagery here and that of the passage on realism in 'The Portrait'. There is the same antithesis of 'man in his beauty' (*prekrasnyy chelovek*) and what is revealed by the 'blade', but this time it is Gogol himself who has chosen the way of the knife, and what he has dared to exhibit is the 'terrible mire of petty detail'.

In chapter 2 Gogol had humorously called attention to his passion for detail: 'But the author loves exceedingly to be circumstantial in everything, and in this regard, despite the fact that he is himself a

Russian, he wants to be as accurate as a German' (VI, 19). Shortly afterwards he gives a typical catalogue impression of Russian reality: 'Scarcely had the town slipped by than the confusion started in the Russian fashion of stuff and nonsense on both sides of the road: hummocks, fir-groves, the low, thin bushes of young pine, the burned trunks of old pine, wild heather and similar rubbish' (VI, 21). Gogol's choice of words is curiously revealing. He adapts the idiom 'the confusion started' (*poshla pisat' guberniya* – literally: 'the province set out to write') by substituting typical provincial sights for 'province' (*guberniya*) itself, and thus through a verbal joke associates the very process of writing itself with a catalogue of bizarre *realia*, which he then dismisses in totality as 'rubbish' (*vzdor*).[54] The description continues and its detail becomes even more bizarre: villages like piles of firewood; fat peasant women looking out of upper windows; calves and pigs peering out of lower ones. Yet, however sharply observed and idiosyncratically presented, it merely adds up to the usual drab face of banality, summed up in the phrase: 'in a word, well-known sights' (*slovom vidy izvestnyye*). Thus in chapter 2 there is already humorous anticipation of that artistic dichotomy which in chapter 6 Gogol will lament with sentimental pathos: the 'particular' and the 'general' views of reality.

Sentimental rhetoric is even more marked in chapter 7, when the author invites pity for himself both on a professional and on a personal level: as a writer whose task is to portray the unflattering side of reality, and also as a lonely, homeless wanderer (like his hero Chichikov). It is implied that the fortunate artist who chooses lofty themes, and the wanderer who is happy are both family men, whereas he is a lonely bachelor. The theme had been adumbrated in lighter comic vein when his hero, on first entering the town of N. had taken a kerchief from his neck of the kind that wives prepare for married men: 'But I am certainly unable to say who makes them for bachelors. God alone knows. I have never worn such kerchiefs' (VI, 9). Yet what in chapter 1 is merely a whimsical aside, in chapter 7 has become authorial self-pity for his position both as an artist and as a man: 'Like a wanderer with no family he will remain alone in the middle of the road. Harsh is his career, and bitterly will he feel his loneliness' (VI, 134).

He inveighs against contemporary judgement which assigns to the comic artist 'a despised corner among the ranks of those writers who insult humanity', but even worse, it will: 'ascribe to him the qualities of the characters which he himself depicts. It will deny him a heart, a soul and the godly flame of talent' (VI, 134). This apparent rejection of a link between the writer's characters and his own personality is at variance with later statements in *Selected Passages from Correspondence with Friends*: 'None of my readers knew that in laughing at my heroes he was laughing at me' (VIII, 293); 'I began to endow my heroes, in addition to their own vileness, with my own worthlessness' (VIII, 294).

The 'heroes' of Gogol's *poema* are 'dead souls', and it is the implication of this for his own character, which seems to cause him concern in his rejection of 'contemporary judgement'; for it seeks to deprive him of 'a heart and a soul' and to deny him artistic ability.

From the middle of part I to its end, the reader is aware of a sense of crisis which permeates Gogol's *poema*. It takes the form not only of authorial self-pity, but of self-justification, which is linked to an attack on others, be it the reader, contemporary judgement, scholars, society ladies or patriots. In *Selected Passages from Correspondence with Friends* Gogol himself commented that all his latest works were the history of his own soul.

Chapter 6, which introduces Plyushkin, marks the onset of this more introspective second half of part I. It begins with the discussion of the author's two views of reality and contains the description of Plyushkin's garden, with all its implications for Gogol's own art. If there is any validity in Gogol's statements on self-identification with his characters, it is above all in Plyushkin that this may be seen.

Plyushkin is unique among the characters of part I in evoking sympathy from the reader. Gogol achieves this by contrasting his past with his present, much as, at the beginning of the chapter, he contrasts his own past with his own present. This regret for his passing years ('Oh, my youth! Oh, my freshness!') becomes generalised in the figure of Plyushkin: 'Today's ardent youth would recoil in horror, if he were to be shown his own portrait in old age. Take with you on the journey, when you leave the tender years of youth for harsh embittering manhood, take with you every human response. Do not leave them en route, you will not pick them up later!' (VI, 127).[55] Ageing brings to Gogol, the cataloguer of detail, a view of reality as mere vulgar exterior; Plyushkin's accumulation of objects in undiscriminating dusty piles is accelerated by the growing grey in his stubbly hair. The process is further associated with loneliness and lack of family, and this also characterises the plight of that kind of artist: 'who dares to summon forth all that is continually before one's eyes, and which indifferent eyes do not see: all the terrible devastating mire of petty details which entangle our life' (VI, 134). Plyushkin the arch representative of this 'mire of petty details' seems at one with the author himself in losing a certain sensitivity through the effects both of aging and loneliness. His is a kind of blindness symbolically expressed by the papering over of more and more windows in his house with each successive year: 'With every year the main areas of estate management receded more and more from view, and his petty gaze was turned to scraps of paper and bits of feathers, which he collected in his room' (VI, 119). In much the same way that the author feels about his own development, Plyushkin, too, has been moving from one view of reality to another. Increasingly his eyes are averted from more imaginative perspectives and fixed on the trivial and banal. Moreover, it seems significant that this 'petty gaze' should be focused on objects which could be interpreted as debased symbols of the writer's trade – 'scraps of paper and bits of feathers' (i.e. 'pens' – *peryshki*) for the vices of Plyushkin are germane to Gogol's fears about his own art.[56]

'The Overcoat' (1842) dates from this same period. Its hero Akakiy Akakiyevich is another 'dead soul', living in complete isolation without family or friends, whose vision is even more limited: it is focused obsessively on the process of writing. Akakiy Akakiyevich is a careful saver, but like Plyushkin is a victim of the paradox that accumulation leads to poverty.

Gogol's self-indulgent musings about his own role in art at the beginning of chapter 7, in which he contrasts his own 'at times bitter and boring road' to that of a writer who rides in a chariot,[57] are abruptly brought to an end by the exhortation to himself to set out once more: 'To the road! to the road! Away with the frown descending on the brow, and the stern gloom of the face. Let us suddenly, and in one go, plunge into life with all its noiseless crackling and horses' bells. Let us see what Chichikov is doing' (VI, 135).

The road as an escape, as a flight from himself, is no mere literary conceit for Gogol, as he confesses in chapter 11:

> Oh, Lord, how good you are at times, you long, long road. How often, like one who perishes and drowns, have I grabbed at you, and each time you have magnanimously borne me out and saved me. And how many wonderful schemes and poetic fancies have been born in you, how many marvellous impressions have been relived and assimilated. (VI, 222)

Thus, for Gogol, the road leads to artistic inspiration, but at the same time it can also be a flight from the condition of Plyushkin, the deterioration of whose sensitivity also evokes the image of drowning.[58]

If there is a road out of Gogol's crisis, it is seen as a new and entirely untrodden way: the inversion of all the old values; the turning of negatives into positives; 'dead souls' must not only be resurrected but become the apotheosis of Russian life: 'And all the virtuous people of other races will appear dead before them, as a book is dead before the living word' (VI, 223).

Gogol does not appear to be aware of the danger that in this process literature ('the dead book') might be ousted by the sermon ('the living word') and in anticipating the coming salvation (and chiding himself for doing so) he has already converted the weaknesses, which he laments in chapters 6 and 7 (his loss of youth, his loneliness, his sense of inner crisis) into strengths: 'It is unseemly for an author who is already a man, and educated through his stern inner life and the refreshing sobriety of loneliness, to forget himself as though he were a youth' (VI, 223). Nevertheless the note of self-reproach suggests that he is not entirely confident about his new-found strength and the change of artistic personality. Unfortunately, so it was to prove.

Social satire and comic devices

The traditional nineteenth-century view, and one still held in the Soviet Union, is that *Dead Souls* criticises Russian pre-reform society at its roots, by exposing the iniquities of serfdom. At the turn of the century, symbolists, formalists and others reacted strongly against this interpretation, and Western critics have largely tended to follow their line, refusing to see any substantial social implications in the work. In its time this view was a welcome counterblast against too crudely a sociological interpretation of the work, but to ignore the social implications permeating the whole fabric of *Dead Souls* is equally to distort the facts in the contrary direction.

In the first place the very theme of the buying and mortgaging of dead peasants, which is only possible because for official purposes they are not yet classed as 'dead', shows the law of the land to be an ass. Chichikov, in introducing his proposition to Manilov (and to the reader) is careful to call these peasants: 'not in reality alive, but alive as regards the legal form', and there is profound irony in his assertion: 'I am not accustomed in anything to deviate from the civil laws...the law, I am dumb before the law' (VI, 35). In a superficial 'formal' sense Chichikov's activities are within the law.

Nevertheless, it would be going too far to suggest that Gogol's work is against the institution of serfdom as such. There is scant evidence for this in the novel, and far too much evidence to the contrary in *Selected Passages* and in his private correspondence. Moreover the peasants who appear in part I do not escape the negative treatment accorded to the other characters. The drive of Gogol's criticism is not against the system as such, but against abuses which prevent its functioning in an ideal way; his chief butt is bureaucracy in all its manifestations. Nevertheless, it is true that the portrait of Koshkarev in part II can be viewed as Slavophile mockery at the reforms of Peter I,[59] and by implication can therefore be read as criticism of the regime of Nicholas I, which looked back to Peter for its inspiration.

Undoubtedly, Gogol would not have wished his mockery to be taken so far. His disquiet is more with the functioning of his society than with its basic premises. Thus a constant theme in part I is the taking of bribes. Korobochka complains of having to grease the palm of the assessor and the existence of bribery goads Plyushkin into religious indignation. But the theme really comes into its own in the latter half of part I when Chichikov has dealings with the officials of the town, and the 'Temple of Themis'. Chichikov, who is himself a pastmaster at extorting bribes, as we are to learn in chapter 11, knows exactly what must be done to get his business through.

The senior officials of the town are all guilty of blatant maladministration. The chairman of the court only charges Chichikov half the legal costs, transferring the remainder to someone else's account. The police chief has merely to wink in the market to provide first-class food for a reception. We are told that he is in some sense 'the father of the town', and that he manages to get twice as much income as his predecessor, yet retain the affection of the townspeople: 'In a word he managed to acquire complete *narodnost'*.' *Narodnost'* might here be translated as 'folk identity', but it is an interesting word in such a context; since it was one of the three ideological pillars of the regime of Nicholas I: *Pravoslaviye, samoderzhaviye i narodnost'* ('Orthodoxy, autocracy and nationality'). Once more, as in *The Government Inspector*, Gogol appears to hint at more fundamental social criticism. A similar 'official' word conditions the quandary in which the officials of the town have been placed by the rumours about Chichikov: 'and what precisely was he? Was he the sort of man whom one ought to seize and detain as someone not well intentioned, or was he the sort of man who himself might seize and detain all of them, as not-well-intentioned people?' (VI, 196); the designation 'not-well-intentioned' (*neblagonamerennyy*) was an official euphemism applied to liberals and would-be reformers hostile to the regime.[60] Its use in this context of moral confusion, hints at the equivocal nature of the concept itself.

The corruption of the officials of the town very soon develops into the theme of *The Government Inspector*, once they begin to question Chichikov's true identity, and like Khlestakov before him, he acts as a conscience. Faced with the enigma of his presence amongst them, they all begin to remember past misdeeds: the epidemic against which no measures were taken; two court cases involving murder which were hushed up for dubious reasons. Thus the police officer Drobyazhkin was killed by peasants, who were never called to account. Legally peasants were not so much human beings as chattels. Therefore to punish peasants by sending them to Siberia, was in effect to punish their owners, since it meant a loss of wealth. In this case the culprits were state peasants, and the decision of the court reveals an interesting legal argument: 'since it was not known, who precisely among the peasants had taken part, and there were a lot of them. Drobyazhkin, moreover, was a man who was dead, therefore there was little advantage for him, if he did win the case, but the peasants were still alive, therefore, a decision in their favour was extremely important for them' (VI, 194). Given such persuasive factors the court concluded that Drobyazhkin had died from apoplexy, a decision which further illustrates the special legal status of peasants, upon which the central idea of *Dead Souls* is based.

The 'Tale of Captain Kopeykin' suffered at the hands of the censor because it was deemed too outspoken. Gogol was certainly on dangerous ground in setting this absurd tale in St Petersburg and imputing inhuman behaviour to some of the highest officials there. It was one thing to ridicule provincial functionaries, but quite another to imply that all was not well in the higher echelons of the bureaucracy. Gogol had to tone his implied criticism down considerably, nevertheless there is still a certain piquancy in the fact that Captain Kopeykin, the crippled veteran of the victory over the

French, is starving in the capital, whilst a French cook prepares a sumptuous meal.[61]

Yet there is always something which undermines the serious impact of social criticism in Gogol's writing. For the most part the absurdities of an unjust social system are exploited for humour, and explicit criticism is frequently reduced to the trivial. Thus in *Dead Souls* (as in *Selected Passages*) the bribery and corruption of officials is attributed to the influence of their wives. One senses that, in Gogol's world, women in their vanity, triviality and extravagance are in league with the devil.[62] When Chichikov suffers his first major set-back he vents his anger on the frivolity of giving balls, but the chief recipient of his spleen is the arch enemy – woman:

> What have they got to be so foolishly glad about? There are bad harvests in the province, and rising prices, so they go in for balls! Akh, What a thing: they have decked themselves out in womanish rags! A wonder, indeed, that one or two of them wrapped a thousand roubles round themselves! But it's at the expense of the peasant tithes, or what is even worse, at the expense of the conscience of chaps like us. Well, it's well known why you take a bribe and go against your better feelings, it's in order to get enough for a shawl for your wife or for various fancy dresses, devil take them, whatever they are called. And for what? So that some goad of a Sidorovna shouldn't say that the postmaster's wife is wearing a better dress, and because of her you squander a thousand roubles. They shout: 'a ball, a ball, what happiness!' But quite simply, a ball is rubbish, it's not in the Russian spirit, it's not in the Russian nature. (VI, 174)

The hint of effeminacy in the governor, with his passion for embroidery and his lap-dog, can now be seen in a new light; for governors are the providers of such feminine amusements, as Gogol himself comments: 'Where there is a governor, there is a ball, otherwise the love and respect due from the nobility would be lacking' (VI, 161). An idea which is later echoed by Nozdrev when discussing the role of the governor general (VI, 214).

If bribery can be ascribed to female vanity, women, in their more basic function, are also to blame for their husbands' corruption, as the postmaster is reminded by a fellow civil servant: 'It's not too bad for you, you have only one son, but as for me, brother, God has endowed Praskovya Fedorovna with such abundance, that every year she bears either a Praskushka, or a Petrushka. Given this, brother, you would sing a different song' (VI, 198).

Gogol, critical of the bureaucracy, emerges as the champion of the landowners. This can be seen more clearly in part II of *Dead Souls*, and is quite unequivocally expressed in *Selected Passages*, but in both he is concerned to show that the only true interest of the landowning classes is the proper management of their estates. He is highly critical of those who are lackadaisical and profligate, such as Khlobuyev in part II, and it is perhaps significant that Chichikov first gets his idea for his bold scheme, when it falls to his lot to mortgage the estate of just such a figure who has let his estate go to rack and ruin, and bought a house in Moscow, squandering all his money on a fashionable décor. Such frivolous expenditure is not fitting for a country squire, and one might again suspect the influence of women. Certainly the female version of the absentee landlord comes in for strong censure, with her marvellously appointed town house:

> Where she will have greater scope to shine intellectually and utter ideas learned off by heart, ideas occupying the town for a week according to the laws of fashion, ideas not about what is happening in her house and on her estate, whose affairs are muddled and run down, thanks to her lack of knowledge of management, but about what political revolution is in the offing in France, and what direction is being taken by fashionable Catholicism. (VI, 58)

Gogol emerges not only as anti-feminist but as the champion of old, feudal values and he is so out of sympathy with liberalism, that he even suggests democratic procedures to be alien to the Russian temperament:

> In general we have somehow not been created for representative meetings. In all our gatherings, from the meeting of the peasant commune right up to all sorts of learned and other committees, if there is not someone in charge, guiding everything, then a regular muddle obtains. It is difficult really to say why this should be, it must be that the nation is like this. Only those gatherings are successful which are formed in order to have a good time or a good dinner, such as clubs and all kinds of vauxhalls on a German footing. (VI, 198)

Gogol's ultimate aims for his *poema* were fixed higher than the plane of social criticism. His title, with its confusion of peasants/souls/death, hints not merely at the social but also at the metaphysical, yet its implications are grotesque: how can the soul be dead? The detail of the *poema* often exploits the grotesque nature of the death of 'souls' to comic effect. Thus Korobochka tells Chichikov that her blacksmith has 'got burned up'. Chichikov's interest is quickened at the thought of a fire in her village, and the prospect of many peasant deaths, but he is soon disabused:

> God preserve us from such a calamity. A fire would be even worse. He himself burned up, my dear sir. He somehow took fire inside himself, he had drunk far too much, only a blue flame came out of him. He smouldered away and went all black like charcoal. And he was such a very skilful blacksmith. Now I have got nothing to ride out on, there is nobody to shoe my horses. (VI, 51)

The truth of this latter remark is borne out during Korobochka's strange midnight journey into the town.

The death of the public prosecutor is also grotesquely comic. He is caught in mid-wink, it seems, and has raised one eyebrow in a questioning expression: 'What the dead man was asking about, whether it was why he had died, or whether it was why he had lived, about this God alone knows' (VI, 210). It was only when he had died, we are told, that people realised he had a soul at all; for when alive, through modesty, he had never shown that he had one. Through such grotesque touches we come back obliquely to the ambiguous theme of 'dead souls' itself.

Sometimes a bizarre comic effect is achieved through a simile, as when Chichikov is jolted up and down in his coach on the loose logs of Plyushkin's roadway:

> These logs, like piano keys, kept moving now up now down and the passenger who did not take precautions would acquire either a bump on the back of his head or a blue mark on his forehead, or it even happened that he might very painfully bite off the tip of his own tongue with his own teeth. (VI, 111)

The humour here is visual and 'slapstick', as it is in chapter 2 when Manilov and Chichikov both get stuck in the door through vying with one another in politeness. It is the humour of physical discomfiture, admirably illustrated when Chichikov wakes up in the house of Korobochka by sneezing because he has breathed a fly up his nose.

Gogol's 'few strokes' method of characterisation affords great scope for comedy of character. Since each landowner embodies a dominant vice, the predictability of his response to certain situations causes a gratification of anticipation in the reader and sometimes a slight shock, when the character, whilst still keeping true to himself, exceeds what can reasonably be expected. Plyushkin is a case in point, with his miser's hospitality and such skinflint economy as a unique pair of boots for all the servants in the house. It is this type of humour which most links Gogol with Molière, whose *L'Avare* readily comes to mind in any discussion of Plyushkin.

The comedy is also one of situation. The plot is rich in comic possibility: the theme of attempting to buy 'dead souls' and the effect produced on the various landowners by Chichikov's outrageous proposal. Moreover the reader has a partial knowledge of Chichikov's motives, and can laugh at the juxtaposition of innocence and guile, aware that many of Chichikov's apparently innocuous questions have a hidden ulterior purpose. There is, too, the essential comic incongruity of treating that which is dead as being very much alive. Comedy of situation thrives on such ambiguities, and is enhanced by the literalness of interpretation, which, in different ways, emerges from the reaction of both Korobochka and Sobakevich to Chichikov's strange request.

Verbal humour permeates the whole fabric of *Dead Souls*. Gogol's names are often chosen for comic effect. Thus among Plyushkin's peasants there is a certain Grigoriy Doyezzhay ne doyedesh′ (i.e. 'try and travel there, you won't travel there'[63]), a strange name which seems like a mocking reminder of the theme of peasants linked to Chichikov's travels and ultimate failure which had been broached at the very beginning in the peasants' speculations on Chichikov's wheel. Korobochka has a peasant named Petr Savel′ev Neuvazhay-Koryto (i.e. 'disrespectful of his trough'). Sobakevich tries to palm off as a male serf a certain Yelizaveta Vorobey (he substitutes a hard sign for the feminine ending 'a', so that she figures on the list as Yelizavet″ Vorobey).[64]

The rumours which begin to circulate about Chichikov cause weird people with bizarre names suddenly to appear in the town: Makdonal′d Karlovich, Sysoy Pafnut′yevich etc. The postmaster has the absurd nickname, 'Sprechen Sie Deutsch'; Nozdrev, on one occasion, calls Chichikov 'Opodeldok Ivanovich' (*opodel′dok* is an ointment used for rheumatism, but Nozdrev is mocking Chichikov's excuse of a business engagement '*yest′ delo*'). A similar pun is used about Nozdrev himself, when the author describes him as 'to some extent an historical figure', exploiting the double sense of *istoriya* as both 'history' and 'scandal'.

A pun on the ambiguity of the Russian verb *uslyshat′* ('to hear' and 'to smell') occurs at the end of chapter 9. The officials of the town try to question Chichikov's servants about their master: 'But they heard only very little. From Petrushka they heard/smelled only the smell of the living quarters' (VI, 196). The very title of the *poema* contains a pun and Gogol develops its ambiguity throughout the work by suggesting that not merely peasants, but the characters themselves are 'dead souls'. Thus Sobakevich's soul appears to lie over the mountains guarded by the wizard Koshchey, and, as we have seen, the public prosecutor only reveals that he has a soul, when he is dead. A similar playing with the concepts of 'dead and alive' is to be found in the final section of 'The Overcoat', a work contemporaneous with the completion of part I of *Dead Souls*. It is also an ambiguity central to the aesthetic preoccupations of 'The Portrait'.

Playing with words is such an essential feature of Gogol's comic style, that one suspects that the idiosyncrasies of the writing at times derive from verbal associations, either explicit or concealed. Thus when the waiter in Chichikov's hotel carries a tray: 'on which sat such a multitude of tea cups, as birds on a sea shore' (VI, 9), the striking image could well derive from a purely verbal association (i.e. *chaynyye chashki* = 'tea cups', and *chayki* = 'seagulls').

Another aspect of the verbal humour is Gogol's love of formulae. The introduction of Chichikov as 'not too fat, not too thin; not too old, not too young' is a verbal pattern which Gogol repeats in many variations. The governor of the town is also 'not too fat and not too thin', and his rank is described as 'not too high and not too low'. The weather on Chichikov's first journey out of town in chapter 2 is characterised as 'not bright and not dull'. Such a formula is the quintessential expression of the mediocrity of the world which Gogol seeks to depict.

Another formula is used for the ladies of the town: one is 'simply pleasant' and the other is 'pleasant in all respects'. Moreover, the latter comes to a conclusion which is 'in all respects unusual'. Later the insinuations of both these ladies goad the governor's wife into an indignation which is 'just in all respects', and in the same chapter Sobakevich asserts that the peasants he has sold Chichikov are 'alive in all respects'. Playing with this particular phrase at this point in the *poema* is not without its significance. The character of Chichikov himself is being interpreted by the townsfolk 'in all respects' (*vo vsekh otnosheniyakh*, i.e. literally 'in all relationships') and correspondingly the simple story-line of part I has been suspended in favour of proliferation in all directions and 'in all respects'.

A comic effect can be achieved when a set verbal formula is repeated to the accompaniment of a mechanical action. Thus

Chichikov and Nozdrev, playing draughts, repeat the same words each time they make a move:

(Nozdrev). We know you, how badly you play.
(Chichikov). I haven't had draughts in my hands for a long time. (VI, 84)

A deceptively placatory rhythm is thus established, which is suddenly broken when Chichikov catches Nozdrev out in a flagrant act of cheating.

Similar instances of formulaic humour accompanied by action can be seen in Chichikov and Manilov vying with one another not to go through the door first, or in Manilov seating his guest in his study to the accompaniment of: 'allow me', and 'allow me not to allow you'. The mutual suspicion of Chichikov and Sobakevich, the one refusing to surrender his money until the other surrenders his list of 'dead souls', is again treated in terms of the comic formula. Earlier Chichikov had referred to such haggling as a 'theatrical performance', and there is indeed something theatrical in this combination of the verbal formula with repetitive action, as its use in *The Government Inspector* demonstrates (e.g. act IV, scene xii).

The humour of *Dead Souls* has much in common with that of the 'shaggy dog' story or Sterne's tale of a 'cock and a bull':[65] the joke is not so much for the reader as against him. This is true of the conversation of the two 'pleasant ladies' in chapter 9 and the absurd tale of Captain Kopeykin in chapter 10, but it is also true, in a general sense of part I as a whole, with its sustained attempt to mystify the reader about the real nature and intentions of Chichikov. Chapter 9, in particular, reveals many of the methods employed by Gogol to sustain his 'joke against the reader'. At the end of chapter 8, he had already planted expectation in his reader's mind by promising that the strange arrival in town of Korobochka could best be explained by the conversation which is to follow in the next chapter, and chapter 9 begins with 'the simply pleasant lady' burning with impatience to impart her news. As the reader has been led to believe that this will explain something vital to the plot, he is, to some extent, in a similar state of impatience as 'the simply pleasant lady' herself, but he is constantly being frustrated in his expectations by the author's love of unnecessary detail, much as 'the simply pleasant lady' is exasperated by the length of her journey to see her friend. Reading time and fictional time are thus equated and, when as she drives past the long almshouse, which for some reason seems even longer than ever, 'the simply pleasant lady' exclaims: 'The accursed construction there's no end to it!', the reader in turn feels like echoing her impatience, but with the 'accursed construction' of Gogol's prose. Even when she arrives there is no relief in sight. The author indulges in a long digression on the inadvisability of giving either of the two ladies names (a completely unnecessary precaution; for their names and patronymics come out in conversation). Moreover, the titles he gives them of 'the simply pleasant lady' and 'the lady pleasant in all respects' also prove, as he himself even suggests, to be completely inappropriate.

The details of the arrival and mutual greeting of the two ladies are inordinately protracted (even encompassing a digression on girls who go to private boarding schools), and when 'the simply pleasant lady' is on the very point of imparting the news which she is in such a hurry to bring, once more she is frustrated: 'But the exclamation, which "the lady pleasant in all respects" made at this time, suddenly gave another direction to the conversation' (VI, 180). This new direction is a stupid and catty discussion of fashion, and 'the simply pleasant lady' is only reminded about the news, which a short while before she had been burning to impart, by a chance remark from her friend. Before she can deliver it, she is again cut short: 'At this point the breath of the guest stopped, words like hawks were prepared to launch into the chase one after the other, and to venture to stop her, one could only be as inhuman, as was her sincere friend' (VI, 182). Such 'inhumanity' practised by one character on another is in effect a barbarism perpetrated on the reader by a mocking author. Indeed when 'the simply pleasant lady' manages to overcome the repeated interruptions of her friend, and finally launches into her tale, it is the author himself who then chooses to interrupt her flow with a long digression on the use of French (an interruption prefaced by the heavily ironical assertion: 'it does not hinder to remark'). For his part the author promises not to use French in this 'Russian *poema*', and, of course, almost immediately does so. His first lapse is the odd Russified version of '*faire la cour*' – *stroit′ kury*,[66] which evokes the comic association of hens (*kury*) and seems strangely to suit the characters of those two poultry-keepers, the arch-priest's wife and Korobochka to whom it is thought to apply. Slightly later we find the Russified forms of *scandaleuse*, and *horreur*, and towards the end of the chapter the actual French expression '*tête-à-tête*'.

Needless to say the reader learns nothing from this conversation, except how foolish the women of the town are and how preposterous rumours are spread. The same is true of the ridiculous story of 'Captain Kopeykin', in chapter 10, which embroiders these rumours and, by illustrating the stupidity of the men of the town of N., serves as a pendant to chapter 9. It is obvious from the very outset that Captain Kopeykin, who lacks both an arm and a leg, could not possibly be the plumply agile Chichikov. Humorous devices such as these call for further discussion of the author's attitude to his reader: 'But better let this conversation be in the next chapter' (VI, 177).

Author, reader, hero

The literary tricks of playing with the reader, of suspending the action by inserted stories or irrelevant conversations, ultimately go back to Sterne. Sternean too is the treatment of narrative time and actual time as identical entities.[67] The device is first used when describing Manilov's reception of Chichikov: 'Although the time during which they will pass through the entrance hall, the hallway and the dining-room is a little short, let us try and see if we can manage somehow or other to make use of it and say something about the master of the house' (VI, 23). Despite this mock warning that real time is hardly adequate for his fictional needs, the author proceeds at a leisurely pace, protesting his inability to describe either Manilov or his wife, but in the process saying a great deal about both. Indeed one or two pages later he even considers that he has time to say: 'it does not hinder to make one more remark that Mrs. Manilov...but I confess I am very afraid of speaking of the ladies' (VI, 26). However, at this point of avowed authorial reticence he is saved from further embarrassment, by suddenly remembering the passage of fictional time: 'But moreover it is time for me to return to our heroes, who have already been standing several minutes before the drawing-room door, each begging the other to go in first' (VI, 26).

The device is used again in chapter 11, when the author says he will profit from the fact, that Chichikov has dozed off in his coach, to tell the reader, for the first time, all about his hero. There is, however, an added dimension; for just as fictional time and real time are here equated, so, too, Chichikov is treated as a real person, who can overhear what is being said about him: 'But we have begun to speak rather loud, forgetting that our hero, asleep throughout the whole time his tale was being related, has already woken up and can easily catch his name which is being repeated so frequently' (VI, 245).

In Gogol's *poema*, as in Pushkin's 'novel', the relationships of author, reader, hero are presented in a playful way, which owes much in both cases to the methods of Sterne, but whereas Pushkin's attitude to his reader is detached, Gogol shows an increasing concern about the relationship. The opening of the *poema* seems designed to mystify the reader, with its laconically formulaic introduction of the central figure in stark contrast to the detailed description of the episodic character with the Tula tie-pin. The oblique, digressive nature of the narrative becomes more pronounced as the *poema* unfolds.

At the beginning of chapter 2 the author feels it necessary to crave his reader's indulgence: 'But about all this, the reader will learn gradually and at the right time, if he only has the patience to read the tale he is offered, which is very long and which later will be able to expand more widely and spaciously, the nearer it draws to an end crowning the whole affair' (VI, 19). In the first half of part I the tone of such authorial remarks, although facetious, is on the whole conciliatory, it is only after the crisis in chapter 6 that a certain hostility towards the reader finds overt expression.

In chapter I the description of the pictures at the inn tactfully distances the reader from vulgarity: 'In one picture a nymph was depicted with huge breasts, such as the reader, undoubtedly, has never seen' (VI, 9). Chapter 11, however, ascribes to him a 'healthy' interest in the sordid details of the hero's toilet. 'It will be pleasant, I think, for the reader to learn that he changed his underwear every two days and in summer, during the heat, even every day' (VI, 234).

In chapter 5 the author suppresses a vulgar word used by a peasant to describe Plyushkin. A word: 'very much to the point, but not used in society conversation, and therefore we will omit it' (VI, 108). A similar expression in chapter 8, however, evokes an authorial attack on the reader for neglecting his native language in favour of French, German and English: 'But if a word from the street has got into the book, it is not the writer who is to blame but the readers, and above all readers from high society' (VI, 164). Although a shift of responsibility is implied as early as chapter 3, when the author foists off his own love of detail upon certain elements of his readership, nevertheless the tone is not hostile but mockingly compliant: 'The author is convinced that there are readers so inquisitive, that they will wish even to know the plan and interior disposition of the box. Well then, if you like why not satisfy them!' (VI, 55). In chapter 4 he saves the reader a boring conversation between Chichikov, Nozdrev and Mizhuyev; yet, as we have seen, devotes much of chapter 9 to an absurdly pointless conversation, which he pretends is germane to his plot. Chapters 9 and 10 represent through their irrelevance a sustained attack on the reader. The disingenuous naivety of an author who could consider such material appropriate suggests Gogol in his old guise of Rudy Panko, but with a certain added sophistication. Indeed the last three chapters of part I are full of devices designed to impede the narrative flow. Gogol is indulging in the dangerous game of playing with the reader's interest and attention, and in the last chapter he confesses that the *brichka* (the symbol of movement and only real vehicle for the story line) has now stayed so long in the town that it might even bore the reader.

At the beginning of chapter 9 the author anticipates hostility from his readers: 'The author is in extreme difficulties as to how he is to call the two ladies, so that people do not once more get angry with him, as they have got angry in the past' (VI, 179). This is quite close to the note of wounded authorial susceptibility which opens 'The Overcoat'. But Gogol's protestations that he must treat his reading public with respect and caution, are merely a mocking prelude to a sustained attack on the reader's patience, credulity and ultimately his intelligence: 'It is sufficient to say merely that there is in a certain town a stupid man, and this is already a personality; suddenly a gentleman of respectable appearance will jump up and will shout out: "but I too am a man, therefore, I also am stupid". In a word, he will see the point at once' (VI, 179).

A similar attitude to the reader informs chapter 10, but here, at least, Gogol does allow that his readers might object to his absurd story of Captain Kopeykin: 'Perhaps certain readers will call all this improbable. The author, too, to please them, is prepared to call all this improbable, but unfortunately everything happened precisely as is related, and it is all the more astounding in that the town was not in the back of beyond, but on the contrary, not far from both capital cities' (VI, 206). Thus the author, pretending to placate the reader, merely insists more firmly on the 'realistic' detail of this bizarre intercalation into the plot. As the chapter continues still in the same vein the reader's patience is in danger of coming to an end:

But this, nevertheless, is incongruous! This does not correspond to anything! It is impossible that civil servants could so scare themselves; concoct such nonsense; wander so far from the truth, when even a child can see what it's all about. So will say many readers and will reproach the author with incongruity, or will call the poor civil servants fools, because people are generous with the word 'fool', and are prepared to serve their neighbour with it twenty times a day. (VI, 210)

The play with the plot and the reader reaches its apogee in chapter 11. Here Gogol inverts the novelist's usual procedures, only giving the biographical details of his hero, and the motive for his behaviour, at the very end. At the same time he confesses: 'It is very doubtful that the readers have liked the hero we have chosen' and is particularly sure that lady readers will not like him. Yet for all these authorial doubts, Gogol very soon expresses a conviction in a contrary sense: 'But what is irksome is not that they will be dissatisfied with my hero, but that there lives in my heart an irresistible conviction that the readers might be satisfied with this same hero, this same Chichikov' (VI, 242). At least, this would be the case, argues Gogol, if the author were not to take a deep inner look at his hero, but were merely to show him as he appeared to Manilov and the other landowners.

In this strange argument Chichikov both does, and does not, please the reader, and the author attempts to resolve the contradiction by a psychological insight, which is even less flattering to his readership: 'Who among you, full of Christian humility, not publicly, but in silence, alone, in moments of solitary conversation with oneself, will not probe the depths of his own soul with this severe enquiry: "Is there not a part of Chichikov even within me?" Yes, how could it be otherwise!' (VI, 245). If Gogol here hints at a vital link between hero and reader, the relationship of author and hero is no less important – it is the hero who is responsible for the author's theme: 'And thus it was that this strange plot was formed in the head of our hero. I do not know whether the readers will be grateful to him for it, but the gratitude of the author for it is difficult to express, since, whatever you say, if this thought had not come into Chichikov's head, this *poema* would not have appeared in the world' (VI, 240).[68] In chapter 2 Gogol had mockingly described himself as 'filled with conscience at occupying his readers so long with people of low class'. Now in chapter 11 he shirks all responsibility for his characters: 'So the readers should not be indignant at the author, if the personages who have appeared up to now have not been to his taste. It is the fault of Chichikov. Here he is complete master, and wherever he takes the fancy to go, there we must drag ourselves also' (VI, 241).

The final chapters of part I are marked by an ever growing tendency towards authorial self-justification, and although 'the heavy masses' of didactic prose are 'freed' by the sharp 'blade' of the comic tone (the playing with the relationships of author, reader, hero) the contorted shapes which result suggest the presence of a real artistic problem, as yet unsolved. A dominant note is observable in the comic devices themselves: the playful desire to shun responsibility for a work, which was conceived as a comic masterpiece, yet which somehow, because of a change within the author himself, must take a completely new turn and become a work of moral and spiritual regeneration. Hence the teasing view that it is not the author who is to blame for the coarse expressions of his characters, but the reader; that the author has not conceived the novel's plot, but rather Chichikov himself; that it is the hero, and not the author who is to blame for the unregenerate characters who people the first part of the *poema*. Moreover, the events of Chichikov's earlier life are perhaps now something of an embarrassment to an author wrestling with the problem of portraying a positive hero. Certainly Chichikov's biography is presented baldly and without the conciliatory effects of humour. Yet, even so, such a sordid detail as the quarrel over a woman is to become the responsibility of the reader himself: 'What the matter was in fact, God knows, it is better to let the reader, with a mind to it, concoct the details himself' (VI, 237). Such moral lapses of the hero obviously interest the prurient reader far more than an author who now has his sights on higher things.

Nevertheless Chichikov is still necessary. If the great work of the author's life is to be saved and given a clear moral message, the author, unlike his reader, cannot afford to be at odds with his hero:

> It makes little difference to the reader, whether Chichikov gets angry with him or not, but as for the author, he must not quarrel with his hero on any account. There is still quite a journey and a good deal of road which they will have to cover together, hand in hand. There are two large parts ahead and this is no bagatelle. (VI, 245–6)

Such a project is indeed no mere bagatelle, and the difficulties which Gogol will experience on the new road ahead indicate a crisis both of content and of method. The work is to assume a new 'inwardness' as many of his statements at the end of part I imply, and when expressing his fears that his hero will not appeal to his readers, Gogol also reveals his own secret fears: 'However deeply the author were to peer into his soul, even were he to reflect his character more clearly than a mirror, there would still be no value placed on him' (VI, 223). If Gogol feels that he must take on the unaccustomed role of an author who looks deep into the souls of his characters, a similar depth of vision is also required of his readers. Gogol accuses them of hypocrisy. They are friendly with Chichikovs in real life, but reject his portrayal in literature. They would do well to look deeply into the soul of every character – a theme which is later developed into the need for the reader to look deeply into his own heart: 'Why mince words. Who indeed, if not an author, ought to speak the holy truth? You are afraid of the deeply-penetrating gaze. You yourselves are scared to fix a deep gaze on anything. You like to skim over everything with unthinking eyes' (VI, 245). Gogol feels the need to speak the 'holy truth', but significantly it is 'truth' about the reader, not about himself.

One senses in this attack on the reader the same flight from responsibility and involvement that characterises the whole tenor of the play with the relationships of author/reader/hero. Who is it really who is afraid to look deep within himself? Is it the reader, or is it the author who in chapter 6 had contrasted two ways of looking at reality, had regretted the fresh imaginative vision of his youth, and deplored the vulgar exterior which reality presents to him in middle age? Such short-sighted, such faded susceptibilities, hardly augur well for the deep and penetrating gaze which artistic ambition now demands. Yet the new Gogol, the author of the projected parts II and III of *Dead Souls*, is striving everywhere for depth. His worthless hero, Chichikov, might be saved if the author were to look more deeply into his soul; the reader, too, by the same process might recognise the Chichikov within himself.

Through a breathtaking inversion of values, Gogol overcomes self-pity and the envy of those authors who choose positive heroes, which had momentarily welled up and found expression at the opening of chapter 7. In chapter 11 he firmly rejects the virtuous hero as an over-used work horse: 'There isn't a writer who would not ride on him, urging him along with a knout and anything that comes to hand' (VI, 223). Indeed, Gogol claims that this hero has been ridden so hard that: 'there is not now a shadow of virtue upon him, there remain only ribs and skin instead of a body' (VI, 223). The traditional 'positive hero' appears to have become just another 'dead soul' and Gogol concludes 'So let us harness a rogue.' Such a hero is not new in Gogol's stable, but now he is harnessing a rogue for a pilgrimage of virtue – a journey with an inner spiritual sense. He who cultivates the most beautiful of passions 'enters more deeply into the limitless paradise of the soul' and Gogol hints that the passion which sways Chichikov is still a mystery.

The tone of such writing is close to the second version of 'The Portrait', as is the artistic and moral purpose behind the drive to penetrate the surface of things. Unfortunately such inwardness runs counter to the true thrust of Gogol's art, up to now he has shunned all effort to get inside his characters: his is the art of surface.

In *Dead Souls* the author actually views himself as a painter and playfully confesses that there are characters whom he can only depict superficially – the ladies of the town of N.: 'About their characters, it is obvious that we must allow someone to speak, who has more lively colours and more of them on his palette, but we ought to say maybe a couple of words about outward appearance and about what is more superficial' (VI, 158).[69]

The 'couple of words' about outward appearance and what is more superficial recall the methods employed for the landowners in the first six chapters of part I, who are pinned down by Gogol's few strokes like 'trussed up hares' offered up to the readers' laughter (see p. 9 above). Yet if this is the medieval function of his social and moral comedy, we have also seen that there is another comic sensibility at work – a Sternean one, associated with Sentimentalism and fashionable in the writings of many of Gogol's contemporaries (Pushkin, Baron Brambeus, Veltman). The comic manner of Sterne, which questions the very devices of fiction themselves, increasingly took on a new seriousness for Gogol: it presented a means of coming to terms with the suppositions of his own fiction, of examining his own relationship as an author to his reader, his reader's relationship to his hero – but, most important of all, his own attitude to the characters of his *poema*, since for the medieval gargoyles of part I he had now pledged himself to construct a colossal edifice capable of uplifting the soul.

Taking his readers to task for objecting to the sort of Russia he has presented, Gogol suggests that there are two distinct spatial perspectives in fiction:[70] 'It is easy for the reader to make judgements, looking from his quiet corner and from a height, from where the whole horizon is open on what is happening below, where a man can only see objects close to him' (VI, 210). Yet the author himself is not in contact with the reality of Russia; his, too, is the distant view, as he confesses in chapter 11: 'Russia! Russia! I see you, from my wonderful, beautiful distance I see you' (VI, 220). We have seen that at the beginning of chapter 6 Gogol discussed his own two views of reality, but what we have here are three different perspectives corresponding to the three relationships with which he makes play. The hero's view is from close at hand, the reader's from above, whereas that of the author himself is from a great distance (Italy). Like the reader, the author, too, is dissatisfied with the down-to-earth pettiness of his original conception of the work. He hopes that a long view and new breadth of vision will refocus the reader's critical gaze. The reconciliation of these three perspectives presents Gogol with an artistic problem but there is yet a fourth perspective, the inner view, and this is his greatest challenge.

Gogol's physical separation from his native land does not prevent him from launching into a grandiose daydream about Russia's vast space and power, and his own mysterious role in her destiny, from which he is rudely awakened by the words: 'Hold back! hold back, fool!' – the words of his hero Chichikov to the coachman Selifan. The 'reality' of the fiction bursting into the author's own thoughts in this way is a commentary on those thoughts themselves; it introduces a note of self-mockery.[71] A parallel suggests itself with the ending of chapter 6; for it is as though the author is now in the position of that twenty-year-old youth returning from the theatre in a romantic daydream, only to be brought suddenly down to earth by the coarse expressions which assail his ears.

Authorial self-mockery can again be seen in the postmaster's introductory remarks to his absurd tale of Captain Kopeykin: 'There could come out of it a whole *poema* of some sort, extremely interesting for some writer or other' (VI, 199). The idea that a writer may turn the story of a wandering brigand into a '*poema*' is no more ludicrous than that the adventures of Chichikov are assigned to this lofty genre, and Gogol immediately reinforces the effect of self-mockery by repeating, in his role of author, the postmaster's absurd designation of his tale.

Authorial self-mockery is a welcome element in the *poema*, particularly in view of the increasing tendency towards didacticism and hostility to the reader, but is also reveals Gogol's innermost fears for his work: that it may not amount to more than the ludicrous adventures of a brigand; that the hero himself might cry: 'Hold back, hold back, fool', when Gogol is at his most ambitious; that Chichikov's wheel might get as far as Moscow, but not as far as Kazan.

Thus the Sternean preoccupation with the nature of fiction itself merges laughter with tears, and is in danger of turning from a comic mode into a vehicle for authorial neurosis. The tendency to minimise recent work, to reinterpret it, even to reject it, is noticeable throughout Gogol's career; it is particularly striking in the case of *Dead Souls*. But the twice-repeated burning of part II, and with it the destruction of Gogol's ambitious hopes, should not blind us to his real achievement. Part I stands as an indestructible monument to the author's unique genius: a work which will never fail to amuse, tease, fascinate and perplex its many readers.

Conclusion. Art is a reconciliation with life

Even the most ardent champion of Gogol as the sober realist must concede the neurotic nature of the author's personality. The circumstances of his death alone are vivid testimony, but his life is no less permeated by symptoms of neurosis. There is his obsession with illness; his apparent asexuality; his flight from passion or from stagnation through constant travel; the strange treatment of his friends; his many deceptions; the search for a role: civil servant, actor, writer, teacher, lecturer, preacher; the burning of manuscripts and the obsessive attempts to reinterpret his works.

The central figure of Gogolian fiction is the 'nonentity', but often, as in the case of Khoma Brut, Kovalev, Akakiy Akakiyevich, he is a character, without obvious psychological processes, yet subjected to grave psychological stress. In the view of the historian of Russian literature, D. S. Mirsky:

> Gogol's stories of everyday life of contemporary Russia are introspective – not in the sense that he analysed and described his psychic experience as Tolstoy, Dostoevsky, or Proust did, but because his characters are exteriorized and objectivated symbols of his experience. His inferiority complex and his deep roots in the animal, or rather vegetable, life of a rural squiredom gave these symbols the form of caricatures of grotesque reality.[1]

Mirsky is only partially right: it is not just a simple matter of characterisation – the whole texture of a Gogolian story is to varying degrees 'psychological'. Thus in a letter to A. O. Smirnova Gogol himself said of his early stories: 'There are, indeed, in them here and there tail-ends of my spiritual condition at that time, but no one will notice them or see them, unless I acknowledge them myself' (XII, 419).[2] In *Selected Passages from Correspondence with Friends* he went further, claiming that all his latest works were the history of his own soul.

Illness is the most obvious external symptom of Gogol's own lack of well-being; there is more than a suspicion that psychological inadequacy expressed itself, whether consciously or unconsciously, as a physical defect. Thus when presenting himself for audition as an actor, and later when required to conduct university examinations, for which he was ill-prepared, Gogol tied a bandage round his jaw and claimed he had toothache. Abroad, hypochondria became almost a way of life, as he went from one European spa to another in search of a cure. Moreover, in *Selected Passages from Correspondence with Friends* a section is devoted to 'The Significance of Illnesses' in which Gogol argues that illness is the concomitant of greater spirituality and is necessary to him for the significance of his art.

Gogol's hypochondria is closely connected with his writing. On 20 July 1832 he wrote to Pogodin from the Ukraine: 'My health is exactly as it was when we met, except that my diarrhoea has stopped and I now have a tendency towards constipation' (x, 237). Some six months later, in another letter to Pogodin, he describes his writing in similar terms: 'I am inactive and immobile. I don't want to do anything small and I can't think up anything big! In a word, intellectual constipation. Have pity on me and wish me well, and may a word from you be more effective than an enema' (x, 257). Gogol is obsessed by his stomach. He claimed that he had been examined by doctors in Paris who had found that his stomach was upside down. Thus the author believed himself to suffer from one of the central devices of his own art – inversion. The most clearly disturbed of all his fictional characters, Poprishchin, demands spiritual food from 'letters' before he plunges into the final stage of madness. Gogol, the great bon viveur, deprived his stomach entirely of food during his last spiritual crisis, much as his own Pulkheriya Ivanovna had brought about her own death in 'The Old World Landowners'. This attempt to concentrate spiritual life on the stomach is mirrored in an art which expresses the psychological in terms of the physical. *Zhivot* ('belly', 'stomach') in an older and more elevated meaning is 'life' itself, as such it hints at another device of Gogol's art – synecdoche. The nose is another organ which causes Gogol concern (on two occasions he indulged in the fantasy of becoming merely a nose). Artistically he explores the organ's synecdochal potential in a story about inadequacy: 'The Nose'.

A symptom of Gogol's illness was 'coldness' (*zyabkost'*) (in some sense it seems the antithesis of the great heat which he claimed would reduce him to ashes were he to give in to passion).[3] In the 'Old World Landowners' such 'coldness' is ascribed to the reader after a putative amorous pursuit. The hall, where this same reader comes to warm himself, has a door which creaks the words, 'fathers, I am freezing', and it is this voice which evokes for the narrator the idyll of this life in its essence: food in a romantic setting.

Many theories have been advanced about the nature of Gogol's neurosis: incest, necrophilia, homosexuality, impotence, existential anxiety.[4] To explain art in the light of the author's vices has obvious pitfalls. In the first place such an approach is often conditioned by a relentlessly proselytising monotheism (or, perhaps more accurately, monodiabolism). A second and more fundamental reservation may be advanced: 'The personal life of a poet cannot be held essential to his art – but at best a help or a hindrance to his creative task. He may go the way of a Philistine, a good citizen, a neurotic, a fool or a criminal. His personal career may be inevitable and interesting, but it does not explain the poet.'[5] Jung's caveat, however, has only partial relevance to the case of Gogol: the neurosis is obvious in the writing, whereas the personality of the writer himself is an enigma, so that, for the most part, it is not the facts of Gogol's life which critics use to explain the poet, but rather the 'poetry' to shed light on the personal life. Nevertheless it is salutary that words of caution should come from a psychologist; for the problem centres on unconscious 'psychological' values. The idea that such consciously held views as Christianity, Marxism, feminism, could (even should) influence a writer's work, would largely go unchallenged by those who would not allow art to be a legitimate outlet for unconscious drives, as well as by those who would consider such drives incompatible with the lofty nature of art itself. On the other hand, one of the first theoreticians of the nobility of art, Aristotle, came dangerously near to an aesthetic theory based on neurosis in his concept of *catharsis*: the purging of base emotions. Moreover, the two critics who, more than anyone else, were responsible for the traditional view of 'Gogol the realist' were fully aware of the subconscious element in art. Belinsky spoke of Gogol as a 'somnambulist' and N. G. Chernyshevsky in his influential *Essays on the Gogol period in Russian Literature*, stressed the importance of the intellect in art, but also paid respect to the romantic theory of unconscious creativity.[6]

Gogol's first theme, the Ukraine, appears to raise, not personal, but national issues. On the face of it Gogol's attitude to the Ukraine is the same romantic phenomenon as Walter Scott's depiction of Scotland. Yet, at the same time, there is a curious tendency to distance himself. Gogol's flight from his homeland is not merely physical – to Great Russia (St Petersburg) at the earliest opportunity; followed by the flight from Russia itself to Europe (Rome), it is also cultural and linguistic. Gogol's father wrote comedies in Ukrainian: his son wrote only in Russian. Gogol was a fervent collector of Ukrainian songs, and claimed to be proud of the Ukrainian language, yet his letters to family and friends are all written in Russian.

He learned about the Ukraine's heroic past from the stories of his paternal grandmother (the prototype for Pulkheriya Ivanovna). He recreated this legendary history in 'Taras Bulba', but in its later revision the nationalistic sentiments became those of Great, rather than Little, Russia. He planned a history of the Ukraine 'in six small and four large volumes', but it was never written. He had ambitions for the chair of world history at the newly founded University of Kiev, and thought of this ancient cultural capital as his 'promised land'. His friend and fellow Ukrainian, Maksimovich, had been appointed to the chair of literature at the new university, and in December 1833 Gogol wrote to him: 'Let's go there, there! to Kiev! To ancient beautiful Kiev!' It is ours, it is not theirs. Isn't that so? The deeds of our past were enacted there or in the region round about' (x, 288). Some six months later Gogol sought to give Maksimovich advice on the way he should teach literature and exhorted him through an appeal to his nationalism: 'For the sake of everything that is ours, for the sake of our Ukraine, for the sake of our fathers' graves' (x, 326). There is, indeed, something darkly atavistic in Gogol's attitude to the Ukraine. The 'graves of fathers' is a dominant motif in 'A Terrible Vengeance': his poetic evocation of the Ukraine's legendary past. These ancestral graves are threatening and the story is about the progressive degeneration of a Cossack line. Explicitly it is about incest.

Gogol's mother, who was widowed when Gogol himself was sixteen, was a mere eighteen years older than her son. Aksakov records his impression of her youth and beauty; how she looked more like Gogol's elder sister[7] (at thirty Gogol actually looked older than his forty-eight year old mother). The gap between Marya Ivanovna and her husband had been almost as great: she married Vasiliy Afanasevich when she was fourteen and he twenty-seven. Gogol was brought up with the notion that love could jump barriers of age. According to family tradition, his father (as the result of a vision) had singled out his future bride when she was a baby of seven months, and had been her constant play-fellow and companion until she was old enough to marry. As we have seen, love and the generations is a theme woven into Gogol's first collection of Ukrainian stories, and its very title hints at Gogol's home, for the family's own village was itself not far from Dikanka.

After the death of his father Gogol was the only male member of the household. His mother not only looked up to him, but her attitude even seems permeated by the sort of naive hyperbole found in her son's writing. Thus she considered him to be the author of almost every book of merit published in Russia (a claim not unlike that made by Khlestakov to impress the ladies of a remote provincial backwater). She also appeared to think that her son had invented the steamboat, and the railway.[8]

Gogol, for his part, seems to have wished to keep his mother at arm's length. He wrote to her constantly, but some of his more glaring exercises in misinformation were practised against her (e.g. the 'reasons' for his trip to Germany in 1829, and the series of wrongly dated letters designed to conceal his arrival in Moscow in 1839).

In a remarkable letter of 2 October 1833, in which he discusses his childhood, he appears to reproach his mother for her youth during his upbringing, and confesses that the love he feels for her is only that demanded by 'nature' (*natura*): 'I remember: I did not feel anything strongly. I looked at everything as on things created to please me. I did not love anyone in particular, except you, and then only because nature itself inspired the feeling' (x, 282).

It is as though Gogol is owning up to repressing emotion and merely according his mother what propriety demands. This love inspired by nature alone seems perverse, it is coldly 'unnatural' – like nature in 'A Terrible Vengeance' immersed in the cold waters of the Dnepr. As we have seen, inversion there hints, not at the wizard's desire for his daughter, but at Katerina's desire for him. A further inversion is possible – a reversal of the sexes – pious daughter and wizard father could become 'pious' son and witch 'mother': the two protagonists of 'The Old Woman of Berkeley', which was refurbished by Gogol in his fairy story 'Viy'. Like the Gogol of the letter, Khoma Brut is a 'schoolboy' devoid of feeling, who looks on everything merely as objects created for his pleasure. Thus in terms of authorial confession 'A Terrible Vengeance' and 'Viy' are complementary; for if one is explicit about the sin, the other gives a greater hint of the true protagonists. In the letter already quoted Gogol reveals his indifference to religion as a boy (his 'unawakened sight' in church) and claims that the one religious experience which 'shook' him was his mother's account of Domesday.[9] This 'terrible judgement' (*strashnyy sud*) seems to have left its mark, not only on 'A Terrible Vengeance' (*Strashnaya mest'*), but also on 'Viy'. The motif of 'old woman: sexuality: death' is encountered more than once in Gogol's Ukrainian stories. Its fullest treatment is in 'Viy', but Katerina's mother, apparently murdered by her father, is an enigmatic figure haunting 'A Terrible Vengeance'. Another shadow of death is cast by the old crones who dance at the wedding of the young couple at the end of 'The Fair at Sorochintsy', and in 'The Old World Landowners', when Pulkheriya Ivanovna is confronted by the sexuality of her cat she interprets it as her own death.

Incest is a theme of both sentimental and romantic literature, but the poetic intensity of 'A Terrible Vengeance' and of 'Viy' marks out Gogol's treatment of this theme as more than a fashionable literary exercise. Simon Karlinsky has eloquently argued the case for considering Gogol to be homosexual (the strongest evidence is in the fragment 'Nights at the Villa'). Nevertheless, in a Freudian view, such an interpretation would not be incompatible with an early concern about incest.

Sexual anxiety elsewhere in Gogol is seen as overt fear of marriage (e.g. Shponka and Podkolesin). In 'The Overcoat' the 'marriage' of Akakiy Akakiyevich is to a coat (the only other alternative is to an old woman – his landlady). Critics have pointed to the theme of the 'demonic power of woman' in such stories as 'Taras Bulba' and 'Viy', and Hugh McLean has written of Gogol's flight from love in *Mirgorod*. As narrator, Gogol himself has many asides (particularly in *Dead Souls*), proclaiming his inability to deal with women – at least artistically. Gogol's characters are predominantly childless. It is only Chichikov who desires descendants, and that seems more for reasons of status.

It is not, however, sexual anxiety alone which is stirred in Gogol's atavistic attitude to the Ukraine. Two sins are punished in 'A Terrible Vengeance'; besides the terminal one of incest there is also the original crime – betrayal of the oath of Cossack brotherhood. The story of Petro and Ivan is set in the sixteenth century. They are Cossack comrades in the service of the Polish King, Stephen Batory. In 'Taras Bulba', and in 'A Terrible Vengeance' itself, the Poles are the great enemy of Cossackdom, not its sovereign lords, yet here their quarrel is not with the Poles, it is between themselves. Through his act of betrayal Petro (Peter) becomes the founder of a cursed dynasty.[10]

The Gogols traced back their own ancestry (and claim to nobility) to a certain Colonel Gogol of Mogilev. He, too, was in the service of the King of Poland. Unfortunately, Gogol's research into Ukrainian history must have revealed that the Colonel Gogol of history also had dealings with the Turks. Thus the Cossack virtue of the supposed originator of Gogol's line was compromised by his association with the two arch-enemies of the Orthodox Ukraine. In 'A Terrible Vengeance' the betrayal of *tovarishchestvo* is portrayed in individual terms. It is the crime of the founder of a family against Ivan (the stock name of the 'Russian') and for this betrayal the descendants of Petro, particularly the last in the line, are doomed to suffer.

In an illuminating essay Leon Stilman has demonstrated that the claim of Gogol's grandfather to be descended from Andrey Gogol, colonel of Mogilev, is entirely spurious. The family name was, in fact, Yanovsky, and originally they were clergy. When, however, Afanasiy Demyanovich married into the noble family of Lizogub he acquired a small estate. In the 1760s Catherine the Great regularised serfdom in the Ukraine, and her edicts made it necessary to prove noble origin in order to own serfs. Accordingly, Afanasiy Demyanovich produced a Polish royal letter naming a certain Colonel Gogol, whom the writer's grandfather identified as Andrey Gogol, and his own great-grandfather. On the strength of this he claimed noble descent.

The real name of the 'colonel of Mogilev' was not Andrey, but Ostap,[11] and his son, Prokop, by one of those dislocations of logic so typical of Gogol the writer, displaced Afanasiy Demyanovich's true great grandfather – Yakov. (When Gogol again treated the theme of the betrayal of *tovarishchestvo*, in *Mirgorod* he gave the defector the name of Andriy, whereas the true Cossack son he named Ostap.)

Thanks to Gogol's grandfather, therefore, the family became known by the hyphenated surname Gogol-Yanovsky, but there seems to have been an urge to forget the associations of this last component, their true surname. Thus Afanasiy Demyanovich's little estate, originally known as Yanovshchina, was renamed Vasilevka, after the birth of his son Vasiliy. It was left to 'the last in the line' to complete this process. When as a private tutor in St Petersburg pupils addressed Gogol as 'Mr Yanovsky', he retorted: 'Why do you call me Mr Yanovsky? My surname is Gogol. Yanovsky is only an appendage stuck on by the Poles.'[12] In a letter to his mother in February 1832 he wrote:

I beg you to address letters to me simply as Gogol, because I don't know what has happened to the ending of my name. Perhaps someone has picked it up on the highway and is carrying it about as his own property. However that may be, I am not known anywhere here by the name of Yanovsky, and the postmen always find it difficult to find me under this sign. (x, 219)[13]

Besides reinforcing the claim to Cossack nobility, there were probably other reasons for discarding the Polish sounding Yanovsky in the aftermath of the Polish uprising of 1831. Nevertheless the writer was left with a single surname to which he had a dubious right and which, like many Ukrainian names, sounded comic to Russian ears, in as much as it had meaning – the name of a species of duck ('golden-eye').

In 'The Old World Landowners' the narrator speaks disparagingly of those Ukrainians of humble origin, who come to St Petersburg to make a career and even change their names (converting the typical Ukrainian ending in '-o' to the Russian '-ov'). Nevertheless there is an element of self-mockery in Gogol's attitude to his own name, which may be detected in his works. That Gogol was capable of laughing at himself can be seen from a letter which he wrote from school in Nezhin to his mother. In it he discusses, with a certain pleasure, the apparent enigma of his personality, the various *personae* he has presented to different people:

In truth, I am considered a riddle for everyone. No one has guessed at me fully. With you I am considered wilfully capricious, a sort of unbearable pedant who thinks that he is more intelligent than anyone else, and that he has been created in a different fashion from other people. Will you believe that, inside, I myself was laughing at myself along with you? (x, 123)

One of the first pseudonyms he adopted as a writer was the quadruply self-deprecating O O O O, derived from the four dominant vowels in the name Nik*o*lai G*o*g*o*l-Yan*o*vsky. Aksakov has recorded that when travelling by coach Gogol would refuse to admit that he was the famous writer and would attempt to preserve anonymity by insisting that his name was Gogel or even Gonol.[14]

In his writing, on the other hand, there is often sly self-identification with a character through his name. We have seen that the comic bee-keeper of *Evenings in a village near Dikanka* can be related to Gogol through the patronymic Panenko, and as Karlinsky has observed there is also identification through a bird in the name Kurochka (little hen):[15] the narrator credited with having the full version of 'Ivan Fedorovich Shponka and his Aunty'. Nor is Gogol above open mockery of his 'noble' name. In a letter to Zhukovsky (12 November 1836) he describes how he scratched it on a column in the dungeon of the Castle of Chillon: 'some day a Russian traveller will make out my bird's name, if an Englishman doesn't squash it out' (XI, 73). It is interesting to note where the bird itself crops up in Gogol's fiction. The golden eye is introduced at the end of the revised version of 'Taras Bulba', and Leon Stilman links this to the element of 'expiatory sacrifice for the deeds of the author's pseudo-ancestor' which he sees in the work.

The idiomatic expression *khodit' gogolem* (literally 'to walk like a golden-eye duck') means 'to strut', 'to swagger'. There is obvious self-irony in Gogol's use of the phrase in the second version of 'The Portrait' (1841–2) to describe the self-satisfied behaviour of the artist on succumbing to the diabolical gold.

Both these revisions date from the same time and reflect in some measure the self-reappraisal Gogol was undergoing in his struggle with his new conception of *Dead Souls*. It is, therefore, perhaps significant that concern about a 'bird's name' and noble ancestry should surface just before the crisis chapter 6 of part I. Plyushkin has been called a name by peasants which causes the author to speculate about such soubriquets in general:

> and no matter how much you try to be clever later on, and how much you ennoble your nickname, even though you get scribblers for a fee to deduce it from some ancient princely family, nothing can help it: the nickname will croak for itself in full crowish voice, and will clearly tell where the bird has flown from. (VI, 109)

Apart from meaning a species of duck, Gogol's name seems phonetically to echo the sound ascribed in Russian to a gander: '*go, go, go*'.[16] In the quarrel of the two Ivans, Ivan Ivanovich not only complains that he has had the appellation 'gander' added to his surname, but feels it to be an insult both to his rank and status as a nobleman, which he vigorously defends by reference to the parish registers, even though in his ridiculous complaint he reveals that (like the family of Yanovsky itself) he is really of clerical origin.

If there is here a strong element of self-mockery, there is also an evident anxiety about status. It is this theme which comes increasingly to the fore in the St Petersburg tales: social insecurity is the underlying concern of such quadruple zeros as Poprishchin, Kovalev and the 'significant person'[17] of 'The Overcoat' (later of course Chertokutsky and Chichikov too). Gogol himself sought status in a university chair but had to be content with the rank of *adyunkt-professor* (assistant lecturer). He realised that academically even this was beyond him, and it has been argued that he then turned to the theatre as his *cathedra*. Nevertheless, in the story of the nose, which served in education and did not know its place, Gogol not only expresses self-mockery but genuine anxiety.[18]

Later, in *Dead Souls*, he would have his revenge on the academic profession with his gibe at the self-deception of professors who turn mere supposition into hard facts (significantly in an area in which Gogol was unwillingly called upon to teach – ancient history).[19] In part II the university education of Tentetnikov is depicted in disparaging terms, and there is surely an authorial self-echo in the figure of the professor who reads a course of lectures on the general history of mankind, but in three years only gives what amounts to an introduction!

It is obvious that in the varying aspects of Gogol's self-mockery he is laughing at much which causes him pain: we are back with the formula 'laughter through tears'. In the introductory chapter this was interpreted as a medieval consciousness in collision with a new sensibility. Laughter in that perspective was seen as a social force. Nevertheless, it has become increasingly clear that laughter for Gogol also has an intensely private function and that the 'medieval' features of Gogol's writing are in fact a vehicle of expression for his neurotic personality. The procedures of such an art offer symbol instead of analysis and substitute logical dislocation for clear statement; characters are reduced to sociological generalisations or mere cyphers of rank, and in this process rank itself (*chin*) assumes a function closer to *lichina* (a mask). It is an art which offers 'psychology without psychology' to an author who dare not look deep within himself; it projects a bizarre outer world that is, in effect, an inner one; it generates laughter which, while ostensibly aimed at society, is to a significant extent directed back at the author: 'None of my readers knew, that in laughing at my heroes he was laughing at me' (VIII, 293).

Gogol's writing had to bear a great burden; it was art, it was therapy, it was to some extent social comment, but also it conferred status. Increasingly writing itself became a source of anxiety. Gogol seems to have been inordinately obsessed by the production, reception, and interpretation of *The Government Inspector* (perhaps because, as a play, it appeared so readily to become the property of other people). Gogol seemed compelled to explain both the play and himself over and over again. In one of these pieces, 'The dénouement of *The Government Inspector*' written ten years after the first performance of his play, Gogol appeals for respect for his art of 'laughter through tears':

> Fellow countrymen! I too, like you, have Russian blood in my veins. Look I am crying. As a comic actor, before, I made you laugh, now I am crying. Allow me to feel that my professional career too is just as honourable as that of each one of you, that I am serving my land in the same way that all of you are serving, that I am not some worthless clown, created for the amusement of worthless people, but an honourable civil servant of God's great state'. (IV, 132)

These words from the long final speech of 'the first comic actor' are the apology of Gogol himself, they correspond closely to the idea of serving the state which he puts forward in the 'author's confession' (VIII, 241–2). The choice of vocabulary is revealing: 'professional career' – *poprishche* (a term frequently used by Gogol in his letters and in *Selected Passages from Correspondence with Friends* to denote his own activity as a writer) and the identification of the artist as *chinovnik* (civil servant) evokes the image of the civil servant Poprishchin, whose sense of status is based on his ability to write. Poprishchin, in his writing, is a muddler and, in confusing the outer world with his inner life, he ultimately goes mad. Another *chinovnik*, Akakiy Akakiyevich writes beautifully, but it is only outward form – real meaning eludes him.

In 'The Overcoat' the play on the words denoting meaning: *znachitel'nyy*, *znachitel'nost'*, *znacheniye* seems to be echoed in the section on the meaning of illnesses in *Selected Passages*:

> and I myself see that now everything that will come from under my pen, will be more significant than before. Were it not for the heavy torments of illness, would I not have got carried away! What a significant person I would have imagined myself to be! But hearing every moment that my life hung by a thread, that illness could suddenly suspend that labour of mine, on which was based all my significance. (VIII, 229)

It is this search for inner meaning which so torments Gogol in later life. The verb to write and the verb to paint are identical in Russian, and more than once in his works Gogol expresses the desire to be a painter. It is in terms of painting that the artistic dilemma concerning the relationship of surface to content is discussed in the two stories 'Nevsky Prospekt' and 'The Portrait'. In the latter work the artist–monk exhorts his son: 'Subject everything to your brush, but know how to find in everything an inner idea.' Yet art also has another instrument – the cutting edge (*rezets*), a word frequently used by Gogol in discussing aesthetic problems. In 'The Portrait' this blade is the anatomist's knife; it reveals the danger of trying to penetrate beyond the beautiful surface.

Gogol's failure to make an academic career is also linked to his inability to 'get inside' his subject. At the end of his brilliant general introductory lecture on the middle ages (the importance of which for subsequent history, he likens to the role of the heart for the body) he ends by promising facts and detail in his next lectures: that he will 'arm himself with the anatomist's knife' (VIII, 752–3). Unfortunately, he never did!

The relationship between 'dead and alive' in art haunts the aesthetic argument in 'The Portrait'; its presence can be sensed behind all his later writing: 'The Overcoat', *Rome*, *Dead Souls*. Gogol felt the need to destroy almost as keenly as the urge to create. In *Selected Passages* he 'publicly announces' that he has burned all the works he had in manuscript as 'weak and dead, written in a constrained, ill state' (VIII, 222) (a few pages later he will proclaim illness to be beneficial to his writing!). In his 'Testament' he expresses a very real fear of being buried alive, and later confesses that when he 'tried to open a part of himself' to his friends, he was so misunderstood, that he felt like a man in a lethargic sleep witnessing himself being buried alive (VIII, 334).

In 'The Portrait' the fear associated with the concept: 'dead and alive' is closely linked to the portrayal of reality in art, and in chapter 6 of his *poema*, significantly entitled *Dead Souls*, he again raises the question of the artist's attitude to reality, but the argument now is couched in personal terms. It has acute significance for Gogol both as artist and man; for, as we have seen, he subjectivises reality, so that in depicting the external world, he is to a large extent describing himself. In this process the device of inversion plays an important role: the neuroses, perversions, anxieties which Gogol feels within himself are projected onto the external world so that they may be purged through mockery. It is as though Gogol is saying: 'it is not I who am odd, it is the world that is odd'. In this way his writing brings personal reassurance. Gogol, critical of himself, appeared to be critical of external reality, and so it came about that his works were interpreted as an indictment of Russian society and its values. Indeed, for Gogol to see the world as odd he needed the corroborative evidence of the incompetence, abuses and injustices of the real world itself. Thus there are genuine elements of social criticism in Gogol's work; but their function is not all it seems: they stem from personal need – they are the firm areas of support for the distorting mirror focused on his own soul. Although Belinsky's assessment of Gogol is understandable, it is only partially right; it could never recommend itself wholeheartedly to the author himself.

Art for Gogol was 'a reconciliation with life' (a title he wished to give to the so-called 'author's confession').[20] Nevertheless, in the creative part of his literary activity it was negative reconciliation. In *Selected Passages* Gogol is quite frank about the self-purging nature of his art: 'I have already got rid of much of my own filth, by transferring it to my heroes. I have laughed at it in them and made others also laugh at it' (VIII, 296–7). Here, ostensibly, he is referring only to the 'dead souls' of his last great work, but the implications are obviously wider, and the statement also explains why Gogol is haunted by a sense of deadness permeating 'reality' in his art – it is composed of what he rejects in order to live.

In later life his search for significance and his growing religious convictions led him to look to art for a positive 'reconciliation with life', a vindication of the *status quo*. The external projection of psychology, so vital to Gogol in his youth, became less and less acceptable to him in middle age; it presented a mere vulgar exterior. A new inwardness was called for, yet the way of the 'anatomist's knife' was even more revolting: it revealed man in all his ugliness. Gogol was caught in an artistic impasse made even more intolerable by his drive to become the great teacher.

The crisis which Gogol experienced in writing *Dead Souls* was in part a question of content: the need for a positive message, convincingly embodied in art, and the concomitant problem of the positive hero, but it was also one of method; for Gogol promised his readers an inner spiritual exploration of his characters. All these were areas foreign to an author whose art up to then had been the oblique projection of neurosis. The positive message in the second part of *Dead Souls* is trite, the new heroes are lifeless and unconvincing, and the most sustained attempt to get inside the mind of a positive character up to this point (*Rome*) is really only at the level of impressions of life and opinions on art: a subjective didacticism nearer to Gogol's articles in *Arabesques*.

If his art could not penetrate to the 'inner idea', then it could only be that like the artist monk of 'The Portrait', he was as yet an unworthy vessel and must purify himself through ever greater asceticism. As Gogol reminded his readers in *Selected Passages*, Jesus Christ himself had fasted for forty days before undertaking to preach his message. Gogol's behaviour during Lent of 1852 is entirely understandable. He was undergoing an artistic crisis which had already led to the burning of part II of *Dead Souls*, but artistic failure was also identified as a spiritual crisis, and in a very real sense it was. To purify himself as man and artist, Gogol had to undertake a rigorous fast, from which he never recovered.

As we have seen, Gogol's artistic personality was driven by more than one neurosis. Sexual fears loom large in the earlier period ('A Terrible Vengeance', 'Ivan Fedorovich Shponka and his Aunty', 'The Old World Landowners', 'Viy'); concern about identity and status are identifiable with a 'middle' period (the tale of the two Ivans, *The Government Inspector*,[21] 'The Nose', 'The Diary of a Madman'); anxiety about art and writing dominate the later works (the second version of 'The Portrait', *Selected Passages from Correspondence with Friends*, but above all *Dead Souls*). Nevertheless the fact that most of Gogol's work was either written or conceived within a very short span of years suggests that the effect of distinct periods may be largely an illusion – the result of his concentrating on three successive themes: the Ukraine, St Petersburg and the Russian provinces. Gogol's anxieties are not held in watertight compartments. Sexual fears associated with the theme of the Ukraine (his origins) revolve round the taboo of incest. The inbred 'ancestral' nature of such fears raises the question of Gogol's own antecedents, and this in turn poses the problem of status and ultimately of identity. If, however, like his hero Poprishchin, Gogol can only base status on his ability to write, a further burden is placed on art as a vehicle of therapy.

Gogol's anxiety is a composite: its various elements are often found side by side, especially in such stories as 'The Diary of a Madman' and 'The Overcoat'. When religion is ultimately grasped as a salvation, anxiety is compounded; for if artistic greatness depends upon the purity of the artist's soul ('The Portrait') the new turn results in a vicious circle.

Although the areas of neurosis are linked, there is progression, and the changing depiction of 'nature' throughout Gogol's work is in this sense instructive. Natural description abounds in his portrayal of the Ukraine.[22] *Evenings in a village near Dikanka* opens with the description of a Ukrainian summer day which, as Hugh McLean has pointed out, is overtly sexual[23] (the voluptuous sky bends over the earth and seems to have fallen asleep, plunged entirely into bliss; embracing and squeezing the beautiful one in its ethereal embraces – the earth too has fallen in love – and the description ends: 'How full of voluptuousness and sweet bliss is the Ukrainian summer!' I, 111–12).

Yet sexuality in nature later yields to fear; monsters lurk in it. They are mythological in 'A Terrible Vengeance' (the 'forest grandad' and the *rusalka*); in 'The Old World Landowners' it is the wild wood which through a cat becomes associated with sexuality and with death. Nature in this story seems inexplicably fertile, the old couple oddly unsexed. Yet the strangest scene of all is the romantic setting for their one physical enjoyment – food, in which there are no people but the trees outside hold terror. This unexplained terror seems to hint at the strange panic to which the author himself admits, when, as a boy alone in a garden on a still summer day, he would hear a frightening voice. Here the bright Ukrainian summer day is not unlike that described in such sexual terms at the beginning of *Evenings in a village near Dikanka*, but as in the 'idyll' of the old world landowners themselves, nature seems in stasis: 'not a single leaf on a tree stirred in the garden; there was a dead silence' (II, 37).

In 'Viy' the monsters have assumed distinct forms and seem independent of nature. Yet nature seeks to trap Khoma Brut when he attempts to escape through the overgrown garden. At the end it engulfs, in their frozen death, both Khoma Brut and the monsters themselves. In 'Taras Bulba', with its wonderful descriptions of the steppe, nature appears to have less symbolic content, but not entirely so. The steppe, which Taras and his sons cross, becomes a hill which covers up all behind them: 'Farewell both childhood and games, and everything and everything!' (II, 52). The July night when Andriy deserts his comrades for a woman reveals bizarre horrors amid its beauty (II, 88).

When, however, Gogol turns to the theme of status, nature barely figures at all. (The magical landscape at the end of the 'Diary of a Madman' leads the hero back to his mother! III, 214.) It is not surprising that stories set in St Petersburg or that a play (*The Government Inspector*) should be wanting in descriptions of nature, but they have only a minimal role in *The Carriage*: a story which is set in the country. Thus Gogol's 'flight from love' is paralleled by a subsequent 'flight from nature', and this appears to be announced symbolically in the narrator's departure from a 'tearful' countryside at the end of the story in which 'status' first becomes a real issue: 'The tale of how Ivan Ivanovich quarrelled with Ivan Nikiforovich'.

When nature again appears as a real presence in Gogol's writing it reflects his concern about art. The natural phenomena of the Russian countryside, in chapter II of *Dead Souls*, 'set out to write', and the theme of the garden, which in 'Viy' and 'The Old World Landowners' inspired fear, has now turned into a metaphor for art itself with the description of Plyushkin's garden and its pendant – the garden of the supposed neighbour, where artifice and artificiality cause nature itself to be indignant.

The new hope, part II of *Dead Souls*, is ushered in with a long natural description which with its mountains is somehow un-Russian. Here Gogol resorts to his old device of reflection, but it is significant that it is a golden-domed church which is now inverted in the river, and that nature itself, in the form of misshapen willow trees, is admiring it, in as far as nature already in the water (aquatic plants) will allow (VII, 8). It is almost as though Gogol has returned to 'The Idyllic Pictures' of *Gants Kyukhelgarten*; for his very first *poema* had opened with a similar foreign landscape in reflection, but with a church that was less prominent (I, 61).

In 'Viy' nature had run riot through a church, but at the opening of part II of *Dead Souls* a church, for the first time, dominates nature (even distant villages can be sensed through the golden glint of their churches). Nevertheless there is the curious hint of a secondary theme; for the five gilded cupolas of the reflected church, with their gold crosses and golden chains seem to hang in the air 'like shining, burning, ten-rouble-pieces of gold'. This composite image seems emblematic of the positive message of part II, whose chief mouthpiece will be Murazov – the religious millionaire. If the church has to bear such a temporal load, it is scant wonder that its crosses are seen as inverted!

Natural description in Gogol is, for the most part, not naturalistic. His landscapes are 'psychological'. Their symbols convey the inner world of his characters, and the shifting emphases record the private obsessions of the author himself. Gogol's position in Russian literature is unique. He may be said to be the first to have explored the neurotic personality. Yet although he did this obliquely, he opened the way for the intense interest in psychology so characteristic of the Russian novel. Pushkin had touched on the theme of madness in *The Bronze Horseman* and *The Queen of Spades*. In *Eugene Onegin* he had introduced the unconscious through Tatyana's dream, but on the whole the world of Pushkin is balanced and sane.

The neurotic personality is one of the central themes of Russian nineteenth-century literature: Rudin, Oblomov, the underground man, Levin, the hero of *The Kreutzer Sonata* are all characters who in some sense are psychologically inadequate or whose inner life, at the very least, is at variance with life around them.

England in the nineteenth century was by and large a stable society, self-confident, sure of the rightness of things. The heroes of its literature largely reflect such values. Even when they are at odds with society (as say Arthur Clennam in *Little Dorrit*) the spiritual and social malaise does not seem fundamental. By contrast, Russia in the nineteenth century was caught between the old rigid values of a medieval consciousness and a newly awakened awareness of the individual. It was a divided society: on the one hand were the illiterate masses of its vast countryside; on the other, the highly civilised élite of its capital cities. It was a sprawling empire searching for an identity between East and West. The soul-searching, the neurosis, both private and national, the theme of alienation itself were scarcely understood by contemporary readers in Western Europe. It took the twentieth century to discover the 'modern' literature that had been produced in Russia a century before.

Dostoevsky was the first to realise Gogol's latent psychologism and to bring it into the open; each of his early stories is a rewriting of Gogol in a more explicitly psychological way: *Poor Folk* ('The Overcoat'); *The Landlady* ('A Terrible Vengeance'); *The Double* ('The Nose' and 'Diary of a Madman'). With the perception of genius Dostoevsky 'psychologised' Gogol, but he could only do so because he understood what was already there.

The suggestion that Dostoevsky and his generation 'came out of Gogol's Overcoat' has its own truth. Gogol may not have invented the 'little man' in literature, but in Akakiy Akakiyevich he decisively influenced the theme's future development. Yet a 'medieval' need for absolutes prompted Gogol's attempts to transcend the mere individual: his last great work was to be about Russia itself, and even in his earlier writing the interpenetration of the personal and the national is typical of his treatment of both the Ukraine and Great Russia. Here, too, Gogol left a legacy; for alongside the preoccupation with the individual, Russian literature would also be concerned with the fate of Russia: the marrying of these two themes is one of the hallmarks of the great nineteenth-century tradition.

If Gogol's greatest contribution is to prose fiction, he, nevertheless, influenced it both as a poet and a dramatist. At the end of the century the symbolists experimenting in poetic prose would turn to Gogol as a master; on the other hand, as Richard Freeborn has strongly argued, *Dead Souls* conditioned the dramatic way the Russian novel would portray character: 'In *Dead Souls* a process of theatricalisation can be seen to be at work both in the portrayal of the landowners, and in the gradual emergence of Chichikov as the dominant portrait. The Russian novel after Gogol tended to owe much to theatrical example.'[24] The direct legacy here is again that of Dostoevsky, but each writer took from Gogol what he needed. Turgenev learned his pictorial skills and eye for detail from the strange man who had once lectured to him in history. Goncharov came out of Gogol almost in entirety. Leskov listened to the idiosyncrasies of Russian speech with a Gogolian ear and further developed the comic distorting viewpoint of the *skaz*. Tolstoy admired *Selected Passages* and in his own great novels carried on the Gogolian search for self-perfection and universal salvation. Chekhov proclaimed Gogol the greatest Russian writer, and the major influence on his early writing was undoubtedly Gogol; he was the springboard that launched Chekhov into new areas of the short story and a revolutionary technique of theatre. Moreover there was always that side of Gogol which was promoted by Belinsky and Chernyshevsky. As Henry Gifford has said: 'With Gogol, whether he understood it or not, the sensibility of urban Russia, the mood of protest and denial, forced its way into prose fiction.'[25]

As a satirist Mikhail Saltykov-Shchedrin was the direct beneficiary of the protest and denial. With Gorky the tone became more serious, more urgent, and it is this legacy, the sensibility of urban Russia, which Soviet literature has largely inherited. To the outside eye the mood of protest and denial in Gogol's writing was certainly there, but for the inner needs of Gogol himself the contradictory aspects of his art were always an attempt, in their different ways, at 'a reconciliation with life'.

Appendix A

Rank in Gogol's Russia

In 1722 Peter the Great introduced a table of ranks for the civil service, corresponding to military and naval ranks. In the nineteenth century court ranks were added at the higher end of the table (ranks 2, 3, 5) but with minor alterations the table survived until the Revolution of 1917.

Table of ranks

Class	Civil ranks	Military ranks	Naval ranks
1	Chancellor	General-Fieldmarshal	General-Admiral
2	Actual Privy Counsellor	General	Admiral
3	Privy Counsellor	General-Lieutenant	Vice-Admiral
4	Actual State Counsellor	General-Major	Rear-Admiral
5	State Counsellor	—	—
6	Collegiate Counsellor, Military Counsellor	Colonel	Captain (1st class)
7	Court Counsellor	Lieutenant Colonel	Captain (2nd class)
8	Collegiate Assessor	Captain (Major), Captain of Cavalry	—
9	Titular Counsellor	Staff Captain, Staff Captain of Cavalry	Lieutenant
10	Collegiate Secretary	Lieutenant	Midshipman
11	Ship Secretary	—	—
12	Government Secretary	Second Lieutenant, Cornet	—
13	Provincial Secretary, Senate Registrator, Synod Registrator, Cabinet Registrator	Ensign	—
14	Collegiate Registrator	—	—

In spite of these parallels between the various services, the table established the precedence of military and naval ranks to civil ones. Hence the higher civil servants were referred to as 'generals', and Poprishchin ('The Diary of a Madman') thinks of earning the rank of 'colonel' through service (III, 198). In 'The Nose' the collegiate assessor, Kovalev, always calls himself 'major'.

In Gogol's time even the lowest rank (14) conferred 'nobility' on the holder, but for nobility to become hereditary, it was necessary to attain rank 8 (collegiate assessor). Poprishchin and Bashmachkin ('The Overcoat') are both titular counsellors (rank 9) and thus are at a career threshold. Kovalev appears to have crossed this barrier, but by doubtful means (III, 54). Chichikov (*Dead Souls*) is also a collegiate assessor and is therefore greatly concerned about heirs.

For classes 14–8 promotion from rank to rank occurred, in theory, at the end of a three-year period in each case, but Bashmachkin is referred to as the 'eternal titular counsellor' and there seems scant hope of promotion for Poprishchin. For classes 8–5 inclusive promotion was normally at the end of a four-year period. Appointments to ranks 4–1 were made only by the tsar himself.

The various levels of rank had appropriate formal styles of address. Ranks 14–9 were addressed as 'Your honour' (*Vashe blagorodiye*) and this courtesy extended to their wives. For ranks 8–6 the correct title was 'Your high honour' (*Vashe vysokoblagorodiye*). Rank 5 had its own special contraction of this title – *Vashe vysokorodiye*. Ranks 4–3 carried the title 'Your excellency' (*Vashe prevoskhoditel'stvo*); ranks 2–1 were 'Your high excellency' (*Vashe vysokoprevoskhoditel'stvo*).

In *The Government Inspector* Khlestakov has the very lowest rank on the scale – collegiate assessor, but is addressed by the mayor as 'Your excellency', even though his servant Osip correctly addresses him as 'Your honour'.

See *Bol'shaya sovetskaya entsiklopediya* (*The Great Soviet Encyclopedia*) (2nd edn, Moscow, 1956), vol. 41, pp. 446–7; and *Tolkovyy slovar' russkogo yazyka* (*Explanatory Dictionary of the Russian Language*) (edited by D. I. Ushakova) (Moscow, 1935), vol. I, pp. 149, 504, vol. 3, p. 706.

Appendix B

The writing of 'The Nose'

The writing of 'The Nose' is closely connected with the attempt of Pogodin and other Moscow intellectuals to set up a new magazine. Gogol was enthusiastic about the idea. In a letter to Pogodin of 2 November 1834 he called the project 'our magazine': he was full of good advice and promised a contribution. Nevertheless, he was busy bringing out *Arabesques* and *Mirgorod*, and repeatedly said he could not give them anything before the third number of the new magazine (letters to Pogodin of 31 January and 20 February 1835 (x, 351, 354)). In his letter of 31 January he tells Pogodin that he has already begun his tale, but that he will not have time even to think about it for another two weeks. Gogol sent Pogodin 'The Nose' for the new journal, *The Moscow Observer*, on 18 March 1835, and it is obvious from Gogol's letters to Pogodin and Shevyrev (nos. 238, 240, 241, 242, 243) (x, 351–5) that serious work on 'The Nose' could only have taken place in February and March of 1835. Yet, in spite of this, N. L. Stepanov dates the first full draft not later than the end of August 1834 (III, 651, 655). Stepanov's argument for this early date is based on the speculation that, since the fantastic plot is explained as a dream in this manuscript (which he designates as RL2) and since the polemical ending is also absent, it must, therefore, antedate Bulgarin's attack on Pushkin's *Tales of Belkin* (in particular the dénouement of the dream in 'The Undertaker' (*Grobovshchik*)) which appeared in the *Northern Bee* (*Severnaya pchela*) 27 August 1834.

In the first place, however, it must be said that RL2 seems more likely to be the draft for the version sent to Pogodin (who rejected the story). RL2 originates from Pogodin's archive (III, 65) and the opening date of the story, as given in RL2, 'the 23rd of this February' seems to reflect the actual time of writing – i.e. late February 1835. The exclusion of the 'explanation' as a dream and the polemical epilogue are both features which may be seen as a gesture towards Pushkin, and are more likely to have been introduced a year later for the version printed in Pushkin's *Contemporary*. Certainly in introducing Gogol's story Pushkin speaks of having to persuade its author to let him print it (*Sovremennik* (St Petersburg, 1836), III, 54). Moreover, for the 1842 edition of his works, Gogol revised the polemical ending, and incorporated it into the work without the title 'Epilogue' (suggesting that this might have been specially written for Pushkin's *Contemporary*).

A second point is the fact that RL2 is bound into the same notebook with a sheet bearing the water mark 1835. This sheet (designated RL3) is a fair copy of the opening of the story, and Stepanov admits that he does not know whether it relates to the manuscript sent to Pogodin or to the one later sent to Pushkin (III, 651).

Although the first rough sketch of the opening of the story (designated (RL1) (III, 380–1) may well be quite early (Stepanov thinks the end of 1832, beginning of 1833) (III, 650), it is quite short, and quite separate, and does not suggest how the story will continue.

A third point is that Gogol spoke of writing something specially for *The Moscow Observer* (letter to Pogodin, 9 February 1835 (X, 352)), and that earlier he had told him that *Arabesques* was an attempt to throw all the old stuff out of his writing desk, so that he could begin a new life (22 January 1835 (X, 348)). In this letter Gogol asks Pogodin (a Professor of History at Moscow University) for his opinion on the history essays in *Arabesques*, saying that a word from him could help him as he has acquired 'academic enemies' (*uchenyye nepriyateli*). It is obvious that the whole period of the promising and the writing of a new tale for *The Moscow Observer* was a time of difficulty for Gogol at the University.

In this respect the very first letter in which he promises something to Pogodin is of great interest (2 November 1834). He stresses that the new magazine must be filled with laughter, and that it must be laughter 'to score a bull's-eye' (*I glavnoye, nikak ne kolot' v brov', a pryamo v glaz*) (X, 341) – a phrase which he would later use about the deflation of Kovalev's social pretensions (III, 64). He promises to write something once he has got his affairs sorted out; then immediately passes to an attack on a German professor, Arnold Heeren (Pogodin was about to publish his own lectures on the German historian's views): 'I don't know why you want to occupy yourself with, and fuss round, Heeren, who can't see further than his German nose and "trade". An eccentric fellow: he imagines that politics is some sort of tangible object, a gentleman in a dress-coat and shoes' (X, 341–2). Thus the three elements of: academic dissatisfaction; the 'learned' 'nose'; and the personification of the academic are all present in Gogol's mind when he first addresses himself to the question of contributing to the new magazine (which in his view must be permeated by 'laughter').

In his next letter to Pogodin (14 December 1834) Gogol claims that his remarks about Heeren were a joke, and he goes on to reveal his own difficulties as a University lecturer, complaining that he is not listened to, that he encounters no sympathy and that the students are colourless. His mood seems almost schizophrenic: 'Why do nature and man move apart before me' (*otchego zhe peredo mnoyu razdvigayetsya priroda i chelovek* (X, 344)). He confesses that he has been put into a position where in the New Year he has to take on the teaching of ancient history, which earlier he had tried at all costs to avoid, and begs Pogodin to send him his lectures on Heeren's ancient history, even in proof.

It is obvious that Gogol's university career was rapidly disintegrating and about a month after sending 'The Nose' to Pogodin he was already applying for early leave from the University to go to the Caucasus for health reasons. (See letters of 17 April to Pogodin, and of the end of April to G. A. Fonshverin (x, 363–4); also the commentary (x, 493).)

Gogol had long nursed a desire to go to the Caucasus (see letter to M. A. Maksimovich, 2 July 1833 (x, 274)), and now the Caucasus seemed to beckon as an escape from the world of learning. In his story the 'flight' appears to be inverted: it is the 'learned part' which seeks to escape from the qualifications of the 'Caucasus'. Given this background, the 'Freudian' slips of 'collegiate professor' for 'collegiate assessor' in RL2 (III, 385) seem significant.

Even if one accepts Stepanov's earlier date of the end of August 1834 for the first full draft (RL2), it must still be borne in mind that Gogol was appointed *adyunkt-professor* on 24 July 1834, and that he viewed the new post with some anxiety. Thus the day before he had written to Pogodin asking for copies of the latter's lectures on the middle ages: 'It would not be at all a bad idea if you took an exercise book from one of your students in which he has written down your lectures, particularly on the middle ages, and sent it to me right away with Red'kin' (x, 333).

The lost university career of the 'nose' did not end even after the story's completion. From a letter of 17 April 1835 to Pogodin, it appears that it might also have gone astray at Moscow University. 'The devil only knows what's happened to the nose! I sent it, as I should, sewn up in oil cloth, and addressed to Moscow University. I cannot think that somehow it has got lost' (x, 363).

Notes

Unless otherwise stated all references to the works of N. V. Gogol are to the Complete Edition, *Polnoye sobraniye sochineniy* (Akademiya Nauk, SSSR, Leningrad, 1937–52) which, in both the text and the notes, will be recorded as a volume number (roman numerals) and a page reference (arabic numerals).

Introduction

1 For an excellent account of the varying critical attitudes to Gogol's writing see R. A. Maguire (ed.), 'The legacy of criticism', the introduction to his *Gogol from the Twentieth Century* (Princeton, New Jersey, 1974), pp. 3–54.

2 Gogol's interest in ritual found expression in a commentary on Orthodox liturgy. See N. V. Gogol, *The Divine Liturgy of the Russian Orthodox Church*, tr. Rosemary Edmonds (London, 1960).

3 It is interesting to compare Lomonosov's 'Inscription for a Statue of Peter the Great' (M. V. Lomonosov, *Sochineniya* (Moscow and Leningrad, 1961), p. 153) with Pushkin's poem on the equestrian statue of the same monarch, *The Bronze Horseman* (A. S. Pushkin, *Polnoye sobraniye sochineniy* (Leningrad, 1948), v, 131–49). In the eighteenth-century tribute the poet's own individuality is subsumed in the figure of the emperor: Lomonosov, as a man of the people and a man of science, praises him for qualities which are his own. Pushkin's poem projects individual values and those of the great statesman as inimical and antithetical.

4 Even that great champion of humanitarian and peasant values L. N. Tolstoy records in his memoirs (*Vospominaniya*) that in the 1840s no one in his circle questioned the moral right to own serfs. Given such a situation, he points to the influence that Gogol's 'Letter to a Landowner' could have. See L. N. Tolstoy, *Polnoye sobraniye sochineniy* (Moscow, 1952), XXXIV, 383.

5 Gogol forced his servant Yakim to get married for his master's convenience, and when he began to drink Gogol beat him. Cf. letter to his mother, 22 November 1832 (x, 245) and commentary (x, 454).

6 See Henry M. Nebel Jr, *N. M. Karamzin, A Russian Sentimentalist* (The Hague, 1967), p. 31. Also G. P. Makogonenko, 'Puti literatury veka'

introductory article to *Russkaya literatura XVIII veka* (Leningrad, 1970), p. 39.

7 N. A. Berdyayev, *Russkaya ideya, Osnovnyye problemy russkoy mysli XIX veka i nachala XX veka* (Paris, 1946), p, 30.

8 'Sterne makes his points by subtle touches, persiflage, intimate conversations with the reader. Radishchev usually harangues him with all the emphasis of passionate conviction.' (D. M. Lang, 'Sterne and Radishchev: an episode in Russian Sentimentalism', *Revue de Littérature Comparée*, XXI (1947), 256).

Sterne, however idiosyncratically, gives a picture of French society before the Revolution. Yorick has direct contact with all classes from beggars to countesses. He wishes to depict 'the millions of my fellow creatures born to no inheritance but slavery' and goes on to establish himself as an enemy of that important symbol of oppression the Bastille, even adding his symbol for the oppressed prisoner, the starling, to his own crest of arms. ('The Passport: the Hotel at Paris', 'The Captive: Paris', 'The Starling: the Road to Versailles'). It is significant that Tolstoy's first attempt at literature was a translation of Sterne's *A Sentimental Journey.*

9 N. M. Karamzin, 'Pis′ma russkogo puteshestvennika', *Izbrannyye sochineniya* (Moscow and Leningrad, 1964), p. 141.

10 Thus Leskov admitted employing the manner of Sterne and Hoffmann to avoid the censor. N. S. Leskov, *Sobraniye sochineniy* (Moscow, 1958), IX, 643.

11 See A. G. Cross, *N. M. Karamzin: A Study of his Literary Career 1783–1803* (Carbondale and Edwardsville, London and Amsterdam, 1971).

12 The 'English' Sentimentalism of Karamzin also became associated with a cult of nature. In A. A. Shakhovskoy's short comedy *Novyy Stern* (*The New Sterne*) a Russian count who venerates nature falls in love with a peasant girl (an obvious pastiche of *Poor Liza*). When his servant Ipat asks a friend of his master's father, Sud′bin, to explain this 'devil's brew of Sentimentalism' (*sentimental′naya chertovshchina*) Sud′bin replies:

> It was formed in England, ruined in France and really got out of hand in Germany, and it has been imported into our country in such a pitiable state that...
>
> IPAT That it would make a hen laugh. I pity the people who get it after us.

See A. A. Shakhovskoy, *Komedii, stikhotvoreniya* (Leningrad, 1961), p. 745. *The New Sterne* is also mentioned in Narezhny's novel, *The Russian Gil Blas.* See V. T. Narezhny, *Rossiyskiy Zhilblaz ili pokhozhdeniya knyazya Gavrily Simonovicha Chistyakova* (*The Russian Gil Blas*) (Moscow, 1938), p. 11.

The social interpretation of English Sentimentalism can also be seen in the Russian attitude to another novel: 'Richardson's *Pamela*, the story of a serving girl's successful aspiration to an upper class life, was interpreted by the Russians as a defense of the virtues of the lower classes', Nebel, *N. M. Karamzin*, p. 73.

13 For a discussion of the importance of Narezhny for the development of the Russian novel, see R. Freeborn, *The Rise of the Russian Novel. Studies in the Russian Novel from 'Eugene Onegin' to 'War and Peace'* (Cambridge, 1973), pp. 5–6.

14 Narezhny, *Rossiyskiy Zhilblaz*, p. 15. In choosing the name Prostakov, Narezhny seems to be polemicising with Prostakova one of the least humane of characters in Fonvizin's comedy *The Minor*. Goncharov said of Narezhny after reading *The Russian Gil Blas*, 'He is of the school of Fonvizin, his follower and the forerunner of Gogol.' (I. A. Goncharov, *Sobraniye sochineniy v 8-i tomakh* (Moscow, 1952–5), VIII, p. 8.)

15 Narezhny, *Rossiyskiy Zhilblaz*, p. 134.

16 *Ibid.* p. 124.

17 Taras Bulba places military honour higher than paternal love, and kills his own son, whereas in Karamzin's story *The Island of Bornholm* individual love breaks such sacred taboos as those against incest. (Karamzin, *Izbrannyye sochineniya*, I, 663.) 'The laws condemn/The object of my love/But who, O Heart can/Defy you?' A garbled version of this is quoted by Khlestakov in act IV, scene xiii of Gogol's *The Government Inspector*.

18 *Domostroy* was not rediscovered and published until 1849. Gogol himself regarded the work highly and recommended Anna Vielgorskaya to study old Russian so she could read it. See letter of 30 March 1849 (XIV, 110).

19 '*Putevyye vpechatleniya* (*i mezhdu prochim gorshok yerani*) *rasskaz v rode povesti*', *Povesti A. Vel'tmana* (published M. D. Ol'khina (St Petersburg, 1843), p. 259. This is a story of considerable interest and merit.

20 For a discussion of other interpretations see: Victor Ehrlich, *Gogol* (New Haven and London, 1969), pp. 133–4.

21 Henri Troyat, *Gogol, The Biography of a Divided Soul*, tr. from the French by Nancy Amphoux (London, 1974), p. 13, and A. N. Stepanov, *Nikolay Vasil'evich Gogol', Biografiya pisatelya* (Moscow and Leningrad, 1966), p. 9.

22 V. G. Belinsky, *Polnoye sobraniye sochineniy* (Moscow, 1953), I, p. 58.

23 See A. Slonimsky, 'The Technique of the Comic', in Maguire, *Gogol from the Twentieth Century*, p. 332.

24 F. D. Reeve, 'Through Hell on a Hobby Horse. Notes on Gogol and Sterne', *Symposium* (Syracuse, New York, 1959), XIII, 75.

25 D. S. Likhachev and A. M. Panchenko, '*Smekhovoy mir' drevney Rusi* (Leningrad, 1976), p. 76.

26 I.e. the concept of an inverted world '*iznanochnyy mir*' *ibid.* pp. 18, 21, 23; laughter at self, *ibid.* p. 18; use of rhythm and inverted names, *ibid.* p. 27; heroes as dolls, *ibid.* p. 28; the theme of the double, *ibid.* p. 52; comic clothes and possessions, *ibid.* p. 74.

27 In 'O srednikh vekakh' (VIII, 25).
28 D. S. Likhachev, *Chelovek v literature drevney Rusi* (Moscow, 1970), p. 30.
29 *Ibid.* pp. 38, 151.
30 *Ibid.* p. 77.
31 *Ibid.* pp. 7–8.
32 *Ibid.* pp. 75, 76.
33 *Ibid.* p. 116 (cf. p. 86).
34 *Ibid.* p. 133.
35 See F. C. Driessen, *Gogol as a Short Story Writer: A Study of his Technique of Composition*, tr. Ian F. Finlay (Paris, The Hague and London, 1965), pp. 76, 84, 85; Vsevolod Setchkarev, *Gogol, his Life and Works*, tr. Robert Kramer (New York, 1965), pp. 95, 119; Ehrlich, *Gogol*, p. 35.
36 This is one of the many features which link the story with the 'medieval' poem *The Lay of Igor's Campaign* (*Slovo o polku Igoreve*), i.e. battles described as feasts; sudden shifts in the narrative; rhythmical prose.
37 See note of K. D. Muratova in *N. V. Gogol, Sobraniye khudozhestvennykh proizvedeniy v pyati tomakh* (2nd edn, Moscow, 1960), I, pp. 336–7.
38 Zagadchenko, a Ukrainian in Bulgarin's novel *Ivan Vyzhigin* claims that he is simple and straightforward, but the author comments: 'It is a usual trick of the Little Russians to assume the appearance of simplicity' Faddey Bulgarin, *Ivan Vyzhigin: Nravstvenno-satiricheskiy roman* (St Petersburg, 1830), part IV, p. 164.
39 See Driessen, *Gogol as a Short Story Writer*, pp. 70–1, 74; Ehrlich, *Gogol*, p. 39.
40 Driessen, *Gogol as a Short Story Writer*, pp. 109–11.
41 In the scene between the wizard and the soul witnessed by Danilo, the wizard does say: 'Katerina shall love me!' (I, 259), but this scene itself has the confused nature of a dream sequence. Thus the wizard appears to arrive both by boat (I, 255) and on foot (I, 256). Danilo himself wonders whether he is asleep (I, 257). He escapes when the soul looks directly at him. It might be that she is about to betray his presence (I, 259) but an opposite view is given by A. Bely, *Masterstvo Gogolya* (Nachdruck der Ausgabe Moskau, 1934) (Munich, 1969), p. 61.
42 The soul is glad that Katerina has fallen asleep, because she wants to see her mother, but instead she is summoned by her father (I, 258).
43 I.e. '*lyubo*'' = 'pleasant', but it is a word obviously connected with '*lyubov*'' = 'love'.
44 The 'forest grandad' was another version of the wood spirit or *leshiy*. Pomerantseva describes a *dedushka lesovoy* as a huge old man with a long grey beard. See: E. V. Pomerantseva, *Mifologicheskiye personazhi v russkom fol'klore* (Moscow, 1975), p. 33. Here, of course, the beard is green. Forest spirits were regarded as people who had been cursed, or even, at times, as fallen angels (*ibid.* pp. 32–3), they also stole children (*ibid.* p. 38).

45 The figure of the wood spirit is also associated, especially in the Ukraine, with 'The Guardian of the Wolves', *pastyr' volkov*. See Pomerantseva, *Mifologicheskiye personazhi*', p. 31.

46 I.e. *Nechistyye dedy – ded* is the identical word used for the wood spirit, and *nechistyy* has the sense of 'unclean'. A. Bely comments: 'Are they only his?' (*ego li lish'?*) Bely, *Masterstvo Gogolya*, p. 58.

47 The full flavour of this passage can only be appreciated in the original: *Nezhas' i prizhimayas' blizhe k beregam ot nochnogo kholoda, dayet on po sebe serebryannuyu struyu; i ona vspykhivayet, budto polosa damasskoy sabli; a on siniy snova zasnul* (I, 269).

'*Posineli usta, spit kozak neprobudno*' (I. 267) we read at the death of Danilo, when, wielding his 'sabre of Damascus steel', he is treacherously shot by his father-in-law.

The death of Danilo is presented with initial ambiguity, as though it is the wizard himself who has been shot ('The musket thundered – and the wizard disappeared (i.e. *propal*) behind the mountain', I, 267). Moonlight is also described as 'Damascus muslin' – *damasskaya kiseya* (I, 246).

48 The forest spirit and the *rusalka* were often identified with one another in Russian folklore. See Pomerantseva, *Mifologicheskiye personazhi*, pp. 33, 39.

49 Katerina's child is also called Ivan.

50 I.e. *Zadushit'* a verb implying suffocation which seems linked to the cry of the ancestors who rise from their graves: '*Dushno mne, dushno!*' (I, 248) 'I am suffocating'. The dungeon in which Katerina faints after releasing her father, is not 'dank and cold' but 'suffocating' as the old woman who rescues her states: 'I bore you in my arms from the stuffy basement' ('*iz dushnogo podvala*' I, 264).

51 Horseshoe (*podkova*) has yet a further resonance. Ivan and Petro were supposedly in the service of Stephen Batory against the Turks, and in this campaign they were led by Ivan Podkova. The campaign was an embarrassment to Stephen Batory, and in order to avoid war with Turkey he seized and executed Podkova (1578). See K. D. Muratova in *Gogol, Sob. khud. proiz.* I, 368, 370. The treacherous murder of this Ivan may well have served as the basis for Gogol's 'mythological' story of the betrayal and murder of a Cossack comrade-in-arms, Ivan, and his ultimate vengeance from the 'horseshoe'. The geological formation of the Carpathians is in itself suggestive and the torments in the earth of Petro are also given a 'geological' explanation.

52 It is *mera* that the third black horseman of the Apocalypse holds in his hands (cf. Lebedev's words in *The Idiot*: F. M. Dostoevsky, *Sobraniye sochineniy* (Moscow, 1957), VI, p. 228.) The laughter at the time of retribution also seems to link the horseman with the figure of the forest grandad. One of the frightening features typical of him was loud laughter. See Pomerantseva: *Mifologicheskiye personazhi*, pp. 35, 38.

53 His view of 'salvation' appears to invert Christ's teaching on the grain of corn: 'But a man of dishonourable breed and descendants, is like a seed of corn, cast into the earth and needlessly perishing in the earth. It has no shoot. No one will know that a seed was cast' (I, 281).

54 Driessen describes the process as 'gnawing at the tree of the family'. Driessen, *Gogol as a Short Story Writer*, p. 102.

55 But perhaps 'Little Russia' should be interpreted in the sense of Russia Minor. See W. E. D. Allen, *The Ukraine: a History* (New York, 1963), p. 64.

1. Mirgorod

1 For a discussion of the date of writing see the notes to the complete works by N. L. Stepanov (II, 752–3) and V. V. Gippius (II, 682–3).

2 See N. L. Stepanov (II, 754–6), also the comments of V. F. Pereverzev in V. T. Narezhny, *Izbrannyye romany* (Academia, 1933), pp. 664, 724, 749; and N. A. Engel′gardt, 'Gogol' i romany 20-kh godov' *Istoricheskiy vestnik* (1902), II, 572–3, 578.

3 'On the Russian tale and the tales of Mr Gogol', Belinsky, *Polnoye sobraniye sochineniy*, I, 303–4.

4 Before the Revolution the two meanings were differentiated orthographically by the two written forms of the vowel 'i'.

5 M. Yu. Lermontov, *Sobraniye sochineniy v 4-kh tomakh* (Moscow, 1965), vol. IV, p. 47.

6 The story was apparently inspired by Gogol's visit to the Ukraine in the summer of 1832. A letter to I. I. Dmitriyev shows that he responded to this experience in Karamzinian terms (X, 239).

7 (II, 698–9). See also L. Stilman, 'Nikolaj Gogol and Ostap Hohol', *Orbis Scriptus: Dmitrij Tschizewskij zum 70 Gerbürtstag* (Munich, 1966), p. 813.

8 A. S. Pushkin, 'Novyye knigi', *Sovremennik* (St Petersburg, 1836), no. I, p. 312.

9 Belinsky, *Polnoye sobraniye sochineniy*, I, 292, 297.

10 The literary device of the would-be portrait painter of mythological characters comes from Sentimental literature. Cf. *The Island of Bornholm*, N. M. Karamzin, *Izbrannyye sochineniya* (Moscow and Leningrad, 1964), I, 670. A similar desire to be a painter is expressed in 'The Tale of how Ivan Ivanovich quarrelled with Ivan Nikiforovich' (II, 242) where it develops into an absurd parody of itself (cf. R. A. Peace, 'The laughter of the "Tale of the Two Ivans"', Exeter Tapes, 1977). See also Paul Debreczeny, 'Gogol's mockery of Romantic taste: varieties of language in the "Tale of the Two Ivans"', *Canadian–American Slavic Studies* (1973), VII, 339.

11 Ovid, *Metamorphoses*, bk. VIII, lines 618ff. Renato Poggioli also points to Goethe's version of the myth in part II of *Faust*. See R. Poggioli,

'Gogol's *Old Fashioned Landowners*: an inverted eclogue', *Indiana Slavic Studies* (1963), II, 68.

12 Narezhny, *Izbrannyye romany*, p. 746.

13 (X, 239) and (II, 698–9).

14 Cf. the use of voices (descant, tenor, bass) at the beginning of 'Viy' to characterise the various levels of maturity of the seminarists (II, 177).

15 I.e. '*Kogda prozyabnuvshi ot presledovaniya za kakoy-nibud' brunetkoy, vbegayesh' v nikh, pokhlopyvaya ladonyami.*' This is the text of the 1835 edition which V. Gippius, the editor of volume two of the Complete Works, considers canonical. There are other variants (1842, 1855) which ascribe such chasing to 'ardent youth' (*pylkaya molodezh'*) and the manuscript source omits the amorous incident as a reason for feeling cold (II, 461, 696–7).

16 Members of the higher clergy were celibate as they invariably came from the ranks of the monastic priesthood (black clergy). Peter III was murdered with the connivance of his wife Catherine II. Moreover after his death he became a cult figure for the Castrates, whose leader, Kondratiy Selivanov, actually claimed to be Peter III.

17 See H. McLean, 'Gogol's retreat from love: toward an interpretation of *Mirgorod*', *American Contributions to the Fourth International Congress of Slavists* (The Hague, 1959), p. 239. Afanasiy means 'deathless' (Afanasiy Ivanovich, unlike Ovid's Philemon, lives on after the death of his wife). The surname Tovstogub is perhaps suggestive of the couple's one great passion, eating. In Ukrainian the name suggests 'fat mouth' (cf. also *vin lyubit' tovsto isti* – 'he is fond of fat foods' and *zhiti na vsyu gubu* – 'to live in comfort').

18 I.e. *bremya* – a word connected with pregnancy – *beremennost'* (cf. *razreshitsya ot bremeni*).

19 McLean, 'Gogol's retreat from love', p. 239.

20 Belinsky interprets this as a subtle attempt by Afanasiy Ivanovich to divert his wife's attention from his 'terrible appetite'. See Belinsky, *Polnoye sobraniye sochineniy*, I, 294.

21 Being burned to ashes as a metaphor for being consumed by passion is a commonplace in Gogolian criticism. Cf. V. Bryusov, 'Ispepelennyy', *Gogolevskiye dni v Moskve* (Moscow, 1909), p. 157. See also Driessen, *Gogol as a Short Story Writer*, pp. 37, 163.

22 I.e. *vot uzhe i poshel*: the phrase is ambiguous (cf. earlier: *poyti na voynu*), it could suggest that by his remarks he has already begun 'hostilities'. Belinsky takes this teasing at face value. See Belinsky, *Polnoye sobraniye sochineniy*, I, 294–5.

23 The incident with the cat was apparently told to Gogol by the actor Shchepkin as something which actually happened to his own grandmother. When Shchepkin read 'The Old World Landowners' he jokingly reminded Gogol of the origin of the incident by saying: 'But the cat is mine.' To this Gogol retorted: 'Nevertheless the tom-cats are mine' (II,

698). Gogol's own acknowledgement of his addition to the original anecdote is surely significant.

That belief in such omens was not uncommon can be judged from the ethnographer V. Dal′: 'Here and there people have assured me many times that dogs, horses or any other domestic animal have sensed and guessed beforehand the death of their master, and that animals have shown this by howling, bellowing, neighing, nocturnal stamping, unusual timidity, fear etc.' (V. I. Dal′: '*O pover′yakh, suyeveriyakh i predrassudkakh russkogo naroda*', *Polnoye sobraniye sochineniy* (St Petersburg, 1897–9), X, 397.) In Gogol's story the narrator does not explain the cat's behaviour as a premonition, he ascribes its estrangement to purely amorous causes. It is Pulkheriya Ivanovna herself who interprets this as a sign of her own death.

24 It is also the colour of the tailcoat worn by the houseboy, who had earlier been linked (with a note of incredulity) to the pregnancies of Pulkheriya Ivanovna's maids.

25 He complains of this condition in *Selected Passages from Correspondence with Friends* ('Four letters to various people on the subject of *Dead Souls*' letter 4, 1844) (VIII, 299), also in a letter to A. P. Tolstoy, 28 March (n.s.) 1848 (XII, 469–70).

26 Constance Garnett translates *strakh* in this passage as 'tremor', but this is a stylistic gloss which masks the real nature of the word. See *Taras Bulba and other stories*, translated from the Russian by Constance Garnett (New York, 1962), p. 157.

27 Passion and death are often linked in Gogol. See A. de Jonge, 'Gogol', *Nineteenth Century Russian Literature: Studies of Ten Writers*, ed. J. Fennell (London, 1973), pp. 81–2.

28 Dostoevsky, *Sobraniye sochineniy*, X, 365–70. A similar experience is described by Varvara in *Poor Folk*, Dostoevsky, *ibid.* I, 175.

29 Victor Erlich, for example, relates the theme of habit versus passion to Tolstoy's *War and Peace* and *Family Happiness*. Erlich, *Gogol*, p. 59.

30 See commentary (VI, 716–26).

31 Stilman, 'Nikolaj Gogol', p. 813.

32 See his introductory article to Narezhny, *Izbrannyye romany*, p. 12.

33 Cf. Katerina's 'mad' song in 'A Terrible Vengeance' (I, 273–4).

34 The 1835 version has other comparisons of warfare and weddings, e.g. 'And now my brother gentlemen let us drink *gorelki* before the great hour, because our fate is now like a wedding, at which every man must make merry' (II, 327); and later as they go into battle: 'They advanced to the whistle of bullets as though to wedding music' (II, 329).

35 The same is true of Narezhny's depiction of the *Sech′* in his novel *Bursak*. Thus the Cossack Yermil is punished for concealing his wife there: 'The horror of those searching was indescribable. They were amazed that the *Sech′* had not been swallowed up by the earth, or consumed by celestial fire like Sodom, for the fact that a woman had defiled the hallowed place

with her presence.' V. T. Narezhny, *Izbrannyye sochineniya v dvukh tomakh* (Moscow, 1956), II, 133.

36 I.e. he appears to dismiss his son's meeting with the Tartar maid as merely an amorous assignment (II, 316) (cf. II, 93).

37 Danilo in 'A Terrible Vengeance' puts his wife in her place with the words: *nasha zhena lyul'ka da ostraya sablya* (I, 247) and later Gorobets' says of Danilo's son: 'He has not yet grown out of his cradle and he is already thinking of smoking a pipe' (*Eshche ot kolybeli ne otstal, a uzhe dumayet kurit' lyul'ku*) (I, 271).

The phrase *neotluchnaya soputnitsa* was added to the 1842 edition, and the same year saw the publication of 'The Overcoat' in which another female object (an overcoat) takes on the attributes of a woman and is called 'a lifelong female friend' (*podruga zhizni*) (III, 154).

38 I. S. Turgenev, *Polnoye sobraniye sochineniy i pisem* (Moscow and Leningrad, 1961), Pis'ma, II, 60.

39 A. de Jonge, 'Gogol', p. 82.

40 'Philosopher' is merely the designation of one of the grades in the seminary, as Gogol makes clear at the beginning of his story. The various classes are: 'grammarians' (*grammatiki*), 'rhetoricians' (*ritory*), 'philosophers' (*filosofy*), 'theologians' (*bogoslovy*). Nevertheless Gogol uses the term with obvious ironic intent, cf. 'He addressed them with questions, but the Cossacks, undoubtedly, were also philosophers, because their reply was to keep silent and smoke their pipes, as they lay on the sacks' (II, 191). The double sense of 'philosopher' is taken quite seriously by Narezhny in *Bursak* for his hero Khlopotinsky, but with more irony in the two Ivans (cf. Narezhny, *Izbrannyye romany*, p. 861).

41 See commentary (II, 745) also Yu M. Sokholov, 'V. T. Narezhny', *Besedy* (1915), I, 96–109.

42 Cf. II, 186 and II, 218 with E. T. A. Hoffmann, *Werke* (Frankfurt am Main, 1967), I, 126, 129. The commentary of V. P. Petrov also points to *Die Prinzessin im Sarge und die Schildwache* of the brothers Grimm (II, 736, 741).

43 Narezhny, *Izbrannyye romany*, pp. 724, 728.

44 See commentary in V. A. Zhukovsky, *Izbrannoye* (Leningrad, 1973), p. 440; also V. Setchkarev, *Gogol, His Life and Works* (New York, 1965), p. 145; and S. Karlinsky, *The Sexual Labyrinth of Nikolai Gogol* (Cambridge, Massachusetts and London, England, 1976), pp. 87, 92, 97.

45 See commentary (II, 735–44) and Driessen, *Gogol as a Short Story Writer*, pp. 136–51.

46 I.e. *chara*. The word is ambiguous in Russian too.

47 Narezhny, *Izbrannyye romany*, p. 704. Sexuality and the monsters of Ukrainian folklore are constantly associated in *Bursak*. See Narezhny, *Izbranyye sochineniya*, II, 28, 29, 30, 57, 88, 91, 111.

48 Garnett (trs.), *Taras Bulba and other stories*, p. 228.

49 I.e. 'krupnoy gorokh' (literally 'big peas'), a seminary punishment consisting of beating with leather thongs.

50 Belinsky, *Polnoye sobraniye sochineniy*, I, p. 304.

51 *Ibid.* p. 303.

52 I.e. 'unknown to him himself' (*nevedomyye yemu samomu*). The feelings Khoma experiences when he first sees the body of the witch seem oddly suggestive: 'As though suddenly amidst a whirlwind of merriment and a milling crowd, someone had sung a song about a persecuted nation' (II, 199). These contrary emotions seem to carry on the idea of the mixture of fear and delight associated with the ride itself, but the strange reference to the persecuted nation (changed by the censors to 'funeral song' (II, 562, 735)) points to the theme of the Ukraine itself, central to all these stories. There is a further echo of the ending of 'The Fair at Sorochintsy', where old women like symbols of death intrude into the merrymaking of the wedding and strike a different note (the contrast is not unlike that embodied in the witch herself: old woman/young love) (I, 135–6).

53 Yu. M. Lotman has pointed to the confusion in the text about the actual time of the witch's death. Yu. M. Lotman, 'Problema khudozhestvennogo prostranstva v proze Gogolya', *Trudy po russkoy i slavyanskoy filologii, Uchennyye zapiski tartuskogo gosudarstvennogo universiteta* (Tartu, 1968), XI, 35–6.

54 (II, 737, 749); also Driessen, *Gogol as a Short Story Writer*, p. 144.

55 Driessen, *Gogol as a Short Story Writer*, p. 143.

56 *Ibid.* p. 144.

57 The sotnik's words have an ominous, satanic ring. He promises to reward Khoma if he will read prayers over his daughter's body for three nights: '"but if not, I don't advise the devil himself to make me angry". These last words were pronounced by the sotnik so firmly, that the philosopher fully understood their meaning' (II, 198).

58 Virtually the same phrase is used here as later to describe Viy (cf. *besprestanno ostupayas'* (perpetually stumbling) (II, 214), and *pominutno ostupayas'* (continually stumbling) (II, 217). Cf. also *staryye korni* (old roots) (II, 214), and *krepkiye korni* (strong roots) (II, 217), also *krot* (a mole) is semantically connected with gentleness (*krotost'*), i.e. submissiveness.

The description of this overgrown garden is strangely evocative. It is covered like a roof with 'a net of hops' (II, 214). *Khmel'* besides meaning 'hops' also means 'drunkenness', and thus seems to look back to Khoma's first attempt at flight on the journey out which had been inhibited by drunkenness (II, 193). Ominously, these hops hang down 'in coiling snakes, along with wild bluebells'. This motif seems to look back to the nocturnal ride itself, for not only had Khoma heard the ringing of such 'bells' (*kolokol'chiki*) (II, 186) but when he starts beating the witch at the end of the ride her groans become 'more pleasant and purer' and almost ring 'like fine silver bells' (*kolokol'chiki*) (II, 187).

There is water in the dream landscape of the nocturnal ride, which is 'clear as a mountain spring'. The garden also contains an unexpected silver spring, and as Khoma is refreshing himself from it, he is caught.

Above all the overgrown quality of the garden, inhibiting escape, seems to prefigure Khoma's own end, in the church which becomes so overgrown that no one can find a way to it.

59 Yavtukh is also the name of the servant of the seminary, who is ordered by the rector to tie Khoma up so that he will not escape (II, 190).

60 Constance Garnett has: 'the devil himself must dance at the master's bidding' (*Taras Bulba and other stories*, p. 204) but the verb is *skakat'* 'to gallop': the same verb which is used for Khoma's nocturnal ride (II, 186).

61 The image of the nail will recur as he attempts to escape through the overgrown garden (II, 214).

62 Gogol calls the dance *tropak*, cf. *tropat'* (Ukr. *tropati*) 'to stamp, trot, run'.

63 Dostoevsky, *Sobraniye sochineniy*, V, 437.

64 Cf. the words of Kokh in *Crime and Punishment*: 'Heigh, Alena Ivanovna, old witch! Lizaveta Ivanovna, beauty indescribable!' *ibid.* p. 89.

65 See M. Kravchenko, *Dostoyevsky and the Psychologists* (Amsterdam, 1978), also R. D. Laing, *Self and Others* (Harmondsworth, 1972), pp. 61–7, 165–73.

66 Nebel, *N. M. Karamzin*, p. 175.

67 Karlinsky, *Sexual Labyrinth*, pp. 86–103.

68 Thus the wizard has an underground lair (*zemlyanka*) (I, 269). He is incarcerated in an underground dungeon (I, 260); near his lair bodies rise from the ground (I, 248) and the evil ancestor, Petro, is locked up in the earth (I, 282).

69 See L. Stilman, 'The all-seeing eye in Gogol', in Maguire, *Gogol from the Twentieth Century*, pp. 376–89.

70 The idea of old women as witches (with sexual overtones) is present in the conversation of the Cossacks (cf. II, 202, 204).

71 Cf. (I, 271, 275) and (II, 204–5).

72 E.g. 'of very shameful origins' (*i proizkozhdeniya ves'ma ponosnogo*). The adjective *ponosnyy* means 'abusive', 'defamatory' but it also contains the root '*ponos*' (diarrhoea).

In the phrase 'frenzied nobleman' (*neistovyy dvoryanin*) the adjective might also be read '*ne istovyy*' – 'not proper', just as the description of Ivan Ivanovich's parents as 'extremely lawless people' (*prebezzakonnyye lyudi*) could also be taken as 'extremely illegal'. The first reference to his enemy in his complaint is to 'Ivan, son of Ivan Pererepenko who calls himself a nobleman' (II, 253), a formula repeated in the second complaint (II, 262).

73 The device of the double was later developed by Dostoevsky for both comic and serious effect (i.e. in *The Double*, *et passim*).

74 See: Stilman, 'Nikolaj Gogol', pp. 824–5.

75 Cf. Narezhny, *Izbrannyye romany*, pp. 781–5. The incident in Gogol may also be taken as a comic example of conscience manifesting itself as 'the supernatural' (cf. 'Viy').

76 Narezhny, *Izbrannyye romany*, p. 780.

77 *Izhitsa*, a very scribish letter of the old orthography.

78 Cf. Narezhny, *Izbrannyye romany*, pp. 687, 829, 859.

79 *Ibid.* p. 671.

80 See notes to N. V. Gogol, *Sobraniye khudozhestvennykh proizvedeniy v pyati tomakh* (Moscow, 1960), II, 426, 434.

81 These incidents caused Pushkin to write his chauvinistic poem of 1831, 'To the Slanderers of Russia' in which he warns the West to keep out of a purely Slav quarrel, reminding them of the ancient rivalry between Russia and Poland, and that Russia had not always had the upper hand. Gogol was close to Pushkin at this time. Both were out of the capital to avoid the cholera epidemic. (See Troyat, *Gogol*, *Biography*, pp. 72–3.)

There is a curious oblique reference to the Polish situation in a letter to his mother on 16 April 1831: 'I am not writing to my sister Mariya because [I should have to speak about a Pole frequently mentioned by her in her letter, and they are now people who are suspect]' (x, 196). The 'Pole' in question is P. O. Trushovsky, who later married Gogol's sister Mariya. Ominously the last words (in square brackets) have been crossed out by someone unknown. See commentary (x, 432). It is from 1831 that Gogol began to drop the Polish sounding 'Yanovsky' from his hyphenated name (x, 219, 445).

A curious sidelight on Gogol and the Turkish question is provided by a letter of the previous year (Feb. 1830), which reveals that Gogol's gardener acted as a postilion for Turkish emissaries (x, 168, 425).

82 These un-Cossack-like connotations are compounded by the very derivation of the coat's name. The *bekesha* was named after Caspar Bekes, a general of the Polish king, Stephen Batory, who had tried to press the Cossacks into Polish service. The fact that Bekes was a well-known atheist also adds ironical point to the professed Christianity of Ivan Ivanovich. See F. A. Brokgaus, I. A. Efron, *Entsiklopicheskiy slovar'* (St Petersburg, 1891–1903), v, 342.

83 Elizabeth A. Warner, *The Russian Folk Theatre* (The Hague and Paris, 1977), p. 97: 'in later times when the *raison d'être* of the Cossack ferocity was beginning to fade the character came debased and only negative qualities remained – boastfulness, over-fondness for drink and indiscriminate violence...

There are many scenes in the Ukrainian *vertep* in which the Cossack is represented as the champion of Ukrainian orthodoxy and nationalism.' *ibid.*

84 The alogism, which first introduces the reader to these breeches, suggests that in some way they have supplanted his bravery (see p. 74).

85 Other 'military' terms are korpus (II, 256), *kompaniya* (II, 268, 270), *raznokalibernyye* (II, 264). See Paul Debreczeny, 'Gogol's mockery', 335–6.

86 See (II, 758–9), also Debreczeny, 'Gogol's mockery', p. 331.

87 (II, 190, 194). Given the un-Cossack-like nature of the Jews, as depicted for instance in 'Taras Bulba', it seems significant that the coach (*kibitka*) is described as the sort that Jews in their scores ride to fairs (II, 190).

88 The emphasis on houses and possessions is not fortuitous in this story. It is in marked contrast to the attitudes of the Cossacks of 'Taras Bulba' for whom, as Lotman points out, both walls and things are 'enemies'. See Lotman, 'Problema khud. prostranstva', pp. 32–3.

89 This assertion carries on the association of witches with sexuality; it progresses from the narrator's denial that Ivan Nikiforovich had ever been married. Cf. also 'Viy': 'People who know about learning say that a witch has a little tail' (II, 202).

90 The first version was even more explicit. Taras substitutes statement for question: 'a man lives in order to defend the faith and custom' (*Na to zhivet chelovek, chtoby zashchishchat′ veru i obychay*) (II, 326).

91 Hugh McLean calls these two statements 'the positive–negative poles of lyric charge'. McLean, 'Gogol's retreat from love', p. 225.

92 I.e. '*Iz zapisok odnogo puteshestvennika*', which according to Lotman is a 'Karamzinian formula'. See: Lotman, 'Problema khud. prostranstva', p. 22.

2. The St Petersburg Tales

1 Nevertheless when the humble hero of *The Bronze Horseman* thinks of his bride to be, Pushkin says 'he became lost in dreams like a poet' (*On razmechtalsya kak poet*). Pushkin, *Polnoye sobraniye sochineniy*, V, 139.

2 The sort of picture which will evoke an odd awakening of feeling in the hero of 'The Overcoat' is also alluded to: 'From the low windows of shops would peer out those prints, which would not dare show themselves during the day' (III, 14).

3 Piskarev sees the tragedy of the life of the beautiful prostitute in terms of madness: 'Can the life of a madman be pleasant for his relatives and friends, who once loved him?' (III, 30).

4 In Hoffmann's drunken riposte: 'I have a king in Germany' there is an echo of that other symbol of self-affirmation in 'The Diary of a Madman' – the King of Spain (III, 207).

5

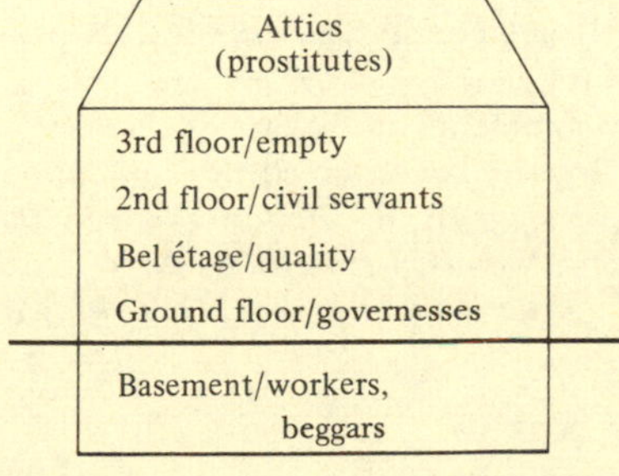

Cf. the opening of Pomyalovsky's novel *Molotov* (1861), N. G. Pomyalovsky, *Polnoye sobraniye sochineniy* (Moscow and Leningrad, 1936), I, 139. Gogol himself may have been influenced by the French writer J. Janin. See commentary of B. M. Engel′gardt (III, 647).

6 A claim Gogol would later make about his depiction of reality in youth. Cf. *Dead Souls*, chapter 6 (VI, 110–11).

7 In an earlier version the gulf between surface and content is explicitly stated (twice): 'Where is she – a picture painted correctly, but deprived of inner poetry' (III, 353).

8 'If Pirogov had been in full uniform, then respect for his rank and calling would probably have stopped the violent Teutons' (III, 44). Censorship would not allow the beating of an officer in uniform. Nevertheless the suggestion that clothes would have impressed more than the man himself, is typical of the values of 'Nevsky Prospekt'.

9 Cf. Schiller's own diet: 'He would in no circumstances increase his expenditure, and if the price of potatoes rose too much above what was usual, he would not add a single copeck, he would only reduce their quantity, and although he would sometimes remain a bit hungry, he would, nevertheless, get used to it' (III, 42).

10 Cf. the theme of 'pity' (*zhalost'*) in Piskarev's attitude to the prostitute (III, 22).

11 Belinsky, *Polnoye sobraniye sochineniy*, I, 181. Hoffmann too had a painter's approach to writing (W. F. Mainland introduction to E. T. A. Hoffmann, *Der Goldene Topf, Ein Märchen aus der Neuen Zeit* (Oxford, 1967), p. x) but Hoffmann's writing was also characterised by *synaesthesia* (mingling of various sense impressions) (*ibid.* p. v). The theme of the town was important for Hoffmann (*ibid.* p. xi) and like Sterne he liked to play tricks on his reader (*ibid.* p. xii). For more detailed studies see: M. Gorlin, *N. V. Gogol und E. T. A. Hoffmann* (*Veröffentlichungen des slavischen Instituts*, IX, Berlin, 1933); also Norman W. Ingham, *E. T. A. Hoffmann's Reception in Russia* (Würzburg, 1974).

12 It is perhaps further significant that the *uzhasnoye mnogolyudstvo* ('terrible crush') of this setting echoes the phrase used to explain prostitution: 'begot of the tawdry level of education and terrible crush of the capital' (*porozhdennyy mishurnoy obrazovannost′yu i strashnym mnogolyudstvom stolitsy*) (III, 21).

13 Cf. the authorial statements of the wish to be an artist in the tale of the two Ivans and 'The Old World Landowners' (II, 15, 242), (particularly the passage which, in a comic *synaesthesia*, the 'painter' depicts: smells, sounds, dreams) (II, 242).

14 N. Mashkovtsev comments on Piskarev's 'interior': 'In this description it is as though Gogol has combined the content of two pictures *Seven O'Clock in the Evening* by E. F. Krendovsky, and *The Studio of the Artist Brothers G. G. and N. G. Chernetsov* by A. V. Tyranov.' N. G. Mashkovtsev, *Gogol′ v krugu khudozhnikov, Ocherki* (Moscow, 1955), p. 39.

Plates of the relevant pictures are to be found *ibid.* pp. 37, 38. Mashkovtsev also sees the inspiration for Piskarev's portrait of an old woman in a picture by one of Venetsianov's pupils, *The Head of an Old Woman* by Lavr Plakhov: 'I will note that here Gogol, underscoring the "insentient expression" of the model contrasts the psychological problems of portraiture and genre painting, which remained beyond the abilities of the school of Venetsianov' *ibid.* p. 40 (for the plate of this portrait see *ibid.* p. 47). Mashkovtsev also sees certain biographical details of the life of Plakhov in both Piskarev and Chartkov ('The Portrait') *ibid.* p. 40.

15 Cf. use of *sozdatel′* (creator) (III, 13, 25, 25, 29, 30), *tvorets* (creator) (III, 28), *venets tvoreniya* (III, 21).

16 This is a well-known Romantic theme: in A. Pogorel′sky's work *The Double, or My Evenings in Little Russia* the 'Third Evening' describes 'the disastrous consequences of an unbridled imagination' – a young count falls in love with a doll. There is also a social message: 'Look at society: how many dolls of both sexes will you not meet, who do nothing and are capable of doing nothing more than strolling about the streets, dancing at balls, bowing and smiling.' See Antoniy Pogorel′sky: *Dvoynik ili Moi vechera v Malorossii: Monastyrka* (Moscow, 1960), p. 84. (Cf. also V. Odoevsky: '*Skazka o tom, kak opasno devushkam khodit′ tolpoyu po Nevskomu prospektu*' in his *Pestryye rasskazy* of 1833.)

17 V. Solovyev saw 'dreams as a window into another world'. See N. O. Lossky, *History of Russian Philosophy* (London, 1952), pp. 90–1. Gorky might even be added to this list. Cf. the portrayal of Tanya in the story *Twenty six and a girl* (*Dvadsat′ shest′ i odna*), M. Gorky, *Polnoye sobraniye sochineniy, khudozhestvenyye proizvendeniya* (Moscow, 1970), V, 7–21.

18 Vasiliy Gippius, *Gogol′* (Leningrad, 1924) (reprinted Brown University Press, Providence, Rhode Island, 1963) p. 53. For a discussion of the influence of De Quincey's *The Confessions of An English Opium Eater* on 'Nevsky Prospekt' see V. V. Vinogradov, *Izbrannyye trudy, Poetika russkoy literatury* (Moscow, 1976), pp. 45–62.

19 K. D. Muratova identifies Perugino's *Bianca* as the fresco of the Adoration of the Magi in Santa Maria dei Bianchi in Pieve with the Virgin at its centre. See K. D. Muratova, in *Gogol, sobraniye khudozhestvennykh*, III, 483. However, the madonna in this fresco is dwarfed by other detail, and it is doubtful whether the fresco would be well known in St Petersburg in the early nineteenth century. A more likely 'Bianca' would seem to be Mashkovtsev's supposition that it was a picture ascribed to Perugino which was in the collection of Gogol's friend A. O. Smirnova. Mashkovtsev, *Gogol′ v krugu khudozhnikov*, p. 58.

20 There are further hints of this theme during Piskarev's pursuit of the girl: 'For one heavenly glance for which he would be prepared to give up his whole life...He felt no *earthly* thought, he was not inflamed by

earthly passion, no, at that moment he was pure and unsullied, like a virginal youth, in whom still breathed an undefined *spiritual* need for love' (III, 19), (my italics).

21 In *The Idiot* Dostoevsky discusses Pirogov as the embodiment of 'the effrontery of naivety', Dostoevsky, *Sobraniye sochineniy*, VI, 524. The phrase 'the power of weakness' (*mogushchestvo slabosti*) contrasted to the 'power of strength' (*mogushchestvo sily*) (III, 10) has a very Dostoevskian ring.

22 See commentary of V. L. Komarovich (III, 635–6).

23 In the second version these details are made more plausible, more 'motivated'.

24 The name might be thought to suggest devil (*chert*) but Mashkovtsev derives it from *cherta* and *chertit'* 'to draw' arguing that the analogy is with Palitrin the name for the artist in the drafts for 'Nevsky Prospekt' (*palitr* = 'palette'). Mashkovtsev believes that Gogol only changed the name after becoming acquainted with the Chertkov family in Rome. Mashkovtsev, *Gogol' v krugu khudozhnikov*, p. 44.

25 Psyche was punished for looking at the beauty of Cupid. Mashkovtsev points to the statue of Psyche on view at the Academy exhibition of 1833 and comments that the theme of Psyche was characteristic of Academy art. Mashkovtsev, *Gogol' v krugu khudozhnikov*, p. 14.

26 It seemed as though an incensed heaven had sent this terrible scourge to earth on purpose, wishing to deprive it of all its harmony (III, 425).

27 In the first version Petromikhali himself makes terrible suggestions and wants to give 'an infernal direction' (*adskoye napravleniye*) to the painter's art (III, 437). Antichrist is 'without form on earth' (III, 444). The artist's sin is that he is skilful enough to let half of Petromikhali's life go into the portrait (III, 436).

28 Mashkovtsev, *Gogol' v krugu khudozhnikov*, p. 49.

29 Thus he hasn't entirely managed to penetrate beneath the 'surface' of the old master: 'As yet the dark façade (*oblik*) laid over old paintings had not entirely disappeared for him' (III, 85). He disagrees with his professor, feeling that the nineteenth century has in certain areas (e.g. imitation of nature) overtaken the old masters. Mashkovtsev sees this wavering between realism and academism as typical of the pupils of Venetsianov. Mashkovtsev, *Gogol' v krugu khudozhnikov*, p. 48.

30 Disharmony which is a 'wild cry' is expressed more concretely in the first version: 'a wild feeling, not fear but that inexpressible sensation, which we feel at the presence of a strangeness representing a disorder of nature, or to express it better, a sort of madness of nature. This very feeling made nearly every one cry out' (III, 405). Such disharmony, it should be noted, does not reside in imitation of nature: it is in nature itself. The word for nature in the second version is *natura* (cf. *priroda* of first version (III, 404), a word suggestive of the term coined for Gogol's own art *Natural'naya shkola* (The Natural School).

31 'There is a canvas of Kramskoy in which he wonderfully depicts human faces. Suppose he eliminated the nose of one of these faces and substituted a real one. The nose will be "realistic" but the picture will be spoiled.' (The words of Chekhov as reported by Meyerhold.) See Ernest J. Simmons, *Chekhov, A Biography* (London, 1963), p. 430.

32 Nevertheless the idea that the disharmony of the painting is because it is a copy of nature is refuted almost immediately: 'It had gone beyond a copy of nature, it was that strange liveliness which might illumine the face of a corpse which has risen from the grave' (III, 88). Curiously we have returned to the idea of the strange life of the dead as the root of Chartkov's unease about the picture; an effect produced, not by the sun (of talent?) but by the odd light of the moon which brings with it the 'fever of day dream' (*bred mechty*).

The artistic problems of realism and the 'strange life of the dead' may be related to Gogol's own struggles with the second part of *Dead Souls*.

33 In his 'testament' Gogol spoke of his 'Farewell Tale' (*Proshchal'naya povest'*) as not having been written but sung from the soul (*ona vypelas' sama soboyu iz dushi*) (VIII, 221). In *Selected Passages* he returns to the theme of the 'song' to explain the lyrical ending of *Dead Souls* (VIII, 289).

34 Cf. the importance of the term 'creator' in 'Nevsky Prospekt'. For an excellent account of Belinsky's aesthetic development and his debt to German thought see: Sigurd Fasting, *V. G. Belinskij: Die Entwicklung seiner Literaturtheorie*, I, *Die Wirklichkeit ein Ideal* (Bergen, Oslo, Tromsø), 1972.

35 See letter to P. A. Pletnev, 17 March 1842 (XII, 45).

36 The religious sentiment of the first version is not so much Christian as pagan and magical. Thus the demonic power in the painting will disappear if the story is solemnly told at the first new moon after a lapse of fifty years (III, 444) and the artist's immersion in religion is explained almost in terms of a therapy: 'You must not be surprised at the strangeness of his words. I saw that he was in that spiritual state which possesses a man, when he experiences mighty and unbearable misfortunes, when, wishing to gather all his strength, all the iron strength of his soul, and not finding it sufficiently powerful, he plunges entirely into religion, and the more he is driven by misfortune the more ardent are his spiritual contemplations and his prayers' (III, 442).

37 An idea repeated in *Selected Passages* at the conclusion of 'On the Lyricism of Our Poets' (VIII, 261).

38 In February 1852 Gogol continued his fast against the spiritual direction of the Metropolitan of Moscow ('Salvation is in obedience not in fasting'). See Troyat, *Gogol*, *Biography*, p. 428.

39 Perhaps Gogol in his attempt to continue *Dead Souls* experienced some of the torments of Chartkov, when he tried to go beyond the bounds of his capabilities (III, 115).

40 The problem seems relevant for 'The Overcoat', in which an article of

clothing not only assumes the nature of a new personality for the hero, but is also likened to a bride (both versions of 'The Portrait' identify 'true art' as 'a bride' (*nevesta*) (III, 111, 421).

41 See V. I. Shenrok. *Materialy dlya biografii Gogolya* (Moscow, 1895), III, p. 228; and (1898), IV, 322, 324.

42 The imagery of the first version is less striking: 'They seem like living bodies which contain within them a corpse' (III, 421).

43 Mashkovtsev, *Gogol' v krugu khudozhnikov*, p. 14. But Chartkov does not betray his calling as much as his 'school' (*napravleniye*) *ibid.* p. 48.

44 First published with the subtitle 'Fragments from the notes of a Madman' in the second part of *Arabesques* (1835).

For a more detailed analysis of this story see my article: 'The logic of madness: Gogol's *Zapiski sumasshedshego*', *Oxford Slavonic Papers, new series*, IX (Oxford, 1976), 28–45.

45 The word *shishka* ('lump') suggesting a painful disorder, could be seen as a reference to the abdication of Charles X after the revolution of 1830. Cf. earlier: 'What a stupid nation the French are! Well, what do they want? I would take the whole lot of them, I swear, and birch everyone of them' (III, 196).

Because of difficulties with the censor Gogol substituted the Bey of Algiers for the King of France, but still managed to preserve a political allusion; for in 1830 Hussein Pasha, the last Bey of Algiers, had been deposed by the French. See D. Magarshak, *Gogol: A Life* (New York, 1960), p. 120.

46 See appendix A.

47 A significant expletive. The notebook version was the more usual: 'Devil take it!' (III, 555).

48 Cf. the earlier: 'Only a nobleman can write correctly' (III, 195).

49 'The clumsy mongrel resembles the clerk, just as his title (*dvornjaga* "mongrel") resembles Poprishchin's own (*dvorjanin* "nobleman").' R. F. Gustafson, 'The Suffering Usurper: Gogol's *Diary of a Madman*', *The Slavic and East European Journal*, IX (1965), 271.

50 In Russian the ending in *-ya* would denote either the genitive singular or nominative plural of the word, but in Ukrainian it would be nominative singular.

51 I.e. '*Pod per'yami*' – 'under its feathers/quills' (III, 213).

52 A word frequently encountered in Gogol's letters and in *Selected Passages from Correspondence with Friends* when referring to himself as a writer. See V. V. Yermilov, *Geniy Gogolya* (Moscow, 1959), p. 230.

53 Notably I. Yermakov in his essay on 'The Nose' in Maguire, *Gogol from the Twentieth Century*, pp. 165–6, 170; also Gippius, *Gogol*, p. 167.

54 Cf. 'The Diary of a Madman':
'October 3rd.

Today an unusual adventure took place.' (III, 193)

with

'On the 25th of March an unusually strange event happened in St Petersburg.' (III, 49)

55 Cf. the later headings of Poprishchin's 'notes' and the possibility of confusing *Ispaniya* with *pisaniya*.

56 In the epilogue to the story which Gogol wrote for *The Contemporary*, the effect is even stronger: 'I, I confess, cannot understand how I could have written it' (III, 400).

57 If taken figuratively *plevat' v potolok* merely means 'to idle'.

58 I.e. *Chúdnaya* – 'wonderful' (even perhaps 'strange' – *chudnáya*).

59 The doctor's words produce shock in Kovalev, which finds expression as synecdoche: 'Kovalev did not even notice his face and, completely deprived of all feeling, only saw the cuffs of his shirt, white and pure as snow, sticking out of the sleeves of his black dress-coat' (III, 70). Kovalev himself seems to be characterised by his shirt cuffs (*manishki*) (III, 53, 56).

The effect of the doctor's words parallels that produced by Petrovich on Akakiy Akakievich in 'The Overcoat', when in a state of shock he sees only the snuff box in the room (III, 151).

60 The civil rank of collegiate assessor was equivalent to that of major, but military rank was considered to have more prestige. (See appendix A.) Thus Poprishchin muses that a civil servant is not the inferior of any officer (III, 194) and believes himself capable of becoming a colonel (III, 198).

Kovalev regrets that the loss of his nose has no military explanation – that he has not lost it in warfare or in a duel (III, 64).

The local policeman (*chastnyy pristav*) is not impressed, even by 'majors'. He points out to Kovalev: 'that respectable people don't have their noses ripped off, and that the world is full of all sorts of majors, who don't even possess underclothing which is in a decent state, and who go the rounds of all sorts of unseemly places' (III, 63–4). This insult to status is seen as affecting another of Kovalev's vital organs: '*to est' ne v brov' a pryamo v glaz*' – 'he scored a bullseye' (literally 'not in his eyebrow, but right in his eye') (*ibid.*).

61 The *ekzekutor* was in charge of the day-to-day affairs and discipline of a civil service department. Yaichnitsa, the collegiate assessor in *Marriage* is an *ekzekutor*. Mikhail Saltykov-Shchedrin, who became a vice-governor, had the rank of actual state counsellor (rank 4 as opposed to Kovalev's rank 8). In the first draft Kovalev talked of even becoming a governor (III, 388).

62 Cf. also the use of the word in Kovalev's letter to Podtochina: '*vnezapnoye ego otdeleniye s svoyego mesta...esli upominayemyy mnoyu nos ne budet segodnya zhe na svoyem meste*' (III, 70).

63 The nose had already stated his independence through a similar construction *ya sam po sebe*. In the first full draft version the nose is finally apprehended on its way to Riga with a passport made out in the name of a director of schools from Tambov (III, 397).

Kovalev's 'rival' for the hand of Podtochina's daughter (Filipp Ivanovich Potanchikov) is described by Podtochina as: 'of good, sober behaviour and great education' (III, 71). It is perhaps significant that it is he, to whom she thinks Kovalev is referring in his complaint about the 'nose'.

64 Originally the scene in the Kazan Cathedral was not allowed by the censors, it had to be transferred to a shop (*gostinyy dvor*). Gogol already sensed this danger when he sent the story to Pogodin and his suggestion that, if they objected to an Orthodox cathedral, a Catholic one could be substituted, shows his wish to preserve a religious setting (X, 355).

Kovalev's attitude to beggars at the cathedral door seems to recall the 'charity' of Ivan Ivanovich: 'He hastened into the cathedral, made his way through a row of old beggar women with bandaged faces and two apertures for eyes, at whom he used to laugh so much before, and went into the church.' His beating of the cabby so that he in turn will beat his horse (III, 59) foreshadows Dostoevsky's image for the abuse of power in Russia. (See F. M. Dostoevsky, *Dnevnik pisatelya za 1876 god* (Paris, n.d. *c.* 1950) pp. 37–9 and *Dnevnik pisatelya za 1877 god*, p. 537.)

65 Cf. Kovalev himself: '*kak zhe mne byt' bez takoy zametnoy chasti tela*?' (III, 61).

66 See especially Yermakov, 'The Nose', in Maguire, *Gogol from the Twentieth Century*. The literary obsession with noses goes back to Sterne. Vinogradov deals with the nose as a literary theme in his essay 'Naturalisticheskiy grotesk: Syuzhet i kompozitsiya povesti Gogolya *Nos*'. See Vinogradov, *Izbrannyye trudy*, pp. 5–44. Victor Ehrlich has speculated that: 'the plot of *The Nose* could be described as a literal enactment or "realization" of Pushkin's witticism' (i.e. on the loss of a nose through venereal disease). See Ehrlich, *Gogol*, p. 86.

Krayevsky's unmarried mother lost her nose according to Bulgarin. See M. Lemke, *Nikolayevskiye zhandarmy i literatura 1826–1855 gg. Po podlinnym delam tret'yago otdeleniya sobst. Ye I. Velichestva kantselyariy* (reprint of 2nd St Petersburg edn, 1909; The Hague, 1965), p. 302.

67 I.e. *istoriya naschet moyego nosa* – the phrase used by Kovalev in his letter of complaint to Podtochina (III, 70) (*istoriya* in this sense means 'scandal').

68 See appendix B.

69 Buttons, like noses, are a symbol of status. The nose points to the difference between Kovalev and itself by reference to the buttons on their uniforms (III, 56). Kovalev himself is perplexed at the loss of his nose which is not like the loss of a button (III, 65) and at the end of the story he can afford to feel superior to a military man whose nose is no larger than a waistcoat button (III, 74). The barber Ivan Yakovlevich, who is accused of 'taking' the nose is suspected by Kovalev merely of having hands which are not clean: 'Tell me beforehand, are your hands clean?' (*Govori vpered: chisty ruki*?) (III, 73). (Cf. the expression '*on na ruku*

nechist' – 'he is lightfingered'.) Earlier the policeman had accused him of stealing a whole breast-front of buttons (III, 66–7).

70 Kovalev refuses to give his name at the newspaper office and the clerk turns *nos* ('the nose') into the surname of a person, Nosov.

71 Cf. the way the two main strands 'fit' through the association of drinking and shaving. Thus it is suggested that Ivan Yakovlevich had cut off the nose while drunk, and the same two elements figure in Kovalev's search for his explanation. See p. 131 above.

The theme of the story of Ivan Yakovlevich is not 'inexplicable loss of status', but 'inexplicable guilt'. It might, as Leon Stilman suggests, ('Nikolaj Gogol and Ostap Hohol', p. 811) be connected with the loss of a name. See also the concluding chapter of this work.

72 Dostoevsky, *Sobraniye sochineniy*, I, 294. Cf. the words of Kovalev: 'It is not the same as some little toe or other, which once in a boot, no one will see whether it's there or not' (III, 61). Little toe in Russian is the same as little finger (i.e. *mizinnyy palets*).

The phrase *ya sam po sebe* ('I am independent') is used both by the nose and by Dostoevsky's Golyadkin. (See Dostoevsky, *Sobraniye sochineniy*, I, 252, 254, 269.) Both drive around in coaches, but Golyadkin is more like Kovalev in not wishing to be seen by people he knows. Cf. Dostoevsky, *ibid.* p. 214 and (Gogol, III, 54). A little disingenuously, Dostoevsky claimed that his story 'The Crocodile' (*Krokodil*) was written in the manner of Gogol's 'Nose'. See: Dostoevsky, *Dnevnik pisatelya za 1873 god*, p. 213. (It seems more likely that the story is a polemical allegory directed against Chernyshevsky.)

73 Notably by V. V. Rozanov, *Legenda o Velikom Inkvisitore* (reprint of St Petersburg 1906 edn, Munich, 1970); and B. M. Eykhenbaum. *'Kak sdelana Shinel' Gogolya'*, *Skvoz' literaturu* (The Hague, 1962), pp. 171–95. For a fuller analysis of the story see my article: 'Gogol and Psychological Realism: *Shinel'*', *Russian and Slavic Literature* (eds. R. Freeborn *et al.*) *Selected Papers in the Humanities from the Banff 1974 International Conference* (Cambridge, Mass., 1976), pp. 63–91.

74 The formulaic effect is clearer in the Russian: *'Neskol'ko ryabovat, neskol'ko ryzhevat, neskol'ko dazhe na vid podslepovat* (III, 141).

75 He saves half a copeck for each rouble he spends and by this means has already accumulated forty roubles (representing a gross expenditure of eight thousand roubles!).

76 'Even during those hours when the grey sky of St Petersburg grows completely dim, and all civil service folk have eaten and dined, each in his own way according to the salary he receives and his own particular whim, when everything is at rest after the scraping of departmental pens and the flurry of their own and other people's necessary business and all that an indefatigable person willingly takes upon himself, more even than is necessary, when the civil servants rush off to devote the time which remains to enjoyment; a more spirited one will head for the theatre,

another into the street allotting his time to the examination of various hats, another will go to a party to waste it in compliments to some pretty girl, the star of a small civil servants' circle; another, and this happens most frequently of all, will go simply to see a colleague living on a third or second floor in two small rooms with a hall or a kitchen, with one or two pretensions to fashion, a lamp or some other such thing, which has cost many sacrifices, the foregoing of dinners and outings; in short, even at that time, when all civil servants are scattered in the small apartments of their friends playing *shturmovoy* whist, sipping tea from glasses along with cheap rusks, inhaling smoke from long pipes, and, as the cards are being dealt, relating some piece of gossip retailed from higher society, something which a Russian can never do without in any circumstances, or even when there is nothing to talk about, retelling the eternal anecdote about the commandant, who was informed that the tail of the horse of the Falconet monument had been fractured, – in short, even at a time when everyone strove to enjoy himself, Akakiy Akakiyevich did not surrender himself to any diversion' (III, 146).

77 Cf. the description of Petrovich's wife (III, 148); also *Kolyaska* (*The Carriage*) (III, 178), and moustaches as a recurrent motif in 'Nevsky Prospekt'.

78 The police in the Russia of Nicholas I did not appear to regard their chief duty to be the apprehension of thieves. See Lemke, *Nikolayevskiye zhandarmy*, pp. 325, 326.

79 See Ehrlich, *Gogol*, p. 147. (Ehrlich slyly suggests that the choice of name was dictated by the 'circumstances' of his christening.)

80 See: Driessen, *Gogol as a Short Story Writer*, p. 194; also John Schillinger, 'Gogol's *The Overcoat* as a travesty of hagiography', *Slavic and East European Journal*, XVI (1972), pp. 36–41; and Anthony Hippisley, 'Gogol's *The Overcoat*: a further interpretation', *ibid.* XX, 2 (1976), pp. 121–9.

81 See appendix A.

82 But the author himself creates much interest for the etymologist around the figure of his hero. Cf. Eykhenbaum, '*Kak sdelana Shinel' Gogolya*', p. 178.

83 Eykhenbaum, '*Kak sdelana Shinel' Gogolya*', pp. 183–4, 189–90.

84 In *Selected Passages* Gogol defends his own inner world from the attention of his readers with the question: '*Zalez ty razve v moyu golovu*?' ('You surely haven't got inside my head?') (VIII, 296), and claims that people assert that Pushkin was a deist, just as though they had been inside his soul (VIII, 274). Cf. Gogol's reluctance to get inside his characters in 'A Terrible Vengeance' (I, 277).

85 For a discussion of its history see Driessen, *Gogol as a Short Story Writer*, p. 185.

86 In *Poor Folk* the poverty of the titular counsellor is put in perspective by the fact that there are people much poorer than himself in the story.

Cf. the description Devushkin gives of his quarters: 'The back staircase is damp, filthy, the steps are broken; and the walls are so greasy that your hand sticks when you lean against them. On each landing stand trunks, chairs and broken cupboards; rags are strewn all over, and windows smashed in; wash-tubs stand filled with all kinds of dirt, filth and litter, with egg-shells and with fish entrails. The smell is ugly' Dostoevsky, *Sobraniye sochineniy*, I, 90.

Gogol's description of the typical St Petersburg 'backstairs' is less 'naturalistic'. The presentation is more humorous and the distorting viewpoint distances the reader from the grimness of the scene described: 'Climbing the staircase which led to Petrovich's, which, one must give it its due, was all anointed with water and slops and penetrated through and through with that smell of spirits which stings the eyes, and which, as is well known is inseparably present on all the back staircases of St Petersburg houses...The door was open, because the mistress of the house in cooking some fish or other, had created so much smoke in the kitchen that you couldn't see even the black beetles' (III, 148).

3. *Theatre*

1. For a discussion of this see E. L. Voytolovskaya, *Komediya N. V. Gogolya 'Revizor': Kommentariy* (Leningrad, 1971), pp. 21–6; See also Gippius, *Gogol*, p. 97, and V. Shklovsky, *Povesti o proze; razmyshleniya i razgovory* (Moscow, 1966), II, 116–17.
2 I.e. Anna Petrovna (the niece); Milof (her suitor); Otchetin (her guardian).
3 In first two rough drafts Khlestakov does indeed begin with the mother (IV, 205, 326–9).
4 'Whippersnapper' might convey some of the flavour. The name begins with the Russian letter identical in form to the roman 'X'. Khlestakov may, therefore, also be thought of as the 'mysterious X' (*tainstvenny iks*).
5 The story which Chistyakov tells Likorisa to gain her favours (i.e. that his father is the ruler of India – Narezhny, *Rossiyskiy Zhilblaz*, pt. III, p. 464) is similar to the story of the two *Yuriy Miloslavsky*'s of Khlestakov (IV, 49).
6 Cf. Harold Skimpole in Dickens's *Bleak House*. Both Khlestakov and Skimpole blandly assume that the world owes them a living, and their arguments on the need to be fed are in essence the same (cf. Dickens, *Bleak House*, ch. 15, 'Bell Yard' and Gogol, IV, 29–30).
7 There are in these characteristics disturbing resemblances to Gogol himself. He, too, loved to eat well, to travel in comfort and expected the hospitality of his friends as a right, requesting 'loans' from them which he never repaid. After the hostile reception of *Selected Passages*, Gogol compared himself to Khlestakov (letter to Zhukovsky, 6 March/22 Feb. 1847 (XIII, 242)).

The address attributed to Tryapichin in the play is Gogol's own at the time of the writing of *The Government Inspector*. See Voytolovskaya, *Komediya N. V. Gogolya*, p. 219.

8 In an analogous speech in Fonvizin's *Brigadir*, the counsellor merely says that not to take bribes is against human nature (act III, sc. vi). See Makogonenko, *Russkaya literatura XVIII veka*, p. 303 (earlier, act I, sc. i, the Frenchified son of the Brigadier had claimed that in France God did not even interfere in marriages, infidelity and divorces, *ibid.* p. 292).

9 *Priezzhiyy iz stolitsy* (act IV, sc. i). See *Dramaticheskiye sochineniya Grigoriya Kvitki* (*Osnov''yanenka*) (St Petersburg, 1862), II, 345. Cf. also the judge in the tale of the two Ivans (II, 245) and the judge in A. F. Vel'tman's novel, *Serdtse i dumka* (Moscow, 1838), pt. I, pp. 129–30.

10 V. V. Kapnist, *Yabeda*, act I, sc. i (Makogonenko, *Russkaya literatura XVIII veka*, p. 489).

11 Cf. a similar hint of immorality about the judge in *The Carriage* (III, 179).

12 'The judge is a man who has read five or six books and is therefore a bit of a free-thinker' (*Observations for the actors*) (IV, 10). *The Acts of John Mason*, according to Nabokov: 'refers to a book of adventures concerning John Mason (or attributed to him), an English diplomatist of the sixteenth century and Fellow of All Souls who was employed on the Continent in collecting information for the Tudor Sovereigns'. V. V. Nabokov, *Nikolai Gogol* (Norfolk, Conn., 1944), p. 39. Nevertheless the title *Deyaniya Ioanna Masona* does have a 'masonic' ring and the reference is not clear. Thus another possibility is: *Self-Knowledge. A treatise, showing the nature and benefit of that important science, and the way to attain it* (London, 1745). Its author, John Mason, was a nonconformist minister. It was translated into Russian as *Poznaniya samogo sebya*, by Ivan Turgenev (a member of the same masonic lodge as N. Novikov) and published by Novikov in 1783 and 1786. See Voytolovskaya, *Komediya N. V. Gogolya*, p. 219.

13 However obliquely, Gogol seems to be singling out the date 1825:

AMMOS FEDOROVICH. By wish of the nobility I was chosen for a three-year term from 1816 and have continued in office up to the present.

KHLESTAKOV. It must be advantageous, then, to be a judge?

AMMOS FEDOROVICH. For three three-year terms I was awarded the order of St Vladimir, Fourth Class, with approval on the part of the authorities. (IV, 59) (Act IV, sc. iii)

14 In earlier drafts the names are assigned to different professions. Thus Zemlyanika is the Superintendent of Schools, Lyapkin-Tyapkin is the Curator of the Charitable Institutions, whilst the judge himself is called Pripekayev (IV, 239).

15 Fonvizin, *Nedorosl'* act III, sc. viii, sc. ix; act V, sc. vi, sc. vii. See Makogonenko, *Russkaya literatura XVIII veka*, pp. 326–7, 337–8.

In an earlier draft Gogol had written a scene mostly in German for his doctor (IV, 317). In view of the fact that Baltic Germans (and they included Count Benkendorf, the head of the 'Third Section' – the political police) were highly influential in court and bureaucratic circles, it could be inadvisable to mock a German accent. See Lemke, *Nikolayevskiye zhandarmy*, pp. 72–3.

16 Zemlyanika distorts the phrase 'all, die like flies' (*vse kak mukhi mrut*) into 'they all get better like flies' (*vse, kak mukhi, vyzdoravlivayut*) (IV, 45).

17 Perhaps there is a distinction drawn between the only two children mentioned by name. Cf. the phrasing of Anna Andreyevna: *Ya u vas krestila vashego Vanechku i Lizan'ku* (IV, 41).

18 The subject was a delicate one at the time. Nicholas I was against such legalisations. See Voytolovskaya, *Komediya N. V. Gogolya*, p. 199.

19 *Ibid.* pp. 115–16.

20 Applause in the theatre was only allowed in 1828. See Lemke, *Nikolayevskiye zhandarmy*, p. 239.

21 Makogonenko, *Russkaya literatura XVIII veka*, p. 490.

22 The civil servants do not address one another formally, nor are they addressed formally by their subordinates (with the exception of the policeman in act. V, sc. vii) (IV, 86).

Khlestakov confesses that his father expects him to have the order of St Vladimir in his buttonhole straightaway (IV, 35–6) – a decoration already gained by Lyapkin Tyapkin for nine years of service.

23 Kvitka, *Dramaticheskiye sochineniya*, p. 316. Cf. the use of this phrase in Kapnist's *Yabeda* (See Makogonenko, *Russkaya literatura XVIII veka*, p. 506).

24 Kvitka, *Dramaticheskiye sochineniya*, p. 316.

25 A similar lapse is experienced by Vral'man in Fonvizin's *Nedorosl'* (act III, sc. viii). See Makogonenko, *op. cit.* pp. 326–7.

26 IV, 186.

27 See Voytolovskaya, *Komediya N. V. Gogolya*, pp. 88, 89.

28 Almost a quotation from the statute of Catherine II on the duties of the *gorodnichiy*. See Voytolovskaya, *Komediya N. V. Gogolya*, p. 90.

29 Cf. the first rough draft: *skol'ko chistotoyu i poryadkom soderzhaniya* ('as much as by cleanliness and the order in which they are kept') (IV, 177). The final version has much greater ambiguity.

30 Belinsky, *Polnoye sobraniye sochineniy*, III, 454. The idea was first put forward by P. A. Vyazemsky. See P. A. Vyazemsky, *Polnoye sobraniye sochineniy* (St Petersburg, 1879), II, 263.

31 The mayor is already in a receptive mood. He confesses that he had a 'premonition' (*ya kak budto predchuvstvoval*) as the night before he dreamed of two unusual rats (IV, 11).

32 Cf. the irony of the heading 'Last Scene' (*Yavleniye posledneye* – literally 'last appearance') (IV, 95).

33 *Preduvedomleniye dlya tekh, kotoryye pozhelali by sygrat' kak sleduyet 'Revizora'* (IV, 112).

34 It is scarcely surprising that Meyerhold should have made such a feature of doors in his famous (notorious) production of 1926. See E. Braun, *Meyerhold on the Theatre* (London, 1969), p. 215.

35 I have in mind the cathedral clock in Lübeck with its life-sized figures which so impressed Gogol on his first trip abroad. See letter to his mother of 25 August 1829 (x, 156).

36 Gogol cut out two scenes 'as slowing the flow of the play' (iv, 105–8).

37 Fonvizin's *Brigadir* ends with a remark addressed to the 'groundlings': 'They say that to live with one's conscience is bad. But I myself have now learned that to live without conscience is the worst thing on earth.' Here, of course, the counsellor's remarks are directed against himself, although addressed to the audience. See: Makogonenko, *Russkaya literatura XVIII veka*, p. 311.

38 Chekhov makes good dramatic use of the opening quotation from *The Government Inspector* in his play *Uncle Vanya*, act iii.

39 Perhaps the device is there too in his non-dramatic writing: 'Gogol's first volume of stories opens disarmingly with an act of double ventriloquism – the voice of a hypothetical reader filtered through the voice of a fictive narrator.' Donald Fanger, 'Gogol and his reader', *Literature and Society in Imperial Russia*, ed. William Mills Todd III (Stanford, California, 1978), p. 77.

40 A similar parallel of surprised proposals takes place in *Brigadir*, act ii, sc. iii and act v, sc. ii (there is even a 'prelude' in act i, sc. iii). See Makogonenko, *Russkaya literatura XVIII veka*, pp. 297, 309 also p. 294. A comparison of these scenes with *The Government Inspector* reveals Gogol's greater sense of rhythm and pace.

41 In act ii, sc. xviii, Agafya Tikhonovna muses about marriage in terms of children: the trouble they represent seems a discouragement from marriage (v, 55).

42 Boots also are connected with status: 'Boots seem as though they are unimportant things, but if they're badly made, and the polish is ginger red, then there will not be the same respect in good society. It's somehow not as it should be' (act i, sc. v) (v, 11).

43 Fekla seems as little impressed by court counsellors as the policeman (*chastnyy pristav*) in 'The Nose' is unimpressed by 'majors': she claims that a court counsellor has already been refused because he couldn't refrain from lying (act i, sc. viii) (v, 13). Fekla has to admit that the bride is only a merchant's daughter, but claims that when she puts on her silk dress on Sundays she looks like a princess.

44 See: Elizabeth Warner, *Russian Folk Theatre*, pp. 43–66.

45 In act i, sc. xi Kochkarev says: 'Well, you see, You yourself have got to the heart of the matter' (*Nu, vidish' sam raskusil* (v, 17) – *raskusit'* – 'to get to the heart of the matter' literally means 'to bite').

46 The sequel to this (act ii, sc. xix) opens with a parody of a banal

conversational formula: i.e. seeking assurance that someone will not find strange something which has not yet been divulged (v, 56).

47 The wheel also has connotations of 'Fate'. It will recur as a symbolic detail in the journeys of Chichikov.

48 Karlinsky points to another homosexual reference in an earlier draft. See S. Karlinsky, *Sexual Labyrinth*, p. 174. It is Kochkarev's own bad experience of marriage which seems to prompt his desire to see his friend married.

49 L. N. Tolstoy, *Anna Karenina*, pt. VI, ch. 5.

4. The Carriage *and* Rome

1 The story is related by V. A. Sologub (III, 695).

2 Setchkarev sees in Pifagor an example of Gogol's peculiar use of names non-existent in Russian usage. See: Setchkarev, *Gogol, Life and Works*, p. 163.

Karlinsky rejects the derivation of the element *kut* from *kutsyy* – 'dock-tailed', relating it to the word *kut* – 'corner' or 'nook'. See Karlinsky, *Sexual Labyrinth*, p. 133.

3 'He is in a fetal position; threatened with exposure, he subconsciously acts out a return to the womb.' John G. Garrard, 'Some thoughts on Gogol's *Kolyaska*', *Publications of the Modern Language Association of America*, vol. 90, no. 5, p. 853. In modern Russian *kolyaska* also means a baby's pram. There is more than a hint of this in Chertokutsky's own description of it: 'and when you get into it, it's simply as though, if your excellency will allow it, a nurse were rocking you in a cradle' (III, 182).

4 Belinsky, *Polnoye sobraniye sochineniy*, VI, 427.

5 See letter to S. P. Shevyrev, 1 September 1843 (XII, 211).

5. Dead Souls

1 Cf. the play on words: '*Derevnya Manilovka nemnogikh mogla zamanit' svoim mestopolozheniyem*' (VI, 22).

2 E.g. Erast (Karamzin), Aristion (Narezhny).

3 I.e. '*podavalsya na stol*' (VI, 25).

4 See Ye. S. Smirnova-Chikina, *Poema N. V. Gogolya 'Mertvyye dushi'* (2nd edn, corrected, Leningrad, 1974), p. 76.

5 *Ibid.* p. 79.

6 I.e. '*popol'zovat'sya naschet klubnichki*' (VI, 66). The arms of one lady he describes as *samaya subtil'naya syuperflyu* (VI, 75).

7 The village is only mentioned when Chichikov is escaping from Nozdrev in great haste (VI, 89).

8 Koshchey is an evil wizard encountered in many Russian fairy-tales.

9 Also the names Mikhail Potapovich and Mikhail Semenovich (as here).

10 Cf. *mashinishcha*, *silishcha*, and *plechishche* (VI, 103). However he addresses his wife with the diminutive of the word for 'soul' – *dushen'ka* (VI, 96, 98).

11 Although Plyushkin's Christian name can be deduced from the patronymic of his daughter – Aleksandra Stepanovna.

12 *Gorlyanka* is also the same as *gorlinka* – 'turtle dove', a bird synonymous with 'love'. Cf. the turtle doves (*gorlitsy*) in the love poem received by Chichikov in chapter 8 (VI, 160).

(Nabokov sees romantic leanings in the Greek subjects of Sobakevich's pictures. See Nabokov, *Nikolai Gogol*, p. 97.)

13 I.e. *dushen'ka* – 'little soul'. See note 10 above.

14 'A well-known dish which is served with cabbage soup and consists of a sheep's stomach stuffed with buckwheat, brains and feet. "A nurse like this", he continued turning to Chichikov, "you will not eat in the town. There devil knows what they will serve you!"' (VI, 98). Such a 'well-known' dish has something in common with the 'well-known Schiller' of 'Nevsky Prospekt'. It seems fitting that a dog (in the manger) is an avid devourer of his own 'nurse'.

15 I.e. *v meru* – 'in measure', 'moderately'.

16 But cf. the Russian expression for 'dirt cheap' – *deshevle parenoy repy*, literally 'cheaper than a steamed turnip'.

17 The spider's web, as a symbol, is here the reverse of the 'economic web' of the 'industrious spider' of his younger days. Equally odd is that on two occasions Gogol associates Plyushkin's accumulation of dirt and rubbish with the cleanliness of good housekeeping. The piles of bric-à-brac in Plyushkin's house are introduced by the strange comparison: 'It seemed as though the washing of floors was going on in the house' (VI, 114), and we are told that when Plyushkin has been out foraging for rubbish, there is no need to sweep the street after him (VI, 117). As we shall see, Gogol's attitude to 'acquisition' is ambivalent.

18 Charles Dickens, *Great Expectations* (chapter 8), and *Bleak House* (chapter 5, 'A morning adventure').

19 In *Selected Passages* Gogol talks of Plyushkin figuring in the third volume of *Dead Souls* (VIII, 280).

20 See Pereverzev in Narezhny, *Izbrannyye romany*, p. 44.

21 Bulgarin, *Ivan Vyzhigin*, pt. III, ch. 1, pp. 14–15, 21.

22 See A. I. Herzen, *Sobraniye sochineniy v 30-i tomakh* (Moscow, 1956), VIII, 242–3.

23 Pereverzev, in Narezhny, *Izbrannyye romany*, pp. 44–5.

24 I.e. *konfektnyy bilet* – a doggerel verse included in the wrapper for a sweetmeat. Cf. Pushkin's use of *konfektnyy biletets* (*Slovar' yazyka Pushkina* (Moscow, 1956), I, 113.

25 Andrey Bely has noted the many references to 'sideways', 'slanting', 'oblique' in the presentation of Chichikov. See Bely, *Masterstvo Gogol*, p. 90.

26 I.e. *izvedayet ego do pervonachal'nykh prichin* (literally 'gets to know him to his very origins and causes').

27 Narezhny, *Rossiyskiy Zhilblaz*, p. 454 (the interior of this house, which 'from the outside resembles a palace, but inside was worse than a barn' is worthy of the pen of Gogol himself. Instead of furniture Kuroumov has barrels and boxes of foodstuffs, p. 455).

28 Cf. the role of 'habit' (*privychka*) in *Mirgorod.*

29 Dobrolyubov called Ulin'ka 'a pale copy of Poor Liza', and saw Murazov as a repetition of Karamzin's charitable peasant – Frol Silin (to this extent Karamzinian Sentimentalism seems to have influenced Gogol's depiction of positive types). See N. A. Dobrolyubov, 'O stepeni uchastiya narodnosti v razvitii russkoy literatury', *Sobraniye sochineniy v 9-i tomakh* (Moscow, 1962), II, 262.

30 Petukh has also been compared to Paramon in Narezhny's novel *Aristion.* See Pereverzev, in Narezhny, *Izbrannyye romany*, p. 45.

31 This chapter is from an earlier version than the other chapters in part II.

32 Bulgarin, *Ivan Vyzhigin*, pt. II, p. 205.

33 *Ibid.* p. 196.

34 In his essay 'What is Oblomovism?' ('Chto takoye oblomovshchina?') See Dobrolyubov, *Sobraniye sochineniy*, IV, 321–4, 329, 330.

35 'To go forward or to remain behind?' is seen as a question more profound than Hamlet's. I. A. Goncharov, *Sobraniye sochineniy v 6-i tomakh* (Moscow, 1972), IV, 193.

36 See Goncharov's essay. 'Better Late than Never' (*Luchshe pozdno chem nikogda*) *ibid.*, VI, 453.

37 The prototype was probably D. E. Benardaki, a millionaire of Greek origin, whom Gogol met in Marienbad in 1839. See commentary on letter of 15 August 1839, to M. P. Pogodin (XI, 416).

38 Goncharov, 'Better Late Than Never', VI, 453.

39 Cf. also *Selected Passages* (VIII, 416).

40 Dostoevsky, *Sobraniye sochineniy*, IX, 550 and VII, 271.

41 *Ibid.*, V, 480.

42 See also Shklovsky, *Povesti o proze*, p. 135.

43 See *Uchebnaya kniga slovesnosti dlya russkogo yunoshestva* (VIII, 478–9). For a discussion of this view see Smirnova-Chikina, *Poema*, pp. 33–5. See also Carl L. Proffer, *The Simile and Gogol's 'Dead Souls'* (The Hague and Paris, 1967).

For a discussion of Gogol's work in relation to Dante's *Divine Comedy* see Gippius, *Gogol*, pp. 216–17.

44 Nevertheless he did in a letter to M. A. Maksimovich, 10 January 1840 (XI, 272). In *Dead Souls* itself, at the beginning of chapter 2, part I, he refers to his work as *povest'*, i.e. 'tale' (VI, 19).

45 See Setchkarev, *Gogol, Life and Works*, p. 183.

46 E.g. 'The roads crawled out in every direction, like caught crayfish, when they are emptied out of a sack' (VI, 60).

47 I.e. *rafinad* (refined sugar). Cf. the use of sugar as a comparison for Agafya Tikhonovna in *Marriage*.

48 I have borrowed the terms 'tenor' and 'vehicle' from Carl Proffer, *The Simile*, p. 23. The usage derives from I. A. Richards.

49 Cf. the many references to sugar in the description of Manilov: 'having eyes sweet like sugar' (VI, 16); 'but there seemed to have been too much sugar put into this pleasantness' (VI, 24); 'An expression not only sweet, but cloying, like that medicine which a skilful society doctor sweetens without pity, thinking to please his patient by it' (VI, 29).

50 The wheel is a recurrent motif. When Nozdrev blurts out Chichikov's secret at the governor's ball, and he experiences his first setback, we read: 'Everything went like a crooked wheel' (*vse poshlo kak krivoye koleso*) (VI, 173). A wheel is also one of the items which holds Chichikov up in the town of N. when he wishes to make his escape (VI, 216).

At the end of part I Chichikov's coach appears to become identified with Russia itself. See: A. Bely, *Masterstvo Gogol*, pp. 81–2, 91, 102.

51 Cf. the theme of boots in an amorous context in *Marriage* and 'The Overcoat'.

52 Nabokov translates this passage in full as a prime example of Gogol's innovatory skill at pictorial description. See Nabokov, *Nikolai Gogol*, pp. 87–9.

53 Human artifice and nature are contrasted as antithetical forces in yet another garden described in this chapter – that of an assumed neighbour: 'What did he lack: theatres and balls; all night the garden shines, decorated with lights and lampions, deafened with the thunder of music. Half the province is dressed up and is happily strolling under the trees and nobody thinks it a wild and threatening thing in this contrived lighting, when from the dense wood there jumps out in theatrical fashion a branch deprived of its bright green and darker towards the top and more forbidding, and the night sky seems twenty times more threatening because of this and the forbidding tree tops, stirring their leaves on high and into the distance, receding deeper into the eternally sleeping gloom, are indignant at this tawdry brilliance, which illumines their roots below' (VI, 120). Thus if man intrudes into nature too rudely with the 'illumination' of his art, it evokes a hostile even threatening response.

54 Cf. the use of *vzdor* (rubbish) to describe the objects painted by Piskarev in 'Nevsky Prospekt' (III, 17).

55 The passage continues in the vein of 'dead/alive' and even seems reminiscent of the ending of 'The Fair at Sorochintsy': 'Old age, striding ahead, is threatening and terrible. It gives nothing back, returns nothing! The grave has more pity. On a grave there can be written: here a man lies buried. But you can read nothing in the cold, insentient features of inhuman old age' (V, 127).

56 Cf. the 'pens' which conceal Ispaniya/pisaniya for Poprishchin and the bunch of goose-quills and the quire of white official paper which constitutes the bulk of Akakiy Akakiyevich's legacy to the world (III, 168).

57 He it is who shows 'man in all his beauty' (i.e. positive man) – *prekrasnyy chelovek*. (Cf. the artistic problems discussed in 'The Portrait'). He it is whose very name makes ardent young hearts flutter.

Here, too, as at the beginning of chapter 6, Gogol feels himself alienated from the ardent receptiveness of youth and condemned to depict that which the indifferent gaze fails to see.

58 Cf. Gogol's injunction to Yazykov on how to pray: 'Pray not like one prays sitting in a room, but as one drowning in the waves prays, seizing the last piece of wood' (letter to N. M. Yazykov, 15 February 1844) (XII, 260–1).

59 Gogol's own view of Peter I was not, however, that of a Slavophile. In *Selected Passages* Peter I is seen as an instrument of God (VIII, 369–70).

60 See Lemke, *Nikolayevskiye zhandarmy*, p. 65.

61 In Leonov's *The Thief* the civil-war hero Vekshin is humiliated by the 'old enemy' in the form of a well-dressed wife of a *Nepman*, as he hungrily admires smoked sturgeon in a Moscow shop window. See: L. M. Leonov, *Sobraniye sochineniy v 9-i tomakh* (Moscow, 1961), III, 62.

62 In 'The Diary of a Madman' Poprishchin asserts that woman is in love with the devil, and that the devil hides in a decoration and makes signs to her (III, 209).

63 Nabokov translates the name: 'Drive-to-where-you-won't-get', *Nikolai Gogol*, p. 101.

64 These names reflect themes in the *poema* itself: travel, food, and indeterminate sex (i.e. Plyushkin).

65 See: Laurence Sterne, *The Life and Opinions of Tristram Shandy, Gentleman*, bk. IX, ch. 33.

66 The phrase was in use at the time. Cf. M. Gershenzon, *Griboyedovskaya Moskva* (The Hague and Paris, 1970; reprint of Moscow, 1918, second edition), p. 66.

67 L. Sterne, *Tristram Shandy*, bk. II, ch. 8 *et passim*.

68 It is true that the idea of the plot, according to Gogol's own admission (VIII, 439–40) was not conceived in his own head, nor yet of course in the head of Chichikov, but in that of Pushkin.

The bizarre phonetic similarity between the names Pushkin and Plyushkin is therefore all the more disturbing. Has the 'generous Pushkin' of the *Author's Confession* become the 'miserly Plyushkin' through Gogolian inversion?

69 Cf. the constant references to the writer as painter in 'The Old World Landowners', the tale of the two Ivans, 'Nevsky Prospekt' and 'The Portrait'. The difficulty to understand, or even talk about, women, had also been jokingly mentioned, when the author was faced with his first real female character – the wife of Manilov. Indeed his hostility towards

his readership seems partly to be conditioned by the knowledge that there are women amongst them. He is sure that the ladies will not approve of his hero and he ends his first open attack on his readers (the question of unseemly expressions) by comparing his readers' capriciousness with that of the ladies: 'Of course the female half of the human race is difficult to fathom, but the respected readers, one must admit, are even more difficult' (VI, 165).

70 See Yu. M. Lotman, 'Problema khud. prostranstva', pp. 5–50.

71 The author–reader relationship as a didactic or polemical device was further developed by both Chernyshevsky (*What is to be Done?*) and Dostoevsky (*Notes from Underground*). At times in this latter work the 'authorial' hectoring of the 'reader' is not unlike that in *Dead Souls*.

Conclusion. Art is a reconciliation with life

1 D. S. Mirsky, *A History of Russian Literature* (comprising a History of Russian Literature and Contemporary Russian Literature) edited and abridged by Francis J. Whitfield (New York, 1960), p. 151.

2 'Everything I have written is important only in a psychological sense', letter to Pletnev, *Zapiski o zhizni N. V. Gogolya* (St Petersburg, 1856), II, 148–9.

3 See Valery Bryusov, 'Burnt to Ashes' in Maguire, *Gogol from the Twentieth Century*, pp. 103–32.

4 E.g. by Driessen, *Gogol as a Short Story Writer*; V. V. Rozanov, *Legenda o Velikom Inkvizitore*; Karlinsky, *Sexual Labyrinth*; K. Mochul'sky, *Dukhovnyy put' Gogolya* (Paris, 1934).

5 C. G. Jung, *Modern Man in Search of a Soul* (London, 1933), p. 199.

6 See Belinsky, *Polnoye sobraniye sochineniy*, I, 286–7 and N. G. Chernyshevsky, *Ocherki gogolevskogo perioda russkoy literatury* (Moscow, 1953), p. 162.

7 S. T. Aksakov, *Sobraniye sochineniy v 5-i tomakh* (Moscow, 1966), III, 178.

8 Shenrok, *Materialy*, I, 202. Gogol rebuked his mother for her inordinate praise of him to other people. (See letter of 12 April 1835 (X, 361) in which among other things he says: 'literature is not at all the result of intellect, but the result of feeling'.)

9 'I looked at everything with the eyes of indifference [i.e. *besstrastnymi glazami*, literally "passionless eyes"]. I went to church because I was ordered to go or I was carried. But standing there I saw nothing except chasubles, the priest and the revolting bellowing of the sextons. I crossed myself, because I saw that everyone crossed himself. But once, I remember the occasion vividly as though it were now, I begged you to tell me about the Last Judgement, and so well, so clearly and so touchingly you told me then as a child of those blessings which await people for a virtuous life, and so strikingly, so terrifyingly described the

eternal torments of sinners that it shook and awoke within me all my sensitivity. It took root and later produced in me the most elevated thoughts' (x, 282).

10 If there are biblical overtones in 'Peter the founder' these are carried on in the wizard's false comparison of himself to a St Paul converted from great wickedness to great virtue (I, 262).

11 Gogol himself referred to him as Yan (Jan). See L. Stilman, 'Nikolaj Gogol'.

12 M. N. Longinov, 'Vospominaniye o Gogole', *Gogol' v vospominaniyakh sovremennikov* (Moscow, 1952), p. 71.

13 I.e. *vyveska* = shop sign. In 'The Nose' the *vyveska* of the barber Ivan Yakovlevich (a Russified version of Gogol's own great-great-grandfather Yan Yakovlevich) has also lost its surname. See L. Stilman, *Nikolaj Gogol*, p. 811.

14 Aksakov, *Sobraniye sochineniy*, III, 198, 214.

15 Karlinsky, *Sexual Labyrinth*, p. 44.

16 In Act III of Chekhov's *Uncle Vanya* Marina commenting on the quarrel between Voynitsky and Serebryakov says '*Pogogochut gusaki i perestanut*' and repeats the taunt in Act IV: '*Gusak; go-go-go!*' See: A. P. Chekhov, *Polnoye sobraniye sochineniy i pisem v 30-i tomakh, sochineniya*, XIII (Moscow, 1978), 103, 106.

17 In *Selected Passages* Gogol claims: 'A Russian is more frightened of his nullity [i.e. *nichtozhestvo* – 'worthlessness'] than of his sins and failings' (VII, 293).

18 Besides the meaning 'nose', *nos* is also 'beak' of a bird. It thus hints at the insecurity surrounding Gogol's own name: 'but without a nose [beak?] a man is devil knows what, a bird, not a bird, a citizen but not a citizen' (III, 64).

19 See appendix B.

20 Letter to Zhukovsky 10 January 1848 (XIV, 33–9).

21 As we have already seen, a servant of the state (the mayor) has a subconscious need *not* to know the identity and true status of the young man from St Petersburg who passes himself off as the friend of Pushkin and a man of letters.

22 It is interesting that Gogol's admission to Smirnova about the 'tail-ends' of his own psychological state to be found in his stories, was in response to her curiosity about whether he felt himself to be Ukrainian or Russian: a question which Gogol evades by talking about 'nature' ('both natures are too generously endowed by God' – *obe prirody slishkom shchedro odareny Bogom*) (XII, 419).

23 McLean, 'Gogol's retreat from love', p. 226.

24 R. Freeborn, *The Rise of the Russian Novel*, p.88.

25 H. Gifford, *The Novel in Russia: from Pushkin to Pasternak* (London, 1964), p. 52.

Biographical table

1809	Nikolay Vasilyevich Gogol-Yanovsky born at Sorochintsy in Ukraine.
1821–8	Educated at Nezhin High School.
1825	Death of Gogol's father, Vasiliy Afanasyevich.
1828	December: Gogol leaves for St Petersburg with friend A. S. Danilevsky.
1828	23 March: Gogol publishes poem 'Italy' anonymously in *Syn otechestva* (*Son of the Fatherland*). May: private printing of poem *Gants Kyukhelgarten* under pseudonym, V. Alov; and subsequent burning of copies. August–September: mysterious trip to Germany on money entrusted to him by mother for mortgage repayments. Unsuccessful auditioning for profession of actor. November: appointed to minor civil service post.
1830	Gogol's first Ukrainian tale, 'St John's Eve', published anonymously in February/March issue of *Otechestvennyye zapiski* (*Fatherland Notes*).
1831	February: appointed teacher of history at school for daughters of high-ranking officers (The Patriotic Institute), also acted as private tutor to rich families. Leaves civil service. May: meets Pushkin. September: first part of *Evenings in a village near Dikanka* published.
1832	Second part of *Evenings in a village near Dikanka* published. Summer trip home to Vasilevka. Breaks journey in Moscow; makes friends with Aksakov family and Slavophiles, also actor Shchepkin. October: returns, via Moscow, to St Petersburg with sisters to be educated at Patriotic Institute.
1833	Following example of Maksimovich, attempts to get appointed to Chair of History at Kiev University.
1834	July: appointed assistant lecturer in history at St Petersburg University.
1835	January: *Arabesques* published. April: *Mirgorod* published. May: Gogol goes home to Vasilevka, via Moscow, then on to Crimea.

	September: returns to St Petersburg.
	December: leaves University.
1836	April: première of *The Government Inspector* in St Petersburg. *The Carriage* published in vol. I of Pushkin's new journal, *Sovremennik* (*The Contemporary*); 'The Nose' published in vol. III of *Sovremennik*.
	July: Gogol leaves Russia with Danilevsky. Will spend three years in Europe, mostly based in Rome.
1837	February: In Paris learns of death of Pushkin.
	Autumn: (in Rome) receives financial subsidy from tsar.
1839	September: spends eight months in Moscow and St Petersburg. (His letters to his mother designed to make her think he is arriving later.)
1840	Gogol receives financial subvention from the Heir Apparent.
	June: leaves for Europe. On way back in Vienna – illness and spiritual crisis. Further travel cures him.
1840–1	Gogol in Rome completing work on part I of *Dead Souls*.
1841	October: returns to Moscow with manuscript of *Dead Souls*. *Rome* published in *Moskvityanin* (*The Muscovite*).
1842	February: *Dead Souls* passed by censors, appears in May.
	May: Gogol leaves for Europe. Collected edition of Gogol's works published (including 'The Overcoat' and revised version of 'Taras Bulba'). Revised version of 'The Portrait' appears in *Sovremennik*.
	September: first performance of *Marriage* in St Petersburg.
1842	May to April 1848 Gogol restlessly travels Europe in search of 'a cure'.
1845	Part II of *Dead Souls* completed, Gogol burns manuscript.
1847	Starts correspondence with priest, Father Matvey Konstantinovsky. Publishes *Selected Passages from Correspondence with Friends*.
1848	January: pilgrimage to Holy Land.
	April: return to Ukraine. Works on second version of part II of *Dead Souls*.
1852	4 February: starts severe fast.
	11 February: burns new version of part II of *Dead Souls*.
	21 February: Gogol dies.

Index

Titles of works are listed under the names of the authors